Urarina Society, Cosmology, and History in Peruvian Amazonia

UNIVERSITY PRESS OF FLORIDA

Florida A&M University, Tallahassee
Florida Atlantic University, Boca Raton
Florida Gulf Coast University, Ft. Myers
Florida International University, Miami
Florida State University, Tallahassee
New College of Florida, Sarasota
University of Central Florida, Orlando
University of Florida, Gainesville
University of North Florida, Jacksonville
University of South Florida, Tampa
University of West Florida, Pensacola

Urarina Society, Cosmology, and History in Peruvian Amazonia

Bartholomew Dean

University Press of Florida
Gainesville/Tallahassee/Tampa/Boca Raton
Pensacola/Orlando/Miami/Jacksonville/Ft. Myers/Sarasota

Copyright 2009 by Bartholomew Dean
All rights reserved
Printed in the United States of America on acid-free paper

First cloth printing, 2009
First paperback printing, 2013

Library of Congress Cataloging-in-Publication Data
Dean, Bartholomew, 1963–
Urarina society, cosmology, and history in Peruvian Amazonia/
Bartholomew Dean.
p. cm.
Includes bibliographical references and index.
ISBN 978-0-8130-3378-5 (cloth: alk. paper)
ISBN 978-0-8130-4951-9 (pbk.)
1. Urarina Indians—Material culture. 2. Urarina cosmology. 3. Urarina
Indians—Social life and customs. 4. Shamanism. 5. Loreto (Peru : Dept.)
6. Loreto (Peru : Dept.)—Social life and customs. I. Title.
F3430.1.U83D43 2009
305.898'085449–dc22   2009019225

The University Press of Florida is the scholarly publishing agency for the
State University System of Florida, comprising Florida A&M University, Florida Atlantic University, Florida Gulf Coast University, Florida
International University, Florida State University, New College of Florida,
University of Central Florida, University of Florida, University of North
Florida, University of South Florida, and University of West Florida.

University Press of Florida
15 Northwest 15th Street
Gainesville, FL 32611-2079
http://www.upf.com

To my parents, Stella Keeper and Warwick Randall Dean, for the gift of life, and to Luz Angélica, Maxwell Eric Amauta, Isadora Ursula Beatríz, and Gideon Jack Malachi Dean for making this life worth living.

"Straying maps the path"

Mawlānā Jalāl-ad-Dīn Muhammad Rūmī, thirteenth-century Sufi poet

Contents

List of Figures xi

Acknowledgments xiii

Introduction: Power, Belief, Wealth 1

1. The "People from Downstream": The Chambira Basin and Urarina Society 27

2. Ninichú: Homeland of the Ancients 54

3. Historicizing Amazonia: Domination, Unequal Exchange, and Value Extraction 85

4. Localizing Webs of Power in the Chambira Basin: The Urarina and Forest Extraction in Contemporary Perspective 116

5. "When There Were No Women": Gender and the Experience of Peonage 132

6. Forbidden Fruit: Affinity and the Economy of Kinship 157

7. Multiple Regimes of Value: Unequal Exchange and the Circulation of Palm-Fiber Wealth 185

8. Mitayo, Myth, and Meaning: Alienation and the Circulation of Urarina Forest Game 207

9. Chanting Rivers, Fiery Tongue: *Ayahuasca* Shamanism and Resistance in Amazonia 234

Notes 261

Bibliography 273

Index 313

Figures

I.1. Urarina women and man, Chambira River Basin   10
1.1. Cross section of Pangayacu River, Chambira River Basin   36
1.2. Urarina husband and wife, fishing from canoe on the Pangayacu River   36
1.3. Map of the Native Community of Santa Beatriz, Pangayacu River   37
1.4. Urarina family, Pangayacu River   39
1.5. Urarina children, Chambira River Basin   43
1.6. Layout of Native Community of Santa Beatriz, Pangayacu River   49
1.7. Longhouse drawing, viewed from above   51
1.8. Longhouse frame structure   52
2.1. Urarina geographic terms   56
2.2. Urarina man with *majas* (capybara)   67
2.3. Urarina woman and iguana   70
2.4. Oil pipeline system, Bajo Marañón River   79
4.1. Urarina man making a canoe paddle, Pangayacu River   128
5.1. Urarina hunter   135
5.2. Urarina woman weaving a palm-fiber fan   135
5.3. Headman reconstructing longhouse, Pangayacu River   140
7.1. Urarina woman weaving palm fibers with back-strap loom   187
7.2. Urarina baby sleeping in hammock   188
7.3. Chambira palm tree and woven net bag   191
7.4. Urarina girls and young women in canoe, Pangayacu River   195
7.5. Transporting the dead (shrouded in woven palm-fiber fabric)   199
7.6. Urarina cemetery, Chambira River Basin   199
7.7. Urarina ritual chest   200
8.1. Urarina ritual stave, stool, and blow-dart quiver   211
8.2. Urarina hunter with the head of a tapir   213
8.3. Boat, Chambira River Basin   214
8.4. Urarina boy and necklace   223
9.1. Urarina shaman, Chambira River   238
9.2. Headman playing music, Pangayacu River   244
9.3. Urarina boy and peccary "pet"   249

Acknowledgments

The research for this book was made possible through the generous financial support of the following institutions: Harvard University (Department of Anthropology, Sheldon Traveling Fellowship, Peabody Museum of Archaeology and Ethnology, Committee on Latin American and Iberian Studies, Graduate School of Arts and Sciences); IIE-Fulbright Fellowship; U.S. Department of Education Fulbright-Hays Fellowship; Wenner-Gren Foundation; Emslie Horniman Scholarship, Royal Anthropological Institute; Tinker Foundation; the Sigma Xi Research Society; and the Fundación MAPFRE America. Follow-up research and the final writing of the text were made possible by the critical support of the University of Kansas (Carroll D. Clark Research Fund—Department of Anthropology, Chancellor's Office—Peru Fund, College of Liberal Arts and Sciences, Hall Center for the Humanities, International Studies Program, Latin American Studies Center—Tinker Foundation, Museum of Anthropology, University General Research Fund).

At the outset of my fieldwork in Peru, I was first affiliated with the Centro de Investigación Antropológica de la Amazonia Peruana (CIAAP), Universidad Nacional de la Amazonia, Iquitos. I am deeply obliged to Federica Barclay Rey de Castro and Fernando Santos Granero for first encouraging me to do field research among the Urarina. In addition to Flica and Fernando, Camino Moran Power, Alberto Chirif, Lucy Trapnell, Clara Santos, Jacoba Sucher, and Padre Joaquín García provided my former wife, Michelle McKinley, and me with a stimulating and vibrant intellectual environment in Iquitos, Peru. I also warmly recognize the friendship and steadfast support of my Iquiteño *compadres*, Mauro Arirrua Nasnate and Luzmilla Torres, as well as their dearly beloved family. Invaluable field support and technical advice was provided by Alejandro Herrera, Jorge Timoteo, Santiago Rivas Panduro, and Johnny Davila. Marcia Koth de Paredes of the Fulbright Commission in Lima provided logistical help during the early years of fieldwork; she was instrumental in securing the support of the now defunct national petroleum firm Petro-Perú, whose transport facilitated the safe completion of the fieldwork. Travel to the Chambira Basin is no small feat. As such, I appreciate the efforts of the crew members of the countless airplanes, helicopters, and boats who were responsible for ferrying us to the Chambira Basin and Bajo Marañón. I would also like to recognize the support of Henry Harman, the current executive director for the Fulbright Commission for

Educational Exchange Between the United States and Peru, for his assistance during the later stages of field research for this book.

My travel to the Urarina was dependent on more than just transportation. Indeed the journey began long before, during my days as an undergraduate at Washington University, where I was blessed with superb teachers, in particular Evelyn Hu-Dehart, Silvia Pedraza, Leonard Green, and Richard Walters. While a graduate student in Latin American studies (politics and anthropology) at Oxford I benefited from the keen thinking and guidance of Allan Angel, Malcolm Deas, Rosemary Thorp, Peter Rivière, Herminio Martins, James Dunkerley, the late Edwin Ardner, and Rodney Needham. As a doctoral student at Harvard, I profited from the encouragement and invaluable contributions of many, including the late Juan Carlos Aguirre, Paul H. Gelles, the late Julie Goldman, Margot Gill, Richard Grinker, Michael Herzfeld, Carmen Hess, Jennifer Krier, Lida Junghans, Mike Lambert, Jerome Levi, Valerie Long, Kathy Skelly, Parker Shipton, Chris Steiner, Penny Rew, Alan Trevithick, Cynthia Verba, and Marilyn Zax. I am forever thankful to my graduate supervisor, the late David Maybury-Lewis, whose humane scholarship and vitality shaped my thinking and acting in the world. I owe warm thanks to Sally Falk Moore, Kenneth George, and Nur Yalman for their intellectual mentorship and steadfast support.

I also owe special thanks to the scholarly advice of many colleagues and friends: Manuel Burga Díaz, Gisela Cánepa Koch, Michael Chibnik, Luz Angélica Dean, Hastings Donnan, Shane Greene, David Guss, Erwin Frank, Michael Herzfeld, Jean Jackson, Kenneth Kensinger, Jerome Levi, Claude Lévi-Strauss, Theodore MacDonald, David Maybury-Lewis, Michelle McKinley, Thomas Myers, Jaime Regan, Peter Rivière, Santiago Rivas, Raul Romero, the late Steven Rubenstein, the late Richard Evans Schultes, Stanley Tambiah, and R. Tom Zuidema. I am particularly appreciative to those who provided me with their exceptionally helpful critiques of various portions of the book. I also deeply acknowledge the assistance of Lawrence Boudon, the former editor of the *Handbook of Latin American Studies*, Hispanic Division, U.S. Library of Congress.

In formulating the ideas that have been expressed in this text, I value the conversations that I had in Peru with Cristóbal Aljovín, Benedict Anderson, Jean Pierre Chaumeil, Roberto Da Matta, the late Carlos Iván Degregori, Oscar Espinoza, Salvador Flores Paitán, César Germaná, Padre Gonzalo González, Shane Greene, Peter Klarén, Nicholás Lynch, Raul Mayorga, Guillermo Nugent, Knut Olawsky, Norma Rodríguez, Michelson Peréz Rojas, Richard Chase Smith, Gustavo Solís, and Bladimiro Tapayuri. While "back in the States" at Harvard, my mind and my spirit benefited greatly from the camaraderie of my "Boston buddies": E. J. O'Neil IV, Keith Maurizi, Jon Shriber, and Ellen Lawton. A subsequent postdoctoral fellowship in urgent anthropology at the Royal Anthropological Institute (RAI) in London, and the resolute encouragement of Jonathan Benthall, the former director of the RAI, as well as Stephen Nugent and the late Olivia Harris at Goldsmiths College, University of London, proved most conducive to the analysis of my field notes.

My colleagues at the University of Kansas have provided me with a wonderful intellectual home to further my understanding of Urarina culture and society. In particular, I would like to thank Michael Crawford, Beverly Davenport-Sypher, Nancy Erickson, Laura Hobson Herlihy, Al Johnson, John Janzen, Robert Hemenway, F. Allan Hanson, Joshua Homan, Zach Holden, John Hoopes, Abdelmajid Hannoum, Darcy Morey, Felix Moss, Joan Nagel, Donald Stull, Howard Sypher, and Akira Yamamoto, all of whom lent their support in some way to the research, crucial feedback, and writing of this book. In addition to my anthropology quarters at the University of Kansas, my project has been deeply inflected by my academic experiences in Lima, Peru, particularly as they pertain to the establishment (1998–99) of the Maestría de Estudios Amazonicos at the Universidad Nacional Mayor de San Marcos (UNMSM). Over the past ten years, I have had the privilege and great honor of working with a diverse group of Peruvian faculty and students committed to developing a socially relevant program of scholarship and engaged practical action in Amazonia.

In terms of this book, I am ever indebted to the editorial staff at the University Press of Florida, especially Eli Borz, John Byram, Derek Krissoff, and Jacqueline Kinghorn Brown, as well as a number of anonymous reviewers, for providing me with useful "prods" and essential feedback at critical stages in the writing of this ethnography. My gratitude to Christine Sweeney, my wonderful copy editor, who managed to infuse the book with consistency and a modicum of readability. I trust their tireless efforts and crucial insights are reflected in the finished book, although any misinterpretations of and errors regarding Urarina society and culture are, of course, my own responsibility.

During all of the years leading up to the writing of this book, my family and friends have provided me with generous expressions of love and support that can never be repaid. I am grateful to my parents, Warwick and Stella, for their love, and most importantly for demonstrating to me the inherent dignity of humanity and the value of struggling against that which undermines it. My siblings—Melinda, Gregory, Adam, and Aurelia—inspired me to question authority and to follow my dreams. My extended family in England, particularly my deceased maternal grandfather, John William Keeper (who was instrumental in introducing me to Karl Marx when I was a schoolboy), my uncle Michael Keeper, and my dear cousins Kevin Kirk and Crispin Keeper, all provided me with a sense of moral indignation against the blind abuse of human hierarchy.

This book would never exist if it were not for the critical perspective and tenacious support of my beloved wife, Luz Angélica . . . *nadíara kumazái*. A Chayahuita native of Peruvian Amazonia, Luz Angélica has been my moral compass and loving partner, and she is the reason that this book finally saw the light of the day. Along the way, Luz Angélica has shared in the joys and in the hardships—both real and imagined—of the "anthropological endeavor." Moreover, my work has profited from the many undertakings and countless insights of my children, Maxwell, Isadora, and Gideon, as well as my former feline companions Janu'laudi and Abdoul.

Final thanks belong to my many friends and acquaintances on the Chambira. In particular, I would like to thank the late Biña, as well as Kiriná, Najlegue-kuktíri, Ujkuaizíri, Calísto, and Raguití for their willingness to share their stories and for their liberal patience in fielding countless questions, which I am sure had little to with their own personal "agendas." While few, if any, Urarina really understood why I had traveled so far from my "home" to learn their language and their stories, and about their distinctive ways of life, they nevertheless welcomed me with gracious warmth and abundant gestures of hospitality. Indeed, no period in my life has been more personally challenging and at the same time as rewarding than that spent with the Urarina communities on the Pangayacu River, or Ajadiyú, as they fondly call it.

I took the photographs that appear in the text during the course of fieldwork in the Peruvian Amazon. All line drawings were done by my *compadre*, Santiago Rivas Panduro. Parts of this book were previously published, in different form, in the following places: "Ambivalent Exchanges: The Violence of Patronazgo in the Upper Amazon," in *Cultural Construction of Violence: Victimization, Escalation, Response*, edited by M. Anderson (West Lafayette: Purdue University, 2004); "At the Margins of Power: Gender Hierarchy and the Politics of Ethnic Mobilization among the Urarina," in *At the Risk of Being Heard: Identity, Indigenous Rights, and Postcolonial States*, edited by B. Dean and J. Levi (Ann Arbor: University of Michigan Press, 2003); "State Power and Indigenous Peoples in Peruvian Amazonia: A Lost Decade, 1990–2000," in *The Politics of Ethnicity: Indigenous Peoples in Latin*

American States, edited by D. Maybury-Lewis (Cambridge, Mass.: Harvard University Press, 2002); "Brideprice in Amazonia?" *Journal of the Royal Anthropological Institute* 4(2) (1998): 345–47; "Forbidden Fruit: Infidelity, Affinity, and Brideservice among the Urarina of Peruvian Amazonia," *Journal of the Royal Anthropological Institute* 1(1) (1995): 87–110; "Multiple Regimes of Value: Unequal Exchange and the Circulation of Urarina Palm-Fiber Wealth," *Museum Anthropology* 18(1) (1994): 3–20. Subsequent insights are presented, including recent data, interpretations, and analyses.

Introduction

Power, Belief, Wealth

This book is an ethnographic investigation of the Urarina, an indigenous Amazonian society occupying the Chambira Basin of northeastern Peru. The interplay between the cultural and the material conditions of Urarina society is the book's primary focus: it explores the ways in which an indigenous peoples of Peruvian Amazonia organize their existence with regard to production, exchange, and the consumptive desires framing their lives. I assess the historical reproduction of Urarina society as it has both been inspired by and resisted the violence of the colonial and postcolonial encounters. In offering a history of local-global interconnections, I document the Urarinas' involvement in regional and international political economies, namely petty-commodity production mediated through relations of debt peonage.

By addressing the Urarina in terms of what Lyotard (1997, 47) calls a "stream of cultural capital," I provide an ethnographic account of the social construction of Urarina marginality and resistance.[1] Marked by relations of internal colonialism, unplanned hydraulic and agroforestry development has been the rule rather than the exception in Peruvian Amazonia (Dean 2002b). Throughout much of the twentieth century, the Urarina continued to exist at the margins of Peruvian national society, in spite of their active participation in the region's commercial economies. By the end of the twentieth century, the Urarina found themselves facing a "developmentalist ideology" embraced by the national bourgeoisie, local elites, and the rural poor alike, and whose slogan could perhaps best be summed up as "assimilate, move, or die, because the progress of Peru [can] no longer be stemmed" (Brown and Fernández 1991, 66; Dean 2000, 2006a; Huertas Castillo 2005). Like other Amazonian peoples, such as the Yanomami (Early and Peters 2000), the Urarina see themselves in a life-or-death position, with their health seriously in jeopardy by contact with infectious disease and oil contamination, and their land being expropriated by outsiders.

Throughout the nearly 740,000 square kilometers comprising the Peruvian Amazon, indigenous peoples have long faced centuries of missionization, unregulated streams of colonists, violent land-grabbing, decades of formal schooling in an alien tongue, pressures to conform to a foreign national culture, and more recently, explosive expressions of social conflict fueled by a booming underground coca economy. Disruptions accompanying the establishment of commercial economies, coupled with the Peruvian state-sanctioned civilizing project, led to a devastating impoverishment of Amazonia's richly variegated social and ecological communities. Anyone who has spent even a short time among putatively "uncivilized" peoples of the Peruvian rainforest is well aware of the high operating costs accrued by those who are made to suffer such dehumanizing distinctions.

The vulnerable indigenous societies of Amazonia have long been susceptible to the social and demographic distortions associated with the Peruvian state's coercive assimilationist policies. Assimilation has also occurred in Amazonia because of the state's benign disregard for indigenous communal interests (T. Turner 1996, 67–70).

Ignorance has been a major obstacle to social justice in Peru's benighted policy toward its indigenous peoples. Local and national elites have variously ascribed the economic impoverishment of native Amazonian peoples to their idleness, to their scavenging "mentality," to their "Indian blood," and to their non-European modes of agronomy. But their poverty has rarely been attributed "to their status as an exploited and non-autonomous class created by the systematic commercialization of the cultural ecology of the Amazon Valley" (Ross 1978, 193), or to the ruinous processes of extractive development and "frontier expansion" (Schmink and Wood 1984; R. Anderson 1999). Poverty tends to affect indigenous peoples disproportionately, especially in rural zones of Amazonia where malnutrition and illiteracy as well as increased health and environmental risks accompany the limited availability of basic social services.

From the perspective of indigenous peoples, the actions of the Peruvian state have been arbitrary and profoundly unpredictable (Burga Cabrera et al. 2005). State intervention in Amazonia has often followed on the heels of particularly brutal entrepreneurs, many of whom have operated above the law that they swore to uphold. The infamous Putumayo scandal involving allegations of abuses by station managers in La Chorrera and El Encanto, Julio Arana's rubber camps, is a good case in point. The surfacing in 1907 of wild allegations of brutality, slaving, and genocidal murder of Bora (Bóóraá) and Huitoto (Uitoto) peoples by the henchmen working for Arana's Peruvian Amazon Company set into motion an international scandal that focused world attention on Amazonia (Hardenburg 1913; J. Arana 1913; Rey de Castro 1913; Lagos 2005).[2] A century later, large-scale exploitation of natural resources and raw materials in indigenous territories remains commonplace.

Inundated every year to a depth of up to thirty feet, the Amazon floodplain is ever more threatened by unrestrained agricultural expansion and ranching, and its natural resource base is being damaged by inappropriate land-use practices (N. Smith 1999). Most recently, encroachments on indigenous territories have come from a variety of sources: Andean colonists; peasant and indigenous communities displaced during the civil war; coca growers (*cocaleros*); rebels in search of new bases of operation; business interests; and adventure seeking eco-tourists. In addition to the staggering negative socioeconomic and ecological impact of the recent coca boom, which has led to significant deforestation and erosion, some of the most egregious cases of environmental degradation in Peruvian Amazonia have been committed by multinational lumber, mining, and oil companies (Bedoya Garland 1991; see also Wood and Porro 2002).

While marginality indicates that some forms of human experience are inconsequential and peripheral, I adopt the term to underscore the Urarinas' positionality—defined not in geographical terms, but rather with reference to their limited access to what Eric Wolf (1990) called "structural power"— for example, the capacity to govern consciousness and structure political economy. Indicative of the dilemma of marginality (Tsing 1993, 26), the Urarina are simultaneously inside and outside of the state. While some native peoples in Peruvian Amazonia see government as a high-status project, the Urarina are marginalized in official state discourse, which until very recently represented indigenous peoples as beyond the pale of civilization. Nevertheless, I contend that the Urarinas' marginality does not necessarily derogate from their agentive capacities, especially in determining essential aspects of the present, nor does it erase the control that they exert over key features of production, exchange, consumption, and social reproduction. Turning to the "internal" dynamics of Urarina society, the book critically examines how affinity and consanguinity are both mediated and constituted by larger processes of marital and communal exchange (*cudiaca*), the creation of value, and interpersonal desire. Analysis of the Urarinas' kin economy illuminates critical institutional arrangements (for example, debt peonage or *habilitación*) while also alerting us to the Urarinas' creative adaptations to the region's varied geographical and societal topographies.

In the Chambira Basin, a heightened concern with market forces offers a privileged view into the networks that unite the local and the global, and that help to sustain the linked asymmetries of gender, generation, ethnicity, class, and state rule. Urarina economics are socially embedded in a wider nexus of relationships determined not only by kinship, but also by politics, cosmology, and the global economy. Notwithstanding their active participation in economic activities driven by supralocal market forces, I contend that the Urarina do in fact exemplify what Maybury-Lewis has aptly deemed a traditional society: their moral economy is "permeated by personal and moral considerations....[Here] exchanges define [social] relationships" (1992, 85).[3] Examining the creation of Urarina cultural value through the optic of circulation illustrates that power is, as Clastres noted, "faithful to the law of exchange which founds and regulates society" (1987, 38). As such, the book follows the analytic shift within anthropology, from a concern with reciprocity—or why things are given—to study of inalienability—or why things are kept. Analysis of inalienability provides insight into "that universally familiar thing which seems to endanger the practice of *gift*-exchange and to penetrate the sacred only to profane and destroy it: money" (Godelier 1999, 9).

By attending to the Urarinas' long engagement with purveyors of domestic and international capital, and by charting popular responses to the overtures of what I clumsily call the outside world, this work is intended to help undermine the popular idea of the isolated and atomistic Amazonian society. In so doing, I argue that the mutually constituted nature of power, belief, and wealth are more readily apparent from the perspective of subaltern actors in a "pre-cash economy" than in monetized societies where the ultimate example of a fungible item—money—dominates. Of course, it would be patently absurd to claim that Urarina are unfamiliar with money. My intention in using the phrase "pre-cash economy" is to draw attention to the local scarcity of money: petty commodity exchanges are primarily nonmonetized. It could perhaps be held that in my insistence on the interstitial relationships between the kin and regional economies I advance an overly enveloped view of two discrete economic systems. Arguably, I could have viewed the Urarinas' remove from industrialist modes of production and alienation from market logics as credible proof of their economic isolation. Nevertheless, to do so would not only defy the ethnographic evidence culled from my own fieldwork, it would also contradict the insights of recent debates in exchange theory, political anthropology, and gender studies. As a representational stance, viewing the Urarina in isolation would perpetuate the anthropological tendency to romanticize and freeze frame the "primitive" out of time, history, and economic activity (Fabian 1983; Dean 2002a).

Method: Experience and Crafting Representations

My empirically grounded account of the Urarina falls squarely within the modernist cannon of ethnographic description. Rather than a narrow theoretical orientation, I have opted for a multi stranded, eclectic theoretical approach to understanding Urarina society and political economy. At the same time, I embrace what Francoise Michel-Jones deemed the "Absolute Subject." In part this is a reflection of my academic training in social anthropology during the 1980s and 1990s (Oxford, Harvard). But more important, this is tied directly to my overall concern with linking multiple levels of analysis to demonstrate articulations at every level within Urarina society, and between the Urarina and their neighbors and more distant actors. Written intentionally as a reactive move to postmodernism's and cultural studies' obsessions with signs, sounds, and text, often at the expense of paying attention to the material conditions of the social organization of life and behavior as it plays out in daily life "on the ground," this multifaceted ethnography emphasizes the structural dynamics of inequality while also paying close attention to the cultural construction of value (both material and symbolic) ranging from interpretations of mythological discourse to symbolic readings of local architectural patterns and sacred landscapes.

This book is based on field research conducted over a thirty-month period (1988–2002) among the Urarina longhouse communities of the middle and upper Chambira Basin, as well as time spent in Urarina, Cocama, Alamas Quichua, Chayahuita, and *ribereño* communities on the Urituyacu, Tigre, Corrientes, Marañón, Huallaga, Paranapura, and Amazonas Rivers. Through actively "forming communities" and engaging in "conversations" (Gudeman and Rivera 1995), the ethnographic portions of this text are representative of a collaborative endeavor. My conversations with young and ambitious men, like Ujkuaizíri, as well as elders—such as the jocular Najlegue-kuktíri, or Kiriná, an enchanting man of solitude and silence yet utterly devoted to the welfare of his people—are all part of the ethnographic material from which I draw to reflect upon Urarina social practices, narrative traditions, and beliefs. Full of panache, Najlegue-kuktíri and Ujkuaizíri were usually willing to descant on just about any topic, even in instances or intellectual domains with which they were—at least from my point of view—seemingly unfamiliar. Additionally, I have relied on the more mundane methods of participant observation and a great deal of intuition to close some of the lacunae that inevitably surface in attempts to chronicle and make sense of the deeply intersubjective life-ways and experiences of any diverse group of peoples.

Besides participant observation, collaborative fieldwork research included the collection of primary linguistic data, ethno-ecological information, material culture, and a large corpus of oral narratives, shamanic chants, music, and stories of doughty deeds conducted by the Urarinas' ancestors and culture heroes. While in the Chambira Basin, I collected many myths, numerous songs, and scores of personal stories. The regularity by which I was told historical and mythological stories during my time in the Chambira Basin is indicative of the high esteem the Urarina place on the performance of verbal art. Storytellers would intensify narrative performances in accordance with my facial expressions and bodily gestures. Their willingness to recount narratives of the mythic past dovetailed with my own research agenda.

Urarina mythology is a cultural system of signification through which reality is mediated. The phonocentric vitality of Urarina myth is invoked through a naming of the lived world, a verbal referencing of the forest and rivers, as in the specific case of the serial listing of the origin of the fish, birds, serpents, and vermin. In Amazonia, the rain forest itself provides an ostensibly limitless constellation of shifting and stable points of reference through which people's stories "make . . . sense of history and cosmologically interpretable historicity" (Whitten 1988, 293). The terms reference and sense are employed here in the manner outlined by Stanley Tambiah (1985, 4–5). Reference marks the entities in the universe "out there," which nomenclatures name or designate. The sense of the individual terms in classificatory schema refers to their place within the nexus of relationships among constituent parts. This way of grasping cultural meaning "sets up a dialectic between the sense and referential axes of a classification scheme" (Whitten 1988, 293). Of the theoretically limitless images of worldly existence, some groupings, such as nourishment, corporeality, maturation, the natural elements, and sociality, are habitually marked as key points of reference. These "universal" lexicons underpin symbolic systems that enable people to make sense out of the everlasting flux and indeterminacy of social life.

The myths and stories appearing in this book are based on tape-recorded versions told to me by various Urarina informants. In some instances, versions were painstakingly translated phrase by phrase from Urarina into Loretano Spanish. I relied extensively on Ujkuaizíri's help to translate taped recordings of Urarina speech and songs. Inevitably cultural meaning was lost, but the simultaneous taping of Ujkuaizíri's oral transcription gave life to the narrative's multiplex meanings, which are dependent on a thick web of intertextuality. Stories rely on a culturally proscribed pattern of knowledge or coda ostensibly known to all Urarina peoples, yet disagreements did emerge when eliciting people's interpretations of the narratives. On the one hand, they signal that the Urarina sustain a strong sense of cultural identity, while on the other hand, they suggest that people are very much capable of adapting to changed circumstances.

While far from rigorous, transcription of Urarina words and phrases appearing herein rely on a phonetic system closely approximating spoken

Spanish that was developed over the course of my fieldwork. Given that I have had no formal training in linguistics, a warning should be issued to the reader. I am confident that this text is marred by gross linguistic inaccuracies and riddled with problems of representation. In retrospect, I remember how I initially resented the animadversions of my Urarina acquaintances about my limited linguistic capacities, particularly since I came to realize their truth. "You have a heavy tongue" (Tú tienes una lengua pesada), I was told in Spanish as I tried to learn Urarina from the men and boys. Over time, I managed to supplement research in Loretano Spanish with a rudimentary understanding of spoken Urarina.[4]

In recounting myths and stories, the rhetorical devices of incremental repetition or redundancy and epistrophe have been minimized for brevity. Nevertheless, I have tried to keep the stories' original tenor and cadence, despite obvious variations in grammar, idiom, and syntax. In translating myths across three languages (Urarina, Loretano Spanish, and English), the interpretation I put forth is but one of many possible readings of the correlations between Urarina social practice and cosmology. Any given variation in orators and audiences reshapes each mythopoeic performance and changes the sense of the myth's meaning, giving it vitality suitable for the moment, the storyteller, and the individual listeners. Inherently recyclable, stories, as Feld suggests, "live lives of reinvention" (1998, 446). They are always subject to "figuring and refiguring in relation to the interpretive desires of both their immediate tellers and hearers and the larger social fields through which they reverberate" (Feld 1998, 446).

The nuanced and complex values of Urarina culture reside in colloquial idioms—the encoded language of the insider that remains elusive to outsiders like me. An ethnographer's understanding, like the knowledge the ethnographic subjects have of their social universe, is always partial and situated (Clifford 1986). Invariably, my rendition of Urarina culture is incomplete, at times lacking the historical context and background information necessary for adequate understanding or interpretation. My rendition is distorted by miscommunication and the missteps accompanying my own biases and academic research agendas. I found that collecting information, like other items of wealth, carried its price. The dialogic extraction of information—which some astute commentators have likened to vampirism (Wachtel 1994; cf. Dean 1996, 111–13)—was intended for a scholarly audience. Just as I intended to transport this information to a wider academic audience, my Urarina acquaintances came to see me and talk about themselves and their lives within a broader political agenda. Despite these different communicative agendas, I am confident that my experience of the shared hardships and joys of life with the longhouse group on the Pangayacu River enabled me eventually to discern—if albeit faintly—some of the general outlines of Urarina culture and social organization.

While doffing my hat to those who promote ethnographic subterfuge (Dean 2005), my book seeks to provide historicized knowledge of consequential processes associated with the ambiguous circulation of wealth items. Corresponding to the term ambiguous, ambivalence refers to the presence of conflicting ideas, beliefs, emotions, or attitudes. The functions of ambivalence and ambiguity as they are found in human nature and society have been the object of considerable anthropological inquiry (among others, see Boehm 1989; Battaglia 1997). Ambivalence for Boehm refers to those individuals who are torn between conflicting desires, emotions, or choices for action (1989).

More generally, ambivalent and ambiguous both refer to uncertainty in comprehending what somebody or something means. The principal difference between the words is that the former is used when speaking about people and their attitudes, whereas the latter refers to something enunciated or written. If the Urarina then are ambivalent about commercial exchanges, they are uncertain about the rewards and drawbacks of participating in the market, whereas if a headman makes ambiguous statements about exchange, his assertions have multiple meanings. The use of the concept of ambivalence in this book signals a conscious effort to destabilize the sense of the word society. It does so by combining perspectives that are usually not embraced at the same time—"insider-outsider, local-supra-local, short-term—long-term, model and event" (S. Moore 1986, 329).

Arrival

> Light has finally burst into the eastern sky, and I now *finally* find myself among the Urarina. Above the buzzing canopy, the sky is at once brilliant . . . now orange-red mottled by swathes of dark ink-blue. Remnants of twilight mist mix with the effused scent of tropical nectars filling the warm musky air. In shadow's security, the forest is alive and I am humbled by my total insignificance in the midst of this monumental grandeur. (field notes, July 1988)

My first encounter with the rain forests of the Chambira Basin inspired romantic imagery, yet the manner in which I arrived in the field was far from pleasant. Given the physical remove of the Urarina communities from distant commercial centers, their contact with outsiders is often with *comerciantes* (traders) and locally established *patrones* (labor bosses). Indeed, my initial entrée into Urarina society was facilitated by a man I was soon to loathe, and then pity, and now finally tolerate, if only cordially: Don Miguel Rojas (pseudonym). The greed and personal brutality of Rojas, and other traders like him, have earned the itinerant merchants the opprobrium of many of the inhabitants of the Chambira watershed. Because I arrived with this corpulent and shiftless "river trader," my position among the Urarina seemed precarious during my initial visit in the summer of 1988. Who could avouch for my integrity or even clarify my murky intentions? Certainly not Rojas, whose personal association with me undermined my callow pretensions of social scientific neutrality.

When I returned in 1989 to live with the longhouse communities on the Pangayacu River it seemed as if the Urarina had—if only momentarily—imbued me with a sense of supra-humanness; I was powerful because I was a master of abstruse knowledge. I knew how to write, possessed Western pharmaceuticals (*gringó kuî*), and had fantastic gadgets (among other things, binoculars, a mini-cassette tape player/recorder, a solar-battery pack, and a Coleman lantern whose brilliant burning white light inspired awe for many).[5] My "expeditions"—or so they were called by the military officers at the Quinta Región Militar—were always accoutered with the finest that the decrepit old storehouses of Iquitos's Belen market could offer. Among other things, this included canned sardines; tins of tomato paste; boiled meat imported from Denmark; sacks of rice (*arruzo*), sugar (*azucarú*), and non-iodized salt (*tevé*); spices; fishing gear; and baubles and bolts of cotton fabric, much of which was destined for barter. Upon reaching the Chambira Basin it seemed as if I were assimilated into the category of trader—with the twist that instead of seeking forest produce and game at inequitable prices, I sought myths, gossip, practical knowledge, and personal narratives. Indeed, I explained to my hosts that I had left my home to chronicle the life stories of a number of Urarina men, women, and children (fig. I.1).

I was often awoken, especially in the middle of the night or the wee hours of the morning, by the clarion shrills of birds, howling monkeys, croaking frogs, crying babies, and the cacophonous sounds uttered by young children. But when I listened carefully—not just to the noise around me but to the human voices speaking—I found that it is not only in momentous events that the quality of life consists, but also in the episodic procurement of life's petty pleasures, and in the triumph over its many inconveniences and mortal threats—namely disease, misfortune, and unwanted encounters with malevolent outsiders and spirit beings. I gave prodigiously to those who were good storytellers, who accommodated me with gracious hospitality,

Fig. I.1. Urarina women and man, Chambira River Basin

who put up with hot afternoon translation sessions, and who looked after my many things when I went away.

Early morning and late evening colloquies with Urarina men enhanced my view of their lives, as well as my own brittle sense of self. This appreciation was anchored—in ways unbeknownst to me at the time—by endless hours of idle prattle and bantering with Urarina children. At first, it was difficult to bate the children's curiosity. They were fully aware that my oversized rucksacks were filled with gifts for them, including *blogos* (balloons) and *confetti* (candy). Boys' apocryphal claims of lost *kajtai* (fishing hooks) and requests to replace broken fishing lines were satisfied through the barter for stories, gossip, and songs, while girls enjoyed swapping honey bananas and papayas in return for beads, combs, and hand mirrors. With time, I eventually learned what goods the Urarina desired and discovered the burgeoning consumerism, sense of style, and assignation of value that accompanied bargaining sessions with outsiders. I also discerned the apportionment of status and personal privileges in internal networks of distribution.

Discussions with Urarina women were more limited and often involved the intermediary communicative role of males. Given our awareness of the inevitable distortion that accompanies translation of "women's worlds" (Abu-Lughod 1993; cf. McCallum 2001, 50–53; Chernela 2003; Corrales Caraval 2005), particularly from a male subject position, I must alert the reader to the indirect and sometimes circuitous route that informs my understanding of

Urarina feminized spheres of social interaction. Women's deafening silence and diffident attitude toward my inquisitive probings proved to be a major obstacle during field research among the Urarina.[6] With time, I gained the trust of a few Urarina women confidents. While the women looked askance at me during my beginning months of residence, I was able eventually to communicate directly with a number of the women from the Pangayacu, such as Aruba, and later her sisters and mother. This small circle of female voices grew over time, but I was never nearly as comfortable negotiating the meaning of women's worlds as I was in participating, and to some extent understanding, the richly textured lives of Urarina men.

The "People from Downstream": The Chambira Basin and Urarina Society

Chapter 1 provides the reader with an introduction to the Chambira Basin, the ancestral "homelands" of the Urarina, the so-called people from downstream. Geographic and ecological contextualizations are followed by a summary of the major contours of Urarina social organization and a characterization of the daily rounds of communal life. Description of Urarina longhouses highlights the architectural and social dimensions of public and private interaction. Chapter 1 also addresses the formation of regional and ethnic identities by attending to the relevance of *ribereño* cultural identities and suggests that social distinctions based on powerful discourses of civilization and progress frame interactions between Urarina and non-Urarina peoples. These discourses are in fact part of a diverse and historically elaborated assemblage of interlinked narratives about civility and progress, modernity and tradition, violence and peace.

This background information not only provides an indication of the fractured nature of ethnic identities, but also helps to accentuate the rich and diverse cultural mosaic comprising Peruvian Amazonia. Consisting of fourteen major linguistic families,[7] forty languages, and at least sixty-three "distinct" societies, the precise population of the native peoples of the tropical Andes and lowlands (*selva baja*) of Peru is difficult to determine (Solís Fonseca 2003, 19). Population estimates for the Peruvian Amazon range between two and three million inhabitants, of whom at least a half a million are considered indigenous peoples (Gray 1997, 75). In Peruvian Amazonia there are numerous indigenous societies, such as the Bora (Bóóraá), the Jebero (Shiwilu), and the once mighty Omágua whose numbers have dwindled radically. During the later half of the twentieth century, eleven indigenous cultures have virtually died, and many others are in danger of soon becoming extinct, such as the Orejón (Maijuna), Munichi, Dukaiya, and Ibo'tsa (Ocaina), or the Taushiro (Pinchi), of whom only a handful remain (Solís Fonseca 2003).

The subjects of this book, the Urarina, are a semi-mobile, hunting, and horticultural society whose population I estimate between 4,000 and 6,000, a more realistic (albeit imprecise) figure that reflects the "demographic turnaround" noted in other indigenous groups of lowland Latin America (McSweeny and Arps 2005). In the mid-1970s, Kramer estimated that the population of the Chambira River drainage (excluding the Urituyacu watershed, which lies to the west and runs parallel to the Chambira Basin) was about 1,000 to 1,200, which she notes is the same as the Malaria Eradication Service figures (1979, 3). In 1990, the total population of the District of Urarinas was estimated at 8,723 (Odicio Egoavil 1992, 7). Urarina population estimates range from a low of 1,500 to 5,000 by the Summer Institute of Linguistics (Chirif and Mora 1977, 49; Cajas Rojas et al. 1987, 174). More recently, Olawsky puts the number of Urarina speakers at 3,000 (2002, 6).

The Commodification of Land and the Politics of Urarina Autonomy

While the "father" of use-values is labor power, it is not the only source of material wealth, whose "mother" is the earth (Marx and Engels 1978, 50). This is a point driven home in chapter 2, which is devoted to revealing indigenous conceptions of territorial ownership. The critical interplay between territorial integrity, political autonomy, and cultural value is assessed in light of how customary patterns of land use are informed by both cosmological referents and the exigencies of everyday life. Chapter 2 posits that Urarina factionalism and patterns of itinerant residence are consistent with a strategy of autonomy achieved largely through oscillation between polar extremes of "isolation" and "national" integration. Use of the oscillative metaphor is deliberate; I want to imply a single swing from one extreme—incorporation of alterity—to another—isolation through flight. Urarina conceptions of land are shaped both by subsistence patterns and the factionalism exacerbated by the Urarinas' competitive participation in market-driven forest extraction.

The ideal of Urarina society is a fierce insistence on autonomy and independence—much the same way that the dominant political ideal in liberal, post-capitalist societies is individualism and noninterference from government. Here I should mention that my preference is to regard the Urarinas' strategy of political autonomy through isolation as one of selective incorporation. In imbuing subaltern peoples like the Urarina with a sense of political agency, I hope to contribute to reversing the tendency of seeing indigenous societies merely as powerless vis-à-vis all-encompassing or aggrandizing fronts of national expansion.

Political mobilization is an important factor that determines whether small farmer or peasant settlements are able to retain rights to their lands in Amazonia (Thiele 1995; García Hierro, Hvalkof, and Gray 1998). Over the past quarter of a century, the indigenous rights movement in lowland South America has frequently made claims to land based on historical ties to ancestral homelands. The establishment of supra-local organizations that allow the Urarina to defend their human rights through political and legal means has been a slow process in coming. The political unification of Urarina society has been hindered by the Urarinas' geographical isolation, by the nature of their dispersed settlement pattern, and by their long history of intra-longhouse factionalism. Attempts at countermanding or at least subverting the authority of rival groups are common stratagems marking relations among factions. Moreover, the relatively egalitarian character of their social relations mitigates against hierarchical models of political organization. This has been a perennial challenge not only to the Urarina but also to indigenous political organizations that ideally "seek to permit maximum participation with a minimum of concentration of power" (R. Smith 1985, 29).

Not withstanding these challenges, *indigenismo* (pro-indigenous sentiment) continues to be identified—at least in the West—with a discourse of equality, and as such carries with it an enormous moral weight capable of mobilizing collective social action. The Urarinas' level of political organization is mirrored by their ongoing entanglement in grossly inequitable relations of debt peonage. As I demonstrate in chapter 2, the Chambira lands from which forest goods are being extracted or produced is increasingly coming under pressures emanating from market forces.

Historicizing Amazonia: State Domination and Value Extraction

Contextualization of my account of the Urarinas' engagement with Peruvian colonial and national society necessitates a review of the historical record. By providing a conspectus of upper Amazonian colonial and postcolonial history, chapter 3 explores how Urarina society has been shaped by long-term entanglement with missionaries, colonial administrators, and traders, as well as with agents of the "singular" Peruvian nation to which the state gave birth. Following centuries of colonial rule, a pattern of skewed development emerged in Peruvian Amazonia that effectively prevented indigenous peoples like the Urarina from full participation in the Peruvian nation-state. The link between social domination and economies, "based on [the] extraction of value from nature rather than on the creation of value by labor" (Bunker 1988, 12), is examined in light of the colonial encounter and the subsequent emergence of Peru's liberal nation-state. Following Tsing, I employ the term state to "refer to those aspects of the governing administrative and coercive apparatus that are experienced as external yet hegemonic" (1993, 26). The state thus is seen as the system of power and domination through which the interests of various classes are expressed. State and non-state actors have played a long and prominent role in shaping upper Amazonian history.

In assessing the long *durée* of Amazonian history, I have tended to emphasize the material conditions of social life, paying particular attention to the intersection of power, economics, and social organization. This sociopolitical approach assesses the ethnic and emergent class dimensions accompanying the historical struggles pitting elites, *mestizos*, and indigenous peoples. Following a review of the pre-Columbian history of upper Amazonia, my attention shifts to evaluating the role ecclesiastical colonialism had on influencing the basic contours of daily life. Once important centers of production, exchange, and consumption, the upper Amazonian missions conditioned subsequent historical trajectories—namely the growth of commercial economies based on the inequitable system of debt peonage.[8]

Linked to recurring booms in a wide variety of forest commodities Amazonia has experienced countless socioeconomic frontiers, some of which extend over the past 450 years (Rausch 1999; Radding 2005). Amazonian commodities have historically been varied: they include, inter alia, fish poisons (known generically as *barbasco*), coca, gold, shamanic knowledge, turtle oil, slaves, parrot feathers, quinine, salt fish, petroleum, sarsaparilla, rosewood, and indigenous labor power to provide services, such as hunting, farming, gathering forest products, transportation, and soldiering. Peruvian Amazonia's commercial economies have provided fleeting periods of elite prosperity, but more often than not the wealth generated has benefited a small group of elites and come at a hefty social and environmental cost.

During the colonial period, the region lacked a large internal market. Forest commodities made their way to Europe, but intra-regional domestic trade was impeded by the lack of transport infrastructure and by geographic barriers, which have long inhibited communication between the regions of the Amazon, the Andes, and the Coast. A road system was nonexistent at this time, while rivers were not always navigable. In spite of monumental challenges to transport, the ideological construct of "Amazonia awaiting conquest" finds historical resonance in the powerful discourse of El Dorado. Neither of the Spanish centers of regional colonial power—Quito and

Lima—provided much in the way of domestic investment in transport. This situation would not change until the latter half of the nineteenth century, when regular fluvial transport was established. The introduction of steam navigation marked significant shifts in Peruvian Amazonia's social landscapes, in the dominant patterns of land-tenure, and in the structure of markets integrating the region into broader networks of economy and polity.

Many theories of Peruvian underdevelopment, particularly those influenced by dependency theory, have emphasized the importance of external linkages, such as the export of raw materials (silver, guano, wool, sugar, cotton, rubber, coca, and so forth) and the role of foreign capital. In examining the Urarinas' involvement in supra-local economic arrangements, my aim is to deepen our appreciation of the ways in which local actors determine and are shaped by larger-scale regional and transnational economic systems. To this end, I assess colonial and national political projects linked to the establishment of hegemony through the civilization of Amazonia.

National Hegemony: The Civilizing Project in Amazonia

Hegemony is a lived process; it is "a realized complex of experiences, relationships, and activities" (Williams 1977, 112). As an analytical trope, I find hegemony useful because it encompasses domination, accommodation, and resistance.[9] Hegemony is a multifarious process by which the ruling class or group extends its domination throughout society and society's various cultural fields. It implies not only economic and political dominance but also the cultural preponderance of the ruling elite. Typically, this entails a diffuse process in which the dominant class articulates its own interests and those of other social groups. In Peru, hegemonic groups have included a broad spectrum of associations and social units, such as the military, religious institutions, the landed elite, merchants, industrialists, the petite bourgeoisie, and the professional classes. Agents of national expansion have long sought to establish themselves in indigenous territories throughout Amazonia (Henley 1982, 156). The operative word over the past two centuries has been *national*. During the nineteenth and twentieth centuries, seven nation-states vied with one another to exercise national sovereignty over Amazonia (Little 2002, 2).

Upper Amazonian frontiers have been driven by extractive export-oriented economies, as well as by what Stefano Varese (1968, 2002) has aptly deemed the "civilizing project." This refers to global styles of great temporal duration that have been tempered by the violence of modernity. In her analysis of the Inquisition in Peru in the sixteenth and seventeenth centuries,

Silverblatt (2004) reveals how modernity was intimately tied to its origins in colonialism and to its ability to legitimize violence. As such, Silverblatt compels us to consider the extent to which the Inquisition was not only a product of the modern world, but was implicated in the creation of the "civilized" world familiar to us today. In a somewhat similar fashion MacCormack (2006) has demonstrated how Roman and classical concepts helped forge the construal of historical experience in the Andean region, yet the historiography of Amazonia in this aspect remains in its infancy.

The historical circumstances that permit the rise of an all-encompassing, self-conscious national culture out of a diverse array of relatively discrete cultures varies widely throughout the world. Yet everywhere we note that it is "the forging of a shared body of symbols allowing for various, even rival interpretations" that underwrites the creation of national identities (Hirsch 1990, 20; see B. Anderson 1987, 2000, 2003). Historically, the ruling classes' civilizing project has provided citizens of the Peruvian nation in the making with its shared body of symbols and civic rites celebrating la Patria—the Nation. In his account (1997) of nation making in Huaraz, Peru, Thurner posits that the local—or what he deems the "Indian Republic"—was articulated with the "National Republic" through the imposition of a system of taxation and obligatory provision of labor for public works projects. Likewise, David Nugent (1997) has shown in his study of Chachapoyas how a universalist discourse of citizenship was mobilized to conceal the prevalence of coercive labor relations imposed on the region's indigenous peoples. In spite of the rich body of literature that has contributed to our understanding of local perspectives and regional responses to Peruvian state formation (see G. Smith 1989; Jacobsen 1993; Mallon 1995; D. Nugent 1994, 1997; Thurner 1997), few scholars have investigated how indigenous peoples in Amazonia have been bound to agents of the postcolonial order.

A comprehensive study of the creation of Peruvian national identities in Amazonia is well beyond the analytical ken of this work (see Degregori, ed. 2000). Instead, this book assesses the implications that the civilizing project has had for the Urarina in particular, and more generally for rural peoples in Loreto and other frontier zones of Peruvian Amazonia, such as San Martín. In Peruvian Amazonia, the civilizing project has emphasized the social stigma associated with the distinction between those who were Christianized (*las catequizadas*) and those who remained savage infidels (*salvajes*) (Ballón Landa 1917, 144; see also Aza 1922). An entire ecclesiastical, quasi-legal, and ethnological discourse emerged surrounding the use of the notion of barbarian and savage (*salvaje*), as is clearly evident in the work of Máxime Kuczynski Godard (1943, 2004), one of the founder's of Peruvian Social Medicine (Dean 2004b). This is also readily apparent in the voluminous texts documenting Amazonian expeditions, such as the constant references to savages in the account of Colonel Pedro Portillo's journey in 1900 "through the *montaña* of Ayacucho and along the Rivers Apurímac, Mantaro, Ené, Perené, Tambo and Upper Ucayali, under the auspices of the Peruvian Government" (Adamson 1904, 14; see also Castrucci da Vernazza 1854; Goehring 1877; Sabate 1887; Junta Fluvial 1907).

Indigenous peoples who had not been catechized were considered infidels (*infieles*) or pagans (*paganos*) (Amich 1883; Wiener 1884, 58; Carrasco 1901). "Civilizing savages" (*conquistando los salvajes*) in Peruvian Amazonia became a question of inducing Christianity, Castillization, and commerce. In the noted laissez-faire commentator Aníbal Maúrtua's estimation, Loreto's "civilized Indians" (*Indios civilizados*) maintained relations with outsiders, cultivated extensive food gardens, and were conversant in Spanish or Portuguese (1911, 48). According to the geographer Germán Stiglich (1922, 3), in addition to the "Quechuas and Aimaráes," the indigenous peoples of Peru included more than one hundred nations (*naciones*) of *chunchos* who resided in "the east" (*el oriente*). Throughout Stiglich's 1922 geographical lexicon of Peru, *salvaje* and *chuncho* (from the Quechua term *ch'unchu*, meaning "savage man") are used interchangeably (Otero 1929, 56). Four decades later, Capitán Guillermo Faura Gaig continued this practice by referring to the indigenous inhabitants of Amazonia as *chunchos* (1964, 18). It is not until at least the 1970s that popular characterizations of the local peoples of Peruvian Amazonia began to change quickly. Writing from the perspective of liberation theology, Juan Mercier divides the population of the Peruvian Amazon into three primary groups: urban, *ribereño*, and *nativo* (1974, 7). The growth and popular appeal of the international human rights movement has valorized another term in the regional lexicon—indigenous (*indígena*).[10]

For its part, the "Bolivarian state" has failed to acknowledge indigenous peoples' rights to cultural, political, or economic autonomy. Implicit in the Peruvian state's neoliberal and at times populist project is a political philosophy whose imperative is the creation of a national citizenry—a "national community" (R. Rosaldo 1989)—out of a heterogeneous mix of culturally, linguistically, and historically diverse peoples. By promoting the cultural homogeneity of a unified Peruvian citizenry, schoolteachers, military officers, traders, missionaries, bureaucrats, and local elites have long reinforced the naturalizing impulse of the state's relentless attempt to forge the singular nation.

Peonage: Localizing Webs of Power

Chapter 4 is dedicated to providing an understanding of localized networks of power by placing Urarina society and forest extraction in contemporary perspective. The upper Amazon's commercial economies are based on a vast series of exchange relations linking petty commodity producers, like the Urarina, to middlemen, wholesalers, and distributors. The system of patron-clientilism found throughout much of Amazonia has long been predicated on unequal exchanges "made possible through the differential access to the market economy" (Stearman and Redford 1992, 241). By providing a detailed overview of the Urarinas' engagement with various fronts of national expansion—mercantile, political, and ideological—chapter 4 contextualizes Urarina society and the unequal exchange characteristic of petty commodity production.

Constituted by the "self-perpetuating relationship of center and periphery," unequal exchanges are not an explanation of dependent development, but stem rather from "the uneven pattern of capitalist development" (Cooper 1993, 94, 96). In Peru, this lopsided socioeconomic development was perceptively regarded by José Carlos Mariátegui as "the question of regionalism" (1988, 153–81; 1969). Mariátegui's socialist anthropology of indignation and indigenous liberation is significant for its insistence on linking hegemony and class struggle to the political and administrative systems of land tenure, and, more broadly, to nationalism (among others, see Germaná 1995; López Alfonso 1995). In a similar vein, Amazonianist commentators such as Roger Rumrill and Pierre de Zutter have argued that erasure of the marginality that characterizes Amazonia entails repudiation of internal colonialism (1976, 30; Chirif 1980, 1983).

Today, Urarina local longhouse groups continue to be forced—through a system of involuntary servitude based on their indebtedness to creditors—to produce a level of surplus to meet the demands of the itinerant labor and extractive economies. Urarina surplus goods typically include agricultural produce, poultry, lumber, tree balsams and latexes (like *Sangre de grado* or *Brosium* sp., and the anthelmintic agent *ojé*, *Ficus insipida*, *Ficus anthelmentica*), forest game (including fish and pelts), and woven palm-fiber goods. By advancing goods to subsistence producers and by receiving specialized commodities, traders and *patrones* act as the most important agents of supra-local exchange. In Amazonia, the Spanish term *patrón* (or *patrao* in Portuguese) denotes the boss or overlord, and can more generally be said to designate "the superior in a particularistic relationship between people of different social classes" (Romanoff 1992, 123). Much like Kramer (1979),

I tend to think of the Chambira *patrones* in terms of functioning as "labor contractors."

Even though their bodies have been caught up in the vortex of the market, the Urarina are not simply another type of commodity. Indeed, as the Urarina have followed in the wake of market expansion and contraction they have carried with them "memories and customs, beliefs and eating habits, musics and sexual desires" (B. Anderson 1992, 7). Paying attention to the ways in which producers like younger Urarina women, aspiring headmen, and widows, for example, engage in market relations demonstrates the overlapping and mediated value systems of multiple economic arrangements. Based on both historical and ethnographic evidence, chapter 4 concludes by presenting a reconceptualization of debt peonage.

In an effort to push the analysis beyond the ephemera of historical events, I subsequently turn to an examination of the embodiment of Urarinas' production—palm-fiber wealth and hunted forest game. Not only is this an effort to map the Urarinas' multiple regimes of values, but it is also an attempt to plot the processes underlying the commodification of Urarina social life. By examining the close ties between social relations and material culture, I am able to assess the construction of Urarina and *mestizo* social identities through the production, circulation, and consumption of specific items of material culture, such as woven palm-fiber goods.

The production of palm-fiber wealth articulates the female or intra-demic kinship economy with the institution of debt peonage. Chapter 5 assesses Urarina women's partial loss of control over the circulation of one of the most important wealth items that they produce—palm-fiber goods. Ethnographic sensitivity to gendered segregation illustrates the extent to which Urarina women are actively involved as transactional agents within an economic complex that almost always only attends to men's activities. This is clearly evident by women's salient absence from the transcultural negotiations integral to petty-commodity production. Not surprisingly, Urarina women have a relatively limited range of options when it comes to dealing with outsiders.

The circumscribed roles of Urarina women are celebrated and legitimated by an elaborate mythological discourse that authorizes the gendered segregation of production, exchange, and consumption. Collective representations involve ideas about the social aspects of the world: they are composite phenomena whose authority is symbolically sanctioned, and thus they often appear immutable. Urarina mythological contemplation is never the simple mirror of productive relations: it is, as García Canclini notes, "an internal condition of their emergence" (1993, 12; cf. Williams 1977, 75). Urarina mythology is integral to the establishment and maintenance of hegemonic social practices—namely the linked asymmetries of gender and generation, and those associated with relations of indebted servitude, glossed here as *habilitación*. These practices take root in a shared sense of time and understanding of collective tradition. Chapter 5 concludes by pondering the practical and ideological implications that women's exclusion from the "public" sphere has for indigenous political mobilization.

Forbidden Fruit: The Economy of Kinship

Underscoring the prominence of uxorilocal extended family longhouse groups in the Urarinas' kinship economy, chapter 6 emphasizes the importance of affinity and exchange. Study of Urarina domestic units and their patterned trajectories provides insight into mechanisms of cultural continuity and variation, while concomitantly allowing us to analyze different levels of social organization. In retrospect, my decision to pursue the themes of exchange, value, and desire seems now to have been a natural or logical outgrowth of my initial object of inquiry: understanding the politics of uxorilocality and the practice of bride service (Dean 1995, 1998a). Unlike industrialized societies, bonds uniting Urarina society are not forged through the regulation of assets, but rather through the control of people as if they were assets. Examination of bride service and marital infidelity illustrates how Urarina affinity involves men's and women's mutual negotiation of status and obligation. In spite of the fact that women are discursively represented as objects to be circulated, Urarina women are never actually exchanged: affinity in bride service societies involves not only the subjective interests of men, but of women as well.

The reality of gender and age hierarchies revealed from the study of the politics of bride service implicitly informs the subsequent analysis of the processes of ambivalent exchange underwriting the cultural production of Urarina value. While objects are crucial to exchange theory, they are usually portrayed in putatively egalitarian societies as complementary *prestations*. Following Lévi-Strauss's (1969, 65) theory of matrimonial exchange, women are the "supreme gift among those that can only be obtained in the form of reciprocal gifts" (see also Clastres 1987, 38; Gregory 1980, 641; cf. Renshaw 2002, 215). Pursuing this line of reasoning, some Amazonianists have even equated the circulation of comestibles with the symbolic exchange of women. Reichel-Dolmatoff (1976b, 312), for instance, argued that in Tukano society the "ritual exchange of certain foodstuffs come to represent the exchange of women." However, I found absolutely no support for this symbolic evaluation among the Urarina. From their vantage point, the Urarina insist that *prestations* of forest game and the labor power associated with brideservice are not exchanged for a woman in matrimony. Instead, men claim that their labor power—in the form of bride service and gifts of forest game—feeds their wives and maintains their families.

Components of Urarina public rhetoric and social practice embody both aspects of gender symmetry and hierarchy. Uxorilocality and sororal polygyny, which favor solidary matrilines, coupled with a cosmology that celebrates women's capacities, account for the relative degree of female autonomy noted among the Urarina. Detailed review of a specific case of infidelity highlights the importance that access to children plays in bride-service societies. In this regard, the dispute indicates the continuing need to examine how relations of sexual complementarity and antagonism in bride-service societies are mediated not through assets, but rather through a discourse that characterizes people as though they were assets to be exchanged strategically.

Exchange, Value, and the Power of Things: Alienation and the Commodification of Social Life

Urarina society is predicated on the reproduction of a cultural system of wealth—including hunted forest game, cassava beer, woven palm-fiber goods, and the accoutrements of shamanism. These items of cultural wealth "stand as an object code for the signification and valuation of persons and occasions, functions and situations" (Sahlins 1991, 287). Anthropological interpretations of exchange have evolved from specific historical conditions that endowed understandings of "gifts, reciprocity, authority, ownership, and gender" with an expressly Occidental mentality (Weiner 1994, 393). In contrast, I argue that the ambiguity and labiality inherent in the transcultural circulation of the aforementioned wealth items is best captured through a "temporally conscious" (S. Moore 1994, 126; 1983) processual approach stressing the mutable and contextualized nature of exchange. After all, what regulates the process of exchange in any given context are morally, legally, and ritually sanctioned systems of classification. When it comes to praxis, the classification of exchanges is an inordinately unstable field that is "open to manipulation, fixing, deceit—to all sorts of creative and interested chicanery and goodwill" (Davis 1992, 45). Accordingly, this book adopts a phenomenological model of the circulation of wealth that incorporates ambivalence, flexibility, and enterprising manipulation as part of the essence of the moral system underpinning Urarina exchange.

The Urarina exhibit symmetrical and complementary regimes of food exchange: meat is procured by men and distributed by women, while cassava beer (*bardiguë*) is made by women and generally circulated by men. The production, distribution, and consumption of these wealth items are central to Urarina social and political life. Given the importance of cassava beer in ritual and political affairs, those men who can rely on large productive cassava gardens and multiple wives or daughters to make beer are at a distinct advantage in their ability to mobilize attendants at a communal assembly.

Men's hunting prowess is a prominent factor animating the exchange of bushmeats (forest game). In evaluating the significance of bushmeat circulation, I elicited verbal statements attesting to the centrality of obligations and rights within the domus, rather than to reciprocal cycles of *prestation* between domestic groups. Focus on the internal circulation of forest game as objects of *prestation* signals the importance of gendered and intergenerational exchange of other key items of wealth, such as cassava beer. Women's role as cultivators of cassava (*Manihot esculenta*) and primary producers of beer stands in equipoise to bushmeat's gendered valence (cf. Hill 1987, 189). As elsewhere, beer and bushmeats are thoroughly "infused with many symbolic meanings" (H. Moore 1993, 131–32). They are emblematic of the objectified production engendering the longhouse or *ludéri*.

The Urarina have culturally prescribed calculi for determining equivalent values for disparate items entering into exchange—to wit, social *prestations* are bestowed for prestige, gifts are swapped for shamanic favors, and cane alcohol (*aguardiente*) is bartered for petty commodities. In the absence of a cash economy, equivalencies are the primary measure of value for the Urarina. Given that the items entering into circulation have no a priori measure of common worth, such equivalencies are virtually impossible to measure objectively. Subjective experience then becomes the index of value, alerting the various parties involved in specific transactions to the inequities or satisfactory nature of the terms of exchange. This becomes more readily apparent in chapters 7 and 8 when I explore Urarina labor relations in light of the "social life" of cloth and forest game (*mitayo*)—particularly as these items function as fluid currencies of value.

I have isolated woven palm-fiber goods and bushmeats for further analysis because of the proclivity of these items to straddle various circuits of exchange. The Urarinas' wealth of hunted forest game and palm fibers is capable of migrating through multiple regimes of value. The analysis of their circulation gives us a privileged vantage point for understanding the interrelationship between Urarina kinship economy and petty-commodity production. Value is after all never "dissociable" from those wider social processes in which things, agents, and relations mutually "valorize" one another (Thomas 1991; see also Callahan 1999). Urarina value creation (*niya cahuatua*) is a process recursively constituted as the "outcome of acts of substitution, juxtaposition, and transformation" (Thomas 1991, 31). These acts effectively reveal attributes of animals, plants, and other items of exchange, and the capacities of their human transactors.

Rather than imputing occidental notions to the Urarinas' embedded economic relations, my intention is to delineate more clearly the nature of the interaction among the various components of the Urarinas' kin economy. In this fluid, global world, Urarina culture is assessed as a discursive or signifying system; signs and cultural practices are examined as elements in disparate, yet overlapping structures of meaning. Wealth items are signs of embodied qualities that form part of a larger totality. As signs, Urarina wealth items communicate essential aspects of that larger cultural totality. Their value is a function of contrast within a system (Saussure 1966). In addition to Urarina people and their words, fundamental wealth items of what Marx and Engels (1978, 316) called congealed labor power—in the form of forest game, palm-fiber wealth, and shamanic paraphernalia—circulate through multiple regimes of value. The notion of multiple regimes of value is helpful in understanding the cultural construction of Urarina society because it yields insights into the circulation of wealth as it crosses transcultural boundaries.

By focusing on woven palm-fiber, chapter 7 elucidates important aspects of the social production of female wealth. The exchange of palm-fiber wealth stabilizes a host of social relationships, ranging from marriage and fictive kinship (*compadrazco*, that is, spiritual compeership) to perpetuating relationships with the deceased and with extractive entrepreneurs. In exploring the mediation of labor and communal relations through the circulation of palm-fiber goods, chapter 7 illustrate the ways in which cloth—both indigenous and imported—moves through multiple spheres of value.

While the production of palm-fiber wealth integrates the female or intrademic kinship economy with the institution of debt peonage, hunting fulfills a comparable function for Urarina men. By examining the exchange of Urarina forest game within the context of peonage, the book emphasizes the tensions between unfree relations of production and the circulation of goods, labor power, and knowledge, particularly hunting shamanism. The circulation of forest game facilitates the construction of social identities and fosters the collective reproduction of society. Hunters, hosts, and consumers of game are reciprocally defined through their mutual implication in the disbursement, display, and consumption of forest game. Chapter 8 demonstrates how the Urarinas' exchange of forest game is epitomized by strategic action and informed by their cultural conceptions of commensality (*siya lenunejké*), social precedence, and consumerism.

Anthropological contributions to the study of material culture are helpful in sensitizing us to the contradictions and multiplicity in the types of exchange and *prestations* found among the Urarina. Thomas's (1991, 1993) notion of "the instability of things" and Weiner's (1994, 400; cf. Mosko 2000) contention that social hierarchy both surfaces and is undermined through the "paradox of keeping-while-giving" are particularly revealing in the context of gifts, commodities, and alienation (see also Carrier 1990, 1992a, 1992b, 1994). The aforementioned approaches provide useful perspectives on the ways in which the circulation of wealth items both actuates and distinguishes nodules of power and arenas of authority, particularly among Urarina headmen (*kurana*), senior women (*ené biña*), male hunters (*atiya*), female weavers, shamans (*kuichá*), and *mestizo patrones*.

Woven palm-fiber goods or bushmeats do not have fixed identities; they may simultaneously have symbolic, ceremonial, and commercial value. But as Strathern posits, the challenge in all of this economic entanglement is to decipher the process of conversion. As Strathern opined, "What is at issue is not a scale of value but an alteration of identity—transformation" (1993, 91). The degree to which wealth items are themselves transformable is an empirical problem pertaining to the contested topography of commodity flows. As analysts have demonstrated, ranking by wealth is not simply a matter of assigning a quantity through multivariate estimations, "but of plotting locations on a complex map of possible flows of differently constituted forms of wealth" (J. Ferguson 1992, 59; cf. May 1999; Godoy 2001). Additional research is needed that goes beyond exploring just the metrics of market integration, including as well the study of the specific implications of such incorporation (Lu 2007).

Rather than simply establishing determinate economic value for "commodities" I adopt Steiner's insights on "extractive bargaining," which he employs to explore the negotiation of value in the commodification and circulation of African art objects (1994, 62, 176 n. 2). As he convincingly argues, "extractive bargaining" is directed toward coaxing items away from their owners. Through extractive bargaining, *mestizo patrones* and traders transform Urarina wealth items from their noncommodity state into a commodity phase by luring them from an "indigenous milieu into the realm of the market economy" (Steiner 1994, 62).

Analysis of extractive bargaining as it occurs along the Chambira River Basin calls for inclusion of the relational dimensions of exchange. Debt peonage is constituted not only by the "coaxing" efforts of the traders, but also by the strategic efforts of the Urarina to acquire trade goods, in spite of the fact that they find themselves asymmetrically positioned vis-à-vis the rest of Peruvian national society.

Trade is both an intellectual and a social phenomenon: in the words of Marx, commodities are "social hieroglyphs" whose significance is modified through their conventional usage (see Hebdige 1979, 95). In terms of consumption, commodities are liable to double inflection; that is to say, they are open to either legitimate and illegitimate deployment or expenditure (Bataille 1985). Urarina and *mestizo* wealth items exhibit comparable contradictions. Objects can be mystically commandeered, "'stolen' by subordinate groups and made to carry 'secret' meanings: meanings which express, in code, a form of resistance to the order which guarantees their continued subordination" (Hebdige 1979, 18). Symbolically they can be reappropriated and endowed with inherently antagonist significance by those who have produced them, as is clear in both Urarina cosmology and social practice. The linkage between the social order and ideology, production and reproduction is "neither fixed nor guaranteed" (Hebdige 1979, 16). Nowhere is this more readily evident than in the realm of the metaphysical.

Chanting Rivers, Fiery Tongues: *Ayahuasca* Shamanism

The book's final chapter explores one particular response that the Urarina have developed to interpret and deal with the encroaching outside world, namely *ayahuasca* shamanism—which draws its ritual efficacy from the coupling of historical reflexivity and mythopraxis. Based on the ritualized consumption of hallucinogenic beverages made from *ayahuasca*, analysis of this sacred activity demonstrates the significance of cultural heterogeneity and transcultural dialogue.

The persistence of the social order can never be taken for granted: it is the shamans who chant the world into being. Urarina shamans enter into trances in an effort to sustain the homology between the cosmos and society. The essence of Urarina shamanism is knowledge of the cosmos that manifests itself through knowledge of mythology, and through the ability to chant and to sing. Divine afflatus is achieved through the consumption of entheogenic plants. Shamanic ingestion of psychotropic compounds includes tobacco, cayapi, and datura, which are used in curing and in divinatory vision quests. Throughout Amazonia tobacco smoking is an important component of shamanic healing (Wilbert 1987, 97). Among the Urarina, dried tobacco (*enuata*) leaves are wrapped in *tahuari* (*Tabebuia chrysotricha*) bark or Bignoniaceae or banana leaves and smoked as cigars.

Shamanic and political power are not necessarily coterminous—shamans assume positions of leadership only if they so desire. By virtue of their ability to charm, cure, and bewitch, (*kuichá*), shamans possess control over the primary forces of life and of death. Disembodiment and celestial travel are achieved through hallucinogenic trance. During the Urarinas' mythical time of origin the universe was in a state of perpetual daylight. As a result shamans were sent to bring back the night from Lumaí, the master of *ayahuasca*. Perpetuating continuity with a sacred antediluvian past can be read as resistive of the hegemonic claims of Peruvian national culture. In this vein, I illustrate how Urarina communion with the cosmological realm (via expressive culture and shamanism) coexists with what has become known in the literature as "the millennial dream"—the indigenous belief that the conditions of scarcity and human affliction will terminate in well-being and splendorous abundance in the way of trade goods and game animals. I evaluate the role that *ayahuasca* shamanism plays as an interpretive device in Urarina society. Study of Urarina shamanism enhances understanding of how imaginary structures help the Urarina negotiate the internal contradictions accompanying the intrusion of market relations and disease, and the many challenges to the Urarinas' cultural autonomy.

I conclude my examination of the Urarinas' ideological conception of the circulation of commodities in chapter 9 by comparing the prohibition on the commoditization of meat with the increasing commoditization of produce and wealth items traded for Western consumer goods. By surveying how shamanism is integral to Urarina hunting and healing—two arenas of social life at the margins of both the kinship and the regional market economies—the book highlights the contradiction between the commensality of bushmeat circulation and the commercial transactions circulating trade goods. This is useful in contextualizing the Urarinas' apocalyptic cosmology and alerting the reader to the Urarinas' own sense of deep ambivalence toward the outside world.

1

The "People from Downstream"

The Chambira Basin and Urarina Society

East of Peru's capital, Lima, the narrow Pacific coastal plain rises precipitously to join a formidable chain of mountains. From the high-altitude peaks of the Andes, the rugged landscape descends again through a region of richly biodiverse forested plateaus eventually to meet the upper Amazon (Lathrap 1970). This vast area of the neotropics extends beyond Peru's borders with Brazil, Colombia, and Ecuador. It was designated Antisuyu by the Inca empire, and it is commonly referred to today as the *montaña* (high forest) or *selva*.[1] Stretching away from the Andean piedmont, the upper Amazon includes that portion of the Marañón River that descends into the lowlands at the notorious water rapids called the Pongo Manseriche.

Scholars once aggregated Amazonia into two primary habitat types—the interior upland forest (*terra firme*) and the floodplain (*várzea*) (Meggers 1971, 1994; Moran 1982, 30 fn. 11). By overlooking the multiplicity of Amazonian biotopes, this polarizing approach restricts comparison and credible generalizations (Coomes 1992; Moran 1995; Cleary 2001). Although the region was apparently uniform upon first sight, specialists of Amazonia are now taking into account the prodigious variety of ecospheres that comprise the region (Descola 1994, 54).[2] Indeed, far from being a homogenous region of undifferentiated tropical rainforest, the upper Amazon varies tremendously in terms of its topography, annual rainfall, soil composition, seasonal climatic deviations, geology, and faunal and floral compositions (Kalliola and Flores Paitán 1998; Peisa 2003, 10–19, 43–52).

Peru's upper Amazon region is composed of at least three primary morphological zones: 1) *ceja de la montaña*, the higher altitude rain-forested foothills located between 800 and 2,000 meters above sea level; 2) the *selva alta* or high jungle located between 400 and 800 meters above sea level; and 3) the *selva baja* or dense tropical-forested lowlands located below the 400 meter mark. The topography of the *selva baja* (also known as the *llano amazónico*) is characterized by high zones that do not flood. These areas are separated by waterways or *quebradas*. Some of the *quebradas* have water all year-round; others remain dry until the rainy season. The regional climate is characterized by its heat (average annual temperature is 26°C), and high levels of humidity. Perhaps the greatest geographical variation occurs between the riverain regions—whose soils are enriched by annual flooding—and the upland interfluvial zones, whose ancient soils are composed of relatively barren alluvial precipitates. In addition to the upland interfluvial zones, Peru's *selva baja* is also composed of extended areas of low-lying forest that become inundated during the pluvious season, thus posing challenges to agricultural development (Szyszlo 1947, 64–6).

Encompassing a large stretch of humid tropical forest, the Chambira Basin is formed by an array of blackwater rivers,[3] streams, meandering brooks, oxbow lakes, and a complex of alluvial terraces and flood plains. The Urarina say that "blackwater" rivers or *ajcaig jijchúai* originate from the upriver palm swamps. They contrast *ajcaig jijchúai* with the turbid, silt-laden waters of the Bajo Marañón River (or as the Urarina call it, Nutiyú), and its various tributaries. Unlike the Río (River) Marañón, the Chambira is not one of Peruvian Amazonia's primary rivers. The Chambira River drainage extends to the north, to the border with Ecuador, but it does not extend beyond the international frontier.

To facilitate the administration of a vast and wildly heterogeneous imperium in the New World, Madrid divided its American colonial holdings into viceroyalties (*virreynatos*) and audiences (*audiencias*). During the seventeenth and eighteenth centuries, the entire Chambira Basin fell within the jurisdiction of the government of Maynas (Governación de Maynas), a bureaucratic division of the Audiencia de Quito. The term Maynas comes from the name of the indigenous group of peoples the Jesuits encountered south of the Río Santiago, at the foot of the Pongo Manseriche (Ardito Vega 1992, 16; Reyes Flores 1999, 130). Today, the Chambira Basin falls largely within the political boundaries of the province and department of Loreto, Peru. Formed in 1866, the department of Loreto is bounded by Colombia to the northeast, Ecuador to the northwest, and Brazil to the east. The largest of Peru's provincial departments, Loreto includes 368,865 square kilometers of rainforest territory, which accounts for nearly 30 percent of the total area of the country (Peisa 2003, 10).

The Chambira Basin's two main rivers—the Chambira (Ninichú) and Tigrillo (Ajcañe)—are meandering and slow-flowing. They vary in width between approximately 20 and 250 meters. They receive inputs from numerous tributaries including the Airico (Yancó), Pangayacu (Ajadiyú), Patayacu (Anariñe), and Pucuyacu (Lanaá). Average annual rainfall on the Chambira is between three thousand and thirty-five hundred millimeters (on the lower to middle portions of the basin this ranges from two thousand to four thousand millimeters) (see Ferrúa Carrasco et al. 1980, 2; Kramer 1979, 29). The cyclical advent of the rains (*ejlo tabáij*, lit. "big rains") replenishes the Chambira Basin's waterways and heralds the beginning of seasonal food scarcity. There are impressive seasonal variations in river flow, with the lowest levels noted in the dry season months of July and August, and the highest levels occurring during the wet season, between the months of November and April.

For descriptive purposes, the Chambira Basin can be divided into three hydrographic zones: lower, middle, and upper. The lower portion of the Chambira River passes through the Marañón River's silt and nutrient-rich floodplain (*várzea*). Small-scale flooding occurs at least once a year when the Chambira River's discharge exceeds the capacity of its channel and inundates the adjacent low-lying lands of the lower and middle portions of the catchments. As water spills out of the channel, alluvium is deposited on the banks, which over time forms natural levees. Much larger floods occur at intervals on average every decade or so. *Ribereños* from the Bajo Marañón refer to the seasonally flooded, forested wetlands of the Chambira Basin as a huge *aguagal*—that is, they refer to the area as a giant palm-tree swamp (see Ferrúa Carrasco et al. 1980, 2).

Aerial photographs of the region indicate that the lower portion of the Chambira River runs parallel to a series of bluffs that border the flood plain. This portion of the Chambira Basin is composed of a complex mosaic of pools, marshy swamps, sandbars, abandoned channels, and naturally formed levees running along the side of the river channel. At the confluence of the Chambira and Marañón lies the small *ribereño* settlement of Ollanta whose population in 1998 was approximately 230. The Chambira River's embouchure is an ancient oxbow lake prized by local inhabitants for its fish, particularly *paiche*, which are absent from the upper reaches of the Chambira. In the lower section of the Chambira Basin one encounters a series of lagoons that are also valued for their fish stock, aquatic herbs, grasses, and water lilies. The lower and middle stretches of the Chambira channel are inhabited by two types of river dolphins—the *bufeo gris* (grey dolphin, *Sotalia fluviatilis*) and the *bufeo colorado* (pink dolphin, *Inia geoffrensis*)—neither of which are hunted by the Urarina or *ribereños*, who hold these creatures in high symbolic esteem.

The middle stretch of the Chambira Basin begins at the upper reaches of the Marañón's flood plain and continues until it meets the waters of what the Urarina call Anariñe, the Río Patayacu, which is one of the Chambira's primary tributaries. This portion of the Chambira River is characterized by a serpentine course, with many meanders. Here the river's sloping alluvial fans become sandy beaches (*playas*) during the dry season. Throughout Peruvian Amazonia, mudflats (*barreales*) are distinguished from emergent sandbars (*playas*) (Denevan 1996, 675 n. 5). The appearance of beaches, or exposed riverbeds in the Chambira Basin, corresponds seasonally with the dry period and symbolically with the regeneration of life. The dry season is also the time of greatest residential mobility. Of particular importance at this point of time is the search for tortoise (*taricaya*) eggs. The eggs are dug out from their beach nests when river levels are at their lowest.

The upper section of the Chambira begins at the Anariñe River and terminates in the headwaters of the basin located in the luxuriant forested uplands that skirt the Pastaza River. The number of loop-shaped curves or meanders increases in the upper reaches of the Chambira, while the width of the river's channel gradually decreases. The verdant canopy forests of the middle and upper Chambira Basin are crisscrossed by countless streams, rivulets, and braided channels that periodically overflow their banks during the rainy season's heavy daily downpours. This run-off pools in clay-bottomed depressions and replenishes the low-lying palm swamps. As seen from the air, the upper canopy appears unbroken. The rivers that course through the forested lands, the skies above, and the ground below all yield a wealth of animal products (bird feathers, animal hides and game, honey, insects) and aquatic life that forms the basis for the Urarina people's livelihood.

Kachá: The "People from Downstream"

They refer to themselves as Kachá (lit. person, human), and we know them by the ethnonym Urarina. The label Urarina may come from the word *uru-dai*, a term for a comestible tuber from the arrowroot family (*Calathea allouia*?) similar to the *dale dale* or the *papa mandi* (unidentified). According to early European accounts, this plant provided the Urarina with their basic foodstuff (Ferrúa Carrasco et al. 1980, 4; Olawsky 2002, 6). My own fieldwork was unable to confirm this claim. The ethnonym Urarina may in fact be from Quechua—*uray* meaning below, and *rina* referring to *runa*, or "people." Urarina is thus rendered in Quechua as *uray-runa* or "people from below" or "downstream people" (Espinoza Galarza 1979, 305). Quechua was after all the imposed lingua franca of the Jesuit's mission outposts. Moreover, the geography of the Chambira River, whose headwaters are located to the south of two major river basins—the Pastaza River to the west and the

Tigre and Corrientes to the east—suggests that this is a more likely interpretation for the origin of the ethnonym Urarina.

Native inhabitants of the Chambira Basin have also been called various names, including Itukales, Ytucalis, Singacuchuscas, Cingacuchuscas, Aracuies, Aracuyes, Chimacus, and Chambiras (Grohs-Paul 1974, 53 n. 4; Velasco 1960, 267; Figueroa 1904, 163, 177). The Urarina have also been referred to derogatorily as Shimaco—a term etymologically related to the word *cimarrón*. In the Iberian Americas, *cimarrón* originally signified escaped feral livestock, then runaway blacks, Indians, or mixed ancestry people who fled life on the plantation and sought refuge in the inaccessible forests, hills, or outback (Wolf 1982, 156).

Underscoring Urarinas' resistance either to working in the colonial *encomiendas* or living in the missions, the appellation Shimaco conjures up their common strategy of dealing with hostile outsiders through flight into the forest or distant waterways. Spanning more than four centuries, this form of resistive accommodation has structured contemporary relations between those who are Urarina and those who are not. While it is true that the discursive strategies of indigenous peoples are usually elaborated as resistive, a number of other accommodative reactions such as religious conversion, banditry, inter-ethnic conflict, and millenarianism are also constant features of the relations between forest people and the state (cf. Brown 1996). For the Urarina, resistance can be seen in a number of phenomena—ranging from residential mobility to *ayahuasca* shamanism.

During my time on the Chambira, *patrones* (local labor bosses) and *regatones* (itinerant river-traders) frequently complained about the Urarinas' shifting patterns of residence.[4] Seasonal fishing and gathering expeditions in floodplain regions and upland forest, a tradition of headman factional politicking, a defensive strategy emphasizing disengagement rather than confrontation, disease, consumerist desires, and the requirements of labor migration have all promoted frequent population resettlements on the Chambira. For many of the residents of the Río Pangayacu, those Urarina living further upstream are portrayed as ignorant and impoverished—vulnerable to exploitation by the roving *regatones* or more permanently established *mestizo patrones*.

Urarina society and culture have received exceptionally little attention in the burgeoning ethnographic literature of the region and only sporadic references in the encyclopedic genre of Peruvian Amazonia.[5] Neoteric accounts of the Urarina peoples are limited to the data reported by Castillo (1958, 1961), by the information relayed by Tessmann in his magnum opus *Die Indianer Nordost-Perus* (1930, partial Spanish translation 1987), and to the erratic and idiosyncratic observations of missionaries and contemporary adventure seekers (Izaguirre 1925; Quintana 1948; Villarejo 1988). Aside from Kramer's doctoral research (1979) conducted at Urarina settlements along the Tigrillo (San Lorenzo) and lower Pucuyacu Rivers, and her article on Urarina swidden agriculture (1977), the literature on Urarina society and cosmology is relatively scant. The most recent survey works on the Urarina peoples include Ferrúa Carrasco et al. 1980, Cajas Rojas et al. 1987, and Rijke 2000, a study of the ecological impact of oil contamination along the Chambira, yet no comprehensive monograph on Urarina society and culture has ever been published. The linguist Knut Olawsky has written the most welcome and valuable *Urarina Texts* (2002), which includes grammatical information in the form of free translation as well as an interlinearized translation of Urarina stories recorded in the field.

Culturally and linguistically distinct from the societies that border them, the Urarina can be seen as an indigenous island in a diverse ethnic archipelago. They are similar in this regard to lowland South America's Tupi-Guaraní Sirionó and Tapirapé, and to the Karib-speaking Bakirí, all of whom are "small in number or isolated in the midst of culturally different people" (Clastres 1987, 62). The majority of the Urarina are primarily monolingual speakers of Kachá eje, a language that has yet to be standardized through writing. Likewise, Kachá eje remains one of the last unclassified languages of Amazonia (Cajas Rojas et al. 1987; Dávila Herrera and Corbera Mori 1982). Urarina has variously been classified as Panoan (Velasco 1960, 3: 208); as Tupian (Figueroa 1904, 187); as Macro-Tucanoan (Shell and Wise 1971, 14; Bouroncle Carrion 1973, 399); as belonging to the Andean-Equatorial family (Greenberg 1960, 794); and most commonly as an unclassified, linguistic isolate (Loukotka 1968, 156; Kramer 1979, 5; Cajas Rojas et al. 1987; Pozzi-Escot 1998, 158; Olawsky 2002).

Historical sources consistently associate the Amazonian Roamainas with the Zapas. Figueroa and Velasco postulate that in the past the Roamainas and Zapas were a "nation" numbering some ten thousand people living throughout an extensive tract of territory (Figueroa 1904, 136, 149; Maroni 1889–92, 26: 263; Velasco 1960, 3: 263; Grohs-Paul 1974, 60). It is unclear whether they are distinct indigenous societies or, as Figueroa believed, two segments of the same "group" (1904, 136). My fieldwork indicates—albeit tentatively—that the Urarina have considerable ties to the Omurana (Záparoan) peoples, including isolated cases of intermarriage. Omurana territory extends westward from the Chambira to the Pastaza, above the mouth of the Río Huasaga. Omurana settlements are also located to the north on the upper affluents of the Tigre River, whose course comes close to converging with the Pastaza at the historically contested border between Peru and Ecuador.

Group boundaries along the Chambira River emphasize ethnic differences that distinguish the Urarina and other indigenous peoples on the one hand, and *ribereño* and urban *mestizos* on the other hand. For the Urarina I know, native peoples (*gente nativa*) include the Omurana (known to the Urarina as Mañjá); the Jeberos (Debero); the Cocama (Kokwamu); the Cocamilla (Kokwámitsa), who in the 1920s were reported to live at the disembouchure of Chambira; the Lamas (Lamistu); and the Jíbaros and Kandozi (Baxkagá), meaning "savage" (Tessmann 1987, 47). When I asked pointed questions about the nature of ethnic identity, bilingual Urarina men would explain it to me in the following terms: "You are *gringos*, there are also Peruvians, different sorts of people, there are also the Shishaco [Serranos, or people from the Andean Sierra]; we are different classes of people. (Ustedes son personas gringos no, hay también los Peruanos... diferentes personas, hay también los Shishaco, somos diferente clases de gente)" (Kirina, October 1998).

Primordialist notions of ethnicity based on procreative metaphors of shared blood did, on rare occasions, enter into the conversations I had with my Urarina acquaintances, though it is still unclear to me how central this idiom is in their ethno-anthropology. The spatial categories of upriver (*ujkuaä*) and down river (*ujkuái*), however, do serve as prominent indexical signs of ethnicity. The Urarina say that *mestizos*, Inga (Ijiá ídi), and Lamista peoples originate upriver, from the upper reaches of the Marañón River. In contrast, the Urarina note that Cocama settlements are dispersed along the Marañón River, both downstream and upstream, mirroring the settlement pattern of contemporary *ribereño* peoples.[6]

Ribereño or "river dweller" delineates non-native rural residents from indigenous "tribal" peoples such as the Urarina, Kandozi, and Achuar (Chibnik 1991, 167). When considered at all, *ribereños*, much like Brazilian *caboclos*, have most often been portrayed as subaltern, as stagnant, as passive, as "marginal" (Oberg 1965)—and at best—as merely an enfeebled peasantry (see S. Nugent 1990; 1993; see also Parker 1985; M. Harris 2001; Nugent and Harris 2004). Our understandings of *ribereño* and *caboclo* cultures have undeniably been shaped by what Stephen Nugent (1993) has aptly called an "over-determined naturalism" present in the various discursive renderings of Amazonia. While depictions of nature tend to obfuscate and in some instances erase the presence of humans societies in Amazonia, anthropological descriptions of the area have long been engrossed with the micro-study of the region's seemingly "authentic" social formations—that is, indigenous peoples. Much of the Amazonianist scholarship has been influenced by Orientalist concerns with presenting the Other as part of an ancient, enduring, and static culture. Unlike the numerically dominant *caboclo* and *ribereño* societies of Amazonia, indigenous peoples have occupied the attention of ethnologists and explorers alike for centuries. To be sure, the mere existence of hybrid *ribereño* and *caboclo* cultures—creations from the wake of a colonial system forsaken following the collapse of the rubber industry—sets into question popular accounts of Amazonia that persist in envisioning it as an edenic realm (N. Smith 1996; Dean 1998b; Slater 2002).

The *ribereño* versus *nativo* (native) distinction is prominent throughout Peruvian Amazonia due to the comparatively large indigenous population of the region, and to the enduring "Amerindian self-identity" found among contemporary *ribereño* society (Chibnik 1991, 174, 180f.). In Loreto, *ribereño* identity is shaped by multiple cultural and socioeconomic features, including class position, descent, employment, and regional affiliation. When not maligned for their cultural ignorance, crude behavior, and dim-witted ways, *ribereños* (and Loretanos more generally) are represented in national discourse with Arcadian imagery. Loretano women are often portrayed as licentious (*putería*) by many coastal inhabitants, particularly residents of Lima. The image of promiscuity is mobilized in stark contrast to the sexual puritanism inscribed in the popular, national imagery of "traditional" Andean communities.

The widespread *ribereñozation* of Peruvian Amazonia began during the rubber bonanza (circa 1880–1920), nearly a century after it did in comparable regions of Bolivia and Brazil. Given the scant number of recent colonists who have migrated to the Chambira Basin, *ribereño* identity categories continue to frame inter-ethnic relations. On the Chambira, *ribereño* and *nativo* are oppositional categories that people use as a means both of self-identification and for distinguishing others, a practice that is at least five decades old. When communicating with outsiders, bilingual Urarina men will often use the term *nativo* self-referentially. Invariably, the rise of Peru's lowland indigenous political movement has influenced the growing appeal of this term for the Urarina. Gow's work (1993) suggests that the importance in Peru of ethnic categories for "white" Europeans and North Americans, like *gringo* and *blanco*, which are common to much of Latin America, seems to be relatively insignificant in the Chambira Basin.[7]

By 1980 two schools had been established in the Chambira Basin, Nueva Esperanza on the Chambira River (under the auspices of the Summer Institute of Linguistics), and Santa Cecilia, located along the Pucayacu. Along the Tigrillo River, two *mestizo* schools had been established at the sites of the *mestizo fundos* (work camps) of Pandora and Nueva Angora (Ferrúa Carrasco et al. 1980, 48). Throughout the 1990s, however, virtually no state-sponsored schools, health-care facilities, or other public facilities were operational in the Chambira River drainage.

Ribereños from the Marañón River and its tributaries often told me that the Urarina lack schools, and as such are still violent (*bravo*) in their behavior and thoroughly uncivilized (*salvaje*). The Urarina I knew vehemently denied this charge on common-sense grounds. As my good friend Najlegue-kuktíri told me, "We are not like wild forest animals, you can approach us—we don't flee like the animals of the forest." Contrary to what was said to me by inhabitants of Iquitos and by *ribereños* living along the riverbanks of the Marañón, the Urarina I came to know were not savages, they were not aggressive, they were not particularly captious. Tranquility (broken by periodic outbursts during drinking parties) is the social norm of daily existence.

Kaj Laitjíra: Daily Rounds of Urarina Communal Life

Urarina settlements are composed of multiple longhouse groups (*kaj laitjíra*). These are small-scale communities located on high ground (*restingas*) or embankments along the flood-free margins of rivers. The embankments are bounded by low-lying territories (*tahuampa* and *bajiales*) that are susceptible to flooding during the rainy season (fig. 1.1).

Kaj laitjíra band together in settlements that are dispersed along the navigable waterways of the Chambira watershed. Communities typically comprise 40 to 100 members of bilateral kindreds (*kanarai kíri*) living in a combination of multi-family longhouses, single-family *ribereño*-styled dwellings, and temporary shelters perched along the region's immense blackwater river system or situated away from the Chambira's paludal floodplain. While some settlements are said to have up to 150 residents (Ferrúa Carrasco et al. 1980, 26), I never saw an Urarina community with more than 100 inhabitants. Many are only one half or one quarter of this size. Much of the data for this book draws from my experience living with the local longhouse groups of the middle portions of the Chambira, and especially those located on the Pangayacu River or Ajadiú (fig. 1.2).

The alluvial deposits at the mouth of the Pangayacu are fertile; they support a profusion of plant life. It is here that abundant fish can be harvested, since they are attracted by the fruits and seeds from the bank's plant cover. Consisting of three primary local longhouse groups perched on a river terrace, the Pangayacu community is referred to in Spanish by the name of Santa Beatriz. This designation originates from the name given the commu-

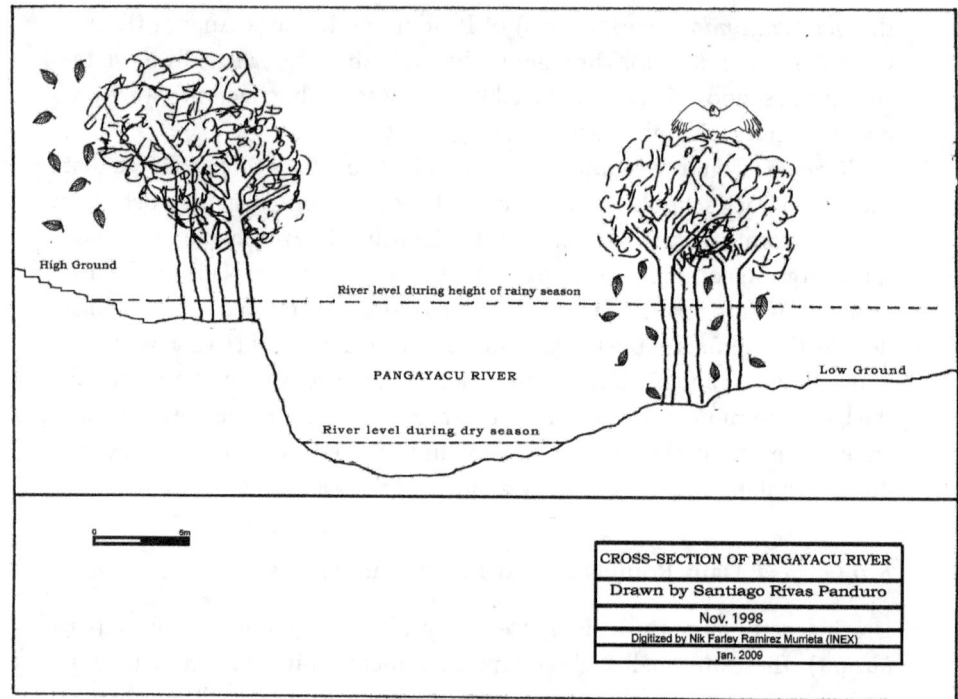

Fig. 1.1. Cross section of Pangayacu River, Chambira River Basin

Fig. 1.2. Urarina husband and wife, fishing from canoe on the Pangayacu River

nity by a *patrón* known as Don Tobias, who worked on the Pangayacu in the 1960s. The current senior female inhabitants have resided at the mouth of the Río Pangayacu since 1977. Throughout the 1990s, Santa Beatriz's population was around seventy inhabitants (fig. 1.3).

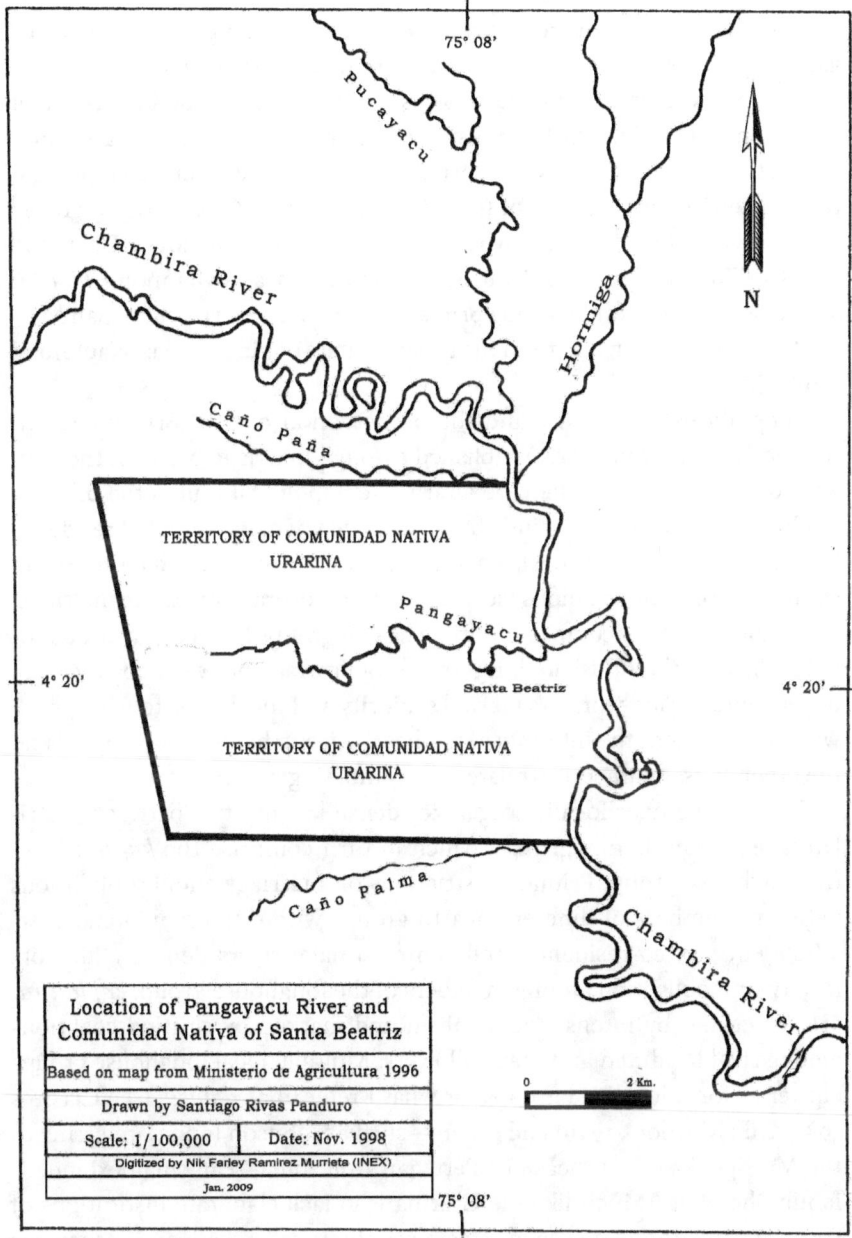

Fig. 1.3. Map of the Native Community of Santa Beatriz, Pangayacu River

Officially registered as a Native Community (Comunidad Nativa), the Pangayacu Urarina obtained legal title to their homelands in 1996. Their community is situated on the south side of the Pangayacu, and is located a short distance (approximately five hundred meters) from the mouth of the river. The Pangayacu's embouchure with the Chambira is approximately fifteen kilometers downstream from the Río Patayacu. It provides the fluvial gateway to a dense stretch of seemingly limitless forested lands.

Urarina swidden agriculture involves the cultivation of food gardens that remain in production until diminishing crop returns require their abandonment. This mitigates against the formation of densely concentrated population nuclei. The inhabitants of the middle and upper Chambira watershed are overwhelmingly Urarina, whereas the residents of the lower Chambira and Tigrillo rivers are both Urarina and neo-Peruvian (Marañón *ribereños* and regional immigrants hailing primarily from the department of San Martín, the Ucayali River, and from the urban centers of Yurimaguas, Nauta, and Iquitos).

Generational continuity and the perpetuation of territorially circumscribed kinship groups are established through marriage between the children of political allies. The core Urarina sociopolitical unit is the bilateral kindred, which is headed jointly by men and women. Post-nuptial residence is overwhelmingly uxorilocal, while sororal polygyny and child bestowal are common. Polygynous unions (sororal and non-sororal) constitute multiplex households. They encompass multiple hearth groups headed by various co-wives. Within the household, rights and obligations between co-wives are dependent on each woman's marital seniority and the degree to which each wife can represent the interests of her hearth group before her husband and the other consanguineously related yet competing hearth groups.

Prescriptive uxorilocality organizes dense kinship ties between matrilateral extended family groups, which in turn comprise the *kaj laitjíra*—the longhouse group. Primary restrictions on marriage entail prohibitions between members of different hearth groups within the same longhouse. While kinship, co-residence, and common natal rivers denote affiliation, loyalty, and obligation among members of the longhouse group, *kaj laitjíra* are structured by intense factionalism and marked by shifting coalitions among rival headmen and their followers. Multiple local longhouse groups cluster to form localized groups, or what I refer to as *demes*[8] (see Clastres 1987, 57ff.; Murdock 1949) and others—such as Johnson (2003), referring to the Matsigenka of southeastern Peruvian Amazonia—call small extended-family "hamlets." Much like the Urarina who lack elaborate institutions of social control, the Matsigenka esteem economic self-reliance, management

Fig. 1.4. Urarina family, Pangayacu River

of aggression within the extended-family "hamlets," and autonomy to act in their own perceived self-interest (Johnson 2003) (fig. 1.4).

Urarina local politics are characterized by a mercurial balance of power between *demes* united through affinal ties and episodic political alliances, exchange relations, and disputation. Comprising a *"plurality* of extended families" (Clastres 1987, 58) Urarina *demes* are dispersed along the Chambira Basin at varying distances that can be covered by canoe trips of one to two days. They appear to be divided into ritual clans or "sibs" bearing mythologically inspired animal and plant names. The descent, localization, and other features of Urarina sibs remain obscure. My acquaintances on the Pangayacu would explain this matter to me by saying, "We are all of different types" (*calidades*), but they were generally very reluctant to elaborate any further.[9] It maybe that the Urarina, in common with other indigenous peoples of Amazonia—as Fejos indicated for the Yagua (1943, 82)—once had a well-defined clan system that has lost most of its distinctive features. Urarina *demes* are often referred to by their river locale, by the name of nearby *mestizo* work sites (*fundos*) or *ribereño* villages (*caseríos*), and, more recently, by their association with or status as an officially recognized Native Community, such as the Comunidad Nativa Santa Beatriz.

Open disputes are most commonly provoked by allegations of shamanic assault (*satiyá*) and by conflicts over the rights and obligations surrounding "marriage" (*ijtaráriga*). The high priority the Urarina accord to the issue of sexual fidelity (*kasháuki*) accounts for a large proportion of the controversy within local groups. This in turn underscores the extent to which the question of access to persons as *assets* and control over their sexuality and reproductive capacities is deemed problematic by the Urarina. Group associations are informed by gender and age hierarchies that are reinforced by a discourse in which women (particularly when young or widowed) and youths—both male and female—are portrayed as objects to be exchanged (*cudiaca*).

Relations between *demes* are publicly identified with affinal ties and with competitive political relationships among headmen mediated primarily by socially mature men. The Urarina do not recognize chiefs, nor do they seem to value the notion of chieftainship. Headmen, or *kurana* as they are called in Urarina, are leaders of semi-autonomous communities (cf. Carneiro 1993, 8 n. 1). Maturity and marital status are directly correlated to a person's political authority. Contact with Peru's ethnic federation movement has begun to change this since literacy, rather than orality, has come to certify public expressions of indigenous authority (Dean 1999). Nonetheless, throughout the 1990s Urarina political power was still authorized primarily through personal prestige rather than through appeals to jural authority. The selection of a headman is not determined by length of residence nor by genealogical seniority, but rather by reliance on a faithful "following." Male leadership is predicated on personal attributes that the Urarina deem especially suitable: social maturity, munificence, oratory skill, hunting prowess, and shamanic knowledge. Leaders garner personal prestige and influence by negotiating exchanges, distributing goods and information, and by promoting intra- and inter-demic associations. Successful men of renown do not command, they persuade—often by way of example, and through appeals based on their personal experiences as socially efficacious, shrewd, and wise leaders. But *kurana* are followed for only as long as people think it is advantageous to do so. Typically, a headman's most important male followers are those considered his *reina caná*—his sons-in-law.

Men of renown are characterized by their adept command of mythopoeic discourse and their mastery of phatic allocution. Urarina men are the ones who tell stories, or *nerejtána*, publicly. *Nerejtána* are performed monologically by a single orator, dialogically by two men of relatively equal standing, or in pedagogical fashion by a senior man (*biña*) and a group of his juniors. Skilled oration is always worthy of praise among the Urarina. The telling of myths and daily narratives are accompanied by gestures and peppered with numerous echoic words. Elaborate bodily gestures enhance the performative dimensions of storytelling, while the articulation of the sounds of animals, climatic phenomena, and machinery (guns, chain saws, boat motors, airplanes, and so forth) enlivens the recounting and gives the narrative the aural texture of everyday life.

The core of Urarina mythology comprises stories that recount the heroic deeds of the divine beings and the primordial ancestor's Herculean struggles to overcome human fallibility. Aetiological myths celebrate a cosmogonic process whose culmination is the metamorphosis of human beings from bestial progenitors. The interval in the distant past when humans were animals (*kachiané nerutúrga lenunej kíri*) is distinct from what is colloquially referred to as "people stories" (*nerejtána kacháire*). Historic contact with non-indigenous society is the concern of this narrative genre, or of what Hugh-Jones, writing about the Barasana, has declared as comprising "popular history" (1988, 140).

Heuristically, Urarina narratives of the past can be divided into the following intervals: the primordial antediluvian and diluvial eras; the cosmic postdiluvian past when people and animals experienced isomorphic transmutation; and the present age, which includes memories of the lived past and historical sagas of malevolent *patrones*, ethnic conflict, and magical hunting trips and adventures downriver in the ports of Iquitos or Nauta. Even though the Urarina distinguish a series of primordial and historical ages, they exhibit no great concern for elaborating a sequential theory of time. The master tropes of Urarina time are neither circadian nor monumental, but rather they are derived from the processes of ontogeny, horticultural production, and seasonal cyclicities. Indeed, discursive time is embedded in Urarina tropes of ontogeny, in the stages corresponding to the ongoing replication of the domus, and those associated with seasonal periodicities, such as ripening of the coveted *pifuayo* fruit and the appearance of tortoise (*taricaya*) eggs. This is also reflected in the Urarinas' understanding of lunar calendrics used for food gardening.

Relative to men, women are not as appreciated for their storytelling competence. Women do recount gender specific stories (*detainéne*), but these tend to be shared more exclusively with those of their own longhouse (*ludéri*), at least during the occasions I lived with the Urarina. While men may dominate public speech events, women have spheres of public discourse open to them, including songs (particularly lullabies), communal complaints, menstrual rites, ritual wailing, and hallucinogenic trance. These discursive practices draw on an epistemology stressing the importance of wisdom predicated on personal experience. Women enjoy symbolic power over the collectivity's mythical beginnings and play key roles in the interment of the dead.

Female prestige is sanctioned through women's roles as mothers, as senior wives in polygynous households, and as post-menarchal mothers-in-law with their own large followings (*yajané kachdecidi*). Like men, women are also recognized as having the capacity to heal and to bewitch (*cutipar*), and they are recognized as well through their active participation in *ayahuasca* shamanism. *Cutipar* in Loreto is associated with contagion and witchcraft (*brujería*) (Castonguay 1990, 32). Women's power is also culturally valorized through women's participation in gender-specific productive activities, such as weaving palm-fiber goods, pottery making, beer fermentation, and their taking part in critical aspects of horticulture. While men are the ones who obtain clay from riverbanks and prepare the hardening agent from the ashes of the bark of the *apacharana* tree (*betáto, Licania genera*), mature women are the recognized potters of Urarina society (Kramer 1979, 102). The influx of plastic containers and metal cooking pots (*cuatárjue*) has undermined this ancient art form, but Urarina women from the middle and upper Chambira Basin remain avid potters and continue to coil, slip, fire, and burnish clay vessels.

As throughout much of Peruvian Amazonia (Bergman 1990), Urarina subsistence and petty-commodity production are typically organized at the domestic level—the *kaj laitjíra*. The Urarina subsist on sweet manioc and plantains, supplemented by gathered wild plant foods (palms, fruits, nuts), insects (such as fat palm grubs), honey, and proteins in the way of ample varieties of fish and hunted forest game, including peccaries, tapir, monkeys, deer, iguanas, armadillos, caiman, paca, capybara, and birds, such as toucans and *perdiz*. While the *kaj laitjíra* is the basic unit of subsistence and consumption, Urarina division of labor exhibits aspects of both gender complementarity and hierarchy.

Prior to puberty, boys and girls learn through following the lead of older children and adults. Young children live blithe, carefree existences, free from the obligations that are to face them in later years. When they reach the age of about eight children begin helping more systematically with the care and harvest of the gardens, gathering firewood and other forest produce, looking after small animals, fishing, and assisting with child-care. Parents take little notice of their children's desultory behavior, but if they misbehave by fouling food supplies or breaking cherished possessions, they are reprimanded. As far as I could tell, the Urarina rarely strike their children. However, to punish disobedient children the Urarina do use two types of stinging nettles, potent red (*ajkisía lanajái*) and mild white (*ajkisía sumajái*). The degree of affection parents express for their children is remarkable. When working in their gardens, mothers will often carry their babies in slings to make the half

Fig. 1.5. Urarina children, Chambira River Basin

hour journey to the garden plot. Parents—both mothers and fathers—caress their young children, rock them, engage them in banter, and occasionally participate in their child's play (fig. 1.5).

Child-care, garden maintenance, transportation of crops, firewood collection, cooking, pottery production, the elaboration and upkeep of clothing, beverage preparation, and weaving are all primarily done by women. Girls begin assisting in adult women's work once they have had their first menses. They are then taught the skill of weaving and the art of pottery making. Men's work includes hunting, forest-cover clearing, working lumber, tool and shelter construction, fine basketwork, fishing, organizing commerce, and the shamanic arts, of which they are the primary practitioners. Teenage boys help in swidden agriculture, hunting, and logging expeditions, and spend time learning from their male elders how to make blowguns and fashion fishing and hunting gear. Women keep chickens (*atahuari*) and men occasionally raise swine, which are exchanged almost exclusively with *mestizos* for trade goods.

In accordance with elaborate ritual prohibitions, men make dugout canoes (*inanjiá*) that provide the Urarina with their primary mode of river transport. Balsa rafts are constructed to transport agricultural produce downstream. The Urarinas' lack of motorboats or funds to pay for the passage aboard the ferryboats (*motonaves* or *lanchas*) that ply the Marañón and Amazon rivers are often cited as the reason why the Urarina do not market their garden and forest produce in the urban markets of Nauta and Iquitos.[10] While on the river, all Urarina are keenly aware of subsistence opportunities, including fishing.

Spear fishing is seen as a quintessentially masculine affair and subject to considerable ritual elaboration. To augment the aim and power of their fishing spears, adolescent boys and young men undergo rites of intensification that take the form of arm scarification (*bijij yuruára*). This extremely painful procedure involves tightly wrapping thin strips of *ninahuasca* or *anguilla caspi* bark around the novitiate's forearms. The caustic bark strips are left in contact with the skin for about twenty minutes. This causes blistering skin wounds to appear that are prone to permanent scarification. Urarina people told me that the larger the scar, the more impressive the effect.

Hunting is a masculine pursuit of prestige. It is done with lances (*cuaderno*), blowguns (*jijchana*), and shotguns (*ijchafua*). Huntsmen are accompanied by hound dogs and assisted by magical amulets. Reliance on hunting and fishing magic is extensive, whereas agricultural ceremonialism appears to be minimally elaborated. Small mammals including monkeys, pacas (*añuje*, *Dasyprocta variegate*), and sloths are tamed by the Urarina and kept as pets. Parrots (*piwicho*, *Brotogeris* sp.) and *chirricles* (*Pionites melanocephaca*) are valued as mascots; their colorful plumage is sought after for the manufacture of ritual headdresses. Adorned with the luminous casings of *elateridae* beetles, parrot feather headdresses symbolize a man's sacred prerogatives. As with ritual headdress, the social construction of Urarina personhood is deeply influenced by ideas and symbolism associated with the body, the natural landscapes, and the cosmos.

The ethnography of Amazonia and Melanesia has amply demonstrated the extent to which male-female differences infuse social organization and permeate foundational beliefs about body imagery, procreation, and conceptions of personhood (Gregor and Tuzin 2001). In the context of Ese Ejja kin relations, "Otherness" is created through matrimony. Lepri (2005) underscores the importance of Ese Ejja kinship filiation and the cultural significance of notions about the transmission of vital substances among this indigenous Amazonian society. Likewise, the Urarina emphasize the social constitution of personhood, defining it primarily in terms of other "selves" composed of vital essences, rather than in terms of social institutions.

Urarina ontology holds that the self is bifurcated: the body is an androgynal composite—a union of male and female elements. The Urarina say that the masculine element is transmitted through semen (*réi nüjëé*, lit. "man's milk"), and the feminine element is passed on through a woman's blood (*nelacdiá*).[11] When ill, women are thought to be incapable of having children since it is said that their blood is cold (*kinaitéri*), rather than hot (*ajátua*). The consumption of banana gruel mixed with the ashes of burnt cockroaches is believed to enhance fertility. The gestation for a male is typically said to be ten months long, while the duration for a female is thought to be nine months.

In preparation for the birth of a child a free-standing birthing house (*jajtá*) sheltering the expectant mother (*asidínia*) from the unwanted gazes of others is constructed from palm fronds (or mosquito netting) and situated either adjacent to or within the longhouse near the hearth fire of the expectant mother. The birthing hut abuts the hearth fire, which, when necessary, is rekindled to keep steady warmth. Inside the birthing hut, a shallow pit (*fatiyá*) is dug. The birthing pit's earthen ground is covered with a sheet of freshly cut *yarina*, *shebón*, or banana tree leaves. Female kin chant and perform *effleurage* like massages to aid the parturient woman, who will give birth squatting over the pit. Before the newborn is collected from the recess in the ground, a female assisting the mother cuts the umbilical cord, leaving a cord approximately twenty centimeters long. The woman who severs the umbilical cord is socially consequential; she is considered henceforth the mother's *cumáire* (an apparent analogue of the Spanish *comadre*, or co-mother). The birthing assistant—known as the *michirá*—then digs another deeper hole and places a few bamboo slats across the opening in the ground.

To protect the newborn from spiritual harm a number of purificatory ablutions are performed. While suspended over the new pit, the newborn child is bathed by the birthing assistant, who then gives the child to the mother for nursing. Bathings continue for the first few days following the birth. The placenta (*misi*) and bloodied banana leaf sheet are placed by the birthing assistant into the deeper hole. As is customary among the neighboring Achuar, the placenta and umbilical cord (as well as fetal still births) are buried near the mother's hearth fire, "thereby becoming a form without an occupant" (Descola 1994, 121). Mother and child remain in the birthing house cum nursery for approximately a week. Experienced Urarina mothers have been known to give birth alone in the forest. Physically disfigured infants are thought to be the offspring of sylvan spirits, and as such are dispatched to the other world by abandoning them near *lupuna* trees. In cases of unwanted or inconvenient pregnancies, abortion is commonly practiced.

In its classic form, the couvade devotes ritual attention at childbirth to the father instead of the mother (Rival 1998; Vilaca 2002). The expectant Urarina father may take to his bed and simulate labor pains. Parturition practices involve both parents being confined and similarly restricted, underscoring the progenitive roles of both parents. To protect the newborn, parents are subjected to food tabu and to various restrictions on their activities, such as tactile prohibitions. The Urarina discourage direct contact with a wide number of plants, such as peppers (which are associated with eye disorders), because they are said to cause harm to their infant children. The Urarina believe that particular trees have strong guardian forces or *madres*, such as *moena* (*urëba, Aniba* sp.?), *lupuna* (*ichyah, Trichilia tocacheana*), *cumala* (*cayajudí, Iryanthera juruensis*), and *marupá* (*virarinigá, Simarouba amara*). In addition to avoidance of *copahiba* trees—which my friend Najlegue-kuktíri blamed for the agonizing death of two of his young children—direct contact with *aguajé, shapaja, yarina*, and *ungurahui* are also strongly discouraged. It is thought that these trees' cosmic forces can damage one's health, or more commonly the health of one's newborn offspring, causing such ailments as scabies and diarrhea. During the "lying in" period, the mother and the newborn are secluded in the birthing hut, and the father remains nearby. Not until after the remaining umbilical cord drops off does the father resume his productive activities. Urarina expressions of couvade are paralleled by postpartum work restrictions that prevent mothers from leaving their newborns until they are partially weaned, a period lasting approximately three months. Throughout this time, mothers are dependent on the female members of their *kaj laitjíra* to provide them with sufficient garden produce, namely, tuberous cassava plants and plantains (Kramer 1979, 81).

Mission and popular Christianity have influenced Urarina worldviews—though their precise significance on the Chambira remains to be fully determined. In the missions, religious festivals such as Semana Santa, Fiesta de Las Cruces, Corpus Christi, and Saint John's Day were observed for hundreds of years. Such occasions continue to inform *ribereño* religious calendars. For the Urarina, the influence of Christianity is perhaps most evident in the anointing of infants in a baptism-like naming ceremony they refer to as *baicha*. This practice combines recitations, solemn adjurations, and truncated water rites. After the child has reached its first birthday, the parents select ritual co-parents and organize a cassava beer-drinking festival attended by guests from the surrounding longhouse groups.

Co-fathers or *compadres* are termed *cumfáire*. A godchild (or in Spanish, an *ahijado*) is called a *caballé* in Urarina. Drum, flute, and panpipe music, and lively dancing accompany the celebration. Paralleling *ribereño* popular

Catholicism, the child is anointed with water and endowed with a Spanish name. In their dealings with *patrones*, traders, evangelists, and *ribereños* in their midst, the Urarina use their Spanish names when addressed by non-Urarina peoples. However, they do not generally use Spanish appellations among themselves but rather draw from a wide range of names, many of which emphasize people's physical appearance.[12]

As elsewhere in Peru, dress creates gendered bodies (Femeninas 2004). Girls' wrists are adorned with a double-strand of blue or black beaded (*chaquira*) bracelets from infancy. At puberty, young women start wearing triple-stranded wristlets. The onset of menarche is also marked by a haircut and confinement (approximately eight to ten days) in a menstrual hutch. During her isolation, the pubescent girl is placed in a prohibitive status: her isolation is undertaken in an effort to avert her unwanted gazes from harming the men. The menstruating girl is attended to by her senior female kin, especially mothers and grandmothers who instruct her in the arts of womanhood, namely the techniques of weaving. After confinement, the pubescent novitiate bathes in the river and her face is then adorned with *achiote*. Food tabu continue for the next few weeks. Menstrual rites are conducted to ensure that girls will eventually become robust and hard-working women.

Coupled with forearm scarification, male rites of passage include instruction in the rituals and knowledge surrounding *ayahuasca* shamanism. In this bride-service society, seniors are the junior's mystagogues; sons, grandsons, nephews, and daughter's husbands are regularly counseled by their elders in the ways of the ancient "grandfathers" (see Tessmann 1987, 64). The few who ever reach old age (and acquire the status of "elder," or *biña*) can look forward to being respected as cultural illuminati, as faithful keepers of the sacred chants, healing arts, and tales of the grandfathers. While the Urarina make relative distinctions between the young (*nyamaña*) and the old (*biña*), they have no elaborate age-set systems as noted elsewhere in lowland South America (see Maybury-Lewis 1984). Relative to the life expectancy of members of the "post-industrial" world, the Urarinas' life cycle is compressed into a shorter time frame. The transition from youth (*nyamaña*) to adult male (*kicha*) and female (*ené*) statuses is achieved when one has married, had children, and lived long enough to learn all that is necessary to assume the rights and obligations intrinsic to the core reproductive, economic, political, and symbolic functions of Urarina society.

In addition to *vivax* and *falciparum* malaria, the Urarina suffer from numerous tropical diseases such as leishmaniasis, intestinal parasites, and toxoplasmosis. With the Urarinas' history of chronic diseases and episodic demographic decline, it is not surprising that much of their mythopoeic discourse is a commentary on fatal illness (likewise among the Matisgenka; see Izquierdo and Johnson 2007). As elsewhere in Peruvian Amazonia (Kuczynski Godard 2004), sojourners to the Chambira River have long complained of disease, as well as the stifling heat and unrelenting swarms of blood-sucking insects. Ron Manus, a missionary with the Summer Institute of Linguistics (SIL, also known as the Wycliffe Bible translators, and known more recently as SIL-International), estimated a decline of 80 percent of the Urarina population that had been exposed to the measles outbreak of 1962 (Kramer 1979). During the cholera epidemic of 1991–92, mortality rates were noted as high as 30 percent among affected longhouse groups of the Chambira, over three times greater than the reported rate of 8.5 percent for Peruvian Amazonia (Rosenberg 1991).

The death of persons of renown—both male and female—precipitates the burning of the center of domestic and public life—the longhouse or *ludéri*. Chanting and wailing in unison and individually, female mourners express profound grief through stylized ritual wailing. Keening consoles the bereaved and reiterates the deceased's social personae. The women's elegiac chants are framed in terms of personal relationships and social obligations. Corpses are interred in canoe coffins that are buried in the forest in a communal cemetery, simulating the form of a miniature longhouse. The body and the house are intimately linked (Carsten and Hugh-Jones 1995, 2–3). After death, the deceased's spirit returns to its natal longhouse and begins another intra-utero existence by reoccupying the placenta. As Descola notes for the Achuar, this represents continuity "between the life of the embryo in its placenta-house, post-partum life in the house placenta, and the life of the 'true' soul after death, again in its placenta-house" (1994, 121) (fig. 1.6).

Ludéri: Sheltering the *Kachá*

A "pre-modern" architectural celebration of the collectivity, the *ludéri* is the nexus point for the circulation of Urarina goods, labor power, and knowledge. It is at once a domestic space and a public one. The traditional longhouse shelters familial hearths and provides the Urarina with their primary forum for the articulation of political discourse (cf. Rival 1993, 643). Urarina shelters may be divided into two primary types: permanent (*ludéri*) and provisional (*luanadí*) (cf. Tessmann 1930, 492; Kramer 1979, 42). *Ludéri* differ from *luanadí* or temporary lean-tos in terms of their architectural complexity, in their intended functions, and in their permanence. *Luanadí* are transitional shelters; they are forest encampments made during the hunt or during trips to fish or fell trees. They are equivalent to the son-in-law's

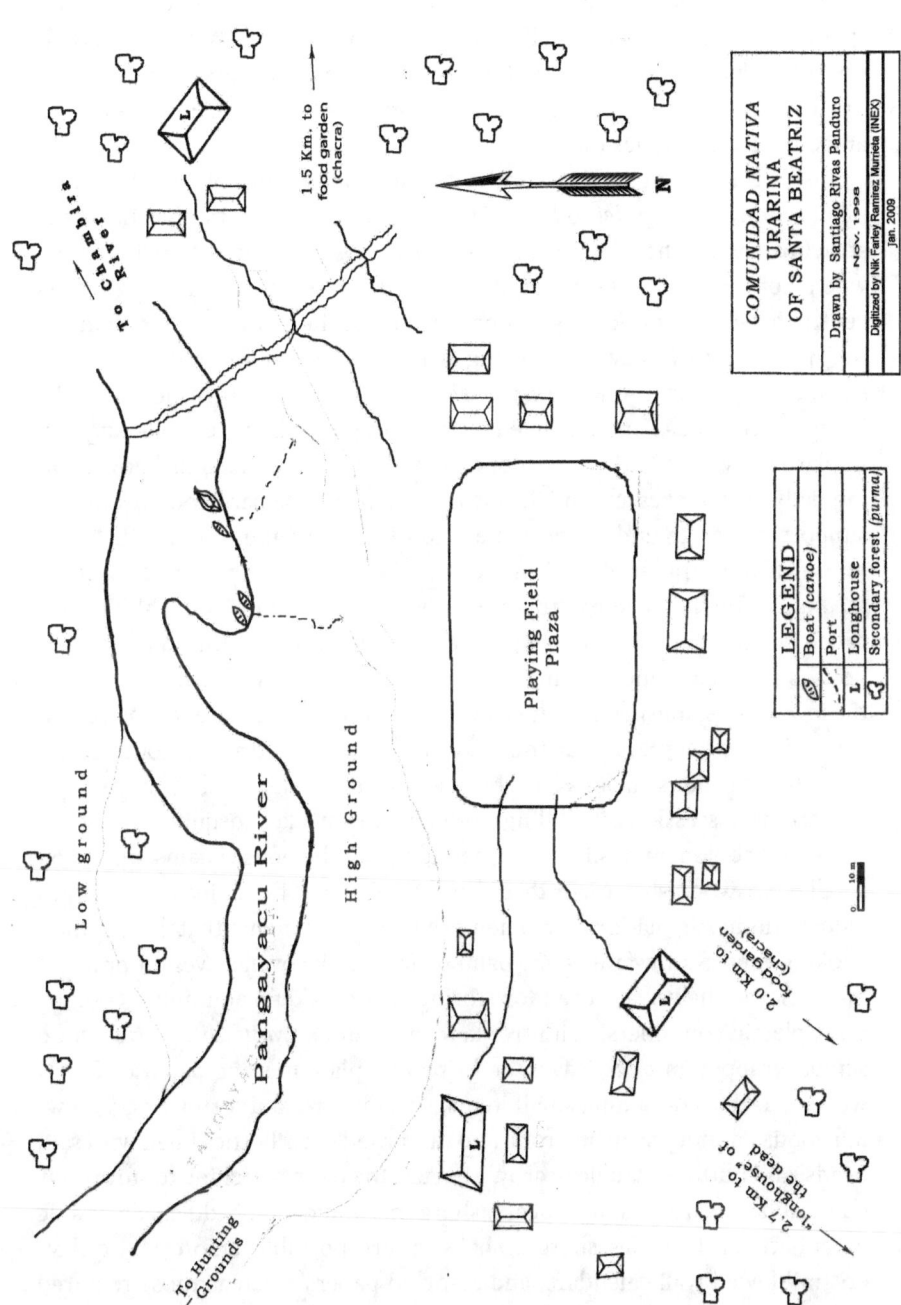

Fig. 1.6. Layout of Native Community of Santa Beatriz, Pangayacu River

shanty or the menstrual hutch. In the region that I am the most familiar with (for example, the middle course of the Chambira), longhouses—both "permanent" and "provisional"—as well as lean-tos and "Marañón styled" houses built on elevated (one to two meters) hardwood stilts can all be seen. The Urarina also construct a variety of shades, potter's shacks, storehouses, and chicken hatcheries (fig. 1.7).

Inside the typical longhouse or *ludéri*, a parallel series of dais-like, hard, palm-wood (*Iriartea deltiodea*) platforms (*ajána*) run from one end of the structure to the other. Supported by *huacapu* posts (*anesíyu*), the slightly elevated (approximately one meter) *pona*-wood platforms flank the longhouse's central aisle, giving the longitudinal surface of the structure something of the appearance of a nave. Consisting of a rectangular frame and palm-wood slats, each platform—or *tarima* in *ribereño* parlance—corresponds to the living quarters of a female-headed hearth group. Holding the projecting roof in place above the horizontal supporting beams are stanchions known colloquially as *horcónes* and in Urarina as *anisijiá*. These hardwood beams are supported at both ends to bear the load of the roof and to brace the longhouse's frame. The fixed vertical props of the frame are referred to as *cutiyá tenanajá*. The thatched rooftop or *cumba* is made from woven palm fronds called *banaáu*. Smoke from hearth fires constantly billows through the longhouse's roof thatching, helping to safeguard it from insect damage. Among the few well-established headmen of the Chambira, *ludéri* are reconstructed every eight to ten years when the thatch has deteriorated and becomes leaky, and when the house beams have been sufficiently consumed by termites.

Various possessions, including clothing, muslin-like mosquito nets, metal tools, and cooking utensils, are suspended from the house beams, placed on small *pona*-wood shelves, or thrust in the palm roof thatching over an individual's domestic platform. Women use the over-hanging thatch near their cooking fires to stow fans, spiny palm boards, and woven sieves for processing cassava. Shelves are used for storing clay crockery, aluminum cooking pots, plastic containers, primitive kerosene lamps (*ramfadi*), gourds, food scraps wrapped in *bijao* leaves, and ripening plantains and papayas. Finely woven baskets containing small items, such as bird and tortoise eggs, sewing goods, laundry soap, mirrors, and discarded glass bottles filled with salt, beads, and buttons, dangle nearby. Men use the palm thatching to store their cultural hardware—fishing spears, shotguns, and canoe paddles. Shamanic paraphernalia, batteries, shotgun shells, curare, portable radio/cassette players, mildewed wall calendars, and assorted papers (such as those required for the registration of births, school documents, and legal declarations or *officios*) are all stowed in small wooden chests (*inia cujcuajon*) placed on

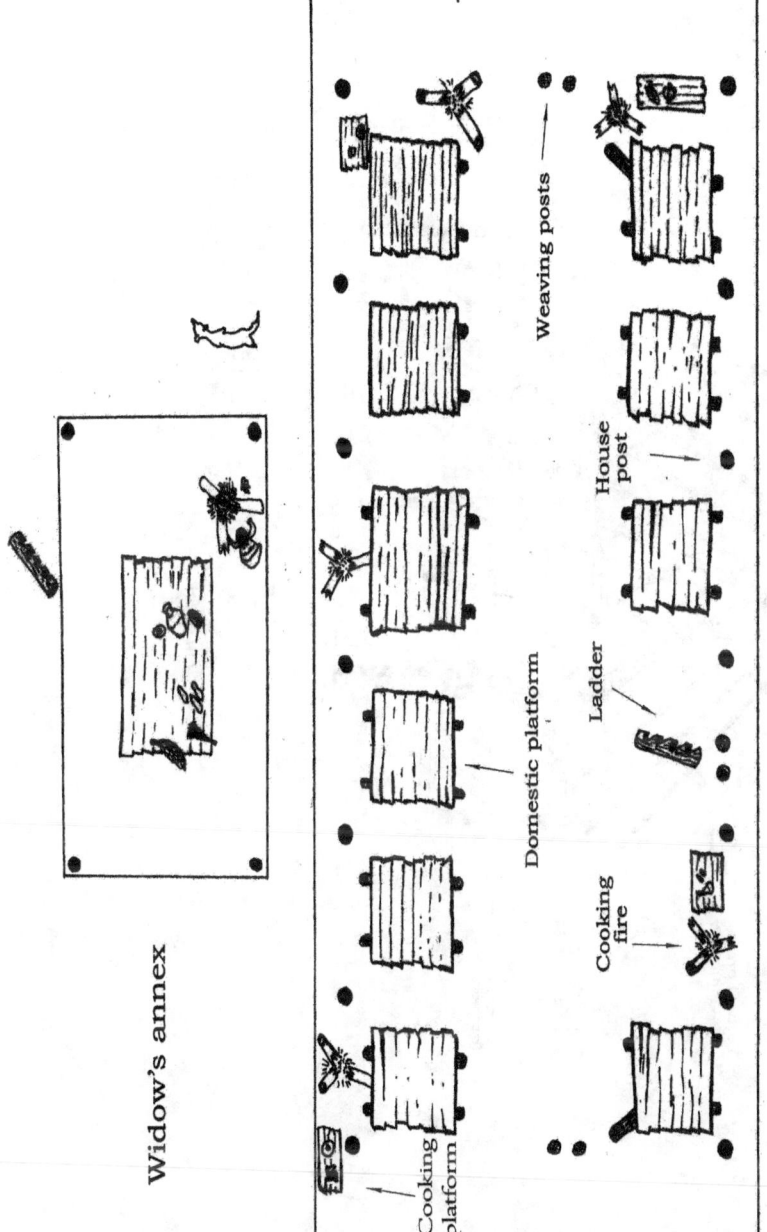

Fig. 1.7. Longhouse drawing, viewed from above

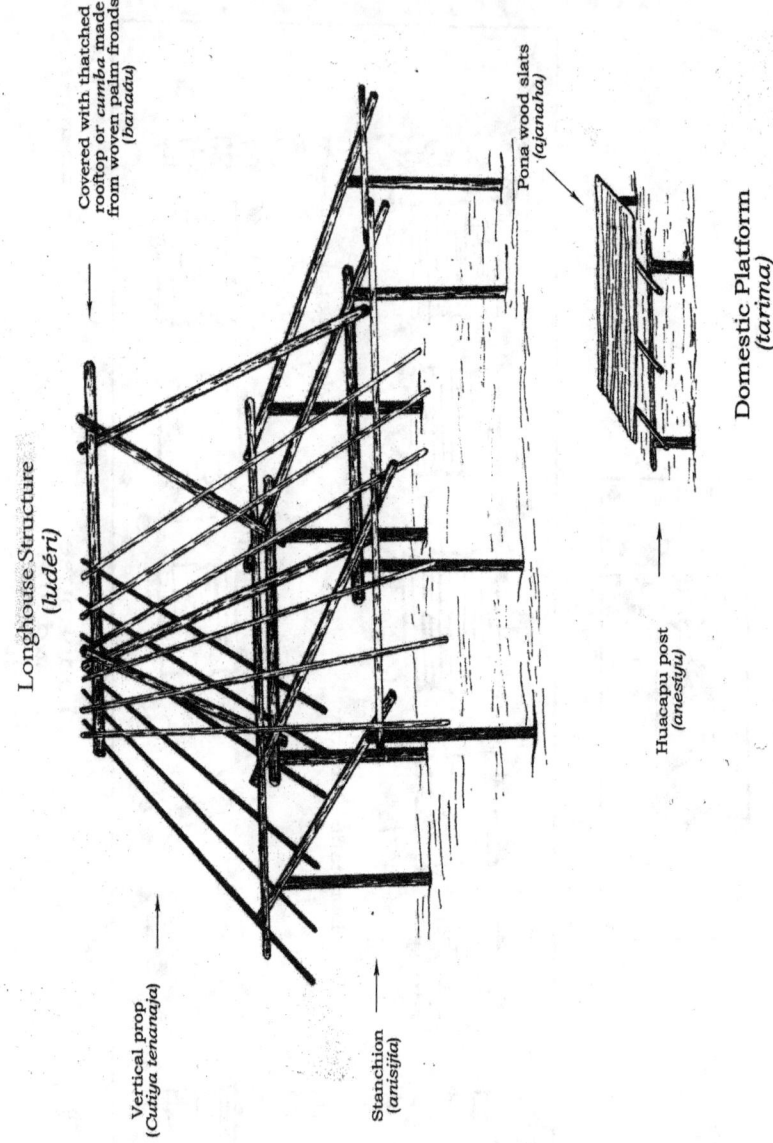

Fig. 1.8. Longhouse frame structure

pona-wood slats suspended from the longhouse's roof frame. Various items, including firewood, bottles, and large ceramic pots are stored below the wooden domestic platforms (fig. 1.8).

People everywhere rely on the built environment to valorize novel forms of wealth, to sustain economic relationships, and to establish competing standards for attaining social status. *Ludéri* are permanent edifices symbolizing the owner's social maturity, standing, and personal worldview. Longhouses signify personal histories and rights to property, and they imply wider spheres of territorial control. Spatial structures facilitate different methods of social interaction: the size of the longhouse, its age, and its spatial proximity to other *ludéri* are all important markers of kinship, affinity, status, and the vagaries of personal intimacy. Citing the estimates of patrón informants, Kramer (1979, 40–41) noted that longhouses customarily measured twenty-five to thirty meters long by eight meters wide. A Pucuyacu longhouse she visited measured twelve by eight meters (with four domestic platforms and one storage platform). My own findings from the middle and upper stretches of the Chambira Basin correspond closely with Kramer's (1979) findings.

Following the insight of Lévi-Strauss that houses themselves can stand for discrete social groups, Carsten and Hugh-Jones (1995) have underscored the importance of analyzing "house systems" in terms of totalizing social institutions. Similarly, in this chapter I have considered the Urarina domus as being inseparable from its homestead. The *ludéri*, at once a physical space and a culturally determined social unit, is also a fundamental component of Urarina production and consumption. The elaboration of indigenous categories of the longhouse is instructive, particularly when it comes to understanding the Urarinas' system of territorial organization.

2

Ninichú

Homeland of the Ancients

Examining the Urarinas' conception of territorial ownership, this chapter assesses the critical interplay between territorial integrity, political autonomy, and the cultural value of sacred geography. Customary patterns of land use are informed by cosmological referents, as well as by the exigencies of everyday life. Urarina communal factionalism and itinerant residence are consistent with a strategy of independence largely achieved through territorial oscillation between polar extremes of isolation and "national" integration. The Urarinas' conceptions of territoriality are shaped by subsistence patterns and by their participation in market-driven forest extraction.

Since at least the time of the colonial encounter (circa 1650s), the Urarina have regarded the entire Chambira River—or Ninichú as they call it—as "the homeland of the ancients" (Reichel-Dolmatoff 1976b, 309). Oral accounts collected (1996) from a headman from the Hormiga River (or *kurana*) assert that the first Urarina were associated with a settlement located near the Urituyacu watershed (upstream from Maipuco, a rural settlement along the Marañón River). According to this *kurana*, the Maña peoples (for example, the Omurana/Roamainas peoples) were the ancient mortal enemies of the Urarina. However, most of the Maña peoples eventually died during the period of the "great epidemics." After disease ravaged the upper Marañón, the Urarina fled downstream and eventually made their way to the headwaters of the Chambira Basin. A number of local acquaintances claimed that the Urarina founded Iquitos. As proof of this assertion, they pointed to the presence in Iquitos (Moronacocha) of *bidi* (*piri-piri, ciperus* sp.), a sacred plant bestowed on the Urarina by their creator god Kuánra. In the 1920s, Urarina informants spoke to the German ethnologist Gunther Tessmann of Kanakwánido diosi. Tessmann renders this as the "God who created everything." They also talked to Tessmann about the Oxpwá diosi, which he translated as the Grandfather God. Tessmann also mentions the Urarina belief that "God's Son" populated the Chambira River Basin. This is a clear reference to the Urarina creation myths I collected more than six decades later (Dean 1994b; see also Olawsky 2002).[1]

For centuries, the upper reaches of the Chambira watershed were largely the Urarinas' own *chasse gardée*. Wedged in between the mighty Pastaza watershed to the west and the Río Tigre drainage system to the east, the strategically unimportant headwaters of this immense blackwater ecosystem provided a zone of refuge for those native inhabitants evading forced labor, fleeing disease, and shunning missionization. Residential groups displeased with their labor boss have frequently absconded to adjacent rivers—from the Urituyacu to the Tigrillo and Chambira rivers, and from the headwaters of the Chambira to the Corrientes River (Kramer 1979, 53).

Historical evidence indicates that the Urarina have inhabited the same region (that is, the middle and upper reaches of the Chambira watershed) for the past three and a half centuries. Oral tradition holds that the Chambira Basin was given to the Urarina by the omnipotent culture hero Kuánra so that they could live serenely and multiply. Territorial dominion is authorized not by delimitation, but rather by the Urarinas' elaborate discourse of origin that relates the abodes of the primal ancestors and divine beings as well as their fantastic deeds. Toponymies spice mythopoeic discourse and loom large in Urarina popular claims to territory. This is clearly evident in the names given to small streams (*caños*) according to mythological and natural referents, as well as historical realities. Not far from the Pangayacu River is the small stream Siñeñe, named in honor of the arboreal *siñe* ant that makes its nests in tree trunks. *Paña caño* or *abeajcaig* is referred to by some as Tobías *caño*, in recognition of a local patrón, Don Tobías Ríos. The small stream bordering the Saldaña *fundo* is referred to as Achúne. These examples are a small indication of the extent to which the Urarinas' natural worlds are part of named universe known to all local inhabitants.

In addition to sites of productive activity, such as prized fishing grounds (lagoons or *najalkadi*) and garden sites (divided between *ujkuaná* or gardens and *ijchugué* or secondary overgrowth, known as *purma*), the Urarina recognize ancestral and mythical locales, such as the spirit charged palm-swamps (*ajláca*), local longhouses of the dead (*ajtánabana*), and turbulent whirlpools (*nesamuná*) in the bends of rivers. The Chambira Basin's many voraginous locales pose practical and spiritual dangers—they are said to link the living with the riverain underworld. Urarina mythology is particularly rich regarding the aquatic underworld (fig. 2.1).

Urarina myths are librettos for ritual action. Following Dundes, myth is defined here as "a sacred narrative explaining how the world or humans came to be in their present form" (1988, 1). Oral narratives and ritual praxis

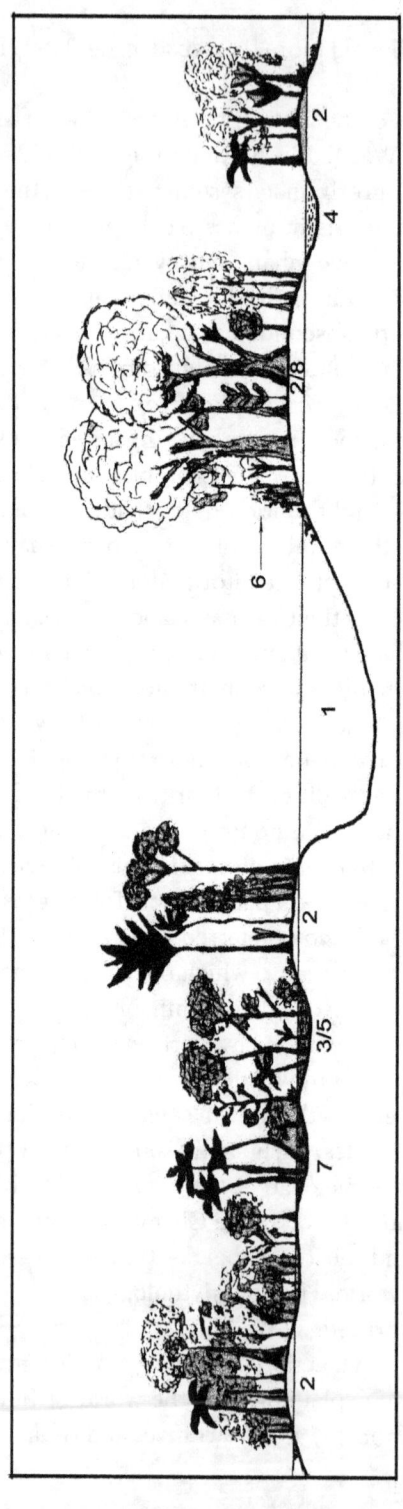

Fig. 2.1. Urarina geographic terms

exhibit an intimate connection between society and geography. Sacred geography finds expression in the Urarinas' historical experience of geographical mobility. This provides the Urarina with a foundational discourse for the negotiation of political autonomy. The sacred or spiritually invested territory is also intersected by sweeping geographic distinctions previously alluded to, including terrestrial divisions (for example, high ground or *ajtáne* versus low-lying inundatable land or *ajcaigjúne*) and aquatic distinctions (for example, oxbow lakes or *najalkadi*, and brooks or *sijtigá*).

Patrones and *ribereños* have long implored the Urarina to "stop living like *huangana*" or peccaries (*Tayassu pecari*) in a migrating herd and to establish permanent villages or *caseríos* (Kramer 1979, 56). This demand is somewhat ironic given the fact that the Urarina say that at the beginning of human time peccaries were created by their god Kuánra from a group of Urarina who had gone to cultivate peanut gardens. In light of the Urarinas' proclivity for local migration, place provides a significant idiom for identity. Najlegue-kuktíri's legendary account of Rurú, the red howler monkey (*Alouatta seniculus*, or *coto mono*), is but one example of the Urarinas' preoccupation with their own patterns of shifting residence and migration as articulated in popular bestiaries.[2]

Rurú: The Monkey Chief

> Rurú, the howler, is today the chief of the monkey world. Ajláu, the black spider monkey,[3] was originally placed on earth by our god Kuánra to be the leader (*kurana*) of the forest . . . not the howler monkey. One day Ajláu went off traveling, leaving behind his stave. Always traveling afar, he had no permanent place. Our God didn't like this: Kuánra decided to change leaders. As a test, our God Kuánra asked the monkeys to swallow a tree fruit. Ajláu's mouth was simply too small to swallow the large tree fruit. Rurú was able to swallow it, and so he was designated the new leader. The stave was given to Rurú who only stays in one place.[4] Kuánra put Howler on this earth to lead all of the forest's monkeys. Rurú sings to please the other animals and the monkeys. God placed Rurú on earth to enliven other monkeys. That's why sometimes when howler monkeys are killed the entire forest is silent. Rurú does not sing (*ninté*), nor do any of the other animals. (Ujkuaizíri, Chambira Basin, October 1994)

One of the neotropic's largest monkeys, the red howler (genus *Alouatta*) lives in territorial groups whose boundaries are marked through howling contests with rival groups. Their enlarged hyoid bone provides a shell-like structure that gives resonance to their ululant calls, which can be heard over a distance of a couple of miles. This emphasis on vocalization perhaps explains why I—the incessantly vocal ethnographer—was called red howler monkey (*ruruu sumajai*) by many of my Urarina friends and acquaintances. These relatively slow-moving monkeys like to inhabit the uppermost branches of the forest, seldom descending to the ground below. When they do move, howlers tend to do so in organized groups led by a senior male.

Emphasizing the fact that howler monkeys have a small natural range, the myth of Rurú is a dialog about what the Urarina conceive of as suitable leadership characteristics. In the eyes of the Urarina, a *kurana*'s capacity to remain in the same residential locale is one of the supreme signs of political prowess. While geographic mobility (particularly for men) affords the acquisition of knowledge about other places, social contexts, and regimes of value, stability in residence—marked by the possession of productive gardens—begets personal identity and provides the material means for the maintenance of the domus.

The Creation of the Food Gardens

No relation between Urarina men and women is of perhaps greater productive consequence and more abundant in its sentimental charge than that established through the cultivation of cassava gardens. A Urarina woman without access to a man's labor power can have no garden. Similarly, a man without access to a woman's labor power can have no beer and hence cannot rely on others to help in opening up new gardens. Both men and women derive prestige from their participation in a mutually complementary division of labor power. In addition to residential stability, the possession of productive food gardens affords self-sufficiency and a means to achieve a degree of political autonomy. As with other critical arenas of productive life, Urarina horticulture is mythologically informed, in spite of its apparently limited ceremonial elaboration relative to the practice of hunting.[5] Banana's (*capirona*) spirit's sister is credited by the Urarina with bringing daylight to the primeval world. The first plantains grew because of the urination of stars that appeared with the night sky. Once the result of divine intervention, food gardens—known as *ujkuaná*—are now the product of Urarina hard work. This is made clear in the following mythical account of the origins of swidden gardening.[6]

Ujkuaná

Before, there were no food gardens. Since there was nothing to sustain life, a man decided to make an *ujkuaná*—a garden. He went off to high grounds (*ajtáne*) in search of good land. Once he found a suitable plot, he began to mark it off. Kane Kuánra Kaj Laui—God's son—appeared and asked the man what he was doing. The man told him, and he was then instructed to go home and to rest. Kane Kuánra Kaj Laui said, "In four days come and see the garden. But first tell me, what do you want to be planted?" The man told the Son of God what crops he wanted cultivated: cassava, corn, papaya, and yams. In four days, the man returned to find the garden free of weedy overgrowth and full of food crops. Many came to see the beautiful food garden. Others soon followed suit and began asking Kane Kuánra Kaj Laui to create gardens for them. This process continued seven times, until one day Ajedi—the lazy one—ruined everything for us. Instead of asking for food crops, Ajedi told God's son that he wanted thorny bushes, *cocona*, papaya, and weedy grasses in his garden—all of the elements of *ijchugué* [secondary regrowth or *purma*]. When Ajedi returned four days later, he found his new garden filled with *ijchugué*. If it were not for that otiose (*aragán*) Ajedi we would be living without a care, but he ruined it for us. This is why we now have to rely on slash and burn agriculture. Until the end of time, we will have to continue to suffer working in our gardens, all because of the ignorant and lazy Ajedi. The people now all have to say, "I have worked ... I am tired, my hands and arms hurt." (Najlegue-kuktíri, Chambira Basin, August 1992)

For the Urarina, the forest is always a teacher bearing the message of vital interconnectedness, diversity, and rejuvenation. Yet because of ancient human fallibility, it now requires the Urarinas' own efforts to transform the forest into gardens yielding edible produce. As Raguití commented to me in 1998, "He who works will see a beautiful garden, he who doesn't work will not" (*El que trabaja se vé su lindo chacra, el que no trabaja, no vé su chacra que esta lindo*).

Communal participation in clearing forest cover for swiddens seems to have little bearing on the Urarinas' conception of the individual ownership and harvesting of garden plots. Land pressures among *ribereño* colonists along the Huallaga, Marañón, and Amazon rivers have forced some to migrate to new "unsettled" zones, including the Chambira and Urituyacu river basins. For example, the late Don Juan Saldaño (originally from the Caserío of San Rafael on the lower Huallaga River) and his Cocama wife, Claudina (formerly of the Caserío of Santa Rita de Castilla on the Marañón River), had established themselves in the early 1970s on the Chambira as *fundo* homesteaders. Before his death during the cholera epidemic of 1991, Saldaño had two bovines and a gaggle of chickens and swine. Saldaño's *fundo*, called Tropezón, was one of the most important extractive estates along the middle

Chambira. Tropezón was the median point between the Chambira's only *ribereño* settlements of any import—Nueva Alianza and Dos de Mayo.

Horticulture

The cessation of the rains and the onset of the dry season in April and May mark the beginning of a new horticultural cycle and a return to relative food abundance. Urarina swidden agriculture relies on crop rotation and on the extensive use of land, rather than on extensive manual labor inputs. The Urarina are unfamiliar with the system of cultivating the floodplains, as is common among the *ribereño* communities of the Bajo Marañón.

Preference for garden plots is given to primary forest located along the banks of rivers and streams. Like the Shipibo-Conibo of the central Peruvian Amazon (Behrens 1989; Tournon 2002), the Urarina are excellent horticulturalists. They are able to assay soil types quickly by using sight, smell, and touch.[7] When planning a new banana garden, men first select swaths of primary forest (*ajtáne*)—flat high ground protected against flooding. Compared with low-lying land (*ajcaigjúne*), *ajtáne* soils are darker and more porous, and as such do well for bananas. They prefer *purma*, or secondary regrowth for planting their cassava gardens, which are usually situated no more than a thirty-minute walk from the homestead. *Purma* has the added benefit of attracting a number of animal and birds, which are regularly hunted (see Flores Paitán 1987).

The Urarina have developed a type of swidden horticulture particularly appropriate for the cultivation of plantains (Kramer 1977; Ferrua Carrasco et al. 1980). Once the garden plot has been cleared of weedy undergrowth, plantain rhizomes are sown using a wooden *cumaceba* digging stick (*jicuñáira*). *Jicuñáira* are multipurpose implements used extensively for horticulture and for the gathering of food. Complementing machetes, wooden staves are used by the Urarina to cultivate crops, to obtain tubers and roots, to exhume animal burrows, and to use as basic carrying yokes. The foliage cover of the primary upland forest (*monte alto*) is retained to conserve the soil's moisture and to prevent too much sun from damaging immature plants. After a few weeks, the surrounding trees are felled, allowing the immature plantains to receive sunlight. Any plantain rhizomes destroyed by falling trees or ravaged by insects are replaced. Leaves, twigs, and branches felled from the high forest are left to dry in the sun and eventually burned at the end of August or the beginning of September. The low-intensity brush fires do not usually damage the plantain rhizomes (see Kramer 1979, 94–96; 1977; Ferrúa Carrasco et al. 1980).

Medicinal plants and food crops, such as the dietary staple sweet manioc (*lanú*), are cultivated in the ashes.[8] In addition, the Urarina cultivate corn (*kajtudí*), peanuts (*kajtuhué*), three types of sweet potato (*ajkií, Ipomoea batatas, Convolvulus batata*?), squash, papaya (*afuayá*), and three types of sugar cane. They also cultivate avocado (*azáru, Persea Americana*), taro (known locally as *sachapapa* or *auca papa*, and in Urarina as *ijchái, Solanum tuberosum*?), cacao (*ijchuridí, Theobroma cacao*), two types of pineapples (*iñuídi, Ananas comosus*), and peppers (a hot variety is known as *inüje*, and a sweet variety is called *inüje ijchúnai, Capsicum*). Medicinal and sacred plants and trees include *ninahuasca* and *Anguilla Caspi*, which are employed for masculine arm scarification; *ojé* (*adijiá*), whose white latex contains eloxanthine and is used as a vermifuge; *ishanga* (*ajkisá*), whose leaf is brushed against the arm to relieve pain; the red and black *huairuro* (*irilé*) seeds that are used in necklaces and ornamentation, and are said to bring good luck; and *achiote* (*jiané*, seed of the annatto tree, *Bixa orellana* L.), which yields a yellowish red dye obtained from the pulp enclosing the plant's seeds and is used as face paint when taking *ayahuasca*. *Sachauiro* (*eruaríjki*) extract is consumed for respiratory ailments, and *Arco-sacha* (?) or "false rainbow" is applied as a poultice for a skin condition called *patico*, which is thought to be caused by the evil rays of a rainbow. The extract from *uña de gato* (*nejküdi*, lit. "cat's claw," which includes any of several prickly shrubs, such as *Mimosa biuncifera* or *Acacia greggi*) is utilized to combat skin eruptions. An infusion made from *sijye* or "cotton" (?) is used to combat diarrhea and labor pains.

Plantain[9] gardens remain in production for two or three cropping cycles, after which they are abandoned due to their diminishing returns. In the more permanent homestead sites, I have seen gardens kept up for considerably longer (particularly if they are located within a short distance of the longhouse). The size of the garden depends upon the age of the cultivator and the anticipated final destination of the garden's produce. Large gardens are typically used for the cultivation of cassava and plantains, which are often grown explicitly for the purpose of trade. Young co-wives may have multiple hectare plots, elderly men and women work small gardens (a quarter hectare), and children take care of a few dozen plantains in a small garden near the longhouse. Kramer (1979) found that domestic gardens located along the Tigrillo River measured one-half a hectare with approximately five hundred plantains (the average amount consumed annually by a household). Gardens whose crop is destined for markets measured between one-half a hectare to an entire hectare. Cassava gardens on the Pucayacu River[10] measured about one hectare (whether this was for domestic consumption or sale). Throughout the 1990s, I noted comparable garden sizes along the Pangayacu and middle portions of the Chambira Rivers.

Agricultural work is the task of both men and women. There are no "crystalline rules" regarding tenancy beyond the understanding that those who prepare and maintain the garden are considered its legitimate owners. Men open gardens for their wives or widowed daughters and on occasion for their widowed sisters. Polygynous males prepare gardens for each one of their wives. Working by himself, a man will spend up to a month to clear and prepare a one-hectare garden. The labor power expended on this work is not continuous. Throughout the year, men will divide their time between various obligations, including garden work, hunting, fishing, tool and shelter construction, and working lumber.

Garden preparation is usually a collective, masculine effort orchestrated by a focal male. Here the practice of bride service comes into play: fathers-in-law orchestrate the work tasks while young, more dependent sons-in-law lend support. Relative to other types of labor (including subsistence and petty-commodity production), junior sons-in-law appear to enjoy more autonomy in determining labor power outputs when it comes to working in their own gardens rather than in those of their fathers-in-law. Invitation to communal work parties—called *mingas*[11]—devoted to opening a new garden are reciprocal and are marked by a convivial and buoyant atmosphere sustained by the liberal consumption of cassava beer, and on a limited number of occasions food. Led by the initiative of the host, and men of renown lending verbal encouragement, men slowly arrive at the host's homestead in the early morning. Collective labor parties or *mingas* are accompanied by the persuasive speech of *kuranas* and their followers. Matutinal utterances of "let's go to work" (*amia niáca*) serve to initiate productive activities and, later on, to moderate their tempo.

While sharpening their highly prized machetes on the homestead's grinding stone, the men of the work party (typically ranging in size from six to twelve) consume a few rounds of tart-tasting cassava beer (*bardiguë*), exchange pleasantries, and then set off to the garden site, which is usually located within walking distance. The workers periodically break off from clearing and felling the forest's thick foliage to slake their thirst with additional rounds of *bardiguë*. While felling trees, junior males guard the beer from the dangerous prospect of spiritual contamination of the beer by *morpho* butterflies.[12] The Urarina say that the spectacular *morpho* butterfly (*Morpho granadensis polybaptus*?) is the corporal manifestation of deceased spirits. The wings of this large blue butterfly are believed to be the hat or cap of an invisible spirit who pollutes the beer by urinating in it, which in turn is said to cause potentially fatal bouts of vomiting. After the sun passes its zenith, the mildly inebriated workers begin returning to the host's homestead to continue drinking until all of the host's fermented beverages are consumed. Large, extended uxorilocal longhouse groups with access to productive gardens can depend on a steady supply of beer necessary for mobilizing labor through competitive hosting. During festive gatherings, it is not uncommon for music to commence: men play two-headed skin drums (*tóntoó*), panpipes (*aynú*), and bamboo flutes (*dadadi*). Male and female celebrants dance (*ranzáig*), sing, and converse into the wee hours of the following day—or until at least the beer supply has been exhausted.

Women make fundamental contributions of labor power toward the preparation and ongoing maintenance of gardens. The arduous task of weeding and harvesting are eminently female tasks, and women assume charge of domestic cultivation, particularly when their men folk are busy hunting, fishing, or felling trees for saw timber, poles, and firewood. In the absence of their husbands, women go to their gardens in the company of other women or young boys, especially their younger brothers. During menstruation, women abstain from all work in the gardens. The constant upkeep of the gardens, including the critical task of weeding (*taujiá*), is accomplished by the matrilines of the uxorilocal extended family longhouse group. In general, the working atmosphere is relaxed and jocular in tone; however mother-in-law/daughter-in-law relations tend to be more reserved and restrained, as are relations between mature senior wives and their younger, junior co-wives. Work is directed by the materfamilias (*ene biña*) who selects plants to be cultivated and segments of the garden to be weeded. The young are responsible for harvesting while the older women weed the surrounding areas of the garden; children unearth tubers and transport them back using woven palm-fiber net bags.

Bananas, cassava, and other food crops consumed by the domestic group are cultivated and carried back to the longhouse by their female owners and occasionally by young boys. Men become increasingly involved in the harvesting cycle when garden produce is marketed as barter crops. Men's negotiation of the barter transaction with a river trader or *patrón* includes carrying the produce from the gardens, such as fifty to one hundred hands of bananas or basketfuls (*paneros*)[13] of manioc and bagfuls (*toneladas*) of rice.

Urarina subsistence hinges on the flexible utilization of varied terrestrial and riverain resources. The Chambira watershed is marked by its environmental heterogeneity and diversity of natural resources: they are unevenly dispersed, creating a vast number of micro-environments. With respect to the politicization of territory, it is *dominion* or territoriality, not "ownership," that up until very recently concerned the Urarina. From their point of view, land does not exist as real property. As a culturally autonomous group inhabiting a sparsely populated area,[14] the Urarina effectively control large stretches of the Chambira River drainage—including an estimated 8,000 square miles (20,720 square kilometers) of primary rainforest. Territorial boundaries are tacitly understood: longhouse groups take offense when other *demes* harvest resources from the forest or waterways directly surrounding local homesteads. *Kaj laitjíras* in close proximity to narrow waterways (streams and rivulets) claim dominion over their use. But multiple communities collectively utilize primary stretches of rivers as well as fluvial headwaters.

Urarina cosmology suggests an interactive relationship among humanity, divinity, and the natural habitat. For the Urarina, flora and fauna are anthropomorphized. In contrast, when *ribereño* or *mestizo* representatives of neo-Peruvian national culture argue about land rights, they practically anthropomorphize the rights and interests in the land. Often they do not even refer to the land itself. Urarina property rights are defined by communal knowledge, itself responsive to various pressures along a series "of interactive 'fronts' among neighbors" (Rose 1988, 290). Customary rules regarding use-rights exist as stated norms, but all Urarina know that they have multiple means at their disposal to adapt the "rules" in actual practice. At times, the Urarina adopt a stance that rejects "ownership" of land. This was the case when Kiriná succinctly and forcefully announced during a drinking party in May 1996 that "the earth has no owner." At other junctures, such as in the face of lumber extractors, the Urarina embrace an idiom of ownership through collective notions of territoriality. The latter posture has coincided with formal state recognition in the Ley de Comunidades Nativas (Law of Native Communities), which has provided a framework for local inter-ethnic relations and a way of thinking and talking about local politics.

Migration, Subsistence, and the Politics of Territoriality

The Urarinas' ability to remain in the Chambira is surely a function of the fact that colonial and postcolonial frontiers of national expansion have historically viewed this watershed as a relatively unimportant geopolitical space. In some respects, this is because the Chambira and Urituyacu rivers are only navigable for a short distance from the south, where they can be entered at their confluence with the Marañón. The Chambira River drainage is of course navigable by canoe (save for the dry season when fallen tree trunks and sandbars that form elongated islands break the surface and inhibit navigation in the upper reaches of the basin). Boats larger than twenty meters can only ply the middle and upper Chambira Basin during the rainy season. Unlike the Pastaza River to the west, or the Tigre to the east, the Chambira and Urituyacu provide no access to the strategic equatorial territory lying to the north. In terms of fluvial navigation, the Chambira River is a veritable cul-de-sac. However, the headwaters of the Chambira Basin are linked with the major parallel rivers (Tigre and Pastaza) through overland trails (*berü* or *trochas* in Spanish) used by the Urarina and Achuar peoples.[15] These overland trails, combined with the Urarinas' extensive knowledge of the zone, enable them to take swift flight in cases of epidemic, explosive disputes, and the reprisals of disgruntled labor bosses and their loyal agents.

The Urarina relocate to the Chambira Basin's headwaters or central forest after the death of individuals of renown, or during outbreaks of serious infectious disease, such as the resurgence of malaria in the late 1990s, the cholera epidemic of the early 1990s, or the deadly measles outbreaks in the early 1960s and mid-1980s. This migratory impulse is in response to what the Urarina see not only as the encroaching "outside" world, but also as the threat of *anekái*, the malevolent spirits of the dead. In spite of their tendency to minimize inter-ethnic contact, it would be patently absurd to suggest that the Urarina are in any sense an isolated, insular, or atomistic society. By portraying the Urarina as a culturally autonomous group tied to a distinct geographic locale—the Chambira River drainage—I do not want to be seen here as advocating the venerable, yet outmoded "culture-area" ethnology of indigenous South America, which tried to classify patterns of cultural similarities identified with sizable yet discrete geographical areas.

Urarina migratory strategies are intimately tied to the matrices of subsistence and to debt-peonage production. Urarina migration is calibrated to mesh with mercantile cycles, with their own subsistence patterns, and with conditions dictated by seasonal periodicities. Urarina domestic groups—including both the uxorilocal extended family longhouse, as well as singular "nuclear" households—have developed strategies for coping with economic duress, including attempts to better their conditions through participation in debt peonage. By diversifying productive activities to include the exchange of labor power for barter goods, the Urarina have maintained a base in subsistence production. Invariably, individual and group resettlement decisions are responsive to the satisfaction of those desires emanating from wanting to establish or maintain access to trade goods and garden produce (particularly in the daily form of manioc and bananas). When a *deme* splinters some of its members will resettle among a new social group—sometimes near a *rib-*

ereño or petty patron's homestead or *fundo*. In these instances, the Urarina will exchange their labor power for access to subsistence crops and a small but periodic stream of trade goods—cane alcohol, shotgun shells, batteries, and cloth.

It is imperative for recent arrivals to obtain the consent of those ensconced in the "community" since newcomers are totally reliant upon the established households' willingness to share their garden produce (at least until the newcomer's own garden plots begin bearing fruit). When parties tire of the constraints imposed on one another, the bonds uniting them through trade, labor exchange, and ritual associations deteriorate. Frequently, the Urarina will relocate after a number of months of living in close proximity to *mestizo* homesteads or extractive encampments. Periodic migration between the Marañón and the Chambira Basin during times of scarcity (for example, during floods) flavors local relations and provides an ongoing social context for the articulation of inter-ethnic relations. *Ribereños* from the Marañón (some claiming Cocama affiliation, others originating from the department of San Martin, or from the Río Ucayali, or little big-towns like Nauta and Lagunas) make their way upriver to trade salted fish, cane alcohol, and baubles for handicrafts and food—including garden produce and forest game.

Residential oscillation is consistent with Urarina patterns of seasonal migration, as well as the area's historical integration into capitalist markets at regional and national levels. In the Chambira River drainage, it has been labor rather than land that has been the critical means of petty-commodity production. Urarina labor migration is glossed locally with the euphemism *contrato* ("contract"), which involves the literal relocation of an extended uxorilocal longhouse or homestead group from one residential locale to another, often to work in seasonal, agricultural labor. For instance, a local longhouse group from San Lorenzo on the Río Tigrillo was relocated by its *patrón* to the settlement of Nuevo Angora were its members were employed in the cultivation of thirty hectares of rice (Ferrúa Carrasco et al. 1980, 40).

Climatic changes are responsible for seasonal flooding of the rivers, particularly the southern portions of the Chambira-Urituyacu fluvial system. On the Pangayacu and the middle course of the Chambira, the heaviest monthly precipitation is usually between November and March. Cessation of the rainy season comes in June and lasts through August and early September. Surface runoff rejuvenates the forest's inland rivulets and palm swamps and creates pools in low-lying areas. Game is most abundant during the dry season, when it is attracted to the river's edge. During the wet season, game animals move upriver to high ground (*restinga*) or to inland forest that does not flood. Inevitably, this reduces the Urarinas' hunting yields (fig. 2.2).

Fig. 2.2. Urarina man with *majas* (capybara)

The Chambira Basin's many waterways supply tortoises (*charapa, matama*, and *taricaya*), numerous varieties of fish, caimans, stingrays, or *ledé* (*Potamotrygon hystrtix*), and enormous electric eels (*Electrophoridae*). The most intensive period of fishing coincides with the dry season, a time also devoted to scavenging. Drugging is used to stupefy fish that are then gathered up in the dugout canoes. The keepers of the ancient lore say that during the antediluvian period before the emergence of the ancient Urarina peoples, the proto-humans were frustrated in their attempts to acquire fish through poisoning. As a result, the divine Creator's son, Kuánra Kájlaui, was dispatched to stock the big fish commonly found in the oxbow lakes and deep channel bends (*pozos*) of the area's rivers. Kuánra Kájlaui's spearing minnows paradoxically generated the larger representatives of the Chambira's piscine life, such as the greatly coveted *tucanaré* fish. While my Urarina friends did not readily acknowledge God's son's behavior in terms of a paradigmatic example of ecologically sustainable spear-fishing versus drugging, they were quick to point out the hazards of depleting fish stocks with excessive use of fish poisons (particularly *barbasco*, *Lonchocarpus* sp., which is effective even on demersal or bottom feeding fish). Barb-tipped spears (*sudiríji*), metal hooks, and nylon line (when they are available) are used daily to catch large fish and aquatic reptiles, such as caiman (*yajkarí*). Fish traps are placed in the drainage canals or rivulets of streams and brooks, while seine and purse seine nets are occasionally used. Fishing primarily supports subsistence demand, though Urarina do sporadically exchange dried, salted, smoked (*curdeé*), and fresh fish with *patrones* or *regatones*.

Fish are widely available and are consumed year-round. Most males and females are proficient anglers, though men and boys tend to dominate piscatory pursuits. The Urarina employ fishing strategies that respond to seasonal fluctuations in the depth of landscape inundation. Fishing success in the Chambira Basin's blackwater ecosystems depends on access to downriver zones, particularly during the dry season when the fish and reptile volume is greatest in the middle to lower reaches of the drainage system. The dry season months of June through August are a time of intensive fishing when shoals of fish swarm up the Marañón and its tributaries. The Urarina use the techniques of poisoning and spearing during the dry season to take advantage of the shallow rivers' increased fish density.

The Urarina calibrate fish procurement methods to offset variations in fish density. Fishing productivity is negatively associated with monthly rainfall. The principal fishing implements used by the Urarina are trident spears, hook and line, machete, and ichthyotoxins. During the time of maximal flooding, hooks and lines and spears predominate, whereas poison is used only during the height of the dry season (see Gragson 1992a, 122, 126). The catch from fish-poisoning expeditions is distributed among the participants and the women who supplied the poison. Commercial fishing by *mestizos* on the Chambira often includes the use of motorboats and on occasion even gas-powered refrigerated vessels. Predictably, this has lead in some instances to the partial depletion of fish stocks—particularly along the Chambira Basin's lower courses. In the community of Santa Rosa, there were conflicts over access to those lagoons with great hydrobiological resources. In spite of Urarina protest, many commercial fishermen worked in the area thanks to official permits from the former Dirección de Pesquería (Ferrúa Carrasco et al. 1980, 50).

Paralleling the rainy season migrations, the Urarina move downstream during the dry season to the lower portions of the Chambira watershed to take advantage of changes in fish densities resulting from the precipitous drop in the basin's water volume. The Urarinas' residential mobility is thus consistent with subsistence patterns, allowing for the harvesting of fish from both the Chambira's blackwater ecosystem and from the white-water ecosystem of the Marañón River (see Gragson 1992b, 428–40; Guallart Martínez 1976).

In addition to influencing patterns of subsistence, seasonal periodicity informs commercial extractive pursuits such as logging. Instead of relying on heavy machinery, non-indigenous loggers mobilize Urarina labor power to fell trees. In an effort to cancel old debts (*debeuca*) and to satisfy their needs for trade goods, the Urarina are actively contributing to the deforestation of the Chambira Basin through selective logging for the commercial market. The Urarina have felled timber trees for external consumption for at least a century. During the first half of the twentieth century, *capirona* trees were cut down for kindling and fuel for the region's steamboats. Stimulated by international and national demand for mahogany and other valuable tree species (*lupuna, moena, cumala,* and *cedro*), a North American firm developed the region's export-oriented lumber industry between the world wars. Emergence of the petroleum exploration industry in the early 1970s spurred a regional surge in construction, and with it heightened demand for timber (Kramer 1979, 120, 130; San Román 1975, 171).

Inundation is beneficial to the extraction of timber since a major problem in harvesting lumber is the transportation of felled trees from the forest to the sawmills in Iquitos. Logging typically occurs in enclaves close enough to the riverbanks where Urarina lumberjacks can remove logs, often with the aid of seasonal floodwaters. In 1996 the *patrón* from Santa Silvia, Tobias Ríos, lent a chain saw to a work group from Santa Carmela so that its members could selectively extract *lupuna*. Similarly, in 1998 Tobias Ríos lent Kiriná's work group a chain saw to extract fifty boles of valuable hardwood (whose worth was estimated by some in the thousands of dollars, or tens of thousands of soles). Kiriná's group was outfitted again in the year 2002 by Tobias Ríos, who provided the Urarina work team with the use of an old dilapidated chain saw for the extraction of fine hardwoods growing along the riverbanks of the Pangayacu.

The wet season involves floating boles from upriver lumber encampments downstream. The logs are lashed together to form rafts and eventually floated down river to Ollanta, a *ribereño* community perched along the confluence of the Chambira and Marañón rivers. Financed by the sawmill owners, the boles are then collected and transported to Iquitos by tugboats or balsa rafts. Although the Peruvian state had an official environmental

Fig. 2.3. Urarina woman and iguana

agency—INRENA (Instituto Nacional de Recursos Naturales)—during my time "in the field" this governmental body did not effectively regulate logging or forest extraction activities in the Chambira Basin. Rather than the bulldozed, deforested tracts commonly seen in areas of concentrated logging and ranching, the Chambira River drainage has "strips" of selective hardwood extraction that has lead to species diminution, the destruction of fruit-bearing trees, and the elimination of nesting areas (Dean and McKinley 1997).

Foraging strategies are responsive to fluctuations in game and food availability: rainy season lumber expeditions coincide with efforts devoted to intensifying hunting, fishing, and foraging during this time of relative food scarcity. The dry season is spent felling trees for the market in hardwoods, hunting, pursuing horticultural activities, including barter-crop cultivation (rice, plantains, cassava, corn, and peanuts), and foraging for materials necessary for domestic production and consumption. Scavenging is sporadic: many items have their "epoch" or seasonality in which ecological conditions permit their abundant collection. Items scavenged include such things as turtles, bird eggs, reptiles, honey, larva, palm-fronds, resins, seeds, clay, and natural dyes (fig. 2.3).

Territorial Disputes

Urarina natural resource management is embedded within the productive and reproductive cycles of the *domus*, which are contingent on the exigencies of supra-local political economies. Due to heightened state and local intervention within their territory, Urarina proprietorship has emerged as a complex web of legal and political relations between persons with respect to cosmo-centric land use versus extractive patterns promoted by the market. A review of lumber extraction in the Chambira Basin illustrates both how and why proprietary rights have crystallized among the Urarina at specific historical moments.

Inter-ethnic conflicts over access to land and natural resources commonly pit the Urarina against lumbermen (*madereros*) as well as commercial fishermen. During the 1990s I noted three primary lumber extractors working the Chambira Basin and its environs: Señor Balzeca, Señor Soto, and the Ocampos family, all of whom are members of the Asociación de Madereros de Iquitos (Ferrúa Carrasco et al. 1980, 50; Dean 1992). In 1980, the government office of natural resource management (Dirección de Flora y Fauna) classified the region as an unrestricted zone for timber extraction (see Ferrúa Carrasco et al. 1980, 2–3). Through their recourse to governmental institutions dependent on record keeping, extractive entrepreneurs like the Ocampos have systematically attempted to sharpen the demarcation of their own private entitlements. Here, bureaucratic records acquire an overdetermined status as unimpeachable sources of juridical facts regarding ownership of land as property. In this regard, both the Peruvian Ministry of Agriculture in Iquitos and the Regional Forestry Department's (Nauta) land registration systems are indicative of deliberate attempts at instituting crystalline regulations. These neoliberal rules, ostensibly favoring efficiency for the sake of simplicity in managing land transactions and the extraction of resources, have enabled a cadre of well-contacted regional entrepreneurs to take advantage of increased access to credit and growing opportunities to migrate to the Chambira Basin. These extractive entrepreneurs are a heterogeneous assortment of persons who have diversified their economic bases through active participation in the business in pelts, plantains, forest produce (resins, latexes, palm hearts, honey, and so forth), and lumber extraction.

For the Urarina, these changes have meant that territoriality has become increasingly heteronymous, that is, increasingly more dependent on the vagaries of postcolonial extractive expansion, such as the national petroleum company's exploration for oil in the zone, or the government's licensing of commercial net fishing along the lower Chambira and its numerous lagoons, as well as the liberal provisioning of lumber concessions. State legislation as embodied in its credit policy, in its support of dubious extractive "contracts" granted private parties, and more broadly in its promotion of the militarization of social life have all conjoined in marginalizing residents of the Chambira from being able to decide the nature and scope of their territorial autonomy.

When multiple matrilateral extended family longhouses groups unite in establishing a permanent homestead (symbolized by a *ludéri senjua* or big longhouse) they have the option of either working with itinerant lumbermen or presenting a united front against encroachment. Since at least the promulgation of the Law of the Native Communities (Ley de Comunidades Nativas) in 1974, which sanctioned communal land tenure, Urarina settlements have been able to speak about the lands they have traditionally occupied as "community property"—in spite of the fact that many Urarina local longhouse settlements do not have official title to their traditional or ancestral homelands. Indeed, in publicly redressing grievances against particularly hard-driving lumbermen, the Urarina will refer to surrounding territory—the trees and riparian resources—as belonging to "the community" (*la comunidad*).

A case in point was the Urarinas' association with a Señor Ahuite, who in 1980 negotiated with a Urarina community from the Río Airico to extract lumber from the area. When Ahuite's state-issued forestry contract expired, he began felling trees in areas the Urarina had previously designated as "off-limits" to lumber extraction. In response to the lumberman's violation of his forestry contract and the goodwill of the Airico community, the local Urarina authority and members of the Proyecto de Apoyo a Communidad Nativa (ORDELORETO—Organismo Regional de Desarrollo de Loreto) lodged an official complaint against Señor Ahuite. Filed in the *ribereño* community of Ollanta, the complaint served only to halt temporarily Ahuite's extractive lumbering on the Airico (Ferrúa Carrasco et al. 1980).

In addition to recourse to legal channels, a variety of other methods are at the Urarinas' disposal to defend their territorial integrity, most commonly involving a simple retraction of exchange relationships through gossip, or less frequently, through violent confrontation, including beatings and in rare cases, poisonings. During my time among the Urarina, I recorded two cases of attempted poisonings of a local *mestizo patrón* and an itinerant *regatón* who was intoxicated with sap from the *catahua* tree. While the poisonings did not prove fatal, they did precipitate intense vomiting, malaise, and diarrhea. In some instances, the Urarina have been able to enforce their dominion of strategic areas by controlling access to the Chambira Basin's affluents through such dramatic means as felling large tree boles to block the passage of boats. This occurred in 1998 when the inhabitants of the Río Huituyacu closed access to a small stream being used by a *mestizo* lumberjack working in the area without community approval.[16]

Land use in the Chambira is determined by the economic options open to groups or individuals, and by the relative balance of power between the labor bosses and river traders, on the one hand, and the economically and politically subaltern Urarina and neighboring *ribereño* petty-commodity producers, on the other hand. Review of one lumberman's experience in the Chambira will illuminate this. In 1979, three lumber *patrones*, including one Señor Balseca, entered into a partnership with one of the few legally recognized indigenous communities of the Chambira Basin—Santa Cecilia—to extract timber from the Pucayacu River.

Within a year the temporary timber extraction permit had expired and the community's goodwill towards the *mestizo* loggers had all but vanished. When the *mestizos* continued to harvest lumber, the Urarina angrily confronted them. A literate *ribereño* "representative" of the community was also dispatched to the District Forestry Department in Nauta where a complaint was lodged and the appropriate written documents delimiting Santa Cecilia's access to the lumber stands of the Pucayacu were filed. In late 1980, the situation had escalated to shows of violent aggression: a number of Urarina from the Río Pucayacu were apprehended by the lumberman's henchmen, who then threatened them with actively running chain saws (Ferrúa Carrasco et al. 1980, 49, 74).

The Pucayacu "community" retaliated by evicting the lumber extractors and temporarily retreating into the forest's interior. Nevertheless, this did not prevent one of the more unscrupulous lumbermen to continue to do business elsewhere in the Chambira. In 1993, I noted that Señor Balseca was attempting to orchestrate another lumber contract with the neighboring though untitled Urarina "community" on the Hormiga River. The adult male members of this local longhouse settlement publicly expressed desires for the promised chain saws and rewards for their labor power in the form of barter goods. But, perhaps more importantly, it was felt by many that the extractive entrepreneurs' official easement to extract wood on the Río Hormiga provided the local *kurana* and his supporters legitimacy as an autonomous *comunidad* vis-à-vis the other neighboring though hostile local longhouse settlements. As such, the Hormiga River "community," in contrast to the Pucayacu community, can be seen as pursuing a strategy of incorporating extractive fronts of national expansion. Local land conflicts in the Chambira Basin must be viewed in terms of a broader political economy, mediated in part by state and non-state actors.

Secure Homelands: From Reform to Reaction?

Coinciding with the rise to power of the so-called Military Radicals, the Peruvian state's most proactive involvement in advancing the rights of Amazonia's indigenous peoples has been in the arena of securing their traditional homelands. General Juan Velasco Alvarado's assumption of power following the *golpe de estado* of 1968, which overthrew the civilian-led Belaunde government, heralded a number of significant albeit temporary changes in the state's historical posture toward indigenous peoples. In addressing the nation's grossly inequitable "feudalistic" social order, Velasco's military government instituted a series of structural reforms that were formulated to diffuse the growing rural agrarian revolt in the Andean highlands. The reformist military regime nationalized key sectors of the economy and initiated one of Latin America's most extensive land redistribution programs. In Amazonia, the Peruvian state embraced a development strategy tempered by strong pro-indigenous (*indigenista*) sentiment. This found expression in the promulgation of the Law of Native Communities (Ley de Comunidades Nativas y Promoción Agropecuaria de las Regiones de Selva y Ceja de Selva). Supplanting legislation passed in 1909 (Ley de Tierras de Montaña N. 1220) that had rendered the tropical rainforests the exclusive property of the state, the Native Communities Law of 1974 was the first instance in modern Peruvian history in which the state recognized the explicit right of its Amazonian indigenous peoples to hold communal title to their ancestral homelands.

Under the combined direction of the Ministry of Agriculture and the state's corporatist popular mobilization agency, SINAMOS (Sistema Nacional de Apoyo a la Movilización Social), a process of indigenous land entitlement began in the Peruvian lowlands. Marred by many contradictions, the implementation of the Native Communities Law in Amazonia echoed the state's model of agrarian reform in Andean peasant communities (for the Andes, see Gelles 2000). While the Native Communities Law recognized semi-mobile patterns of residence and conceded communal rights to territories used for foraging, fishing, hunting, and swidden agriculture, a primary issue not stipulated in the legislation of 1974 was exactly how much "migratory" territory the state was obliged to deed to legally recognized indigenous communities (*comunidades nativas*). Implementation of the legislation resulted, in some instances, in the fragmentation of common property and in the segregation of local indigenous groups. The phenomenon of territorial fragmentation of ethnic groups was by no means universal. Among the Urarina of the Chambira Basin, for example, the presence of SINAMOS was quite limited. During its brief existence, this state agency only titled three Urarina communities.[17]

Throughout this century, governmental influence in the Chambira has been minimal and more often than not has followed on the heels of particularly egregious extractive entrepreneurs. Perhaps the greatest state involvement in the region came in 1976 when SINAMOS entered the Chambira Basin with the aim of implementing the Ley de Comunidades Nativas (Decreto Ley 20653). At the end of 1976, officials of SINAMOS encouraged several Urarina groups from the Hormiga and Pucayacu rivers to establish cash-crop gardens at the mouths of their respective rivers. The organization's efforts at encouraging commercial agriculture on the Chambira were unsuccessful: the Urarina local groups quickly abandoned the newly established plots (Kramer 1979, 18). Between 1976 and 1977, SINAMOS recognized three communities—Santa Rosa, Patoyacu, and Pucayacu (for a total extension of 23,143 hectares)—making them the first Urarina communities ever to enjoy formal legal recognition (Ferrúa Carrasco et al. 1980, 7).

Though significant at the time, the long-term impact of SINAMOS in Amazonia remains poorly understood, especially in Loreto. While a group of well-meaning anthropologists staffed the upper reaches of SINAMOS, those who worked directly in implementing the state reforms often lacked appropriate training, and many harbored romantic if not negative stereotypes regarding indigenous peoples. Often rural extension workers were just as patronizing as the most overbearing of god-fearing missionaries, or as abusive as the local labor-bosses. Their message tended to be altogether not that different: labor not for the *patrón* or for the church, but rather for the state (Dean 1990). In spite of real shortcomings, the Velasquista reforms were a watershed in state relations with Peru's substantial indigenous populace. The legislative reforms implemented during Velasco's government marked a historic recognition of the basic human right of indigenous peoples to be culturally different.

The transformation in the Peruvian state's assimilationist posture toward indigenous peoples was only short-lived. Under new presidential leadership (General Morales Bermúdez), the military government disbanded SINAMOS in 1977 and replaced the Native Community Law with legislation liberalizing the terms under which large-scale extractive industries (mining, petroleum, and lumber) could operate in Amazonia. Laws subsequently enacted further relaxed constraints on land ownership. This in turn allowed the Peruvian state to begin allocating generous land concessions to private investors. Even though the Native Community Law of 1974 was left intact, the process of granting land titles to indigenous communities came to a virtual standstill. In the name of modernity, national progress, and economic prosperity, big business was yet again given a free reign in its quest to develop the Amazon (Dean 1990, 70).

The stampede for nonrenewable natural resources, namely petroleum, natural gas, and gold, has wreaked havoc on ecosystems and local communities in Peruvian Amazonia. During the second government of Fernando Belaunde Terry (1980–85), colonization of Amazonia was reemphasized, and the state-directed indigenous land-titling program came to a grinding halt.[18] The subsequent government of Alan García Pérez (1985–90) publicly expressed greater understanding for the need to provide indigenous communities with land titles, but political crisis, economic chaos, and the growing threat of the Sendero Luminoso's[19] armed struggle prevented a besieged state from doing much in the way of concrete programs for the welfare of indigenous peoples, let alone the vast majority of the impoverished citizenry (Varese 2002). The subsequent emergence of Alberto Fujimori's "narco-state" (1990–2000) did little to change the lives of the upper Amazon's impoverished communities, which now found themselves in the throes of a vicious civil war.

Beginning in the early 1980s, the Peruvian state had initiated a fitful yet savage counterinsurgency campaign that resulted in civil war and the deaths of more than seventy thousand people. Initially concentrating its scorched earth counterinsurgency efforts on the Andean area of Ayachucho, the Peruvian military compelled members and sympathizers of the Sendero Luminoso to seek refuge and new bases of operation in the sparsely populated Amazonian rainforests. Similarly, defeats of the Túpac Amaru Revolutionary Movement (MRTA) in the Andean department of Junín obliged this rebel group to move its base of operations into Peru's *selva central* (central jungle), especially the provinces of Satipo and Oxapampa. By the end of the 1980s and the beginning of the 1990s, the armed insurgent groups had gained significant popular bases of operation in the *selva central* and some regions of the northern jungle, particularly in San Martín.

Black Gold: Oil, the State, and Indigenous Communities

During Alberto Fujimori's decade in power, Amazonian communities witnessed a dramatic upswing in the rate of privatization and parceling of communal areas. By the close of Fujimori's grip on state power in 2000 there were dozens of oil exploration fields, gold mining outfits, and timber companies operating in indigenous homelands throughout the region. Fujimori's brand of neoliberalism—with its lucrative tax abatements, lax environmental standards, and generous territorial concessions—clearly advanced the interests of the primary-product exporters, particularly the foreign-dominated mining sector (such as the Peruvian Copper Corporation, which is based in the United States) and numerous petroleum companies, as well as the profitable marketers in tropical hardwoods. Assessing the Peruvian state's promotion of hydrocarbon exploration in Amazonia illustrates the priorities of the Fujimori government, which tended to emphasize economic "development" regardless of the consequences this had for the livelihood and communal well-being of the region's politically vulnerable indigenous peoples. Fujimori reactivated the national petroleum company's search for Amazonian oil soon after coming to power. The Fujimori-controlled legislature subsequently passed laws that paved the way for the return of foreign oil investors and the eventual privatization of the state petroleum industry, Petro-Perú. To this end, Fujimori signed the Law of Organic Hydrocarbons (Ley 26221), which encouraged the growth of the petroleum industry. According to this law, which was passed in 1993, lots were awarded in concessions spanning from thirty years for oil extraction to forty years for natural gas exploration. Moreover, the concessionaire is the legal owner of the natural resources extracted (La Torre López 1998, 16). Fujimori's neoliberal land titling program in Amazonia appears to have been designed with the aim of dividing the region into "concessionary blocks" to attract tenders for oil exploitation rights. The Peruvian state's recent encouragement of Amazonian oil prospecting differs little from its enthusiastic historical support for other extractive economies, such as the rubber industry.[20]

The personalist political system that emerged under Fujimori depended on the time-honored populist ploy of doling out state resources on the basis of political patronage. Representing up to 40 percent of the annual budget, the special Ministry of the Presidency established by Fujimori was responsible for managing the allocation of targeted social spending aimed at enhancing political support. New patronage networks accompanying Fujimori's corrupt pork-barrel policies took their place in Amazonia alongside older and more localized forms of clientalism. While somewhat limited compared to other indigenous communities, Urarina leaders attempted throughout the 1990s to secure state patronage. This often took the form of soliciting material aid (in the form of food stuffs, building materials, and small boats) from regional and municipal authorities. Reflective of a new sense of entitlement promoted by the growing pan-indigenous movement, these efforts at securing governmental assistance intersected with the political machinations of established and aspiring headmen whose authority increasingly became associated with their capacity to deliver "goods" back to their local constituents (see, for instance, the Municipalidad Distral de Urarinas-Maypuco "Acta de Entrega" for the month of February 1998, which notes the delivery of fifteen kilos of powered milk to the Urarina community of Santa Beatriz).

Some indigenous representatives supported the Fujimori regime in return for direct material assistance. Along the Río Corrientes, for instance, the public expression of support for Fujimori's 2000 re-election campaign by the Achuar community's leadership was directly tied to old-style political patronage. In some instances, similar pacts were made with the petroleum industry (Dean 2002b).

The threat from oil is apparent throughout the Peruvian rainforest, where many indigenous communities find themselves locked in bitter disputes with petroleum companies. This is evident in Peru's northern jungle, particularly in the territory of the Jivaroan- and Urarina-speaking peoples of the upper Amazonian region along the border with Ecuador. To promote and manage the exploration and production contracts, Fujimori's government created a state agency (confusingly called Perú-Petro). Many transnational petroleum companies—including, among others, Chevron, Mobil, Shell, Exxon, and Occidental—vied for concession rights during what some observers have deemed a new Amazonian economic "boom" in hydrocarbons. By 1998, twenty-one million hectares of Amazonian rain forest had been granted in thirty-four exploration and production lots (La Torre López 1998, 16) (fig. 2.4).

For their part, the Urarina do not enjoy any special rights over the use of natural resources, such as the water in their territories (navigable and non-navigable), nor do they enjoy the right to extract subsoil resources in their own traditional homelands. Indeed, the Peruvian state has complete discretionary control over natural resource management. As in the Andes, local peoples in Amazonia often reject state models because they are seen as constituting "a form of cultural hegemony by a nation-state that neither shares nor respects highland cultural values" (Gelles 2000, 156). Neoliberal legislation implemented during Fujimori's ten-year regime countermanded

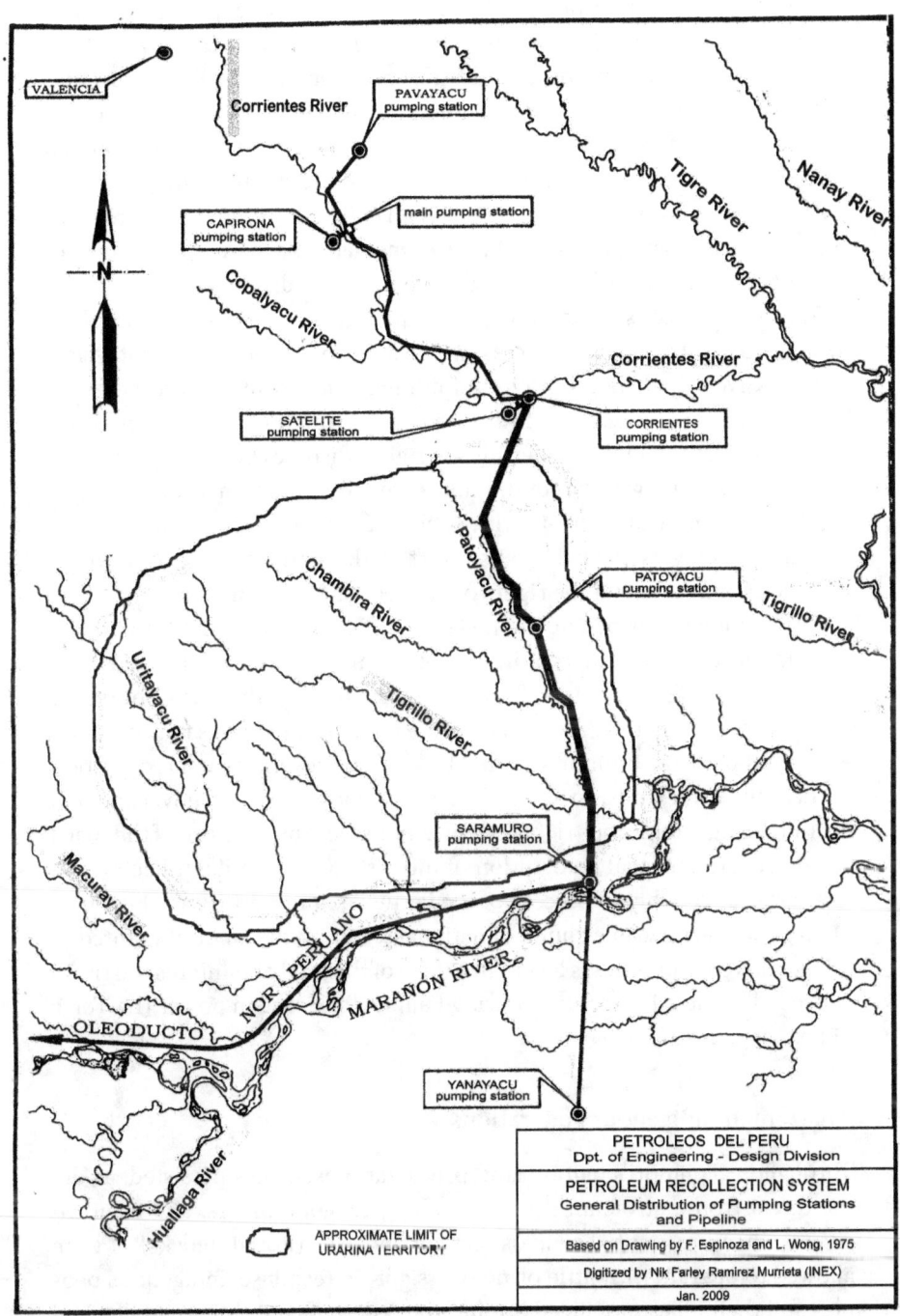

Fig. 2.4. Oil pipeline system, Bajo Marañón River

constitutional and statutory protection of indigenous people's land rights established under previous governments. While the constitution of 1993 guarantees communal property and reaffirms the legal recognition of Native Communities, the inalienability of communally held land was revoked. As a result, the outright sale of communal lands is no longer prohibited under current law. The only right to communal land tenure still remaining intact in the constitution of 1993 is that of "unassignability." In essence this prevents land titles from being reassigned to non-indigenous tenants simply on the basis of the length they have resided on the lands in dispute.

The Peruvian constitution recognizes the state's inalienable and absolute ownership of all mineral resources, which are exploited under a concession system. Given that the promotion of mining investments is considered to be in the national interest, and the fact that communal title to land does not encompass mineral or other subsoil rights, disputes between petroleum companies and indigenous communities are quite common. Moreover, private and commercial interests with sufficient resources and political influence have been very successful at subverting the spirit of those laws, which were designed to defend the rights of indigenous communities.

Titling indigenous people's homelands in Peru is a long and byzantinely complex procedure. Numerous indigenous communities have endured years of bureaucratic red tape, as well as born (often futilely) the cost of pursuing their claims to land title. As a result, there are presently thousands of indigenous and peasant communities that lack official governmental recognition of their ancestral lands. In spite of obstacles, loopholes, and governmental heel-dragging, indigenous rights organizations were by the close of the 1990s able to secure the legal recognition of more than seven million hectares of territory—or roughly 10 percent of the Peruvian rainforest (Brack Egg 1997, 21, 213). While a sizeable chunk of national territory, the amount granted to indigenous communities is less than a third of the total of rainforest territory conceded to the oil companies during Fujimori's decade in power (La Torre López 1998, 20–21).

Amazonian Indigenous Federations

Throughout Fujimori's tenure, land privatization schemes persisted, as did the threat from petroleum companies, loggers, gold miners, and even *co-caleros* who were granted concessions, auctioned territorial "blocks," or were allowed to operate with little or no oversight. In response, indigenous peoples and their allies mobilized around the issues of land titling, intellectual property rights, and rights claims in relation to exploitation of oil, minerals, and lumber, and to community defense. In the last quarter of the twentieth century, *indigenismo* developed in the context of the negative and positive stereotypes of "Indians" that were encoded in existing tropes of Western domination. Influenced by their travels to urban and peri-urban Amazonia, the presence of pro-indigenous and development NGOs in their midst, and the general appeal of *indigenismo*, a new generation of indigenous leaders has come to realize that multiethnic confederations may be one of the most appropriate mechanisms for indigenous societies to articulate and defend their human rights (Verber 1998; Gray 1997; Belaunde et al. 2005).

In light of the limited successes achieved at the national level, struggles for local and regional autonomy have been redirected to the international arena, where transnational indigenous organizations are now asserting their claims to self-determination and sovereignty. An unprecedented rise in political organization and activism by indigenous federations and their advocates in Amazonia has marked the past quarter of a century. National indigenous organizations—such as CIDOB of Bolivia and CONFENIAE of Ecuador—and the transnational pan-ethnic confederation COICA (Coordinadora de Organizaciones Indígenas de la Cuenca Amazónica) have emerged as a vibrant political force in Latin America (among others, see Montoya Rojas 1998; Maybury-Lewis 1997; Varese 1996a, 1996b; Brysk 2000; Dean and Levi 2003; Warren and Jackson 2003). In Peru, indigenous advocacy organizations increasingly pressed their legal grievances by citing ILO Convention 169, which the state officially ratified in 1993. When compared with its Andean neighbors—Bolivia and Ecuador—Peru's indigenous movement is considerably less well articulated at the national political level. Exploring intercultural education, Maria Elena García (2005) has verified how contemporary indigenous politics in Peru are inextricably and simultaneously local and global in nature. Nevertheless, alliances between highland and lowland indigenous political organizations have remained virtually nonexistent in Peru, a country marked by its profound regionalism and mutual antipathy dividing the Andean and Amazonian imagined communities.

Collective mobilization among indigenous peoples in Latin America has required the incorporation of closely knit local communities into a broader national and international framework of political action (Kearney 1996, 5–17; Brysk 2000; Albo 1996; Chango, Whitten, and Whitten 1997, 355–92). Nonetheless, many factors have impeded the ability of indigenous people to participate in, and facilitate their deliberate exclusion from, decision making directly affecting their lands, cultural traditions, and the allocation of natural resources. The centralization of state power in Lima limits the access and participation of indigenous peoples in Peruvian national society.

Cultural exclusion from "mainstream" national *mestizo* society has hindered political unity. Efforts at subverting the authority and political legitimacy of rival groups are common stratagems marking relations among adversarial factions. This in turn has exacerbated factionalism and promoted ethnic rivalry.

The recognition and consolidation of indigenous people's rights to their distinctive ways of life and "traditional" territories are still very much an unresolved matter in Peru. Peruvian legislation is often contradictory when it comes to the rights of indigenous peoples. In some instances, laws recognize indigenous communities' rights, while in other cases laws recognize the absolute authority of the state. More generally, national legislation tends not to favor indigenous people's demands, and the political power of the Peruvian indigenous movement remains relatively weak at the national level, particularly when compared with the neighboring movements in the Andean countries of Ecuador and Bolivia. Problems associated with territorial management, including controlling the access of miners, oil companies, and lumber concerns, continue to plague indigenous communities in Peruvian Amazonia. This is evident from a series of ongoing conflicts over resource use and management. In the southern jungle Department of Madre de Dios unregulated gold mining and lumber extraction is wreaking havoc (Junquera Rubio 1999; Intrator 2006); in the *selva central* the violent aftermath of the civil war has been exacerbated by continued conflicts over coca; and in the northern jungle a series of oil spills by the Argentine oil company Pluspetrol have threatened the livelihood of thousands of indigenous peoples, including the Urarina, the Cocama, and the Cocamilla.

Political mobilization has occurred in the face of the challenges to the cultural survival of Amazonia's indigenous societies. The two primary national ethnic federations representing the interests of indigenous peoples of Peruvian Amazonia are AIDESEP (Asociación Interétnica de Desarrollo de la Selva Peruana or Inter-Ethnic Association for the Development of the Peruvian Amazon) and CONAP (Confederación de Nacionalidades Amazónicas del Perú or Confederation of Amazonian Nationalities of Peru). Established in 1980, AIDESEP is the senior pan-ethnic organization in Peruvian Amazonia. In contrast to the numerically less powerful ethnic federation CONPAP, AIDESEP is resolutely opposed to territorial encroachments by government, commercial, and other interests. For its part, CONAP believes that extractive activities and other development operations are inevitable. Established in 1987, CONAP advocates a more pragmatic strategy that encourages indigenous communities to actively share in the planning and benefits of development initiatives, particularly those activities initiated on their territories. Both AIDESEP and CONAP share similar concerns, even though both claim to be the sole, legitimate, and authoritative voice of all indigenous peoples. Both, for instance, vociferously criticized the legislation in 1995 that allowed for the sale of putatively uninhabited territories or "unproductive" lands in Amazonia. Over the past decade, both AIDESEP and CONAP have requested the creation of communal reserves for hunting and subsistence activities.

Scarcity, Value, and Land as a Commodity

Until very recently, the vast majority of Urarina "communities," as well as territorial "homelands," were not legally recognized. It was not until the late 1990s that attempts were made to title the Urarinas' ancestral territories. The major impetus for this was provided by a Peruvian NGO—the Centro de Desarrollo del Indígena Amazónico (CEDIA). While an important development, the territorial demarcation process alone cannot ensure the ecological or political security of the Urarinas' traditional lands. During fieldwork in 1996 and 1998, I noted that CEDIA's land-titling initiative (that is, "communal" meetings and written materials) was being directed primarily toward a male audience. No effort was made to include or involve Urarina women, and similarly no attempt was made to incorporate spoken Urarina in the mobilization process (cf. CEDIA 1996a, 1996b, 1996c). The autocratic style of those promoting the land-titling effort did little to ensure equal participation in the political process for women or for those who are not conversant in Spanish—arguably most of the Urarina population.

Questions remain whether the land-titling efforts will actually benefit *ribereño* communities rather than the Urarina, who are themselves politically less experienced. The Urarina land-titling campaign of CEDIA followed the physical geography of the Chambira River drainage rather than the cultural topography of Urarina society. Urarina communities on the Urituyacu and Corrientes River basins were not included in the titling efforts (Dean and McKinley 1997).

The classical "scarcity" theory of value suggests that the more socially consequential a specific kind of thing is the greater likelihood that "crystalline rules" will be established to regulate its distribution, use, and consumption. One could assume then that the increased interaction between the Urarina and migrating traders and settlers would generate a series of "crystalline rules"; that is, hard-edged doctrines that provide a framework in which strangers can enter into transactions with one another in a spirit of confidence—especially in the face of multiple regimes of value. I have used the Urarina ethnography to illustrate an ineluctable tendency to substitute ambiguous or mud rules of decision for what appear to be wholly unclouded, clear-cut "demarcations of entitlements" (Rose 1988, 264). In her review of "Western" conceptions of property, Carol Rose suggests that crystal and mud rules are a matched duo: both are derivative of a non-legal commercial context, "where people already in some relationship arrive at more or less imperfect understandings at the outset and expect post hoc readjustments when circumstances require." Crystalline rules are necessary when individuals make deals with strangers. Mud rules or exceptions are called for only subsequently when "things have gone awry . . ." (Rose 1988, 289).

Mud rules are generated in an effort to "recreate an underlying non-legal trading community in which confidence is possible" (Rose 1988, 288–89). Rather than simply driving "hard bargains," individual members of these trading communities are inclined to readjust to real or perceived difficulties. Mud rules echo a system of ad-hoc realignments that people regularly make when they are part of ongoing, long-term relationships. On the Chambira, people cannot simply set out to shortchange their trading partners, to traffic in faulty goods, or to decline to make readjustments on "debts," for to do so would in the long run result in the cessation of *cudiaca*—relations of exchange.

Similarly, the Urarinas' property regime invariably exhibits a tension between "standardization through rules of general application and the negotiability and discretionary arrangements of specific affairs" (S. Moore 1986, 38). The Urarina swing between community defense through autonomy and assimilation to the outside. This is not to suggest that Urarina local culture is merely reactive to the dominant neo-Peruvian "national culture." Urarina cultural practices are composed of internally generated sociohistorical relationships, themselves contingent on broader, supra-local processes and structures.

3

Historicizing Amazonia

Domination, Unequal Exchange, and Value Extraction

Ever since Europe's first encounter with Amazonia, the region has typically been envisioned—both in popular and scholarly renditions—as a remote, uncharted, and even unspoiled tropical rain forest (Léry 1990; Raffles 2002; Slater 2002). Amazonian societies have often been represented as marginal, atomistic, and isolated, a discursive stance linked to the supposition that social simplicity characterized pre-Columbian lowland South America. Such a perspective is neither sustained by impressive archaeological findings nor confirmed by historical accounts left by explorers, missionaries, and fortune seekers, who over the centuries have ventured throughout upper Amazonia. Large and politically intricate social formations situated along the area's primary rivers flourished prior to the advent of Luso-Iberian imperialism (Roosevelt 1999, 326–27; T. Myers 1992a). These included stratified polities, like the Omagua, which numbered in the tens of thousands (T. Myers 1992b; Denevan 1996). Initial European reports described ornately garbed paramount chiefs controlling numerous local settlements, prodigious reserves of food, indigenous slavery, armed canoe flotillas, and well-kept thoroughfares extending from riverain villages well into the forest's interior (see Golob 1982, 6; Markham 1963, 30; Fritz 1922, 48–49).

Humans have been modifying the landscape in Amazonia and managing domesticated plants in the region for well over five thousand years (Balée 1993, 232; Balée and Erickson, 2006; Schultes 1984; Rival 2002). Called the "hearth of significant cultural developments and innovations," such as the invention of pottery, and the elaboration of highly complex iconographies, Amazonia was inhabited by humans at least as early as the settlement of the Andes (Roosevelt 1999, 308, 342). Extensive long-distance exchange networks and craft specialization were critical to the sociopolitical articulation of the upper Amazon's fluvial and interfluvial societies. The Cocama produced and widely circulated palm-bast cloth, tunics, and capes, whereas the Omagua exchanged their painted ceramicware, ornate calabashes, and cotton cloth. Both of these Tupian-speaking peoples obtained blowgun dart poison through barter with the Ticuna and the Peba of the Bajo Marañón region (Métraux 1963b, 697; Cipolletti 1988, 527–40; Reyes Flores 1999, 151). Goods and people also flowed between the tropical regions of Amazonia and the Andean highlands.[1] The Amazonian piedmont of the Andes was an important source of specialized items and tropical produce, which included such things as coca, feathers, pets, salt, *capsicum* pepper, and tapir's feet.

Archaeological evidence indicates that regular contact between Peruvian Amazonia and the Ecuadorian coast was established during the formative period (Braun 1982; Bruhns, Burton, and Miller 1990). At this time, the Chambira Basin supported cosmopolitan communities that participated in the same cultural development as those on the Ecuadorian coast and in the Andean highlands (Myers and Dean 1999). It appears that the Urarina inhabited the middle and upper sections of the Chambira River drainage prior to the Spanish conquest, while the Omagua and Cocama peoples dominated the Marañón floodplain.[2] The extent to which the region's pre-Columbian inhabitants were integrated into a larger polity is presently unknown. It does seem likely that the people of the Chambira and Corrientes rivers participated in intercultural contact, and that the rivers were possibly the routes along which regional contact was established and maintained. The intercultural communication between the tropical lowlands and the Ecuadorian coast was ruptured around 1000 BC (Myers and Dean 1999; cf. Morales Chocano 1998).

In the Name of God: Ecclesiastical Colonialism in Maynas

In addition to thousands of years of indigenous occupation, Europeans, Africans, and Asians have explored and intermittently colonized Amazonia for nearly half a millennia. Compelled by gold fever and the ruthless quest for spices, the Spanish began to explore the seemingly limitless frontiers of western Amazonia in the 1530s (Stanfield 1998, 9). Following their defeat of the Inca Empire in 1533, the Spanish mounted a series of expeditions into the *montaña*. By 1560 the Viceroy of Peru had named Pedro de Ursúa the governor of El Dorado and Omagua, and charged him with exploring the region for the crown. Setting out from the Spanish stronghold of Trujillo, Ursúa's expeditionary force navigated the Huallaga River, finally making it to the Marañón River in September 1560 (Morey Alejo and Sotil García 2000, 137).

European penetration of the South American interior heralded the beginning of profound transformations in the social and environmental landscapes of Amazonia. As the frontiers of the Spanish Empire expanded, disease ravished entire communities, violence intensified, and slave raiding became all too commonplace. This was particularly true for Spanish conquistadors, who frequently mounted campaigns of military conquest against the upper Amazon's native inhabitants. Many of the early campaigns were the result of efforts at pacifying local rebellion.

While scholars have turned their attention to determining if native warfare is an indigenous development or the result of culture contact (Otterbein 1999), it is difficult to dispute that the arrival of "the Leviathan" in lowland South America did in fact "set off crashing waves of violence all around" (B. Ferguson 1990, 248). In addition to increased violent conflict, lethal new diseases such as influenza, malaria, measles, poxvirus, and yellow fever were introduced (T. Myers 1988a). Early chroniclers of Spanish frontier expansion in Amazonia noted large-scale depopulation fueled by rampant epidemics, famine, pillage, and inter-ethnic violence (among others, see Fritz 1922; Uriarte 1952; DeBoer 1986). In a number of cases, the arrival of Europeans led to the virtual annihilation of indigenous societies in the upper Amazon, as among the Maina and Itucale peoples. In the wake of the colonial encounter, some indigenous societies fared better than others. The Carijona, for instance, prospered through their involvement in European trade. By trafficking in human slaves in exchange for trade goods, the Carijona emerged as influential merchants in northern and western Amazonia. At the close of the colonial epoch, the Carijona were wealthier and more powerful than they had been prior to the arrival of the Europeans (Stanfield 1998, 11). The once affluent Carijona eventually entered a period of precipitous decline in the early twentieth century following four lethal epidemics that killed off much of their populace (Stanfield 1998, 217 n. 13; Llanos Vargas and Pineda Camacho 1982, 77–80).

From native Amazonian people's perspective, the so-called Columbian exchange (Crosby 1972, 1986, 1994) introduced contagion, new crops (bananas, cacao, cotton, rice, sugar cane), domesticated animals (such as pigs, cows, and chicken), and novel technologies—from mills for crushing sugar cane (commonly called *trapiche*) to metal tools, gunpowder, and mirrors. The colonial encounter also heralded the birth of new social institutions in Amazonia, such as jails, formal military training, orphanages, seminaries, and mission posts, or *reducciones* (Fritz 1922, 141; Ardito Vega 1992). While Spanish colonists tended to settle in the higher altitude, fertile western valleys of the *montaña* (or *ceja de la selva*), the Jesuit missionaries ventured into the sweltering tropical low country that stretched for thousands of miles beyond the piedmont.

The spiritual conquest of the inhospitable lands lying east of the Andes was designated for the Jesuits, who were relative late-comers to the colonial outpost of Quito. By the time they arrived (1567), most of the desirable portions of colonial territory had already been allocated. The Jesuits soon found that the upper Amazon's fluvial chieftaincies had been all but annihilated. Accordingly, they followed a strategy of establishing *reducciones* located in the riverine areas that could draw on the populations of the inter-fluvial regions to supply them—by force if necessary—with new converts and catechumens (see Fritz 1922; Golob 1982, 13; Marzal 1984; Ardito Vega 1992).

Labor conscription and religious conversion besieged and sometimes completely overwhelmed indigenous societies. Those drawn into the missions were placed at greater risk of dying from infectious disease, and as a result the need for new converts was ever constant. Missionaries combined material inducements—most commonly metal goods—with a strategy of aggressive compulsion to congregate and subdue those unfortunate enough to be deemed pagans. Missionaries also relied on the influence of the *viracochas*, or loyal indigenous leaders, to persuade captive peoples to remain at the *reducciones* in spite of their best interest.

By the early seventeenth century, the upper Marañón and its tributary rivers—the Santiago and Pastaza—had been explored by the Jesuit fathers, and by the followers of Don Diego Vaca de Vega. The creation of the administrative division of Maynas soon followed (Markham 1963, xvi; Anda Aguirre 1995). Maynas was under the administrative control of the Viceroyalty of Peru for a total of 212 years and under the control of the Viceroyalty of Santa Fe and the Audiencia of Quito for 68 years. Settlements and colonial outposts were established along the fringe of the Amazon Basin. In present-day Peruvian territory, gateway towns to Amazonia included Chachapoyas (1538), Huánuco (1539), and Moyobamba (1540). During the ensuing centuries, these communities vied for preferential treatment from the central authorities located in Lima or Quito. Colonial and Republican regimes have long sought to determine the best way into Amazonia, and hence the proposed route was of vital significance for those communities located along the trans-Andean path linking the coast and the Amazon Basin.

The Jesuits were motivated by the need to obtain converts, while also trying to defend the territory of Maynas from the relentless attacks of the Portuguese, who continuously sought to expand their holdings. To this end, permanent Spanish settlements were founded in the lowlands when Vaca de Vega took control of the General Command of Maynas (Comandancia General de Mainas), established by the Spanish in 1619 as the administrative center the Upper Amazon (Izquierdo Ríos 1976, 7).

Encomiendas consisted of hereditary grants of control over territory and indigenous inhabitants allocated to conquistadores in return for their service in conquering new lands and in converting the subjugated population to Christianity. In theory, the *encomendero* was charged with protecting and educating his subjects in return for enjoying the fruits of their labor power. By the time of the Jesuits' arrival in the upper Amazon, there were twenty-one *encomiendas* in the Province of Maynas. Relative to the Andean region, the establishment of *encomiendas* in the Amazonian lowlands was a much more difficult task to achieve. Disease and the local inhabitants' tendency to flee into the forest consistently thwarted Spanish efforts at expanding their imperial reach into the lowlands. In response to native resistance, joint military-ecclesiastical raids, or *entradas*, were mounted. The governor of the General Command of Maynas, Diego Vaca de Vega, sent his son Pedro to direct an *entrada* up the Río Pastaza to the Rimachi Lagoon, where thousands of Maina peoples were abducted and then allotted as the personal vassals of some sixty Spanish *encomenderos* in Borja (see Steward and Métraux 1963, 630; Grohs-Paul 1974, 28; Maroni 1889–92, 29, 191–203).

The arrival of the Jesuit friars Gaspar Cujía and Lucas de la Cueva signaled the launching of the Maynas missions. In 1640 Father Cueva had managed to pacify (literally "reduce") a group of Xeveros (Shiwilu) and obliged them to live in a mission settlement on the Río Apena, which was called Concepción de Nuestra Señora de Xeveros. That same year missionaries arrived in Borja to establish schools for the Mainas' children (Markham 1963, xix). Between 1640 and 1682—a period that Clements Markham calls "the first missionary epoch"—thirty-three villages were established in the upper Amazon (1963, xxi; Rodriguez 1684). This included towns along the Río Huallaga, a major tributary of the Marañón River: Jéberos (1640), Lagunas (1670), and Yurimaguas (1709). The second missionary epoch, according to Markham, spanned from 1683 to 1727, and the third and final missionary epoch extended from 1727 to 1768 (1963, xxxii, xxxv).

In light of the epidemics and indigenous modes of passive and open resistance, the Jesuits were forced to embark on a vigorous strategy of recruitment through continued reliance on the *entradas* to sustain a stable mission population (see T. Myers 1974, 153; Regan 1983, 49; Chantre y Herrera 1901, 495; Markham 1963, xxxv; M. Porras P. 1987; Lehm Ardaya 1992). Besides coercive measures that forced missionization on indigenous communities,[3] native peoples were drawn to the missions by their desires to obtain metal tools. They also wanted to secure a modicum of protection against the incursions of slave raiders.

The Jesuits promoted relations of barter by encouraging local inhabitants to exchange their undervalued produce, including woven palm-fiber goods and forest game, for overvalued imported trade items or goods obtained from or manufactured in other missions, such as turtle-harpoons fashioned from iron nails (San Román 1975, 63–67; Marcoy 1873, 3: 32, 40). In this way, the Jesuits had a hand in influencing the diffusion of productive technologies in the upper Amazon (Reyes Flores 1999). Of particular interest to this study is recognition that the Jesuits encouraged the arts of spinning and weaving using a back-strap loom among missionized native peoples (Golob 1982, 235; Fritz 1922, 60).

Upper Amazonian missions were not only sites of economic production, they also served as the privileged distribution points for trade goods, such as textiles, hammocks, icthyotoxins, tobacco, sugar, tools, curare, and salt[4] transported from Yurimaguas, Moyobamba, Chachapoyas, Lamas, Quito, and beyond (see Martín Rubio 1991, xci; Golob 1982, 232; Uriarte 1952, 1: 100, 184, 213, 217, 2: 161). The missionaries themselves were keenly aware of the magical allure of trade goods. Supply parties were periodically mounted to transport vanilla, bees' wax, resins, pharmaceutical oils, and other forest produce to Quito, Ambato, Jaén, Lamas, Moyobamba, and Chachapoyas. These forest products were then exchanged for trade goods.

The Maynas missions transformed local indigenous production, gearing it toward satisfying not only subsistence needs, but also to generating a surplus to be exchanged for barter goods, which over time became indispensable for indigenous social reproduction. Indigenous converts residing in the missions cultivated sugar cane, coca, tobacco, and cacao, while some raised livestock. They also toiled gathering forest goods, including vanilla, achiote, cascarilla, and other scarce items such as caffeine-containing guayusa and the cacao that consumers demanded in distant colonial towns and European markets (R. Jamieson 2001, 278–79). The Maynas missions maintained commercial links with regional towns bordering the lowlands, such as Tarma and Cerro de Pasco, and promoted long distance trade with those settlements located along the Pacific coast.

A rotating corvee system (*mit'a*) was employed in the Maynas missions to secure the necessary labor power for the care of the Jesuit clergy and for the production of a surplus for trade. *Mitayo* is a term used in Amazonia that derives from the Quechua word *mitayoq*, referring to the practice of providing the missions with comestible forest game (see Ballón Landa 1917, 194–95; Hernández 1946, 16–17 n. 3). *Mit'a* in pre-Columbian Andean Quechua denoted a "turn" of labor owed the Inca rulers. Lasting six months, this labor draft was levied every six or seven years of all adult males under the age of fifty (Stern 1987). *Mitayear*, or *lenune atiyá* in Urarina, now refers to the action of hunting, and *traer el mitayo* denotes bringing or delivering forest game. In the colonial missions, a group of native huntsmen (*mitayeros*) was designated weekly and given the duty of providing the entire community with its supply of meat. Less frequently, groups of men were given the task of obtaining salt or turtles for the mission (Regan 1983, 52; 2000, 13).

Even though they provided indigenous people with protection against the slave raids (*correrías*), as well as access to new technologies and desired trade goods, missions were places fraught with bitter conflicts. The social distortions associated with the spread of European empire initially sparked indigenous revolt, most notably in the Maina attack on Borja in 1635, when a contingent of one thousand warriors destroyed the town, killing nine *encomenderos* and their families. During another siege five years later, the Maina peoples failed to capture Borja, but they did manage to force many of the Spanish from the region, leaving few *encomenderos* behind. The Maina people then sought refuge in the headwaters of the Pastaza River (Grohs-Paul 1974, 29). The uprising of 1640 marked the last successful, large-scale indigenous revolt in the upper Amazon.

During this time, more than a dozen Jesuit missions were established along the Marañón River, particularly at strategic locales, such as the confluences of the Pastaza, Huallaga, and Ucayalí rivers. Even so, it would take nearly another century before a mission was initiated among the Urarina (1738). By 1760, there were over twelve thousand indigenous "converts" in nearly three-dozen *reducciones* in Maynas controlled by twenty-two Jesuit missionaries (Regan 1983, 50). This figure is impressive when taking into account the fact that over the entire 131–year period of Jesuit presence in the upper Amazon there were only about sixty villages that ever actually functioned as mission-run settlements (Golob 1982, 192).

Indigenous peoples could attempt to escape Spanish assaults by disbanding into smaller groups and secluding themselves far into the forest's interior or riverain headwaters, as did the Urarina, or they could confederate and fight back, as the Jivaroan peoples did successfully in 1599. The latter strategy included inter-ethnic alliance. The demographically decimated Cocama and Cocamilla (Stocks 1983) allied with the Ucayalí Shipibo and revolted against the missions and Spanish domination. Although it began in 1649, the Cocama-Cocamilla rebellion was not quashed until after nearly a decade of bloodshed. Military defeat eventually culminated in the collapse of the native confederation, whose leaders were tried and executed (see Grohs-Paul 1974; Anda Aguirre 1995, 87). In 1670 the routed and disease weary Cocama were forced to assist Father Juan de Lucero in establishing the Mission of Santiago de la Laguna on the lower Río Huallaga—the eventual administrative capital of all of the Maynas missions. A decade later, a smallpox epidemic compelled a group of Cocama peoples to flee the mission of Santiago de la Laguna and to seek refuge with their Tupian brethren, the Omagua at the mission of San Joaquín. There they remained with the Omagua until the expulsion of the Jesuits in 1767.

For the Tupian peoples of the upper Amazon, the colonial encounter irrevocably changed their lives: by the seventeenth century the Cocama-Cocamilla were employed in Spanish-led attacks on surrounding peoples, including the Urarina who had sought protection in the isolated headwaters of the Chambira Basin. Throughout the following century, the indigenous inhabitants of the Lagunas mission continued to be drafted into service as soldiers, boat builders, and oarsman, particularly during punitive and commercial expeditions. Many of the descendants of those forced into the missions at Lagunas or San Joaquín de los Omaguas now make up part of the region's *ribereño* population, a culturally diffuse group that today comprises the majority of Loreto's rural inhabitants.

The Urarina and the Missions

The autochthonous peoples of the Chambira are mentioned in the chronicles as two groups: the "Itucalis" (Itucales) and the "Urariñas" (Urarina). Friar Pablo Maroni suggests that the Itucale may have migrated after the Spanish conquest into the Chambira Basin from the Río Samiria, where they had lived with the "Cutinana" and "Chamicura" (1889–92, 26, 231). Similarly, Julian Steward and Alfred Métraux noted that the Itucales may at one time have resided south of the Marañón River, since "they are very similar culturally to the Chamicura" (1963, 557). To date, the ethnological status of the Itucales remains enigmatic, particularly in light of the Pangayacu Urarinas' recognition of a ritual sib they called Itucuaidi.

In 1653, Father Tomás Majano (Maxano?), accompanied by Cocama intermediaries, became the first European to make direct contact with the Itucales (Cajas Rojas et al. 1987). In contrast, Maroni believed that it was Father Majano—with Cocama guides—who was the first outsider to make contact with the Itucales in 1653. This corresponds with the opinion of Chantre y Herrera (1901, 156). A group of Cingacuchuscas (ostensibly a Urarina "subtribe" from the Tigre River) was settled with the Pandabeques, a Cocamilla subgroup, in an annex (*anejo*) pertaining to the mission of the Concepción de Nuestra Señora de Xeveros. Some of these native peoples were sent to Borja, where they were became vassals in the *encomiendas*. Perhaps with this purpose in mind, Father Lucero relocated a group of Urarina in 1680 from the Chambira River drainage to the mission of San Xavier de Chamicuros, where they were subsequently taken to the mission of Santiago de la Laguna (Grohs-Paul 1974, 53; Steward 1963, 557).

The *reducción* of Itucales was finally established on the Chambira River in 1712. Located upriver in an area occupied today by the last important *mestizo caserío* (Apra) on the lower Chambira, the Jesuits maintained the Itucales mission until 1730, when they sent the remaining inhabitants to the missions along the Huallaga River (where they were subsequently known as Aracui) (Steward and Métraux 1963, 557; Grohs-Paul 1974, 49, 53). A *reducción* was established in 1738 in the Urarina "parcel" of the Chambira (that is, the middle and upper reaches of the river). Previously, Father José Alvelda had urged the Cocama to lead the pacification of the Urarina. The Cocama embraced the idea, expounding it to the head of the mission at Lagunas. An *entrada* force of Cocama and Itucale, lead by Alvelda, an elderly, fat, and myopic cleric, and José Vahamonde, were given permission to pacify the Urarina. The *entrada* was planned as a three-day affair; however, the expeditionary force traveled for twenty-five days before seeing any Urarina. The *entrada* force was apparently "welcomed" by the Urarina, who were said to have received their Itucale relatives with hospitality (Velasco 1960, 267; Chantre y Herrera 1901; cf. Grohs-Paul 1974, 54, who notes the year was 1737).

The first Urarina mission post was located on the "south bank" of the Chambira some two days' travel upriver (Chantre y Herrera 1901, 350). The *reducción* of San Xavier de Urarinas had a population of 536 persons in 1745 (Grohs-Paul 1974, 54). Following his appointment to San Xavier de Urarinas, the missionary Bazterra drowned in 1754. Brother Pedro Choneman was then dispatched to replace him. Choneman was subsequently sent to the Napeanos, where he replaced Antonio Yenseque, who in turn was assigned to San Xavier de Urarinas in 1756 (Uriarte 1952, 1: 222–26).

In spite of numerous new converts (or *viracochas*), a series of factors, including infertile soils, meager crop production, and persistent flooding, forced Yenseque to relocate the mission in 1756 to the Río Marañón, at the mouth of the Chambira River, the present site of the *ribereño* settlement of Concordia (Grohs-Paul 1974, 54). Due to seasonal flooding, Nuevo San Xavier de Urarinas was relocated once more in 1758 to the mouth of the Urituyacu, located some two days' travel up the Marañón River (Chantre y Herrera 1901, 350–51). In the 1760s, a number of "pacified" Mainas were settled in San Xavier (Uriarte 1952, 1: 225, 274). The Urarina revolted in 1765 against Father Yenseque's excessive labor demands. They organized a delegation, which traveled to the mission settlement of Lagunas to complain about

Yenseque's abusive regime. Consequently, Father Segundo was assigned to take command from Yenseque. Padre Mauricio Colgari then replaced Father Segundo.

In 1767, the year King Charles III expelled the Jesuits from the Spanish Americas, the mission of San Xavier had an estimated population of 600 residents. The following year that number had fallen to 150 people. The precipitous decline from 600 to 150 residents indicates that without the presence of Jesuits, San Xavier, like other mission villages, could no longer offer trade goods and the modicum of protection it had previously provided. In 1814, the population of the settlement of Urarinas was listed as 205, by 1847 this had dropped to 94, and it remained stable in 1859 (Larraburre i Correa 1905–9, 4: 180, 193, 210; 7: 94; Reyes Flores 1999, 139, 142). These population figures should not be taken at their face value. Gootenberg (1991) has highlighted the historical proclivity of Peruvian national censuses to exhibit the "predictable undercount of Amazonian natives." In the 1836 census, "The inhabitants of tropical Maynas had vanished altogether" (Gootenberg 1991, 111, 116). Even today, demographers often lament the lack of accurate censuses of indigenous Amazonia (Odicio Egoavil 1992, 71).

Twilight of the Missions and the Legacy of the Colonial Encounter

By 1768, all of the Jesuits had gone from the Province of Maynas. The majority of those indigenous peoples who still lived in the missions now feared that agents of the Spanish crown would impose tribute, so they returned to their previous ways of life (Regan 1983, 67; Chantre y Herrera 1901, 669–83). By the late eighteenth century, most of the upper Amazon's mission villages had become secularized. The transfer of control over the Maynas missions to secular clergy marked the total collapse of the mission town of San Xavier de Urarinas. In 1790, the Franciscans of the Province of San Francisco Solano were granted authority over the Maynas missions, and in 1802 control passed to the Franciscans from Santa Rosa Ocopa. Under the tutelage of Franciscan and secular clergyman, the Jesuit's former missions languished during a long stretch of decline and virtual neglect (Marcoy 1873, 3: 3, 113). The late colonial government attempted to maintain the *reducciones* as a source of labor power and foodstuffs for the demands of the region's growing European and *mestizo* populace. But without the Jesuits' disciplined efforts, many of Maynas' "missionized Indians" fled to the security of refuge zones of the *montaña*, or to the inaccessible headwaters of the *selva baja* (Smyth and Lowe 1836, 199).

National, secular clergy from the town of Chachapoyas assisted the missions sporadically. In 1840, however, there were only eleven clergymen in the whole region of Maynas; and only thirteen remained five years later (Larrabure i Correa 1905–9, vols. 5, 6). According to Paul Marcoy there were nearly 150 missions in Peru during the mid-eighteenth century, of which only 9 remained by the 1870s (1873, 3: 23). After the fall of Santiago de la Laguna following the rebellion of 1828, numerous neophytes (*neófitos*) and converts alike deserted the missions along the Río Marañón, including the Urarina peoples. To escape the dominance of their Cocama adversaries, many of the Urarina left the settlements along the Marañón River and returned to their former homelands in the Chambira Basin (Myers and Dean 1999).

The departure of the Jesuits also resulted in an increase in both Portuguese contraband and demands on the labor power of indigenous peoples. Traders from the west and Brazilian smugglers from the east now regularly called at the remote and dispersed Amazonian settlements, bartering for salted fish, hats, and palm-fiber hammocks (Werlich 1990, 139). To stem the advance of the Portuguese westward expansion into the upper Amazon, Don Francisco Requena was appointed in 1791 as the governor general and commander of the Province of Maynas. Ever worried about Portuguese *bandeirante* presence in Spanish-controlled territory, and the continued decline of the upper Amazonian missions under Quito's stewardship, the crown charged Requena with leading the efforts at establishing the boundary between the Spanish and Portuguese empires. Requena thought that the Viceroyalty of Peru, rather than the Viceroyalty of Nueva Granada, was in a much better position to administer the vast Province of Maynas.

Compared to Santa Fe de Bogotá, Lima had greater access to the region via the established route of Trujillo-Cajamarca-Chachapoyas-Moyobamba-Marañón River. Acting on Requena's advice, the Spanish crown ceded legal control of the administration of the General Command of Maynas (the Comandancia General de Mainas), which included the Marañón and all of its navigable tributaries, from the Audiencia of Quito (which was part of the Viceroyalty of New Granada) and placed it under the command of the most powerful viceroyalty of South America, the Virreynato del Perú (Requena 1991a; González Suárez 1913; Ministerio de Relaciones Exteriores 1913; Izaguirre 1925, 8: 38–42; Amich 1975, 502–6). In 1808, the entire jurisdiction of the missions on the Marañón was placed by Royal Law (Real Cédula) under the jurisdiction of the Viceroyalty of Peru (Markham 1963, xxxvi). The following year, Moyobamba became the colonial administrative hub of Maynas, as well as the seat of the bishopric, which was relocated from Jeberos (Izquierdo Ríos 1976, 9).[5]

My rendition of upper Amazonian colonial history is a gesture aimed at situating contemporary Urarina society; its recapitulative tenor has been suggestive rather than exhaustive. Here my intention has been to underscore the influence that the Jesuit missions and extractive entrepreneurs of various ilk have had in shaping the lives of the indigenous peoples of the upper Amazon. The full historical significance of these agents' presence in the region is well beyond the orbit of this study. Moreover, there are significant lacunae in the historical record, compounded by the fact that a fire in 1749 destroyed the Jesuit's archives at Lagunas (Chantre y Herrera 1901, 263, 407–8). In spite of the incomplete archival record, research combining archaeological and ethno-historical approaches has yielded valuable insights on the impact of the missions in Peruvian Amazonia (T. Myers 1990; García Jordán 2001). The Maynas missions—once important centers of production, exchange, and consumption—conditioned subsequent historical trajectories in the upper Amazon, namely the development of commercial economies and coercive forms of labor recruitment. Social relationships in regions of intensive intercultural contact involve a dialectic that is always much more complicated than subaltern versus dominant (García Canclini 2001, 126; Dean 2001). Colonial, national, and indigenous modes of production and circulation have long interacted, even in the far reaches of the upper Amazon (T. Myers 1990; Dean 1994a). With respect to Amazonia, ethno-historical evidence indicates the relative political and cultural autonomy of indigenous communities under Spanish colonial rule and the resultant decline in local autonomy through the emergence of the Andean republics. During the colonial epoch, indigenous concerns were administered under constitutional and administrative legal regimes. Colonial authorities recognized indigenous leaders (*caciques*) through their possession of a staff of office (*bastón*) and their use of honorific titles, including Capitán (Captain) and Don (Sir) (Ardito Vega 1992, 23).

For indigenous peoples of the upper Amazon the colonial encounter led to the proliferation of distinctive and novel social identities: *salvaje, civilizado, cholo, chuncho, indio bravo*, and *ribereño*. Some of these identities, such as *cholo*, had relatively long histories (Mora 1995), while others reflected novel cultural categories. Growth in the magnitude of the colonial and national fronts of expansion saw the emergence of the *ribereños*: the Christianized (*catequizadas*), indigenous (*civilizados*), and in-marrying *mestizo* settlers.[6] In the colonial and republican epochs' racializing discourses of distinction, ethnic groups such as the Cocama peoples of Lagunas were held up as examples of *indígena cristianizado*—Christianized indigenous peoples. In contrast, "infidels" (*infieles*) or "savages" (*salvajes*) like the Omurana of the Urituyacu and the Chambira Urarina remained beyond the margins of colonial governance and

Christian salvation. They were deemed by the Spanish and *ribereños* as truculent savages—or "wild Indians" (*indios bravos*).[7] Indigenous peoples who found it impossible to resist the pressures of traders, *haciendas*, soldiers, and priests either were annihilated or were incorporated into the lowland's new class of peasantry—the *ribereños*.

The reports written by the conquistadores, usually designated as *relaciones* (MacCormack 1999, 122), represented a juridical conflation of barbarism, utopia, and natural order. Elaborate proclamations about the legal status of indigenous communities as vanquished peoples, and the correlative obligations of the crown were but "one part of a larger set of concerns about man's relationship with man and his place in God's universe" (Pagden 1986, 27; 1993). Faced with unprecedented novelty, jurists and theologians invoked antecedent social categories (heathens, heretics, and barbarians) and appealed to their own imaginative capacities for critical reflection (see Pagden 1986; Todorov 1982; MacCormack 1999). The contradictions in the modern state's policies (both de jure and de facto) toward the indigenous peoples in its midst is readily apparent in the imaginings of El Dorado and the birth of the singular Peruvian nation.

El Dorado and National Expansion in Amazonia

Latin American nation-states have an external quality imposed largely from without. Sixteenth- and seventeenth- century colonial offices and boundaries served as precedents for the nineteenth-century establishment of Latin America's various national domains of sovereignty. The new Spanish American states stand in stark contrast to their European counterparts of the late nineteenth century and the early twentieth. As Benedict Anderson has observed (1987, 50–51), one cannot account for the new American states in terms of the two factors that have dominated thinking regarding the emergence of European nationalism: namely language and the bourgeoisie. Language did not differentiate the American *creole* states from their respective imperial metropoles, nor did it ever play a significant role in either the discourse or actual struggles for national independence from Spain (1820–24). Moreover, in early nineteenth-century Spanish America the "middle classes" were by historically comparable European industrial standards virtually nonexistent. Rather than preceding the Peruvian nation-state, the bourgeoisie "took permanent advantage of the state apparatus for its establishment" (Varese and Terrientes 1982, 34; D. Nugent 1997).

The Napoleonic invasion of Spain precipitated the Spanish American uprisings. However, in the staunchly loyalist Viceroyalty of Peru liberation came late and was prompted from outside. Rather than advocating open revolt, Peru's loyalist elite had pushed for concessions within the colonial structure. Ideally, they had wanted the re-establishment of the privileges they had enjoyed prior to the Bourbon reforms (R. Graham 1972, 43–45). Peru was the last of Spain's South American colonies to proclaim independence. Out of the breakup of the Spanish imperium between 1810 and 1830 emerged the cruel despotisms, violent revolts, and civil turmoil that have plagued Latin America to this day (B. Anderson 1992, 3). Military and *hacendado* elites scrambled to assert power—some favored centralized, bureaucratic-rational states, while others were inspired by more localized interests following independence. Ostensibly, this was to be achieved through the political philosophy of liberalism.

In August 1821, a month after having captured Lima, José de San Martin abolished Indian tribute and prohibited all forms of personal service such as *encomienda*, *mita*, and forced labor (*conscripción viral*). Perhaps more importantly, San Martin proclaimed the full citizenship of the indigenous peoples of Peru. By prohibiting the legal use of the terms *indios* and *naturales*, and by asserting that native peoples were to be known as *cuidadanos*—citizens—San Martin began the perpetuation of one of the central "deceptions" in the creation of modern Peru, namely the disparity between the state and the many nations or *ethnie* of Peru. This liberal legislation struck at the core of indigenous communities and inaugurated the long tradition in the Americas "of trying to abolish Indianness by a stroke of the pen" (Maybury-Lewis, ed. 1984, 222).

During the early republican period, liberal Bolivarists framed the "Indian Question" inherited from the colony. Animated by a racialized "ideology of hybridity" (Whitten 2007), Simón Bolívar issued a proclamation in 1825 abolishing forced labor recruitment, personal service (*faenas*, *mitas*, *pongajes*), communal land holdings, and the powers and office of the *cacique* (customary leader). Notwithstanding heady political proclamations and legislative decrees, little social reform ensued during the nineteenth century. Personal service obligations and systems of forced labor drafts such as the *mita* were not abandoned. The much despised Contribución de Indígenas (indigenous tribute) was established in 1826 to help pay the state's debts and to finance the burgeoning government bureaucracy. The liberal tribute was banned in Maynas in 1827. The following year, indigenous and *mestizo* peoples were granted ownership of their lands, and in 1830 forced labor was prohibited (Regan 1983, 74). Nevertheless, these laws usually amounted to nothing more than paper promises. The early republican state and its liberal and populists successors failed to effectively incorporate indigenous communities into the national polity. Indeed, throughout the nineteenth century and the early twentieth, "conquer" (*conquistar*), "pacify" (*reducir*), and "civilize" (*civilizar*) continued to be significant leitmotivs marking the thinking of the elite and subaltern sectors regarding Amazonian society and culture. The "Indian Question" eventually assumed the nationalist tenor of integration and modernization of indigenous populations that continues to characterize it today.

Throughout much of the nineteenth and twentieth centuries, Peru continued to administer its indigenous affairs within a framework of internal colonization, replicating the indigenist policies of the country's Spanish predecessors. Overall, nineteenth-century legislation formulated to protect the rights of indigenous peoples was rarely obeyed and generally not enforced. Under the feudal and mercantilist colonial arrangements of Spanish America, native peoples had enjoyed a modicum of protection through the Law of the Indies (Ley de Indies). It is debatable whether their relative status actually deteriorated following independence. An immediate effect of Peruvian national independence on the regional and local levels was the dissolution of the Spanish *corregidores'* monopoly over indigenous people's labor. Spanish overlords were replaced by local and regional elites, that is, *hacienda* owners, local *gobernadores* (government officials), merchants, and extractive entrepreneurs. During the chaotic decades following national independence, the forest trails (*caminos* or *trochas*) into the former Maynas missions fell into disrepair.[8] As previously noted, most of the missionaries left the area, and the local inhabitants resumed their subsistence-based existence (Smyth and Lowe 1836).

The late colonial and early republican periods in this region of lowland South America are best seen as an epoch of embryonic capitalism in which widely dispersed commercial economies, with their traveling merchants using indigenous slave labor, slowly gave way to the lowland *hacienda* (or *fundo*) form of agro-extractive production. By the early to mid-nineteenth century, a nascent form of mercantile and extractive capitalism had developed in Maynas, a system whereby peasant labor was to some degree at liberty to seek a market dominated by the major traders and *fundo* owners, many of whom were migrants from the San Martin area. Concomitantly, a small group—composed of the owners of capital and the regulators of unequal exchange—had evolved into the economically dominant and politically hegemonic social class of Peruvian Amazonia (San Román 1975; Stocks 1983, 84; Dean 1990, 48; Morey Alejo and Sotil García 2000, 214–16).

The New El Dorado

Comprising nearly 60 percent of national territory, Amazonia has long been presented in Peru's official and elite discourse as a vast and empty frontier simply awaiting penetration, civilization, and finally full national incorporation (Cavero-Egusquiza 1941, v). Tracing its intellectual genealogy to the myth of El Dorado, which first appeared with expeditionary forays, such as Pedro de Ursua and Lope de Aguirre's search for mythical lands of gold—the ideological construct—"Amazonia awaiting conquest"—persists in the Peruvian state's modernist fantasies of development predicated on productive extraction.

While Lima and the regional trading elites were intent on expanding the export of Amazonia's produce, so too did they encourage the liberalization of import restrictions and promote European colonization schemes. Animated by the prevalent racist doctrines of the nineteenth century and the early twentieth, government policy encouraged European settlement of Amazonia. As the fronts of national expansion pushed further eastward across the Andes, conflicts over land and access to vital or scarce resources became as increasingly common as they were inevitable. Throughout the first decades of Peruvian independence, indigenous lands continued to be taken over, despite government efforts at halting this process. Congress passed legislation in 1845 that declared that the indigenous inhabitants of the jungle area of Huánuco were the rightful owners of the territory on which they resided. By this time, explorers, extractive entrepreneurs, and land-hungry Andean highlanders had claimed vast expanses of territory inhabited by native peoples.

The emergence of a professional trading network in upper Amazonia dates to at least the last decades of the eighteenth century. Following the trails and river ways linking the mission cum trading posts of Maynas, merchants began traveling between the Pacific coast and the *montaña* or high jungle, and then made their way down to the lowlands, or *selva baja*. Along the northwestern flanks of the upper Amazon, peddlers were primarily migrants from Quito and the region's major urban center, Moyobamba. At the end of the eighteenth century, the majority of the inhabitants of Moyobamba were considered *mestizos*, while the presence of free blacks (*pardos libertos*) was double the rate found in other areas of Peru (Reyes Flores 1999, 129). Throughout the late eighteenth century and the nineteenth, a hierarchy of traders crystallized in the upper Amazon according to preferential access to local markets and credit opportunities. Near the bottom of the commercial pyramid was the petty merchant, "who soon appears on the scene, trailing in the wake of the explorers, heading his canoe into the farthest reaches of the jungle" (Meunier and Savarin 1994, 40). In Peru, this network included peddlers (*recatistas-alcanzadores*), fluvial merchants (*regatones*), local shopkeepers, and merchandisers who dealt directly with national and international business concerns (Scazzocchio 1978, 40; Cipolletti 1988, 534). Gradually *mestizo* merchants established a presence in indigenous settlements in the *selva baja*, such as Lagunas and Nauta, from where they mounted trading expeditions to communities located along the surrounding waterways (Regan 1983, 75).

State officials—*gobernadores*—came to dominate commerce during the initial years of national independence. Chachapoyas and Moyobamba exchanged tobacco, lona cloth, sugar cane, and *cascarilla* bark (*Croton eluteria*, an ingredient used for making incense) with Lima, Quito, and other regions of the colony (Reyes Flores 1999, 146). Many *gobernadores* took advantage of their position of authority by exploiting indigenous labor power for acquiring salt fish, sarsaparilla, beeswax, balsa, copal, tortoise fat, and woven palm-fiber goods such as hammocks (Maw 1829; Marcoy 1873; San Román 1975, 101; Regan 1983, 73).

While traveling along the Marañón River in the 1820s, Maw noted that the extractive economy of the Urarinas district was devoted to the trade of balsa, white beeswax, sarsaparilla, tobacco, and foodstuffs (such as cassava and plantains). These products eventually made their way to distant markets in Moyobamba and the Brazilian settlement of Tabatinga. In return, local producers were recompensed in the form of knives, cotton goods, and crockery (Maw 1829, 170). In a similar vein, almost thirty years later (1853) Herndon (1952) found that the Urarina were involved in the collection and transportation of sarsaparilla. The pace and scale of external demand on Urarina labor power intensified dramatically following the establishment of the rubber industry.

The commercialization of the region's primary waterways was accompanied by a decline in many important fauna, such as caimans, manatee, turtles, fish, and numerous species of water birds. As a result, itinerant merchants and *hacienda* owners became important not only as a source of manufactured goods, but also of food for a growing *ribereño* and urban-based population, such as in the frontier towns of Iquitos and Tabatinga (Dean 1990, 41; Ross 1978, 210). With the spread of export-oriented, agro-extractive economies, many rural communities abandoned subsistence production in favor of producing goods like salted fish, tobacco, and woven items for the nascent domestic and international markets.

Spurred by the expansion of agro-extractive mercantilism, socioeconomic change accelerated in Amazonia. Nowhere was this more apparent than in the boom in the rubber industry, the so-called *oro negro* or black gold, which set into motion a series of cataclysmic events that irreparably changed the environmental, economic, and social contours of Amazonia. Prior to the meteoric boom in the world demand for wild rubber, state presence in the region had been historically partial and usually contingent on interests emanating beyond Amazonia. Since its inception in the nineteenth century, the Peruvian state has been motivated by nationalist sentiments aimed at guaranteeing territorial dominion. Indigenous unrest, territorial encroachments from neighboring powers, and the decline of the Jesuit missions propelled the central government's desire to promote the colonization and national incorporation of Peruvian Amazonia. In 1832, Gran Mariscal Agustín Gamarra's government approved the creation of the Department of Amazonas, which comprised the provinces of Chachapoyas, Pataz, and Maynas. The creation of the Department of Amazonas would, in President Gamarra's words, facilitate "navigation, commerce and civilization of the savage tribes" (Gamarra 2000). However, civil turmoil during the first three decades of the republic prevented the state from exercising its will in Amazonia. A degree of political stability was finally achieved by General Ramón Castilla, who was president of Peru twice (1845–51 and 1855–62).

During the mid-nineteenth century, Peru's economic fortunes were intimately linked to the extraction and exportation of nitrates and phosphates from guano. Financed by revenue from guano deposits on the Pacific coast, Ramón Castilla was Peru's first president to turn Lima's attention to the economic development and national integration of eastern, lowland Peru. To this end, his government authorized the establishment of a military garrison in the Chanchamayo Valley (Fort San Ramón) and promoted the colonization of Amazonia by immigrants. Lima approved a number of legal mechanisms and financial incentives that spurred colonization of the central *selva* regions of Oxapampa, Palcazu, Pozuzo, and Villa Rica. In some of the larger communities of the *montaña* the state established rudimentary schools and a mail service (Klarén 2000). President Ramón Castilla's government established the military Department of Loreto and authorized the establishment of a naval outpost at Iquitos. Two years later, President José Rufino Echenique approved the creation of the political department of Loreto (Larrabure i Correa 1905–9, 1: 19–20).

Loreto's first economic bonanza of sorts occurred in the regions of Chachapoyas, Moyobamba, and Tarapoto, and was based on the cottage industry of making panama hats. The local hat industry eventually employed nearly one-third of the region's economically active population, who were responsible for producing items representing more than 90 percent of the total value of goods exported annually from Peruvian Amazonia. Tens of thousands of woven panama hats made their way along the established routes of fluvial and land commerce. Dependent on distant markets in the northern and southern Atlantic, Loreto's hat industry never fully recovered after the introduction of mass-produced felt hats in the 1870s, which soon became the fashion rage in Europe and the Americas (Orton 1879, 389–93; Larrabure i Correa 1905–9, 16: 120–30; Kerbey 1906, 291–94).

In the most populous and economically vital region of Loreto—the Huallaga valley—the *hacendados* usurped indigenous people's lands and enslaved workers on their coca plantations located along the eastern Andean slopes. Without any further government intercession, this inhumane practice flourished throughout the nineteenth century (Varallanos 1959, 618; Davies 1974, 26). Rather than the protection of indigenous homelands or the extension of civil rights, the state concerned itself mostly with promoting the conditions necessary for export-oriented economic growth. In practice, this translated into yet another quest in Amazonia for the fabled riches of El Dorado.

Civilization and Steam: The Emergence of Fluvial Commerce

> The Marañon, and most of the rivers which fall into it, are as well calculated for steam-navigation as any waters in the world, and there is an inexhaustible store of fuel growing on the banks of all of them. (William Smyth and Frederick Lowe 1836, 269)

Throughout the centuries, many observers have imagined Amazonia as a cornucopia of productive potentials ready for export; much in the way Isaiah Bowman, a North American geographer thought that Peru's fortunes relied on the future development of the nation's low-lying regions, the Pacific coastal fringe, and the tropical forested Amazonian plain (1916). Like many of his contemporaries, Bowman contended that the economic development of Peru depended on the efforts of entrepreneurs relying on imported technology and foreign capital. Peruvian progress, as such, was to be tied closely to the export of raw materials for the international market (Dollfus 1986, 22).

Oriented towards maritime commerce, Lima had long wanted to build a road or rail link between the Pacific coast and the nearest navigable port on the Amazon.[9] Influenced by the Turner thesis, named after Frederick Jackson Turner, an early advocate of U.S. exceptionalism and vigor associated with the expansion of the American frontier, a zone conceptualized as a space between urbane, civilized society and the untamed wilderness (F. Turner 1893), positivist intellectuals in Lima actively promoted the idea that the socioeconomic problems of the Pacific coast and the Andean highlands could be solved by the development of the Amazon Basin (Walker 1987, 61–89). In addition to accurate cartographic information needed for controlling space, this required significant investments in improving the transportation infrastructure necessary to facilitate the projected increase in the flow of colonists, commerce, and, if necessary, troops.

By the middle of the nineteenth century, many of eastern Peru's primary rivers had been explored by traders, missionaries, and adventurers. Buoyed by popular enthusiasm for the "age of exploration," prominent foreign expeditions to the upper Amazon included journeys by the likes of Charles-Marie de la Condamine, Alexander von Humboldt, William Smyth and Frederick Lowe (1836), Gaetano Osculati (2000), Francis Comte de Castelnau (1850–59) and a Spanish survey (1862–66) of Peruvian Amazonia (Litvak 1984). Mention should also be made of the founder of zoogeography, Alfred Russel Wallace, and the entomologist Henry Walter Bates (1989). The U.S. government also became involved in "scientific" surveys of the Amazon, as was clear from the 1851–52 expedition of Lewis Herndon and Lardner Gibbon (1854).

The Peruvian central government also mounted its own commissions with geographers, naturalists, and surveyors to demarcate boundaries across hitherto unexplored regions of Amazonia (Villanueva 1902, 79–81). Government-sponsored studies conducted by the Italian-born naturalist Antonio Raimondi resulted in some of the nineteenth century's most influential published works on Loreto (1874, 1929, 1942). To promote fluvial commerce and secure jurisdiction over Amazonia, in 1851 President Rufino Echenique's government ratified the Herrera-Da Ponte Ribeyro accord with Brazil (Larrabure i Correa 1905–9, 2: 18–23; Romero 1964, 42; Faura Gaig 1964, 59). Declaring the Amazon River open to free trade and navigation, the bilateral accord established the national boundaries between Peru and Brazil. All goods crossing the designated international frontier at the Río Yavari were exempt from paying duty for the next twenty years. Additional decrees from Lima created the legal mechanisms for granting lands in Amazonia, while others were designed to promote local agro-extractive production (Maúrtua 1911, 26; Markham 1963, lii).

By providing greatly increased access to national and international markets for local produce, the establishment of steam navigation resulted in a dramatic surge in commercial activity, including the export of salt fish, turtle oil, palm-fiber hammocks, wild rubber, tobacco, vanilla, and the best-selling pharmaceutical ingredients at the time, like quinine and sarsaparilla (*Smilax* sp.). The growth of exports accompanied the expansion of imports, including manufactured goods, textiles, matches, tools, foodstuffs, clothing, and generous quantities of rum (Herrera 1905; Maúrtua 1911, 30–31; Flores Marín 1977, 80–81; Cleary 2001). In 1853, a Brazilian owned paddle-wheeler made it all the way to the town of Nauta, located on the north bank of the Marañón River, a few miles from the confluence of the Río Ucayali (Mathews 1879). Established by Cocama peoples following the uprising at La Laguna in 1830, Nauta soon became the primary commercial hub of the *selva baja* (Smyth and Lowe 1836, 204, 258). Nauta's economic heyday corresponded to the period 1853–83, a time when the town served as an international commercial port. Nauta eventually declined in prominence following Lima's selection of Iquitos as the primary Amazonian port, which lead to the relocation of the major commercial houses and public offices from Nauta to Iquitos (Ríos Zañartu 1995).

The growth of steam shipping in the upper Amazon was part of a broader worldwide trend. By the late 1850s, the screw propeller was deemed superior to the paddlewheel, and the steamship began to supplant the sailing ship. Markham observed that by 1857 "there were eight steamers plying on the bosom of the Amazons, carrying passengers, and bearing up and down a ceaseless ebb and flow of commerce" (1963, lii; Raimondi 1942, 70ff.). In 1858, a treaty was signed by Peru and Brazil that further liberalized trade between the two countries (Faura Gaig 1964, 59).[10] To counter the growing influence of Brazilian mercantile power stemming from the liberalization of trade and the success of the Brazilian transport firm (Compañia Brasilera Navegación del Amazona), the Peruvian government created the Departmento Marítimo Militar de Loreto in 1861. This demarcation became the Department of Loreto in 1868. In addition to administrative reforms, Lima promoted the development of Amazonia's fluvial traffic (Morey Alejo and Sotil García 2000, 180). Ramón Castilla's government also placed an order for three English- built steamboats that arrived in 1864. This enabled Peru to establish regular steamer service between Yurimaguas, the frontier town known as the pearl of the Huallaga, and Tabatinga, Brazil (Maúrtua 1911, 37). The advent of steam generated demand for local inputs, such as food to feed passengers and crewmen, as well as coal and firewood for the boilers of passing vessels (G. Booth 1910, 13).

Nationalizing Amazonia: Neo-positivism and the Aristocratic Quest for Modernity

Efforts at integrating Amazonia into Lima's orbit of control were manifest not only through military efforts, but also by the promotion of colonization schemes, commerce and transport infrastructure. Originally from Huánuco, Mariano Prado (president of Peru 1865–68, 1876–79) demonstrated a special interest in advancing the national incorporation of Amazonia. Prado's first government was noteworthy for its role in supporting the Hydrographic Commission of the Amazon—a Peruvian state agency created in 1867. As in many efforts at "putting the Americas on the Map," cartographic representations became "performances of colonization" (Mignolo 1995, 313).

Just as the Hydrographic Commission began its work in Iquitos, the Brazilian Empire proclaimed the Amazon River open to international navigation and trade. By 1868, Peru followed Brazil's lead and authorized the liberalization of navigation in its Amazonian waters (Pennano 1988, 144–45). In 1869, President José Balta commissioned the Swiss engineer Juan Nistron to study the feasibility of developing Peru's *selva central*. Nistron concluded that the most efficient and pacific form of "conquering" the region's indigenous peoples was through the construction of a bridge (over the Perené and Quimiri rivers), which would force the "uncivilized" *chunchos* deeper into the interior of the forest, while those who remained behind he felt could benefit from the "civilizing" impulses of commerce (Larrabure i Correa 1905–9, 2: 485).

While domestic and foreign entrepreneurs scrambled to exploit the economic opportunities presented by the opening of Amazonia to free trade, the Peruvian state turned its attention to war with its southern neighbor, Chile, over control of the nitrate rich Atacama Desert. Prior to the War of the Pacific (1879–83), Peru's intelligentsia, like their Mexican counterparts, the Científicos, were imbued with Comtean positivism. Allied to the ruling elite, the Peruvian literati saw science and technology as a way to recast society. Yet Peru's devastating defeat to Chile discredited the prevalent ethnocentrism of the time and lead to a re-evaluation of the Social Darwinian precept of "the survival of the fittest."

Having been previously neglected in the universities and in literary circles, members of Lima's intelligentsia turned to the romanticized noble Indian for national regeneration. The influential neo-positivist, Manuel Gonzalez Prada, argued that had Peru's indigenous peoples been incorporated into civil society the country would not have suffered defeat at the hands of the Chileans. For Gonzalez Prada, indigenous "assimilation" was to be achieved through education (Davies 1974, 36–38; Gonzaìlez Prada 1966). At the state level, legislation formulated during the nineteenth century to defend the country's indigenous peoples was neither heeded nor embraced by the state and its allies. As the historian Thomas Davies notes, "No coherent Indian policy is evident in the conflicting legislation that characterizes the century" (1974, 42). Paternalism and clientalist relations of dependency characterized relations between Amazonia's indigenous communities and regional power brokers, many of whom were by no means beholden to the edicts emanating from Lima. In spite of the liberal Enlightenment rhetoric of popular sovereignty, the rural Peruvian political order was shaped at this time by the principles of what David Nugent (1997) has called "aristocratic sovereignty." Those who wanted to hold positions of public power were obliged to do so through demonstrating their capacity to use violence and shame in dominating their adversaries. In the Peruvian hinterlands, one notes a continuation in the seigniorial ideology whereby the propertied sectors of society, in collusion with the emergent mercantile groups, exercised monopoly control over the apparatuses of state power during the aristocratic or Civilista Republic (1895–1919).

In addition to promoting a laissez faire economic program favoring extractive production, the Civilista's geopolitical project included nationalizing contested frontiers, particularly in Amazonia (García Jordán 2001, 189–97). Moreover, the formation of a national citizenry was central to Civilista visions of modernity. Akin to the colonial and Bolivarian formulations of the "Indian Question," the Civilista's ideological program included the transformation of the nation's native "barbarians" into "civilized" citizens (García Jordán 2000, 31). Civilista visions of Amazonian modernization were articulated in the publications of the Sociedad Geográfica de Lima, which consistently lobbied for the incorporation of Loreto into the nation-state (Martínez Riaza 1998). By the end of the nineteenth century, the Junta de Vías Fluviales had been established to oversee exploration and colonization efforts in Amazonia (Ballón Landa 1917).

When proceeds from the guano boom began to dwindle in the mid-1860s national leaders turned their attention to tapping the imagined wealth of Amazonia so they could replenish the state's bare coffers. Fortune seekers and agents of the state alike were captivated yet again by the myth of El Dorado (Roux 1994). During the formative period of regional integration into global markets, Lima promulgated legislation supporting extractive enterprises (Maúrtua 1911, 22) and was instrumental in subsidizing Loreto's transport and trade activities (Coomes 1995, 110). Brazilian-owned steam navigation dominated regional commerce until the beginning of the twentieth century. In 1899, a London-based shipping firm established the Iquitos Booth S. S. Company and provided regular steam service between Iquitos, Europe, and North America. The English-owned Amazon Steam Navigation Company serviced the route between Iquitos, Manaos, Pará (Maúrtua 1911, 38).

The tremendous wealth and opulence associated with the boom in wild rubber extraction served to reinforce the myth of the abundant Amazonian frontier. The skyrocketing world demand for rubber transformed regions of Amazonia into a "vast equatorial Klondike" (Gheerbrant 1992, 80; Molina 1906, 83–84). Perhaps this was no more evident than in the establishment of Loreto's most important urban center—Iquitos. Once the site of a Jesuit *reducción*, the city of Iquitos was founded in 1863 and gained national prominence as an urban center in the last years of the nineteenth century when some touted it as the "St. Louis of Peru." While the common fare in the city at that time was "red pepper, rice, beans, bananas and *paichi*" fish, Up de Graff noted that "there was in Iquitos as good a supply of the best quality goods from all quarters of the world as you could find in New York" (1923, 140). During the heyday of the rubber industry, Iquitos was a cosmopolitan center boasting modern services, amenities, and patterns of consumption (Maúrtua 1911, 17).

While the race for the commercial conquest of Amazonia's immense and majestic fluvial system was well underway, so too was the regional trading elite's quest for signs of modernity (Guernsey 1870, 358). By the mid-1870s, telegraph lines that ran from the coast over the Andes into the lowlands had been established. The introduction of wireless telegraphy followed in the early twentieth century, making it possible not only to calculate local time accurately, but also to establish a strategically important means of shaping, and in some instances controlling, the dissemination of news, information, and other forms of cultural capital. Electricity was introduced to Iquitos in 1905, by which time the first leg of a rail line had been built. Under the terms of a Peruvian government concession, the British-owned Booth Steamship and Company constructed a harbor and maintained monthly steamer service to Liverpool (G. Booth 1910, 1, 18). The influx of foreign capital and immigrants (North Americans, Sephardic Jews, Spaniards, Portuguese, Italians, British, Chinese, and so forth) lead to the establishment of nine consulates in Iquitos (Haring 1986; Segal 1999). While the masses remained wretchedly poor, a small elite group could afford to host lavish banquets, import iron structures designed by Eiffel, and hire English nannies for their children, as did the well-off and politically influential Morey family (M. Booth 1910, 42).

Recapturing the Faithful: San León del Amazonas

A renewed quest for spiritual domination of the indigenous peoples residing at the margins of the state's reach accompanied the nationalization of Peruvian Amazonia. As previously noted, the Maynas missions languished following the expulsion of the Jesuits from the colonies. The Diocese of Maynas would remain without a priest until 1838, when José María de Arriaga was nominated to oversee missionization efforts (Villarejo 2000, 17). The bishopric was moved from Jeberos to Chachapoyas in 1843, where a number of secular clerics attempted to promote the word of God (García Jordán 2000, 9; Soria Casaverde 1997). Writing in 1894, Pope León XIII urged the bishops of Peru to rekindle interest in evangelical activities in the Peruvian Amazon. This revitalized interest in promoting proselytism corresponded with the Catholic Church's late nineteenth-century efforts at recapturing its former institutional presence in Latin America following the independence movements, which had resulted in Rome's ex-communication of the new sovereign Spanish American nation states (García Jordán 2001). Under the guidance of Pope Leon III (1878–1903), the Catholic Church's foot soldiers were instructed to multiply the number of messengers of God through mission campaigns worldwide, such as among the indigenous peoples of Amazonia (Schindler Catalao 2002).

Renewed interest in missionization gained momentum in Lima with the establishment in 1896 of the church-run proselytizing group Obra de la Propagación de la Fe en el Oriente. Directed by Father Francisco de Salas Soto, this group of Catholic activists had the backing of the influential Women's Catholic Union (Unión Católica de Señoras), whose members included Eva María de Piérola, the daughter of the nation's president (president of Peru 1879–81, 1895–99). In 1898, Father Salas Soto presented the group's plan for mission work in Amazonia, which included the creation of three new ecclesiastical prefectures (*prefecturas apostólicas*). Evangelization and the civilization of barbarian "Indians" provided the Catholic Church with an opportunity to regain the territorial presence it had lost following the wars for independence (García Jordán 2000).

When it came to securing a foothold in Amazonia, the interests of both church and state converged. With an eye to using Christianity to "civilize" the region's "infidels" and promote national progress, Lima approved governmental funds (three thousand soles annually) for the establishment of three apostolic prefectures in Peruvian Amazonia, including San León del Amazonas in the northern jungle, whose base of operation was Iquitos (Gregorio y Alonso 1951, 16). By the end of 1899, the Augustinians had assumed command of the newly created Prefecture of San León, which spanned three hundred thousand square kilometers (García Jordán 2000, 10). Led by Father Paulino Díaz, the first contingent of Augustinian clergymen arrived in Loreto in 1901 and included Fathers Pedro Pratt, Bernardo Calle, and Plácido Mallo, and Brother Pío Gonzalo Fernández. They were not well received by many of the inhabitants of Iquitos, who nicknamed them *gallinazos*—buzzards—in recognition of their unusual garb (Rodríguez Rodríguez and Álvarez Fernández 2001, 32). Local townspeople thought the missionaries should devote themselves to "civilizing the savage and barbarous tribes of the interior," rather than laboring in the city of Iquitos. In spite of their cold welcome by the local rubber planter elite, the Augustinians established a school in 1903 and soon managed to establish a regionally prominent institution (Villarejo 1965, 388; Lovera Vásquez 2000, 35). In 1905–6 the Augustinians created a mission post at Colonia Fuentes on the Tigre River, an affluent of the Marañón River that runs parallel to the Chambira Basin. By this time, the Augustinians had consolidated their position in Nauta and had managed to establish an institutional presence that continues to this day.

Cosmopolitan commercial centers like Iquitos and Nauta were indicative of the extent to which the rubber economy transformed the social landscape of Loreto. The presence of Europeans, Asians, Africans, as well as Protestants, Jews, Laodicean Catholics, and those professing no faith, challenged the Catholic Church's spiritual authority yet also provided legitimacy to those who advocated a renewed campaign of evangelical missionization (Villarejo 1942). During the late nineteenth century and the twentieth, an alliance emerged between the Catholic Church and a slew of Peruvian presidents who supported the Augustinian's Amazonian mandate. In the first four decades of the twentieth century, forty-seven Augustinians arrived in the Vicarage of San León. Many of the early Augustinian missionaries only spent a brief time in the region, often because they fell victim to disease. The performance of sacraments in rural areas accompanied the distribution of religious paraphernalia and assorted medicines. The first wave of Augustinian missionaries kept very detailed records of the administration of sacraments (baptisms, confirmations, marriages, first communions, and after 1922 last rites). Review of these records reveals the importance attributed to three gradations of "civilization." The Augustinians categorized recipients of sacraments as being: 1) civilized; 2) semi-civilized; or 3) infidels. A general decline in the administration of the sacraments accompanied the collapse of the regional rubber economy (Villarejo 1942, 23–41).[11]

Bleeding Trees and Taking Heads

Agents of national society were interested in not only creating citizens through Christian salvation, but also ensuring the conditions necessary for extractive enterprise. Beginning in the early 1870s and lasting until the end of the First World War, the rubber boom represents the culmination of the epoch of early national penetration of Amazonia (Rumrrill 1982, 157–58; Haring 1986). Far-reaching river-trade networks based largely on relations of debt peonage were consolidated during the rush to extract the black gold from the various latex-producing trees native to the region (*Castilloa* sp. and *Hevea* sp.). In contrast to *Hevea brasiliensis*, found primarily in Brazil, *caucho* is a lower grade of rubber latex from the *Castilloa elastica* tree, which is relatively common in the upper Amazon. *Caucho* extraction involved felling the entire tree, whereas *hevea* (or *jebe*) latex was collected through daily excisions of the tree (Maúrtua 1911, 21). Since *caucho* is collected after felling the *Castilloa elastica* tree, *caucheros* had less incentive to stake permanent claims to lands. Unlike Brazilian rubber estates (*seringais*), *caucheros* were continuously extending their search for virgin stands of rubber trees in new territories (Little 2002, 49).

The rubber boom drew thousands of men and in some cases their families from the Andean highlands to the rainforest of Loreto. Concomitantly, a small group, composed of the owners of capital and the regulators of trade and transport, evolved into the economically dominant and politically hegemonic social class of the upper Amazon (Stocks 1983, 84; cf. San Román 1975). Stimulated by the mass production of the automobile, world demand for natural latex skyrocketed. As a result, hard-driving extractive entrepreneurs—such as the Reyes family of Colombia, Peru's Carlos Fermín Fitzcarrald, and Bolivia's Nicolás Suárez—all amassed immense wealth. The heavy-handed exploits of Carlos Fermín Fitzcarrald during the last two decades of the nineteenth century gained him the monikers "El rey del caucho" (the King of Rubber) and "Señor feudal" (the Feudal Lord) of the Ucayali (Morey Alejo and Sotil García 2000, 229).

The rubber industry in Loreto was controlled by merchant houses that represented the financial interests of members of the regional elite, such as Cecilio Hernández, or the redoubtable Morey brothers—Adolfo and Luis. They also acted on behalf of foreign capital, like Wesche and Company of Germany, the Inca Rubber Company of the United States, and the Peruvian Amazon Company, composed of a mix of British and domestic capital controlled by Julio César Arana (H. Fuentes 1908; J. Arana 1913). The merchant houses subcontracted to local intermediaries—the *patrones, enganchadores,* and *regatones*—who in turn were provided with funds or merchandise that were then distributed to faithful suppliers (*aviados*). The noted commentator and prefect of Loreto, Hildebrando Fuentes (1908, 27), described rubber collectors in terms of three interrelated categories: *caucheros*, *aviados*, and *regatones*. The *aviados* were those who traveled to remote forest encampments in order to obtain the rubber in exchange for industrial goods. The local labor boss or *patrón* was in charge of directing the labor power of indebted peons (*peones*). Itinerant fluvial traders and labor bosses with access to credit dominated local commerce, while the owners of the merchant houses became the pillars of the regional oligarchy. From 1886 to 1920 Iquitos-based trading houses were responsible for annually exporting over one thousand metric tons of rubber, or roughly 80 percent of the total value of items exported from the region. At this time, Peru contributed about 30 percent of the rubber for the international market (Pennano 1988, 100–104, 177).

The associations between the merchant houses and representatives of the Peruvian state were as ambiguous as they were mutually collaborative. At the "fringes of the territorial state," in provincial centers like Chachapoyas, modernity and notions of the nation were in fact embraced as potent moral forces of liberation from the oppression of the aristocratic order emanating from Lima (D. Nugent 1994, 333–69; 1997). In Loreto, the rubber planters were able to wield control at the local level because their extractive enterprises and the financial resources to which they had access were politically essential, albeit independent of, state power. The *caucheros'* power was linked to their ability to portray their own private interests as being synonymous with Peruvian public welfare. Indeed, the rubber planters' unfettered extraction of surplus value became a crucial component of the elite's projects that were designed to secure peace and national prosperity. Amazonian wild rubber producers were eventually pushed out of the international market by a slump in demand, by the advent of synthetic rubber in the early 1920s, and by the more "efficiently" managed and hence cheaper latex from the Malaysian rubber plantations (Dominguez and Gómez 1990; Stanfield 1998; Joe Jackson 2008).

For many indigenous peoples the onset of the rubber industry greatly intensified contact with agents of national society and with the forces of international political economy. Along primary waterways, like the Putumayo and Amazon rivers, total communities were annihilated, and entire ethnolinguistic groups were ravaged by the conditions of forced labor, epidemics, and starvation (Casement 1912–13; Hardenburg 1912; and Great Britain Foreign Office 1913). The rubber boom accelerated the influx of guns into indigenous Amazonian societies, as among the Jivaroan speaking groups (Brown 1984, 23). Increased availability of firearms altered customary patterns of warfare. Guns supplanted spears, and defensive safeguards were modified in response to this new means of violence (Karsten 1923, 4–5; see also Habich 1903, 33). The influx of firearms increased long distance head-taking raids; individuals with guns annihilated those without them (Bennett Ross 1984, 90–92).

Demand for firearms further incited head-taking raids. The foreign-inspired trade in *tsantsas* (shrunken trophy heads) helped to engender a vicious cycle of violence broken only by the natural result of demographic decline. For a time, it was standard practice to exchange *tsantsas* for guns (Karsten 1923, 6; Up de Graff 1923, 238–90; Cressy-Marcks 1932, 140–41, 330; Stirling 1938, 76). Karsten writes that it was "especially North Americans [who] would offer a rifle for each trophy head" and concludes that the market was an important catalyst to Aguaruna raiding from 1916 to 1928 (in B. Ferguson 1990, 247; see also A. C. Taylor 1981, 651; Steel 1999, 773; Rubenstein 2007). It was within this context of the rubber boom and the guns for *tsantsa* trade that the Jivaroan-speaking peoples gained their reputation as ferocious warriors (Rubenstein 2002, 51–53). The cruel irony, as Brian Ferguson indicates (1990, 247), is that the trope of the Amazonian headhunter—the expert in violence—emerged due to the outside demand for exotica, which in turn capitalized the assassins. The image of ferocity continues to frame Urarina views of their Jivaroan neighbors and is readily evident in their rich corpus of oral history.

Circulating Bodies and Labor Power: Slavery and *Habilitación*

In the horrific networks of exchange accompanying the rubber bonanza, humans were commoditized. Alfred Simson, for instance, reports that among the Záparo children were abducted and sold to peddlers in exchange for an axe, a cutlass, fish-hooks, needles and thread, or a few yards of *tocuyo* fabric (1878, 505; see also Clark 1953, 49–62; Marcoy 1873, 3: 10; Taussig 1987, 60–63). In 1902, Manuel Villanueva noted that slave-raiding parties (*correrías*) were organized to obtain women as concubines (preferably under twenty years of age) and adolescent boys. A ten- to twelve-year-old boy was worth five hundred soles, while girls of the same age were valued at between three hundred and four hundred soles (Villanueva 1902, 67–68; see also Up de Graff 1923, 105). Some women abducted in the *correrías* became servants in the rubber encampments or sex slaves for the rubber barons' station managers and their loyal indigenous peons (Santos Granero and Barclay 1999, 41).

Analysis of slavery in Amazonia reveals both its longevity and its propensity to transform, particularly during the rubber bonanza. By the last quarter of the nineteenth century, a mature form of mercantile, agro-extractive capitalism had emerged in which labor was relatively at liberty to seek a market. Yet by comparison to markets based on the division of what might be called "free labor," productive relations at this time were "very much akin to slavery" (Adamson 1904, 19). During the rubber boom the rain forest became increasingly united by a political economy predicated on a form of debt peonage many commentators have equated with slavery. Indeed, "It was not the rivers that bound the Amazon Basin into a unit but these countless bonds of credit and debit [which] wound round people like the vines of the forest around the great rubber trees themselves" (Taussig 1987, 68). While people themselves were generally not bought and sold, the amount that they owed, or allegedly owed, to their employers was "merchantable" (Adamson 1904, 19). As Adamson noted, "The purchaser or owner of an account takes over the man with it, and till the amount said to be owing by the man is paid he is not at liberty to seek other employment" (1904, 19).

Unfree labor relations have endured well beyond the collapse in rubber extraction. Yet peonage had no historic precedents in the Americas; labor was not in short supply until at least a century following European conquest. It arose in colonial Peru because labor power was needed to support the various activities of the conquerors and settlers. In the heartlands of the Spanish American realm, peonage lasted until the end of the eighteenth century, but at the frontiers of empire, it was an entrenched technique of labor recruitment, with a veritable life and force of its own. Indeed, for well over the past 150 years bonded labor has flourished in those areas that have been devoid of a strong state presence, such as the upper Amazon, the Gran Chaco, and the Yucatán peninsula (Dean 1990; Langer 1986; Taussig 1987; Katz 1990).[12]

In the face of massive demographic collapse, early Spanish colonists adopted the *repartimiento* (assessment) system to force indigenous peoples to work. Familiar to many as exploitation through the method of the infamous "company store," *repartimiento* refers to the distribution or allocation of labor or goods. Laborers were obliged to obtain desired trade goods at inflated prices, which in turn placed them in debt. Abuses under the *repartimiento* system were as common as they were flagrant, yet the level of mistreatment was perhaps less pervasive or forceful than the deprivations accompanying systems of bonded labor and peonage that emerged following independence from Spain in 1821. As indigenous peoples went into debt they often forfeited their own lands and were reduced to peonage and obliged to toil for the same employer until their debts were cancelled (and in some cases, the debts of their ancestors), a virtual impossibility. In these instances, the debt peon virtually became a serf yet enjoyed none of the serf's customary rights. To facilitate the extraction of forest resources and the cultivation of foodstuffs, merchants and the landed elite needed to find ways to mobilize labor power. The various permutations of forced labor recruitment—*mita*, *encomienda*, and *repartimiento*—replaced the missions as the primary institutional means through which indigenous peoples were incorporated within the productive regimes of late colonial and early republican Peru. The practice of indebtedness, known in Peruvian Amazonia as *habilitación*, has been a regionally important form of labor mobilization since at least the mid-nineteenth century. The system involves advancing capital or goods from one individual to another in order to facilitate the receiver's performance of extractive or productive activities. One of the most salient features of this system is that all productive activity takes the shape of debt cancellation (Gow 1991, 96).

In the absence of an effective juridical regime, owners of bonded labor resorted to public rituals of intimidation and coercion. Those who fled risked violent retribution—as was clearly the case in the notorious Putumayo atrocities (Hardenburg 1913; Dominguez and Gomez 1990; Stanfield 1998). Maintaining a steady supply of manual laborers was a constant concern of the mercantile elite during the rubber boom. This anxiety is evident in a number of governmental decrees, such as the law of 1910 that required *patrones* to pay a deposit to the Departmental Prefecture for each *peón* or *enganchado* under their control who left the country. Those *enganchadores* and *patrones* caught trafficking in peons were liable to fines and the forfeiture of their boats and inventory (Alayza y Paz Soldán 1910).

Social differentiation in rural Peru has historically been tied to the landlord's customary practice of creating labor hierarchies through designating distinct groups of tenants and farm workers by type of labor or land contract. The system of *enganche* typically involved recruiting Andean laborers through payments that the *hacendado* advanced for travel expenses and a stipulated amount of work. The period of labor required to cancel the advance payment increased as *enganchados* incurred additional debts for food, clothing, and other items of necessity sold to them at exorbitantly inflated prices. In some instances, *enganchadores* attempted to ensure a steady supply of labor power by advancing payment for work to be completed the following season.

4

Localizing Webs of Power in the Chambira Basin

The Urarina and Forest Extraction in Contemporary Perspective

In the Chambira Basin prolonged labor scarcity eventually gave rise to the landed estates, or *haciendas,* which are known in the Peruvian Amazon as *fundos*—and elsewhere in the Spanish Americas as *estancias* (ranches) and *fincas* (farms). In Peruvian Amazonia, these categories—*haciendas* and *fundos*—are historically associated with the broader phenomenon noted in Latin America: *latifundia* (landed estates). Dedicated to the cultivation of a number of commercial and food crops, the processing of sugar cane (with a *traipiche*) for alcohol (*agaurdiente*), and to a lesser extent raising cattle, poultry, and swine, *fundos* have long been the dominant unit of land ownership for the rural elites in Peruvian Amazonia. By the time of the rubber boom, the principal cattle-raising *estancias* of Loreto had been established on the Marañón and Ucayali rivers (Maúrtua 1911, 24).

Peruvian extractive estates arose in intricately "structured fields of power": the factors that both lured workers and propelled them from the *haciendas* and *fundos* were themselves complex and contradictory (Roseberry 1993, 349–50). Following the collapse of the Maynas missions, *fundos* became the primary distribution point for scarce trade items and industrially produced goods in the region. Trade goods were exchanged by the *patrón* or his overseers (*capataces*) with native laborers who were systematically drawn into protracted relations of debt peonage. It was control over commerce rather than monopolistic control over land that "played the natives into the hands of the *haciendas* just as it had played them into the hands of the Jesuits" (Stocks 1983, 87; Brentano cited in Fritz 1922, 141).

In Loreto, *fundos* were usually established along primary waterways and near indigenous communities that could supply the labor power necessary for seasonal production, opportunistic extraction, and defense. For the Urarina peoples, this meant *mestizo patrones* established *fundos* at the mouth of the Chambira River and along the strategically and commercially important

Marañón River at locales such as Vacamarina, Ollanta, Maipuco, and Concordia. Indigenous and *mestizo* residents living near *fundos* supplied much of the labor power necessary to satisfy the oscillating regional and foreign demand for forest products, ranging from rubber, game animals, hides, *barbasco*, lumber, and the raw source of quinine, the dried bark of the cinchona tree. While I am unaware of any reliable figures for the Chambira watershed, in the Tahuayo River Basin rubber estates ranged in size from between ten thousand and twenty thousand hectares (Coomes 1995, 111).

At the close of the nineteenth century, a small number of families from provincial towns, such as Yurimaguas, Lagunas, Nauta, and Iquitos, had established control over the flow of goods and people in and out of the Chambira Basin (Wiener 1884, 108; Castillo 1958; Quintana 1948; Kramer 1979, 129). In the early twentieth century, two *caseríos* (villages)—Chambira and San Cristóbal—thrived at the mouth of the Chambira River (Stiglich 1922, 345). Stiglich claims that the inhabitants of the *caserío* of Urarina (located on the north bank of the Marañón, in front of Huati Island) were Yameos engaged in working in the *caucho* and *jebe* camps (1922, 1106). Urarina communities from the lower Chambira River were at the mercy of *cauchero* slavers who would round them up in punitive raids and put them to work as rubber tappers. According to Kramer, those who were captured became virtual slaves on "feudalistic" estates or *fundos* situated along the Marañón River (1979, 15, 52–53). This included *caseríos* such as Vacamarina, located on the northern bank of the Marañón, upstream from the mouth of the Chambira, which may correspond to the site of San Jose de Saramuro (Stiglich 1922).

This seems to have been a common occurrence during the first half of the twentieth century. As Ujkuaizíri told me in 1998, "During my grandfather's time the *patrones* enslaved the Urarina who were ignorant of any protective laws. They transported the Urarina to far off work sites on the Tigre River—they even went as far away as Madre de Dios and forced them to work for months at a time away from their homes." Typical of such estates was Rocafuerte on the Marañón River (Quintana 1948, 276), or the *fundo* of Santa Rosa located along the Corrientes River. Owned by Don César Guzmán, Santa Rosa was situated across from the overland forest route (*varadero*) to the Chambira Basin. According to Faura Gaig, this portage was referred to as Shimaco and as Patoyacu. When Faura Gaig visited Santa Rosa in the early 1960s he noted that there were only ten inhabitants, but another eighty "Indians" who normally lived in the forest's interior were under its charge. Devoted to the procurement of pelts, the extraction of *leche caspi*, and the harvesting of *aguano* wood, Fundo Santa Rosa also had two hectares of gardens where cassava, squash, plantains, and corn were cultivated (Faura Gaig

1964, 246). As in the past, the Urarina responded to the encroachment of extractive entrepreneurs by periodically disbanding their longhouse groups and escaping to the far reaches of the Chambira headwaters, or to the forested lands between primary waterways.

Adjacent to the Chambira watershed, the Río Tigre provides us with useful comparative data on the role of petty-commodity production. Navigable by steamer, the Tigre River was long coveted by extractive entrepreneurs for its ample stands of rubber trees—both *caucho* and *shiringa* (Villanueva 1902, 111). By the early nineteenth century, a military garrison had been established on the Tigre River (Maúrtua 1911, 11). Owned by one of Loreto's most powerful rubber planters—Luis Felipe Morey—Fundo San Antonio comprised five *caseríos* and had an estimated adult male population of 100. This *fundo* was dedicated to agriculture production and the extraction of *leche caspi* (Faura Gaig 1964, 231). Fundo Piura, owned by Don Heriberto Saavedra, consisted of ten homes, which in 1958 had about 150 people, and was dedicated to agriculture and to the extraction of gums and animal skins. Fundo Piura also had a primary school, indicating a relatively large and stable residential population. Clearly not all *fundos* were as large as Saavedra's or Morey's extractive estates. Don Audaz López's *fundo* on the Río Tigre consisted of only two houses, with a population of 19 who dedicated themselves to the extraction of tree gums and skins (Faura Gaig 1964, 232–33).

Urarina rubber tappers were forced to deliver all of their production to a single *patrón* or *regatón* who monopolized access to transport, credit, and markets. Merchandise, tools, food, and booze were advanced in return for rubber. To keep production on schedule, overseers (*acarabellad*) were employed by the *patrones* to monitor Urarina laborers. To prevent them from fleeing work sites, *patrones* incarcerated Urarina workers in the communal stockade, tied them up, and beat them. A number of elderly Urarina recalled bitterly that some Urarina laborers were hung up side down from their feet, while others mentioned water torture and near drownings. During his mission expedition, Father José Quintana noted that the *patrones* coerced the Urarina to work for them (1948, 279).[1] Escapees and noncompliant peons were threatened with induction into the military or imprisonment in Peruvian jails on trumped up charges—such as practicing polygyny (Kramer 1979, 135, 64). An elderly Urarina man related to Kramer that when his grandfather was young he and a number of Urarina from the lower Chambira River were forced from their homes by slavers who compelled them to tap rubber on the distant Yavari and Mirim rivers (1979, 129). Kramer reports that the only river where rubber was tapped on the Chambira was the Pucuyacu. A *patrón* told her that his father had worked as a *cauchero* on the Río Pucuyacu, where he had Urarina debt-peons tapping twenty-five *estradas* (a unit denoting allotments of one hundred to two hundred trees) of rubber (1979, 129).

In 1998 one of the Pangayacu's headmen recounted to me how his great-grandfather tapped rubber for a *patrón* approximately 120 years ago. He told me that rubber *estradas* were tapped near unidentified Cocama settlements in exchange for trade goods brought from Ecuador by *caucheros*. Over the years, I have collected similar accounts from numerous elderly informants, though this topic does not seem to attract as much attention from the young, some of whom are unaware of this episode in the Urarinas' history. The *patron*-owned *fundo* (known on the Chambira as *el puesto* or "the post") continued to thrive in the Chambira Basin as the dominant mode of commercial production during the first half of the twentieth century. The Urarina were employed at this time in the extraction of *balata*[2] and rock salt, in food production, and in the elaboration of fiber cordage. Fraile Tejedor's 1927 history of the Augustinian missions in Loreto mentions by name the following *haciendas* located along the lower Marañón River: Maipuco, San Pedro, Elvira, Chambira, and Parinari (1927, 49). Oral histories I collected six decades later underscore the importance of these extractive locales in the history of Urarina peonage. Of special note were the *haciendas* of Elvira, which had a sugar-cane press (*trapiche*) for the elaboration of alcohol, and Parinari, whose establishment was closely associated with the German merchant house of Strassberger and Company.

Compared with the extractive estates of the Bajo Marañón, the Chambira Basin had far fewer and smaller *fundos*. Nevertheless, *mestizo*-controlled *fundos* have long been an important factor in structuring local fields of power. The current settlement of San Pedro, for instance, was named for an old *fundo* once owned by Don Pedro Dávila. It was located near the former settlement, known in the mid-twentieth century as Palma. Palma was composed of a small *mestizo* homestead belonging to Don Victor Hugo, and subsequently by Don Sandoval. Dos de Mayo is a *mestizo* community located on the Chambira, upriver from the Pucayacu. It was established by Don Rodolfo Balseca, the former owner of a *fundo* located a short distance from Dos de Mayo. Don Balseca is credited with establishing the community, now primarily made up of Cocama descendents from the *mestizo* community of Nueva San Juan (located near the mouth of the Chambira Basin).

As petty-commodity producers, the Urarina are exposed to the vagaries of market demand and to ever changing ecological and political circumstances. Within the past few generations *patronazco*—an authoritarian mode of forest extraction predicated on debt peonage—has begun to decline. Increasingly, small-scale fluvial traders (or what I have labeled the "petty *patrón*") began competing with the Chambira Basin's established *patrón* families. The system of advancing goods against debts (*rijkigúele rukúrcha*) remained largely intact in rural Loreto until at least the 1960s, when factors such as the liberalization of rural credit, increased literacy, and the proliferation of gas-powered boat motors gradually began altering regional commerce.

In Search of Souls

> In ancient days, nobody of the people of the Marañón River had arrived at this part of the world. People did not wear any clothes. They knew absolutely nothing about those who lived outside, about those who live alone. But there was one priest, who had raised a child and made him a novice. So the priest told his novice, "Let's go to see your people," and so they went and arrived. The people already saw them from afar; so they approached and got angry. (Medardo Arahuata in Olawsky 2002, 234)

Transformations in the nature of petty-commodity production coincided with the renewed interest in spiritual salvation, as evident from the Augustinians' ongoing mission work, as well as the arrival of Protestant missionaries. Father José Quintana's description of his mid-twentieth-century missionary expedition to the Chambira is indicative of the Augustinians presence among indigenous peoples like the Urarina. In 1947, Quintana traveled from Iquitos aboard the steamer *Huallaga* (owned by the merchant house of Kahn and Company) to Concordia, at the mouth of the Chambira River. During his two-month stint in the area, Quintana visited numerous settlements, many of which were extractive encampments (*puestos* and *fundos*). Along the Tigrillo River, Quintana visited the *fundos* and *puestos* of San Pedro, Fortaleza, Esperanza, Cáceres, Cafetal, and Valencia. He made stops at Puerto Puerto Palma, Carabanchel, Agua Blanca, Arequipa, Puerto Franco, and Santa Rita along the Chambira River. On the Pucunayacu, Quintana visited San Antonio and the encampment of Puerto Rivas. Along the Airico, Quintana stopped at Santa Rosa, a settlement that is still in existence to this day. During his time among the Urarina Father Quintana managed to baptize 594 people, confirm 344 individuals, conduct 61 marriages, and attend to 20 first communions. This number is quite impressive given that many Urarina were frightened by the presence of Quintana in their midst, and some fled into the forest to escape. Bucking customary practice, Quintana reportedly did not charge for the administration of the sacraments or for the distribution of religious appurtenances (1948, 276–80).

In the Chambira Basin Catholic missionaries were joined by Protestant crusaders in the search for souls. The Summer Institute of Linguistics (SIL) first made contact with the Urarina in the late 1950s. Two separate missionary teams had previously rejected mission work among the Urarina, but then a North American couple, Ronald and Phyllis Manus, agreed in 1960 to spearhead the SIL presence among the Urarina. The couple set up their mission post on the middle Chambira, in the vicinity of a *patrón* who had gathered numerous Urarina families to work his commercial agricultural plots (Kramer 1979, 16). Feeling somewhat threatened by the presence of the evangelists, the *patrón* protested to the Iquitos bishopric. In response, the bishop appointed Gonzalo Gonzalez, a Spanish Augustinian priest, to lead a proselytizing campaign (1961–63) among the Urarina. The magnitude and range of abuses committed against the Urarina impressed Father Gonzalo Gonzalez to such a degree that he publicly spoke out against the injustice of their exploitation. This marks a significant break from the historically cozy relationship many Augustinian missionaries had with the regional labor bosses. Review of early- and mid-twentieth-century missionary reports from the Bajo Marañón indicate a strategic alliance between the *patrones* and representatives of the Catholic Church, particularly when it came to the question of "civilizing" the region's indigenous peoples and promoting regional "progress" through the establishment of civil authorities, local schools, and sports clubs.[3]

Urarina and *ribereño* informants told Kramer how the Urarina "were mistreated by patrones who threatened, tortured and imprisoned unwilling laborers and kept them in a state of perpetual debt peonage" (1979, 16). This was confirmed by Father Gonzalez during personal interviews I conducted with him in Iquitos in 1992, 2000, and 2002. Accompanied by a number of Spanish-speaking Urarina men, Father Gonzalez went to Iquitos and initiated legal proceedings against the Chambira Basin's dominant *patrón* family, the Ocampos of Iquitos (Ferrúa Carrasco et al. 1980, 7; Kramer 1979, 17; Gonzalez, interviews by Dean, 1990, 2000). The proceedings captured national attention. However, when the case came to trial the Urarina refused to testify, which lead to the dismissal of the case. Having spoken with a number of the principal actors in this dispute (members of the Ocampos family and Gonzalo Gonzalez, the parish priest of Punchana), I conclude that the Urarina involved were probably either coerced or co-opted into not testifying against their *patrones*, the Ocampos. According to the accounts I collected in 1996 and 1998 from a number of elderly men along the middle Chambira, an Urarina group of brothers closely allied with the Ocampos as their overseers gave favorable testimony on behalf of the Ocampos.[4] Some of the elderly men allege that the group of Urarina brothers was "paid off" in the form of clothing, watches, and a boat motor in return for their support of the *patrones*. More than thirty years after the events, the brothers' "betrayal" continues to come up in the course of conversation and appears to influence local patterns of political alliance and intra-communal factionalism.

The Pangayacu's current longhouse settlement of Santa Beatriz was born of the conflict with the Ocampos. During the 1960s and early 1970s, two brothers—Julian and Andres Juartari—labored as peons for the Ocampos on their *fundo* along the Tigrillo. After suffering a severe flogging, they fled into the forest to escape the wrath of the *patrones* and their henchmen. The two brothers managed to reach the headwaters of the Pangayacu after walking for two days through thick forest and palm swamps. The senior members of the Pangaycu longhouses credit the Juartari brothers with establishing the first homesteads along the Pangaycu. The trial against the *patrones* coincided with the apogee of Ocampos power in the Chambira River drainage. The increase in commercial opportunities gave rise to a period of entrepreneur enterprise that in turn fractured the power base of the established *patrón* families. Small-scale *regatones* or petty *patrones* have increasingly undermined the influence of the established *patrón* families such as the Ocampos. Likewise, the "fortunes" of the evangelical mission have declined. In spite of concerted SIL efforts at establishing a bilingual school and offering sporadic medical assistance, the mission has had limited impact beyond its foci of local operation—the community of Nueva Esperanza and the adjoining longhouse groups situated nearby.[5] Moreover, the raison d'être for SIL presence in the zone has never been fulfilled. In spite of nearly four decades of work, the New Testament has yet to be translated into Urarina (though a number of chapters have appeared in print; see Manus and Manus 1973, 1976, 1990, 1996).

Unequal Exchange: *Patrones* and Production

> Toditos los patrones te dan las cosas para que nosotros los ayudemos, ellos nunca ni sudando, ni trabajando, ni agarrando machete, ellos están muy tranquilo (All of the patrones give us things to help them, they never are sweating, nor working, nor using their machetes, they are always relaxed). (Raguití, Río Pangayacu, October 1998)

In the Chambira Basin, labor relations remain decidedly mercantilist: traders or *patrones* act as agents of supra-local exchange by advancing goods to subsistence producers and by receiving specialized commodities. In essence, the *patrones*' objective is to ensure a continuous pool of labor power by guaranteeing protracted indebtedness. Surpluses in commodity peonage are derived not through surplus value but rather through unequal exchange within the system of debt peonage. Acquisition of desired trade goods has become a precondition for subsistence production. This productive entanglement with barter goods has heightened the Urarinas' reliance on commercial intermediaries and the globalized markets for which they labor.

Rubber, *tagua* palm seed,[6] *barbasco* fish poison (rotenone), rice, and timber extractive "booms" have all produced considerable social differentiation along the Marañón River and to a lesser extent the Chambira River drainage system. Items provided on credit to indigenous laborers ensured the circulation of goods, knowledge, and people through regional and international markets. Today, the Urarina continue to be linked to the outside world primarily through their exchange relations with *mestizo patrones* and itinerant traders. Peonage plays a critical role in establishing and mediating relationships between the Urarina and their *mestizo* interlocutors. In the Chambira Basin, the crux of peonage is the receipt of an advance payment or debt (*rebeuca*, apparently from the Spanish verb *debiendo*) to be repaid in labor power. This is accompanied by a proscription against toiling for competing labor contractors while debts are still outstanding. *Patrones* advance loans in kind to socially mature males who are then obliged to make repayment through personal or familial labor service in the form of hunting forest game (*mitayo*), harvesting timber, or cultivating manioc and plantain swiddens. The *patrones* want to ensure a continuous pool of labor power through securing protracted indebtedness (Murphy 1978, 40). Surpluses in petty-commodity peonage are derived not through surplus value, but rather "through unequal exchange within the framework of monopolistic and quasi-tributary relationships" (Wolf 1982, 87).

"Unequal exchange" is used here to reflect the inequitable terms of trade binding the Urarina and *mestizo patrones*. On the Chambira River, unequal exchange means inflated consumer prices (justified by the *patrones* and traders through reference to high transaction costs) and low wages "paid" in kind to petty producers. At the local level, unequal exchanges are sustained temporally through continual advances of goods flowing from the traders to the Urarina. Due to language and literacy barriers, the Urarina are not fully versed in the logic of capitalism. They only partially understand the dominant norms of commercial exchange, including weights and measurements. In the transcultural mercantile context, this obviously puts the Urarina trader in a disadvantageous position. In 2002, for instance, the Pangayacu's senior headman was still trying to pay off a debt incurred several years prior for the "purchase" of a used chain saw and a *peque-peque* (boat motor) (worth less than five hundred dollars) that were "paid" for with one hundred boles of fine hardwoods worth thousands of dollars. Notwithstanding the unequal terms of their transactions, the Urarina are active economic participants in the chain of debt peonage or *habilitación* linking the Chambira Basin to regional and global markets. The virtual absence of hard cash on the Chambira means that the Urarina vigorously seek out relations with traders because traders provides them with access to commodities (*rikelé*) of unsure supply, and because such relations suit their own patterns of barter (Hugh-Jones 1992, 69; see also Muratorio 1991, 151; Siskind 1977, 170–71; Chaumeil 1984, 8; Renshaw 2002, 177).

Goods advanced on credit establish relations of indebtedness and in so doing reinforce social hierarchy. Fictitious kinship is a deeply consequential form of social obligation in Peruvian Amazonia. It has enabled *patrones* to perpetuate their hold over local constellations of power, which in some instances has lasted for several generations (Chaumeil 1984, 15). The familiar system of *compadrazco* (ritual compeership) whereby the *patrón* serves as godfather to his client's children (and therefore becomes *compadres* with his client), coupled with the *patrones'* or local traders' virtual monopoly of cargo transport and access to credit, ensures the viability and temporal duration of debt peonage. The practice of forging *compadrazco* ties to legitimize mercantile relations is at least 150 years old.[7]

Throughout indigenous Amazonia, acquisition of desired trade goods has become a pre-condition for subsistence production (Warren 1992, 92). *Mestizo patrones* and traders advance relatively inexpensive yet necessary consumer articles, including, *inter alia*, ammunition, salt, batteries, and a miscellany of medicines (aspirin, chloroquine, menthol rub, and so forth), baubles, and dry goods to Urarina men who in return provide forest goods that predictably fetch high returns in faraway urban markets. The lure of trade goods that the Urarina consider indispensable or desirable has drawn them into exchange relations with outside intermediaries whose behavior is animated by entrepreneurial desires to profit from indigenous surplus production and forest extraction. This productive "entanglement" with trade goods has heightened the Urarinas' dependence on "cheapskate" (*baratero*) traders who regularly finagle unfair rates of exchange, often with the aid of tobacco (*mapacho*)[8] and stupefying cane liquor or *aguardiente* (*abaríti*)[9] traded at an exorbitantly inflated rate (see Castillo 1958, 28). In August 1993, for instance, one of the regular river merchants arrived on the Pangayacu after an absence of two months. The trader promptly began doling out bottlefuls of cane liquor (*aguardiente*) for which he charged two soles (approximately one dollar) each. The river trader purchases the *aguardiente* in

Iquitos wholesale for seven dollars for forty bottles, thus making thirty-three dollars in "profit."

Over the past generation or so, the pace of social change in the Peruvian upper Amazon, like elsewhere in Amazonia, has quickened at a dizzying rate (S. Nugent 1981, 71). During this time, the penetration of proto-capitalist relations of production exacerbated emergent social distinctions in the Marañón Basin, particularly between those who have prospered and those who have remained impoverished. The structure of patron-clientelism is strained by the expansion of competitive mercantilism (petty *patrones*, small-scale *comerciantes*, and so forth), the development of class distinctions, the spread of literacy, and the slow but perceptible growth in urbanward migration and the globalized economy.

Characterized by strategies of predatory capital mobility that undermine the agentive capacities of local actors, globalization is indicative of the crisis over the sovereignty of the nation-state (Appadurai 2000). Its most apparent characteristic is the high velocity and unbridled nature of global markets, ostensibly free of the customary restraints imposed by the erstwhile barriers of cross-cultural communication, governmental regulation, and the limits of industrial modes of production (Appadurai 2000). The growing integration of the world's economy and the emergence of financial capital rather than industrial production as the cornerstone of capital accumulation have adversely affected rural, agrarian communities throughout the Americas. In particular, the pressures of globalization have lead to diminishing availability of resources for subsistence production (Nash 1994, 7–30). In order to understand how Urarina society and culture have responded to globalization, we need to recognize the nature of unequal exchange at the local level.

Peru's rural extractive economy continues to depend on laborers like the Urarina to harvest forest resources and to grow food crops (Castillo 1958, 28; Díaz Barba 1987, 71; Cajas Rojas et al. 1987). By the Second World War, the cultivation of rice was commercially significant in the upper Amazon (San Román 1975, 197–98). Rice production became important in the Chambira Basin by the late 1950s, and its cultivation continued throughout the following decade. The market for plantains developed in the early 1970s following severe regional flooding. It was bolstered further as it responded to the emergent petroleum exploration industry that stimulated migration into Loreto (Kramer 1979, 115, 132).

The introduction of petroleum exploration in the zone increased the demand for Urarina products, particularly plantains and hunted forest game. An oil pipeline (the Nor-Oriental oleducto) linking the Trompeteros River oil fields with the Pacific coast bisects the lower Chambira River. Unlike other indigenous peoples of the Upper Amazon such as the Huaorani of Ecuador, the Urarina have not worked as wage laborers for the petroleum companies. Interest in the region's petroleum reserves predates the "boom" of the 1970s. For instance, in 1956 the U.S. oil company Texaco was engaged in drilling test wells in the mouth of the Río Tigre (Farua Gaig 1964, 236). Though the presence of petroleum exploration teams has been sporadic, they tend to offer the Urarina better terms of trade for their produce and labor than do the *patrones* or river traders. The Urarina continue to be economically constrained by the concomitant requirements of petty-commodity production (among others, see Wolf 1982, 86f.; and A. Fuentes 1988, 217). The oil exploration teams and petty *patrones* have continued the tradition of trade in cloth and other industrial items, such as salt, shotgun shells, and cast-off clothing. Moreover, the Urarinas' involvement with the market as suppliers of plantains and hardwood lumber[10] has been supplemented over the past decade or so by their increased participation in the expansion of rice production. Currently, a small number of *mestizo fundos* devoted to the cultivation of food crops (plantains, cassava, rice, and corn), cattle ranching (on forest clearings deemed *pastos*), and timber extraction are located throughout the Chambira River drainage. Labor power on these *fundos* is supplied by Urarina groups who relocate their homesteads to work temporally as non-waged peons in return for trade goods, cane alcohol, and food.

Refiguring Peonage

The portrait of extensive peonage and the widespread reliance on usurious debts to bind tenants to estates (*haciendas* or *fundos*) has been undermined by a revisionist literature that problematizes the historical importance of peonage in the Americas (Stern 1987, 145–46; cf. Davies 1974, 10–14). Numerous scholars have highlighted the complex interdependencies accompanying peasant production (Assies 2002; Barham and Coomes 1996, 51–53; Roseberry 1993, 349; Wilson 2003, 221–48).

Questioning conventional beliefs regarding the nature of labor mobilization, credit, and land tenancy systems more generally, the historian Vincent Peloso (1999) has demonstrated the multiple ways in which a diverse cast of social actors—plantation owners, labor bosses, hired farmhands, and sharecroppers—vied with one another in the establishment of rural hegemony and the fissured construction of local communities. Peloso's work is important for it reveals the interdependence of planters, overseers, and peasants or *campesinos* in production and emphasizes the diverse labor and land use strategies adopted to circumvent the planters' tactics of paternalistic persuasion, deception, and naked coercion.

Contrary to the standard depiction of the dyadic patron/peasant relationship in starkly oppressive terms, the Urarinas' economic entanglement with *mestizo* labor bosses was animated by more than mere subjugation. While *patrones* did have to contend with labor resistance and generalized foot-dragging, compliant peons were rewarded for their loyalty to the *patrón* and for their market-oriented achievements. Indeed, both *patrón* and peon alike were keenly aware that negotiation was mutually beneficial. Even though *fundo* residents experienced numerous deprivations, economic hardships, and uncertainty, and evinced deeply felt ambivalence toward the *patrones* and their capricious authority and nocuous ideology of racialized dominance, the long-term relationships established through dept-peonage did provide the Urarina with many choices not previously available. This included real options for limited autonomy, especially in the arena of farming decisions, and in terms of increased opportunities to assert land claims and participate in the *fundos*' overall economic growth. The owners of *fundos* like Louis Morey's Rio Tigre San Marcos *puesto* attempted to maintain their domination by relying on relations of debt, occasional outbursts of coercive violence, and, more commonly, through recourse to cultural prejudice, bolstered by a web of symbolic or theatrically inscribed violence and social distinction. Not surprisingly, at *fundos* such as San Marcos *puesto* a thin line existed between tenant stability and entrapment.

Notwithstanding the questions regarding the historical significance of peonage in the Spanish Americas, it is clear that debts have long been a fundamental feature of labor relations in Peruvian Amazonia. In portraying the inequitable relations between the Urarina and *mestizo patrones* and traders, I do not mean to suggest the absence of any "redeeming" aspects of *patronazco*. *Patrones* and *regatones* will occasionally rent space on their boats, dispatch messages (*pasar la voz*), obtain desired trade goods, and provide limited employment for Urarina in their agricultural fields as peons (*peones*), as traveling assistants (*portadores*; *ayudantes*), and as domestic servants (*empleadas*). Obviously, without these additional "benefits," the Urarina would not be nearly as "supportive" of peonage. But the Urarina are aware that the "benefits" of peonage are derived from alliances with a single *patrón*, rather than from participation in the system of debt peonage. This in turn explains the paradox of the Urarinas' continued active involvement with specific trading partners, in spite of their bitter criticism of the entire system of *habilitación* (fig. 4.1).

Given that the Urarinas' primary contact with *mestizo* national society

Fig. 4.1. Urarina man making a canoe paddle, Pangayacu River

is achieved largely through their association with *patrones*, relations with *mestizos* are characteristically oppositional in nature. The *ribereños* who live along the Chambira River do not generally participate in relations of debt peonage with the traders. On the contrary, they sometimes dabble in trading themselves, and on occasion they have assumed the role of a small-scale *patrón*, exchanging forest produce for costly trade goods. The working conditions under which the Urarina toil for *mestizo* bosses are variable—from frightful abuse to paternalistic benevolence. Urarina labor relations with *patrones* and the region's *fundos* are variable and defy simple classification, but they all share similar elements of intimidation and social subjugation mediated through extractive mercantilism. The overlord is always vulnerable to the parodic mimicry on the part of the Urarina peon. It is no surprise then that the Urarina can exhibit great disdain, anger, and sometimes violence against rapacious traders and labor bosses. The Sironó of lowland Bolivia similarly express displeasure with their commercial relations with outsiders. During trading sessions, they make biting remarks about the commercial deprivations they are suffering (Stearman and Redford 1992, 242).[11] For Stearman and Redford, it is the Sironós' enduring conception of mutual obligation and reciprocity that sustains the patron-client relationship. However, this view effaces the internal social differentiation among indigenous societies, like the Urarina and the Sironó, which results from their differential access to trade goods.

On this note, Hugh-Jones (1994, 34) is certainly right to caution against treating the colonial encounter in Amazonia simply in terms of "white people" versus "Indians." Such a grossly myopic stance omits the internal divisions and conflicts both within indigenous and "white" (or *mestizo*) society. In Amazonia, as elsewhere, the agents of colonialism were not "one-dimensional figures unswervingly dedicated to highlighting the symbolic distance between themselves and those they colonized" (Conklin 1997, 68).[12]

Despite its ubiquity as a term denoting social exclusion and economic oppression, peonage is a continuous, processual phenomenon. It cannot be reduced to a structure or geometry of power that always limits some actors to the margins of social life. After all, power is not simply a binary or dialectical relation of oppressor/victim, nor is it necessarily a function of centrality—it is diffuse and multi-focal (Foucault 1979; 1980). As in other areas of South America, such as Northeastern Brazil, patron-client relationships on the Chambira inhibit the emergence of "strong horizontal links of solidarity between members of the lower classes" (Costa, Kottack, and Prado 1997, 139). The vertical links between patron and client, however, are clearly mutually beneficial in terms of security and defense. "Patrons need their clients, just as clients depend on their patrons . . . the patron-client system is one of reciprocal social obligations that adds social costs to the process of exploitation of the work force and the extraction of economic surplus" (Costa, Kottack, and Prado 1997, 140). The profound ambivalence the Urarina feel regarding traders is captured well in San Román's (1975) now classic historical account of Peruvian Amazonia. "The *regatón* is an individual who is talked about, despised, feared, well regarded, and pursued, all depending on the prism through which he is seen. In any event, he is a figure intimately connected to the [cultural] landscape" (San Román 1975, 102–3, my translation).

Viewed externally, *patrones* are labor contractors. But the Urarina largely conceive of their relations with *patrones* in terms of relations of exchange or *cudiaca*. In their accounts about working for the *patrones*, Urarina men rely on discursive images of exchange rather than labor control. In fact, the

Urarina term *nejkurijtuya* is synonymous with trader (*regatón*) and denotes the act of exchange or trade (*regateando*). In Urarina, to sell is *nejkurtiaka*, and to buy is *kureténecha*. In negotiating a barter transaction with a *regatón* the Urarina will say, "Ja takanareké kuréitáche"—"let's do business" or "hacemos negocio." This corresponds with the way local traders represent their activities. As the wife of one prominent *regatón* put it to me in June 1996, "We are merchants; we bring manufactured goods so that we can do business" ("Somos negociantes; traemos productos para poder vender").

Urarina barter economy refers to the swapping of goods without reference to money (*cúrki*), established rates of exchange, or formal partnerships. Barter occurs primarily between individuals living near one another and who are united by kin ties. It is not only a result but also a mark of sociability. Moreover, the bartered objects are often simultaneously both *commodity* and *gift* (Hugh-Jones 1992, 63; see also Appadurai 1992, 9). Whereas commodities are characterized by impersonal modes of exchange, gifts are personalized individual or collective acts of voluntary bestowal not necessarily solicited by the person or groups who receive them. The Urarina speak of the *regatones*' "trading hooks" (*kuritái rujkué*): for example, *lagniappes* such as alcohol or hard-bread as gifts, which are more than "paid" for in successive transactions.

This is not to imply that the Urarina are unaware of the coercion and inequality in their relations with *patrones* and river traders, nor is it to suggest that the Urarina do not employ as much cunning in their dealings with traders. Honoring debts is constantly deferred on both sides and "settlement" is often achieved through violence, flight, or intergenerational debt transmission. In general, the Urarina obtain trade goods as the *regatón* is making the voyage upstream. They then attempt to cancel the debt by giving the trader forest goods on his return downstream. Those unable to cancel their debts will abscond when the trader passes through on his way downstream. The *regatón* must then try to settle the debt on a return voyage to the area. Ultimately, the surety of repayment for goods advanced lies in the generalized understanding that credit can, like the blackwater rivers of the Chambira, dry up.

Urarina resistance to unequal exchange relations commonly takes the form of heel dragging and occasional outbursts of violence. In the early morning, late afternoon, and evening, Urarina with access to radios and the coveted batteries to power them listen to short-wave broadcasts from Iquitos. This provides Urarina communities with doses of national popular culture, news items, and knowledge of current prices for their petty commodities. As the senior Pangayacu headmen recounted, he knows the "real prices" of trade goods thanks to listening to the Iquitos based radio station Voz de la Selva (Voice of the Jungle), which regularly broadcasts market prices for agricultural commodities and forest produce. For their part, *regatones* respond by saying that these are "rigged" prices and tend to discount them in their barter activities with the Urarina. Bilingual and assertive Urarina leaders have resorted to denouncing the exploits of abusive *patrones* and traders by relying on radio broadcast announcements and legal declarations filed in regional government offices (Maipuco, Nauta, and Iquitos). Seldom has this led to the resolution of debts. More commonly, it has simply prevented particularly abusive traders from "doing business" in Urarina territory for a limited period.

Many Urarina communities have managed to achieve a degree of relative isolation from recurrent epidemics and the exploitation of their labor power by continuing to rely on a strategy of flight and seclusion. Urarina groups discontented with their *patrón* will flee, either by river or along an intricate network of forest trails (*berü, barairú*) linking rivers and communities. By way of extensive overland forest trails and portages, one can move between the region's primary waterways: the Urituyacu, Tigrillo, Chambira, and Corrientes rivers. But the structure of the local labor market, coupled with the Urarinas' own demand for industrial commodities, means that there is ultimately no escape: Urarina individuals, often acting on behalf of their *kaj laitjíra*, eventually enter into unequal exchange relationships with labor bosses and river traders.

5

"When There Were No Women"

Gender and the Experience of Peonage

Debt peonage is a system of labor recruitment in which *patrones* advance consumer goods to Amazonian peoples on "credit" and oblige them to repay their debts by procuring forest goods under vastly inequitable rates of exchange. However, this common portrayal of peonage says little about women's involvement as transactional agents. This chapter is concerned with Urarina women's partial loss of control over the circulation of the most important wealth items that they produce: woven palm-fiber goods. Indeed, it is the production of palm-fiber wealth that articulates the female or intrademic kinship economy with the institution of debt peonage. As I will argue, understanding Urarina women's experience of debt peonage depends on a nuanced analysis of the circumstances and local conditions that give rise to the exchange or commoditization of palm-fiber wealth.

The Urarina exchange palm-fiber goods with *patrones* for industrial products needed for domestic consumption, and women use their monopoly over woven goods to secure items of exclusive "female" consumption (for example, beads and crimson-colored cloth). But as I will show, Urarina women's transactional autonomy is ultimately constrained by their total reliance on men in negotiations with non-Urarina groups and individuals (see Seymour-Smith 1991, 639; 1988).

This chapter draws on the much-debated concepts of *public* and *private* that are central to feminist political theory. While my inclination is to see all social life as composed of multiple and overlapping *publics* and *privates* whose boundaries are illusory, I nevertheless adopt a dichotomous public/private division as an appropriate heuristic when representing the distinctions between the Urarinas' gendered experience of debt peonage. Clearly, my demarcation of public and private sociopolitical and economic domains is linked in this regard to ideologies of power rather than to "any existing divisions of social life" (Gill 1994, 9).

In an effort to highlight women's silence in those episodic yet crucial ne-

"When There Were No Women": Gender and the Experience of Peonage   133

gotiations that implicate the Urarina in broader social processes, this chapter consciously privileges those transactional moments in which men articulate women's commercial interests. In light of women's active participation in and control over other aspects of the kin economy, I want to examine the tensions arising from their total absence from these "public" transactional moments with their autonomy in other economic and social spheres.

A simple focus on those transactional moments linking the Urarina to the broader national economy through *mestizo* intermediaries invariably elides other aspects of subsistence and petty-commodity production that indicate gender complementarity. Notwithstanding the existence of gender complementarity as indicated by Urarina "public rhetoric" and social practice, which embody aspects of both gender symmetry and hierarchy, women's dependence on men to advance their interests in commercial transactions invites provocative questions regarding the allocation and elaboration of power relations between the sexes and generations in what otherwise could be called an "egalitarian" society. To situate the problem of women's exclusion from the public sphere, I turn first to an examination of the spatial context of Urarina gender relations.

The Spatial Context of Urarina Gender Relations

Urarina sexual segregation is readily apparent in their patterns of "visiting," in their sense of architectural space, and in their awareness of the environment, all of which influence the shape of mercantile exchange and petty-commodity production. When visiting,[1] men are the first to approach the longhouses; women and the young will typically linger in the dugout or at the footpath leading up to the settlement. After being received by the *kurana*, mature men sit near the host in the male domain of the longhouse. It is only then that the visiting children and women will begin approaching the host's longhouse. Facing outward, the female visitors position themselves on palm-fiber or *huacrapona* bark-mats (*jau*) spread along the outer fringes of the hostess's domestic platform and hearth space. This behavior initially establishes respect for men's and women's appropriate social spaces. Within a short while, the visiting becomes somewhat more animated, especially if there is ample cassava beer to alleviate initial awkwardness. But notions of gendered space continue to structure relations implicitly between men and women of different longhouses.

The spatial organization of the longhouse is conceptually partitioned according to the space-defining elements or *boundaries* of family and gender (see Norberg-Schulz 1980, 11). The male-oriented province consists of the bamboo (*huacrapona*) slate platforms (*adánah*)[2] and the wooden stools (*üfuiufhua*, which are made from *cedro*, also known as *ajlúnjua* or *itauba* wood) or roughly hewn benches that encircle this slightly elevated space. The fulcrum around which women's activities revolves consists of the cooking fire, the adjacent domestic platform, and the kitchen lean-to (consisting of a palm-thatch roof of a single pitch with the higher end abutting the longhouse's truss). Whether reclining on the bamboo dais, sitting on mats, or squatting on the ground, women spend considerable amounts of their time inhabiting the area adjoining their hearths. Wooden stools, once the shaman's "cathedra" (cf. Girard 1958, 174–75; Tessmann 1987), are now commonly used by women laboring at their hearth-fires.

Mature men and women of the same generation who belong to different longhouses do not publicly speak to each other (see Kramer 1979, 48). While Urarina women (and children) are fluent in the language of covert glances and studied disregard, they are discouraged from establishing direct eye contact with outsiders. By keeping their backs to one another, men and women avoid visual and physical contact and thus further emphasize gendered alterity. However, substantial overlap between men's and women's spaces does occur during festive dancing, which unites the sexes in one of the Urarinas' most exuberant and volatile social contexts.

Beyond the homestead, men and boys frequent the surrounding forest when stalking game, fishing, or working lumber for the regional timber market (fig. 5.1). Aside from accompanying their husbands when visiting other *demes*, or on subsistence expeditions, women seldom venture far from their homesteads and their associated garden and fishing sites. Above all this includes avoidance of *mestizo* settlements as well as cosmically charged locales, such as the spirit-endowed palm-swamps (*ajláca*) and turbulent whirlpools (*nesamuná*) in the bends of rivers said to link the terrestrial world of the living with the dangerous spirits of the riverain underworld.

Women's mobility is more restricted than men's, but women do accompany men on extended hunting and fishing trips. They work away from the longhouse in the gardens and make short excursions into the surrounding forest to gather valuable produce. A favorite wife often accompanies her husband on those infrequent trips to regional centers such as Concordia, Nauta, and even Iquitos. Women regularly call on kin in a nearby *ludéri*. In the company of their mature kinsmen, women will occasionally attend social and work gatherings in surrounding settlements (both with Urarina and *ribereño* groups). During distant scavenging excursions, or when women enter palm swamps to collect palm leaves for cordage, they are accompanied by male escorts (fig. 5.2).

Left: Fig. 5.1. Urarina hunter

Below: Fig. 5.2. Urarina woman weaving a palm-fiber fan

As expected, the separate geographies of Urarina gender relations are a critical component in both the constitution and the mediation of debt peonage. Like the Panoan speaking Cashinahua (Kaxináwa) (McCallum 1990, 417; Kensinger 1998), Urarina men's agency links them with the "external world" where they deal with the *anazairi* (foreigners) on behalf of all members of their *kaj laitjíra.*

I have underscored the restricted nature of the spheres that Urarina women inhabit in an effort to highlight their limited range of options in dealing with outsiders. As other anthropologists working in societies with marked gender segregation have indicated, these restrictions on women's interactions do not necessarily derogate from their ability to move and function autonomously within their own domains. My aim is to draw attention to the strategic negotiations and claims that Urarina women must make with the men who are their interlocutors. As I will now demonstrate, women regularly call in favors and stake claims to the men who are indebted or obliged to serve them in some way—through mobilizing either affinal or kinship ties. These efforts collude with the ambitious machinations of aggrandizing headmen, who, as the managers of supra-local affairs, are the mediators between internal relations of socioeconomic production and the external market economy. Ultimately, the redistribution and allocation of trade goods within Urarina settlements reinforces local hierarchies, and it is to this internal, cultural dynamic of debt peonage that I will now turn.

Engendering Fear

Debt peonage has inevitably modified local relations of production and patterns of consumption. Urarina consumption of industrial commodities, including cane alcohol (*birinti*), cloth, matches, kerosene, batteries, and shotgun shells, has increased demands on male labor power in the form of felling trees for the timber market, hunting game for exchange (*mitayo*), or producing "debt" crops (for example, rice and plantains). This in turn has increased the workloads of women and children to compensate for the episodic scarcity of male labor power in the subsistence realm.

Women's produce figures prominently in the barter for trade goods. In addition to agricultural produce and poultry, woven palm-fiber wealth continues to be the most reliable source of surplus production that women can mobilize for the acquisition of trade goods.[3] Compared with swidden agriculture, weaving affords women greater autonomy since it is a productive activity that is considerably less reliant on male labor inputs. On the Chambira, peonage is not determined by unchanging norms of exchange but rather by situational considerations and personal circumstances. The *patrón* will negotiate the recruitment of labor power with the longhouse's headman, typically electing the eldest male in residence, or if he has entered dotage, his most savvy son-in-law. Deviations from this pattern do occur. A headman's sons will sometimes negotiate for themselves independently or on the behalf of their unmarried sisters. In the absence of a brother or sons, a post-menarche widow will turn to her sons-in-law to manage the commercial exchange of her surplus production. Women instrumentally select those men to negotiate on their behalf that they know are both reliable and shrewd. During a rare expedition to Iquitos in 1998, the Pangayacu's headman was charged with acquiring trade goods for his widowed daughter and mother-in-law in return for their garden produce. In this regard, women must mobilize filial obligations by appealing to the very norms that prohibit their interactions with outsiders. In so doing, they reinforce those normative assumptions that in fact silence and constrain their agency.

At times, those women who are disadvantaged junior wives or widows—but who are concomitantly well-situated daughters—are frustrated by the inability of effete males to secure trade goods. These junior wives will routinely leave husbands who can't adequately provide for them in terms of trade goods. If they are daughters of powerful *kuranas*, like Kiriná, they can appeal to their fathers for inclusion in his trading network. Widows, in contrast, must negotiate other alliances with those *arriviste* headmen with whom it is permissible to associate. But given the complicated tabus that proscribe categories of kin interaction—particularly with regard to widows—they are considerably more inhibited in their associational options. The sexuality of widows is highly regulated and is the subject of much ribald humor and contestation within the settlement. Indeed, internal political affairs remain unsettled until newly relocated widows either find a new husband or elect a *kurana* to serve as their intermediary.

The most expedient route for the relocated widow pending remarriage is to elect her most competent son-in-law to handle her exchange affairs. Indeed, the presence of a competent son-in-law within a settlement is a primary factor that influences both her relocation and affiliation. From the son-in-law's perspective, assuming control of his mother-in-law's affairs has the dual advantage of harmonizing his internal relations with his wives and increasing his prestige as the manager of multiple productive relations within his *deme*.

Women's negotiations are integral to the prestige of aggrandizing *kurana*, but here it is hard to distinguish between men's and women's prestige orders, which are themselves interdependent and complementary in nature.

As I have shown, men's prestige is dependent on women's labor, whereas women's prestige in the form of their access to trade goods—particularly cloth and beads—derives from their alliances with efficacious and fearsome male negotiators.

The *patrones* and traders increase their power over the Urarina by promoting an atmosphere of fear revolving around the potential threat of military incursions into the Chambira Basin. This phenomenon has undoubtedly been influenced by the recent history of armed conflict between government forces and subversive groups (for example, the Sendero Luminoso, the MRTA [Movimiento Revolucionaro Tupac Amaru], and *narcotraficantes* [*nachos* or *narcos*]), as well as the border war between Peru and Ecuador. During the years I have known them, many Urarina have regularly expressed trepidation about the possibility (admittedly remote) of press-ganging and the threat of outside military intervention into the Chambira River drainage, as well as apprehension about the presence of *narcotraficantes* and other extractive entrepreneurs, such as illegal lumberjacks (*madrederos*). Hence, most young males and many adult men were apprehensive of traveling downstream to the Marañón because of the former threat of forced conscription.

Border skirmishes, counterinsurgency efforts, the demands of drug interdiction, and the threat of FARC (Fuerzas Armadas Revolucionarias de Colombia) incursions promoted forcible recruitment (*leva*) and compulsory military service (*servicio militar obligatorio*) in Peru. Military recruiters regularly implemented the *leva*, particularly when recruitment goals were not met due to draft evasion and absenteeism (González-Cueva 2000, 89). The contrast between the universal nature of conscription and its unfair application demonstrates the state's support of coercive social distinctions. Peter Beattie has underscored the extent to which the Brazilian army relied on coercive recruitment to fill its lower ranks (2001). Beattie's research illustrates how enlisted service became linked with concepts of criminality, disloyalty, and perversion, as nineteenth- and early twentieth-century functionaries rounded up the "dishonorable" poor—including petty criminals, drifters, and "sodomites"—and compelled them to serve in the military.

Reinforcing the notion that the Peruvian state is the legitimate monopolizer of violence, the *leva* disciplined citizen subjects by defining certain groups—like indigenous peoples—as hazardous to the social order. Those young men unable to produce their military cards (*liberetas militares*) were forced to serve in the military (Dean 1999).[4] Conscription is a publicly acknowledged sign of inequity: everyone knows that those lacking contacts or financial means must serve. Most indigenous peoples in rural Amazonia lacked basic identity documents such as birth certificates, military service cards, and voter registration papers that normally would certify them as fully fledged citizens—albeit notwithstanding all the ambiguities of citizenship such *national* documents imply (B. Anderson 2000, 2003).

In September 1993, the men of a recently established homestead on the Alto Chambira (appropriately dubbed Pionero) expressed to me their complete reluctance to travel to the lower Chambira. Lacking national identity and military service documents, these men worried about being put in prison or, even worse, being impressed into military service with the Guardia. Likewise, in 2002 and 2003 during my time in Loreto, my Urarina contacts continued to express apprehension about *narcotraficantes* and armed extractive entrepreneurs working in the area. Common throughout the region are reports of the *patrones*—as well as specific Urarina headmen's—illicit use of the regional police force to further their own political and economic interests. Urarina mothers are apprehensive of the local convention of "giving away" their children to *patrones* as a means to cancel the unresolved debts of deceased fathers, a practice that lingers to this day.

Interviews I conducted in August and September 1998 with adult Urarina peoples living in Sinchicuy (a *mestizo* community near Iquitos and a defunct *fundo* or agro-extractive estate controlled by a major *patrón* family operating in the Chambira Basin) confirm the longevity of this practice. The Urarina are keenly aware, as elsewhere in Peru, that adoption of urban patterns of behaviors may enhance women's susceptibility to being victims of domestic violence (Dean 2007). Recent attempts by a merchant to cancel in a similar fashion the debt of a deceased mature male from the Río Pangayacu met with fierce resistance by the senior headmen. Intense political factionalism (which mitigates against the development of strong horizontal ties among longhouse settlements—*kaj laitjíra*) combined with the generalized atmosphere of fear not only increases the *patrones*' leverage over the Urarina but also enables those headmen who are fluent in Loretano Spanish to wield a considerable degree of clout vis-à-vis their monolingual brethren. Senior men beyond the age of military conscription tended to be more mobile than both younger men and women whose opportunities for autonomous action were constrained by their inability to travel beyond the Chambira River drainage, downstream to urban centers located on the Marañón or Amazon rivers. As such, both groups remained considerably more dependent on their male elders to manage their commercial transactions. This in turn helps to constitute the Urarina body-politic by reinforcing gerontocratic and patriarchal proclivities (fig. 5.3).

The shortage of labor power, coupled with the requirements of the re-

Fig. 5.3. Headman reconstructing longhouse, Pangayacu River

gion's extractive economy, has meant that *patrones* are not particularly interested in immobilizing the local labor force except when it comes time to repay the debt (Muratorio 1991, 151, 155). *Patrones*' options for retaliatory action are somewhat limited given the ease with which the Urarina can retreat from disagreeable encounters or grossly unequal terms of trade. Hence, when Urarina men recount their cunning flights from avaricious *patrones*, their narratives about commodity peonage are framed by a broad geographic landscape that encompasses distant points and diverse experiences. One man's story of a legendary evil (*caguachani*) *patrón* clearly illustrates the influence labor migration has had upon the Urarinas' experience of participating in the regional extractive economies.

The Evil *Patrón*

> There was an evil *patrón* long ago. I don't know his name. People didn't want to work for him. But they heard there was *yawari* ... *yawari* ... *yarwari* [cassava in Cocama]. They went with the *patrón* to plant *yawari*, cassava. Then came *caucho* [rubber] ... a big tree ... *caucho*. It's true—they say they traveled far, very far—perhaps to the United States, somewhere below Lima. Then the clothes [given by the *patrón*] were worn. In those times, things were inexpensive. Those who worked with the *patrón* had many things: a chest for each person, an axe, a machete, and all sorts of tools. The evil *patrón* died after having been poisoned with *zuriman* [an unidentified toxin]. One of the men robbed the things and then fled by canoe. The Urarina man began the return home, suffering along the journey. At that time, the Amazon River didn't exist and so you couldn't get to Iquitos by water. One night the Urarina man arrived in Iquitos, but he didn't know where to go. He could only stroll around—for an entire month! Finally he returned to the Chambira, suffering along the way ... months, yes years were spent away from here.[5] (Kiriná and Ujkuaizíri, two Urarina)

Characterized by vertical ties of mutual interdependence, *patronazco* narratives are associated with a broader and more generalized pattern of patron-clientalism found throughout South America. These stories are part of asymmetrical relationships that bind people from distinct economic groups—in this case, traders, labor bosses, and indigenous peoples like the Urarina. Tales associated with *patronazco* display the essential role of violence as an index of differentiation in the negotiation and constitution of the social body. While *patronazco* narratives are told in social contexts, their performance indicates the narrators' privileged position in the social group to whom the stories are recounted.

The story of the evil *patrón* references the area's inter-ethnic relations (Urarina—*mestizo*—Cocama). It can be understood as a commentary on the profound influence extractive economies have had on the area. In the story, rubber displaces the staple food—cassava. This is followed by migration: "somewhere below Lima." The narrative makes clear that those who toiled for the *patrón* had their consumerist desires satiated. Yet, relations with the evil *patrón* are framed by avarice and ultimately murder. The story culminates in Urarina migration and misery.

Attempts at understanding patterns and processes of "interethnic dependency and conflict" have become crucial to the analysis of indigenous cultural and social formations in Amazonia (T. Turner 1993, 11, among others; see also Fernández 1986; Albert 1988; Perrin 1988; Henley 1996). In the "contact zones" (Pratt 1992) of Amazonia, it is simply no longer tenable to represent indigenous and non-native peoples as if they constituted completely separate or discrete social constellations. Neither homogeneous nor uninhabited nor linear in its historical development, the upper Amazon represents what Stanfield has called a "spherical frontier" (1998, 216 n. 8). Examination of the way outsiders are treated in Urarina narratives enables us to assess the extent to which their view of the condition of alterity is in fact a reflection of their own image.

Narratives like the preceding account of "the evil *patrón*" exemplify the Urarinas' intensely dialogic and historical understanding of their own entanglement in petty-commodity production. Further evidence of the pervasive influence of this socioeconomic enmeshment in commodity production emerges in crystalline form when I turn to examine the Urarinas' myhologized imagery of the circulation of trade goods. Urarina headman use fierce talk and narrate myths of violent episodes of *cudiaca*—exchange—to substantiate their claims to power. These myths give expression to unbridled violence, which is athwart to the Urarinas' philosophy of social harmony and familial tranquility.[6] *Patronazco* tales are couched in terms of appeals to fear and threats of retaliatory aggression. This legitimates Urarina headmen's ability to control inter-ethnic trade relations. Urarina conceptions of alterity are part of an ideology that mediates authoritarian power and unequal exchange relations in such a way that essentializes the differences between "native" and "non-native" worlds.

In Amazonia, as elsewhere, institutionalized violence is not a particularly efficient form of social domination (Jean Jackson 1992, 12). But the specter of violence is a dramatically powerful medium because it involves a breach of integrities that are both individual and social. Urarina headmen's fierce talk, replete with narratives of encounters with an inhospitable external world populated by rapacious traders and wicked *patrones*, is clearly aimed at marking cultural distance and discouraging unrestrained social interaction. While the talk of violence delineates social divisions, its narrativization also serves to fortify allegiances.[7] Understanding the Urarinas' ideology of retaliatory vengeance, with its valorization of aggression, enhances our comprehension of discourse, personhood, and power. Urarina headmen use the rhetorical posturing accompanying the dramatization of violence as a way of luring their audiences and captivating listeners. However, by muting alternative viewpoints, their stories facilitate the maintenance of the status quo. By employing imagery that fuses the plausible and the fantastic, tales of violence render three dimensional those zones of shared memory that are generally understood yet typically go unvoiced. In this light, *patronazco* stories are indicative of narrative asymmetries that sanction local patterns of authority, male privilege, and the general contours of the Urarina body politic.

Expertise in the various verbal arts—including expressions of satire, ridicule, burlesque parody, and dissent—plays a significant role in the way indigenous societies like the Urarina have responded to the reality of living with extractive entrepreneurs in their midst. Determining the role that violent narratives play in constituting society enables us to discern how imaginary structures are deployed by the Urarina to mediate the internal contradictions accompanying the intrusion of market relations into their vast, yet geographically isolated ancestral homeland—the Chambira Basin. While further, detailed study of the expressive tropes of metaphor, surreal juxtaposition, and metonymy will undoubtedly illustrate how Urarina male leaders and *mestizo* interlocutors regularly reassign meaning to erstwhile dominant cultural symbols, it is important to note—as Tsing has—that "even distorted or oppositional forms of consciousness can reproduce the contours of power" (1993, 75). And on this point, I want to underscore that Urarina men's narrative accounts of their experiences with notoriously evil *patrones* bolster their own images as fearless negotiators, especially with representatives of the alien and ostensibly dangerous non-indigenous world. It is perhaps not surprising then that a characteristic common to the shamanistic complexes of the region—including the Urarina and the Jivaroans—is that power is conceptually "derived from sources outside the group" (A. Taylor 1981, 672).

Urarina myths about the origin of trade goods and narratives about the circulation of commodities situate men as the primary interlocutors with the "outside world"—that is, the *mestizo* world of the Anazairi and the social universe of the Bajkagá, comprising the Urarinas' arch rivals—the Jivaroan-speaking peoples. Like the neighboring Shuar, Urarina men narrate stories that highlight the ability and bravery of individuals, rather than the collective force of the groups. The political discourse of retributive violence is used instrumentally by headmen to advance their interests, particularly when it comes time to acquire and distribute scarce trade items. By recounting stories of violent exchange, Urarina male leaders legitimize their own monopoly over access to encounters with "alien" human beings and the profoundly alluring trade goods they offer. Successful Urarina leaders have a diverse corpus of stories that celebrate—and thus reify—the retaliatory potential of the *patrones*. By framing the condition of alterity in violent ways, headmen position themselves as the only ones capable of dealing with representatives of national Peruvian society, including (and perhaps most importantly) traders (*comerciantes* or *regatones*) and labor bosses.

Men's narrative accounts of their experiences with notoriously evil *patrones* bolster their image as fearless negotiators. Urarina headmen rely on their reputations for commercial acumen, bravery, and munificence in constructing their social networks and public personae. In contrast, women's dramatic self-presentations and narrative accounts do not as a rule reference extensive geographic knowledge.

In collaborating with the *kurana*, the *patrón* is able to manage the labor of the longhouse's co-residents, a management that is realized through the periodic allocation of merchandise and on rare occasions cash.[8] The knowledgeable and adept *patrón* will employ the discontent within the longhouse and capitalize on communal disputes by playing one faction off against another. The most direct way to do this is to establish separate exchange relationships among rival individuals or groups. While their bargaining position is more restricted, the Urarina can occasionally employ similar tactics when negotiating the most favorable rates of exchange offered by competing *patrones* (especially "petty *patrones*"). At any given time, however, there are no more than a few *patrones* or *regatones* working in the Chambira Basin. Urarina men tend to "work" with a limited number of labor bosses. Depending on the season, they may have no alternative but to do business with the area's only labor boss or trader.

Notwithstanding the fact that trade goods are earned through collective efforts, they are apportioned to various members of the longhouse by the *kurana*. Headmen use their trading relationship with non-Urarina to forge relationships of patronage among their own people, especially their sons-in-laws and dependent unmarried females. Merchandise is employed to establish additional obligations *within* Urarina society itself.[9] As such, the debt (*rebeukön*)—symbolized by the exchange of trade goods—assumes a life of its own. "Debt servicing" is reproduced internally according to the confines of local political alliances.

While women do not enter into the negotiation publicly with *patrones*, their interests, as I have argued, are actively represented by the *kurana*. If the *kurana* were to arrange for the exchange of palm-fiber wealth with a trader and only receive "male" goods (that is, alcohol or trousers) or purely domestic goods (matches, batteries, salt, and so forth) when women's goods were predominant in the calculus of exchange, the *kurana* would do so at his own peril. Indeed, in the next trading cycle he would lose control over the produce of the women whom he had previously shortchanged. In this way, it is counterproductive for a *kurana* to be motivated by purely ego-centered considerations because if he is to maintain his position he has to manage multiple transactions to the satisfaction of each party in his trading network.

How much the *kurana* can conceal the terms of the negotiation is an open question, since the trade negotiations most often occur within the relatively "public" space of the longhouse. Private arrangements undoubtedly do occur, especially between younger men seeking to widen the constraints of their subordinate relations as junior males and free themselves of debt servicing to the elder males. It may be here, with a younger couple, that women's interests are underrepresented, since it is up to their significant males to make covert negotiations. The labor power of these younger women may also be harnessed for agricultural production and consequently they would receive collective "remuneration" in the form of domestic consumption goods. Individual female goods (cloth, beads, mirrors, combs, and so forth) may take a longer time to "trickle down" to them.

To recapitulate, the central problematic animating this chapter has been to acknowledge that Urarina women *need* men to deal with the "outside" world. While women activate a number of options ranging from divorce to remarriage to residential relocation to optimize their transactional positions, we must situate their agency within a broader sociopolitical framework. The Urarina authorize their gendered segregation of production, exchange, and consumption by relying on an essentialist ideology that obfuscates "cultural" power and thus facilitates its exercise. Indeed, the circumscribed roles of women do not occur ex nihilo; they are celebrated and legitimated by an elaborate mythological discourse.

Discursive Formations

The ideology of gender and kinship obligation is central to Urarina myth. Idealized presentations of demanding fathers-in-law, dutiful sons-in-law, and sexually dangerous mothers-in-law are elaborated in myth, such as in the Urarinas' popular tale of the creation of thanatophidia—venomous snakes. In many native Amazonian societies, serpents and humans (notably women) are discursively portrayed in terms of their libidinal relations with one another.[10] Throughout the continent, the anaconda is often a mark of revitalization and self-generativity, "in part because of its ability to shed its skin and replace it with a new one" (Hill 1988, 17 n. 5). Whitten (1988) has argued that the iconic reference to chthonic power in Amazonia and the Andes is to the anaconda and its spectacular capacity to overwhelm and squash life, an act which transforms a living creature of flesh and bones into regurgitated pap fit to eat. This is bolstered by the serpent's other extraordinary attributes, such as "its lair within mud and mire within water, its dormant nature after it has fed, its ability to swell tremendously upon eating, its dual penises, its underwater explosive noises, its violently entangling sexuality, or its vestigial hind limbs" (Whitten 1988, 294).

In indigenous South America, the gendered categorization of the primordial anaconda is variable. For the Kayapo, the legendary anaconda embodies the elemental principle of masculine creativity (T. Turner 1988, 264). Similarly, for the Mehinaku of Brazil, the mythical anaconda has potent masculine correlations (Gregor 1987, 154).[11] This stands in contrast with the western Amazonian association of the boa with the personification of Yacumama (Mother of the Water). The boa is a well-known reptile from the order Ofidios Colubriformes, the Boidos family, genus *Boa wagl*. This genus is composed of a number of species, the boa constrictor being perhaps the most renowned. This snake reaches a length of more than six meters and is distinctive in having nasal orifices in the side of the head, rather than at the point of the nose like the anaconda, the Western hemisphere's largest snake. Spanning over ten meters, the anaconda is from the *Eunectes* genus (*Eunectes murinus wagl*). These snakes like to inhabit the numerous lagoons (*cochas*) of the Amazon, as well as the banks of rivers, where they lie in wait for the birds and small animals on which they feeds. The anaconda is not venomous; it kills its prey by coiling round it and squeezing until the creature suffocates. Anaconda skin is utilized for shoes and luggage. In some parts of Amazonia, though not to my knowledge in Peru, snake meat is eaten and the oils are used as a medicinal balm (Espinosa Perez 1955, 515). The Urarina, like many other native Amazonian societies, such as the Siriono of Eastern Bolivia, have a tabu against consumption of snake meat because they believe it to be toxic (see Holmberg 1969, 78). Samuel Fritz's journal recounts the belief held by Yurimaguas mission residents that their textile and ceramic designs were inspired by the markings of snakes—in particular, the Madre del Agua (ostensibly, Yacumama) (Fritz 1922, 139).

Among the Yekuana of Venezuela, the anaconda (Wiyu) is portrayed as "a polymorphous anima-animus" character appearing "as either male or female, depending on the tale in which he or she is invoked" (Guss 1990, 228).[12] In this respect, the Urarinas' ophidian cosmography is akin to the Yekuana's beliefs, as noted in their account of the genesis of serpents.[13]

Ajkaguiño: The Origin of Ainú

> At the beginning of our time, women were without husbands (*lanas*). It was with Ajkaguiño—boa—that they became pregnant. A single woman beckoned Ajkaguiño by striking the water with her weaving sword. The woman made thumping sounds with the wooden *ubinya* to call Ajkaguiño. He came to the woman bringing her large quantities of "painted Lisa" [a type of fish][14] that we now call Boa Lisa. Ajkaguiño pulled the fish out of the water by their tales. The woman's brother heard his sister and Ajkaguiño laughing, so he went to investigate. He discovered his sister having sex with Ajkaguiño. In utter disgust, the man asked his wife to take his sister to their garden to harvest corn while he attempted to kill Ajkaguiño. The brother called the boa with the wooden *ubinya*, just as his sister had done. Ajkaguiño appeared and the man clubbed it to death. He then cut up Ajkaguiño into small pieces and placed them into a cooking pot on the fire to boil. Soon the man noticed a tremendous quantity of grease bubbling up in the cooking pot, and he saw an egg as well. In the meantime, the sister went off to call her Ajkaguiño as she had done before, but to no avail. She returned to her brother's house only to find her lover boiling inside the pot. The sister then chanted over the egg inside the cooking pot, and a huge quantity of snakes appeared: Ajlaichön [Jergon or Bushmaster[15]]; Utiñú [Shushupe]; Jajnajkánu [Cascabel]; Anúri ajkánu [Loro-Machacuy]; Terenú [Mantona]; Sajkánu [Naca naca]; Ajlajkánu [Aguaje-Machacuy]; Ujkuáinu [Afaninga].... That's why we have so many snakes to this day. And now when we are in the forest, we have to be careful for this type of dangerous snake, they bite us. Sometimes these *ainú* [serpents] are venomous. Sometimes they kill us. (Najlegue-kuktíri, Chambira, May 1992)

The narrative of Ajkaguiño contemplates the inescapable consequences stemming from sexual transgression and unregulated promiscuity—symbolized by the unwed sister. Fundamental breaches of this sort are constitutive of the axis upon which much of Urarina "mythic" thought turns. Indeed, human-animal interactions provide the very "stuff of life." Yet, Urarina myths consistently emphasize the value of asceticism. In an attempt to respond to the perils of unbridled desire, the first Urarina ancestor, for example, is said to have created natural evils, such as the pit viper and the stinging insects to bite him. My Urarina acquaintances drew a parallel between this mythical account and the rites of male socialization, which they remarked are designed to both heighten as well as channel desire.

Urarina social practices and gendered narratives oscillate within what Gramsci dubbed a "compromise equilibrium" (1971, 161). The myth of Ajkaguiño alerts us to the extent that the subject position of woman operates as a figure of "undecidability" in Urarina culture. The Urarinas' notion of woman (*ené*) occupies a site of contradiction: woman symbolizes both knowledge and ignorance, authenticity and simulation, affinity and enmity, proximity and distance.[16] As I have sustained throughout this work, Urarina culture is a productive domain, an arena in which hegemony is realized.[17] In Urarina narratives of gender and stories about unequal exchange, power is exercised through the process of definition: inclusion and exclusion are the currency energizing this operation, which strategically plays itself off against gender and "prestige orders." Like Ortner (1990), I consider "prestige orders" as hegemonies—as culturally pervasive, deeply ingrained, and historically contingent relations of sodality.

Understanding the dynamics of prestige is thus central to comprehending the cultural logic underwriting gender relations. A cautionary note should be sounded; this is by no means a "straight forward" endeavor precisely because of "the multiplicity of logics operating, of discourses being spoken, of practices of prestige and power in play" (Ortner 1990, 45).[18] While mythology is not by itself an indication of women's domination or subordination, in my view it is important to trace the relationship between Urarina gendered practices and mythologically inspired narratives. Myths are an integral part of the ongoing effort to make the arbitrary and contingent aspects of social life appear as if they are immutable, "natural," and legitimate. As conceptual frameworks, myths facilitate some maps of reality and deny others; in the Foucauldian sense, they are discursive formations. However recondite and paradoxical, a culture's maps of meaning are formulated and reformulated according to the orthodox discourses about reality. Even though they are authorized with potentially flammable significance, these "maps" reflect the interests of dominant social groupings.

As maps of individual and collective meaning, myths help define the boundaries of Urarina expression: they engage a larger coda, which perpetually struggles to fix the parameters of thought, language, and action. As discursive formations, myths allude to Urarina sexual differentiation and legitimate women's exclusion from the public sphere. A review—albeit extremely attenuated—of Urarina popular mythology signals the complex relationship between gender imagery and petty-commodity production.

Kijchá jésiane: "When There Were No Women"

> Before we had no women, Kuánra—our God—was watching how men lived among themselves. When the men wanted to have sex (*amijiá*), it wasn't like it is now. Men would insert their penises (*lajé*) in between the toes of other men. That's how we got pregnant (*ñú betuá*) . . . . in our calves (*pijia sedí*). By chanting, Kuánra created women so the men could have sex. The men went into a deep sleep. They seemed to be dead. When they awoke some of them had va-

ginas (*jái*) and breast milk. But they were very unhappy with their new status. They were filled with sadness. Kuánra responded by telling them they would be pleased because they could now be married.[19] (recounted by Ujkuaizíri, Chambira Basin, May 1992)

Based primarily on a version recounted by Ujkuaizíri in 1992, the following is a synthesis of five different renditions (one female and three male) tape-recorded on the Pangayacu in 1991, 1992, 1996, and 1998. Ujkuaizíri responded to my persistent inquiry, "But why were there no women?," with the following words:

> Well . . . there were none . . . Look I am going to tell you. There were none they say; that's why before there were no women, that's why they suffered, copulating here [once again pointing to the big toe]. It is said our god Kane Kuánra told a man and his nephew to go to sleep on their backs. Silence fell. They say the men went to sleep. Kane Kuánra, it is said, then began incanting. He cast incantations upon his hand [demonstrating a clasping gripped fist] and then left the men sleeping. The men awoke to find that their hair was different [touching head]. They had changed. They touched their genitals and found they had no penis but rather a vagina, like a deer's genitals. And this is why we now have women.

Contrary to many Amazonian societies whose myths attest to primordial matriarchy giving rise to contemporary patriarchy, the Urarinas' tale of the origin of women "is a separation event, a partition" (Feldman 1991, 17). "'When there were no women' is a myth of separation because the gendered elements of Urarina society are not reconstituted in any novel way: male parthenogenesis is supplanted by heterosexual reproduction. The myth is an instance of what Da Matta (1991) has aptly called reinforcement. Here "there is a kind of inflation or accentuation of what already exists" (Da Matta 1991, 55).

The Urarinas' myth of women's origin stands in direct contrast to the popular pan-Amazonian matriarchal myth of inversion, which elaborates a shift of gendered elements from one domain to another from which they are normally excluded.[20] Here I have in mind myths of male rebellion found in those societies in Amazonia with elaborate men's cults, such as the Mehinácu of the Brazilian Xingú or the Tukano of Northwest Amazonia. The Arawakan Mehinácu believe that women were the first to possess the symbols of power currently owned by the men's house—magical trumpets, bullroarers, and flutes. Because the women were incapable of caring for the sacred musical instruments, or for propitiating the spirits they depict, the men violently wrested control over the instruments. Women, the creators of culture, lost their political dominance and assumed their current ancillary position to men (Gregor 1987, 113).

The Urarina's myth of "when there were no women" alludes to a primeval time when men's homosexual reproduction obviated the need for women, denying even their procreative abilities. Denial of women's reproductive capacities stands in marked contrast to the importance of children as *assets* in Urarina kinship economy, where notions of wealth rest in claims to persons rather than in claims to things. According to the myth, women's creation culminates in the human acquisition of reproductive knowledge, which is disseminated by Kajtí, the brown capuchin monkey (*Cebus paella*) who instructs women on successful childbirth, which includes how to build birthing huts, tells them why they should follow the post-partum sexual intercourse tabu,[21] and perhaps most importantly, teaches them the art of shamanic incantation (*bagniñá*).

While the narrative of the mythic origin of woman engenders Urarina historicity, it is situated in the primeval "timelessness" of the ancients. Framed by its immutability and temporal distance, the myth of women's origin is beyond debate: it ideologically endorses all subsequent social bifurcations that irrevocably splinter men's and women's worlds to such an extent that the public/private dichotomy seems to us the most fitting for its representation (among others, see Maybury-Lewis 1979, 305, 311; Balée 1994, 168). As a discursive formation, popular myths like "when there were no women" establish as a given Urarina sexual differentiation, including women's exclusion from the most "public" of all public spheres—those exterior relations with non-Urarina men and women. In recounting such stories, people are taught "that women are potentially dangerous and immoral and that a stable and just order in this world depends on their being kept under the control of men" (Maybury-Lewis 1992, 130).

This perspective is elaborated in the Urarinas' myth of postdiluvial creation, which asserts the primacy of men in structuring social relations beyond the longhouse (see Dean 1994b, 22–45). Popular myths about the origin of trade goods and personal narratives about the circulation of commodities position men as the primary interlocutors with the "outside world"—that is, the *mestizo* world of the Anazairi and the social universe of the Bakagá, composed of the Urarinas' arch rivals—the Jivaroan-speaking peoples.

The Urarina not only resist the encroaching "outside world" by engendering society in terms of cultural categories refracted through a mythologized conception of their own past, they also engage with the fronts of national expansion through these discursive formations. Their oral narratives about inter-ethnic exchange relay a sense of the ambiguity of overt symbols of power, such as trade goods, the Spanish language, and literacy. Once when discussing a violent tempest, Najlegue-kuktíri remarked to me that "the Peruvians say it is thunder and wind, but that is a lie. God is punishing those who can not speak to him in Urarina."

The Urarina experience debt peonage both as discrete transactional moments and as an enduring structure encompassing a plethora of hegemonic prestige orders and social roles—from self-aggrandizing headmen and their deferential sons-in-law to *patrones* who are themselves dependent on urban-dwelling creditors. Both men and women participate in extractive mercantilism, though undoubtedly their differential roles in the processes of production and exchange shape their personal experiences of peonage.

Urarina idioms of kinship obligation are still cast in terms of appropriate behavior and respect (*cantána*). In their talk about affinal responsibilities and gendered production, the Urarina frequently say that men are obliged to "maintain" their wives and children, whereas the supreme being Kuánra "made women to serve men" ("Kana kuánra enecuaignele"). Urarina mythic discourse suggests that women were in fact created to serve men. As one male acquaintance remarked rather self-assuredly, "Women serve us—that's why we have wives.... We are not going to serve them; we men are not going to be serving them food." When pressed on the issue of the sexual division of labor and exchange, Urarina men will say that women are incapable of maintaining or supporting men because in the words of one particularly vocal acquaintance, "They don't speak Spanish. How are they going to obtain what trade goods we all need?" This sentiment is echoed in the words of Raguití, the senior head of a longhouse: "Women don't know how to speak Spanish; men are the ones who learn to speak Spanish. Women's tongues are heavy, they can't learn to speak, they only live in the longhouse, they don't travel far from here, and they never leave from here." By equating women with an architectonically circumscribed space, and with a restricted linguistic register (*Kachá eje*, spoken Urarina), Urarina "public rhetoric" privileges men's interlocutory status,[22] which in turn enhances their access to trade goods and claims to prestige.

Male patterns of extensive visiting, coupled with their experience of geographic mobility, help them to command public fora—both inter-demically and transculturally. These politically eclipse women's less extensive social networks. On this point, Ortner's (1990, 56) distinction between encompassing and encompassed "sites of social life" is relevant to understanding the Urarinas' gendered engagement with peonage. When negotiating the terms of trade, Urarina men regularly make encompassing assertions of acting on the behalf of their longhouses as well as of the *deme*. Conversely, women respond to men's assertions by making encompassed claims with respect to their own desires for trade goods. Compared to men's encompassing negotiations, women's encompassed claims operate at a relatively more localized site of action (for example, the hearth or isinéja, and the longhouse or *ludéri*).

The degree to which Urarina men claim to speak for the women of their longhouse group obfuscates women's active participation in the institution of debt peonage. One need only mention women's contribution in the form of cassava beer or food preparation to realize their involvement in facilitating socially conducive contexts for barter and inter-demic relations. Similarly, by foregrounding the transactional moment at which wealth items such as palm-fiber goods enter a commodity state we may in fact do injustice to women's participation in other critical junctures of production, circulation, and consumption.

Moreover, privileging the mobility of men may be a false indicator of power since Urarina interactions with representatives of Peruvian national society are on inequitable footing. Indigenous people such as the Urarina are marginalized and disparaged by national society. Thus, the trepidation that women and men display is grounded in very real fears and historical experiences of what Taussig renders as "the space of terror."[23] Nevertheless, the internal dynamics of mobility and exchange can be extrapolated from the overall network of inter-ethnic relations and appear to be a real index of power given the localized factors I have described herein. This calls for a nuanced explication of the complementary and contradictory discourses—local, regional, national, and transnational—that traffic in mandates for social action, be they exclusionary or participatory.

The troubling question remains one that poses challenges to women's ability to retain power and exercise control over their opportunities for self-actualization when they no longer can flee the encroaching state. By this I don't mean to imply that mythology, gender ideology, or current social practices are determinative of women's ability to assert themselves in novel contexts. After all, the Urarina have withstood the onslaught of missionization and the relentless effects of extractive "booms" for hundreds of years.

Examination of the Urarinas' gendered practices of peonage most importantly alerts us to the need for assessing gender inequalities in terms of the discursive formations and cultural contexts in which they are elaborated. Ultimately, the discursive legitimization of women's silence and exclusion is of vital consequence for women whose position vis à vis men in society is increasingly being undermined as the Urarina become less able to avoid the encroaching outside world. What will this circumscribed exclusion entail for women's prestige and life opportunities as they are thrust into increased interaction with *mestizo* society? Furthermore, when we consider that trade and political negotiations with non-Urarina take place in Loretano Spanish, women's monolingualism is the most formidable of all imposed silences. How can women assert their claims and ensure that their demands will be met in an increasingly diversified linguistic context? The point of this has been to raise—at least tentatively—the issue of the future while painting a more detailed picture of women's active involvement as transactional agents within an economic complex that almost always only attends to men's activities.

Gender and Political Mobilization

There are many reasons to be uneasy with contemporary versions of indigenous rights discourse (*indigenismo*) in Peruvian Amazon, particularly when it continues to conceal the endurance of systematic social distinctions through its appeals to a putatively universal indigenous subjectivity. The illusion of a temporal past and internal social cohesion intimated by the pan-ethnic confederations' reliance on a discourse of ethnic primordialism allows its leaders to conceal both accommodation and resistance to hierarchical organizational structures that often exacerbate gendered disempowerment. In spite of the many successes it has had in securing the social, political, and economic rights of Amazonian peoples, the indigenous movement was until recently characterized by a top-down style of personalized politics that deliberately expunged its critics. Apologists of the movement have long ignored its disturbingly nativist tendencies, turning a blind eye to the monopoly that a few key players and groups exert over the confederation structure. While the Amazonian indigenous movement has been characterized as hierarchical and dominated by a few ethnic groups and individuals, the emergent personalization of power and attendant patron-clientalist style of leadership have come under fire.[24]

In Peruvian Amazonia, the indigenous rights movement is all too often complicit in perpetuating the alleged separation of public and private spheres. Pro-indigenous human rights activists employ a discourse emphasizing state violations, while gendered inequalities and intimate violence within the putatively domestic or private sphere go largely unnoticed. As a result, the exclusions, restrictions, and ill treatment associated with women's lives are largely ignored by the indigenous rights movement in Peruvian Amazonia. In a country where the masculine citizen-subject is privileged, the indigenous rights movement is predictably devoid of women, even in titular positions. Few women actively participate in community assemblies, and until recently none had been elected to serve in any of the ethnic federations' primary political offices (R. Smith 1996, 120; see also Kensinger 1995, 16; Heise, Landeo del Pino, and Bant 1999).

The ethnic political federations all too often bear the determinist imprimatur of their indigenist predecessors: its leaders mistakenly assume that "ethnic" identification can either suppress or overcome the multiple constellations of identity such as gender, class, and hybridty (or in this racialized instance, *mestizaje*) that constitute social being. This is the political scenario in which Urarina men seek to become involved, and in their desire to be assimilated into the ethnic federation structure they anxiously embrace the fetishized hierarchies and gender discrimination that confine women to a restricted domestic sphere (in this case, exclusion from educational opportunities, travel, employment, and so forth).

Intra- and inter-group asymmetries are a manifestation of enduring gender hierarchies that naturalize or depoliticize the subordination of the feminine. Lacking agentive capacity in the definition of group interests, Urarina women are denied the authoritative status of full personhood accorded to those men who are empowered to make decisions and represent the group in supra-local political fora. The indigenous movement's protagonists have rationalized the virtual absence of women in the movement through recourse to the "traditional" cultural roles that prohibit women from participating in external political activities. Deference to "tradition" conveniently excludes women and other less powerful indigenous groups from direct political representation and allows the ethnic federation structure to continue along narrow, clientilist lines rather than opening up the movement to a more democratic, dialogic process with greater possibilities for participation and access to resources for all groups. Indeed, the emphasis on ethnic "authenticity" and cultural brokerage checkmates contemporary *indigenismo* by the moves of its very own players.

By no means, however, is this to suggest that the indigenous movement in Peruvian Amazonia is monolithic. Recent initiatives emanating from the Bilingual Teachers Program in Iquitos have generated a vigorous critique of gender disempowerment that has begun to make its way into local classrooms across Peruvian Amazonia (Dean 1999; cf. Trapnell 2003). Similarly, a new generation of indigenous women leaders who have had access to educational opportunities—particularly in Peru's *selva central* (central jungle)—are beginning to clamor for their voices to be heard on the public political stage.

In the fashionably new social context of pan-ethnic mobilization, leaders of historically subaltern communities like the Urarina face many challenges to effective supra-local political consolidation. Barriers include the absence of any real historical precedence as well as the intensely subjective and at times deeply personalized nature of pan-ethnic identity politics wherein indigenous leaders do not necessarily represent their ostensible constituencies (Montoya Rojas 1998; Kearney 1996; R. Smith 1996).[25] How then can contemporary *indigenismo* in Peruvian Amazonia embrace the margins without losing the centrifugal pull of the core? Can the indigenous movement make strategic accommodation for multiple political and intellectual agendas while retaining its collective strength? Similarly, how can an indigenous identity politics recognize or respect cultural diversity—as well as gender equity—without retreating into an effete relativism?

The circumscription of women to the realm of home and hearth is not unique to Peruvian Amazonia—and the conservative deployment of "tradition" unleashed against women need not be recounted here. However, the point of this chapter is to raise—even if tentatively—the issue of the future. The internal dynamics of Urarina political mobilization and exchange can be extrapolated from the overall network of inter-ethnic relations and appear to be a real index of power. As such, I do not think that the virtual absence of women in communal assembly meetings (which are ritually and episodically convened) or supra-local political life is indicative of women's powerlessness per se. Indeed, close attention to Urarina women's participation in other key arenas of social life demonstrates their capacity to wield power in and thereby redefine the contexts from which they are putatively excluded.[26]

Urarina men and women negotiate the terms of gender equality, intergenerational relations, and political accountability on a daily basis. While the Urarina conceive of the distinction between male (*kicha*) and female (*ené*) in absolute, biological terms, daily life reveals more relativistic distinctions in which elements of maleness and femaleness are continually juxtaposed. Numerous contexts associate gender with fundamental aspects of social life and individual personhood—ranging from kinship terminologies and age distinctions to ritualized behavior and mythology.

Since gender is itself a socially enacted cultural construct, one should not regard the present and future political capacity of Urarina women in predictably fatalistic or overly deterministic ways. Just as we embrace the labiality of ethnic and kinship categories, we must insist as thoroughly that we regard gender as a site of negotiation and disjunctive contestation (see, for instance, McCormack and Strathern 1980; Haraway 1989; Butler 1993). In so doing, we need to provide a counterresponse to the seemingly predestined script that indigenous women, such as Urarina women, inevitably lose out in situations of accelerated contact with the encroaching "outside world." But one should also acknowledge the painfully hard fact that Urarina women do not hold political positions in regional, national, or transnational indigenous organizations—and are not likely to in the near future. As the Urarina become better placed to establish a voice in supra-local politics, the troubling questions remain ones that pose challenges to women's ability to retain power, articulate their concerns in public spheres, and thus have some control over the enjoyment of all human rights—civil, political, economic, social, and cultural. However one responds to these complex questions, clearly access to culturally appropriate educational opportunities will continue to remain at the forefront of the Urarinas' prospects for ongoing cultural survival (Dean 2004d).

6

Forbidden Fruit

Affinity and the Economy of Kinship

This chapter explores the constitution of the Urarinas' economy of kinship through a review of affinity and the obligation it implies. I take up the contrast elaborated by a number of analysts between bride-service and bride-wealth societies (Collier and Rosaldo 1981, Collier 1988, 1997; Knauft 1997; Dean 1998a).[1] Distinguished by the "substitutability of persons and things" bride-wealth societies are said to rely on "exchange through value conversion in the context of asymmetric relations of hierarchy" (McKinnon 1993, 121; Thomas 1991). In contrast, bride-service societies are marked by their "like-for-like equivalences (of persons and things) and competition-in-kind exchanges in the context of symmetrically related (often egalitarian) groups or persons" (McKinnon 1993, 121; Thomas 1991, 39, 44, 75–76, 119–22). Bride service has traditionally been portrayed in the literature as the service rendered to the bride's family by the bridegroom as a "bride price" or part of one. But rather than seeing Urarina affinity in terms of a "compensation" model whereby individuals are exchanged as objects, I highlight people's roles as differentially situated subjects. The politics of bride service and infidelity are useful starting points for investigating the creation, mediation, and maintenance of social inequality in indigenous Amazonia.

Infidelity, Affinity, and Bride Service

In much of indigenous Amazonia, social inequality is not substantiated through property or gifts, but rather through competing claims to the labor power and services of specific individuals and groups. In the anthropological literature, scant attention has been devoted to understanding how women in Amazonia gain access to the fruits of male labor. The term "bride service" appeared first in the literature to denote the services rendered by a man to those people from whom he receives a wife. These services are usually rendered to the groom's father-in-law, though the groom may also be compelled to serve other affines such as his mother-in-law or brothers-in-law. A renowned example of this marriage strategy is the biblical story of Jacob, who obtained his wives Leah and Rachel by serving their father, Laban (his mother's brother), for fourteen years (Frazer 1919; Radcliffe-Brown 1987, 48; Goody 1990, 347–51).

The prevalence of bride service as a foundational discourse and social practice in Amazonia has been confirmed by an extensive ethnographic literature.[2] Many works on western Amazonia emphasize the contrast between the role women play in forging the group's internal unity and the role men fulfill as representatives of the group to the external world (Seymour-Smith 1991, 636, 642, 1988; Kensinger 1989, 25; McCallum 1990; Pollock 1992, 35; A. Taylor 1993, 673). In a similar vein, this chapter underscores the importance of paying special attention to the realm of female sociality in indigenous Amazonia. Through a detailed account of one incident of Urarina adultery, this chapter examines women's conjugal claims over their husbands, an important cluster of rights frequently disregarded in the study of bride-service societies. I examine how marital confrontation can lead to fission of Urarina longhouses (*ludéri*) and in some cases to the fragmentation of multiple longhouse groups or *demes*. Drawing from the life histories of a select number of Urarina men and women, I demonstrate how bride service (*amianiaca, kaneajkána amiané*) is embedded within the productive and reproductive cycles of the domus—cycles that are themselves conditioned by the exigencies of regional and supra-local political economies. Urarina marriage (*ijtaráriga*) is interpreted not as an eternal, ahistorical structure of exchange, but rather as a strategic alliance that allows individuals to pursue their own subjective ends and in so doing generate the very relationships that both liberate and restrict.

In an effort to redress the skewed compensation model of bride service, I illustrate how women get and keep spouses by paying particular attention to accusations of infidelity that account for a substantial proportion of local disputes. In this regard, bride service is explored from the perspective of negotiation—I treat it here as the relationships between persons and domestic groups with different resources, motivations, and strategies (Bourdieu 1986, 58–71). Marital infidelity provides the study of bride service with a privileged point of entry: its examination highlights competing claims to the labor, services, and emotional bonds of specific individuals.

Given the competing and divergent interpretations of the functional or practical significance of bride service (Kracke 1976; Maybury-Lewis 1967; 1979; Murphy 1956; Rivière 1984), it seems inappropriate to look for a single sociological explanation for this practice. This is not an attempt to seek a universal explanation for all of the various permutations of this elementary "organizing principle." Indeed, one could argue that the very notion of bride-service societies is like the label "matrilineal societies," which Leach noted is about as useful as the category "blue butterflies" is for zoologists (1961, 4). Nevertheless, I do question whether bride service is best understood in terms of men's establishment and maintenance of claims to women as wives. In an influential essay (1981) Collier and Rosaldo argued that in "bride-service societies" men are more dependent on women to be their spouses than women are dependent on men to be their husbands. In their estimation, marriage facilitates men's achievement of status. However, this approach pays little attention to men's and women's differential access to offspring as a component in the social relations they create and how this access in turn affects the exchange activities of "parents" (Mukhopadhyay and Higgins 1988, 482–83).

In the context of Urarina society, Collier and Rosaldo's model does not account for the concomitant roles that uxorilocality, sororal polygyny, and child bestowal play as mechanisms for ensuring social continuity. Yet despite its shortcomings, their model of bride service is relevant to the study of Urarina affinity because it insists upon seeing marriages as public assertions of status. By so doing, their model is able to link the actions of men and women to politically volatile contexts determined by particular individuals in the ongoing negotiation and management of alliance. Moreover, Collier (1997) is correct to insist that social inequality in classless societies is usually organized on the basis of rights in people. Perhaps most importantly, the Collier and Rosaldo's model of bride service provides insight into the nature of inequality by demonstrating that some individuals are in a better position to exact services in the form of labor from others.

Inequality and Bride Service in Amazonia

Unlike bride-wealth or dowry systems, marriage in lowland South America is generally not legitimized through the transfer of rights over resources, nor through the elaborate exchange of goods. Jean Jackson's observation that in the Vaupés Basin of Colombia "no goods can be given in lieu of a woman" holds true for many societies of lowland South America (1983, 127). In Amazonia, items do not stand for labor or for persons. Instead, individuals mobilize a variety of claims on the acts of others, including labor in the form of obligatory services due one another. Bride service is frequently performed in conjunction with an interval of uxorilocal residence. The length of uxorilocal residence and the duration of bride service are contingent upon negotiations between the concerned parties, the outcome of which has been characterized as an enduring commitment or permanent debt (Rosengren 1987, 127). The power wielded by those who "give" wives over those who "take" them is also said to be a significant part of the political relationships in societies where bride-service obligations are prevalent (Rivière 1977, 41; Mentore 1987, 511–27).

Arguably the leading explanation of bride service is the compensation model: a groom serves his wife's kin in order to obtain the right to remove her from her natal home eventually (Murdock 1949, 207; Steward and Métraux 1963, 646; Ember 1973; Smole 1976, 106; Chevalier 1982, 294–95; Whitten 1976). This theory is an intellectual model whose genealogy dates to Victorian social evolutionism: bride service was first conceptualized as an intermediary phase of social development emerging between the stages of marriage by capture and marriage by purchase. Early commentators maintained that bride service is a "contract" between a husband and his wife's kin obliging the husband to "compensate" his in-laws for the privilege of marrying their daughter (McLennan 1970, 23; Tylor 1937, 132; Lubbock 1978, 86). Westermarck noted that "among most existing uncivilized peoples a man has, in some way or other, to give compensation for his bride" (1901, 390). It is within this context that Goody has argued (1973, 4) that in cases of bride service a man uses his daughter as bait to ensnare a son-in-law. In Amazonia, the appearance of bride service has even been equated with enthrallment. In the words of Up de Graff, "He who aspires to her hand becomes to all intents and purposes the slave of his future father-in-law for a term of five or six months until he proves his worth" (1923, 220).

In summary, the compensation theory of bride service posits that bridegrooms are compelled to serve affines in order to obtain rights in women, whereas parents (especially fathers) are propelled by their desire to achieve appropriate compensation before relinquishing control over their daughters. This quid pro quo interpretation sees bride service as the means by which a man is provided with a wife—an arrangement that simultaneously benefits the bride's family, which receives additional labor power without enduring the loss of a daughter, at least temporarily (Århem 1981, 163). The compensation model contends that through bride service, parents are granted in personam rights in their son-in-law, while grooms are granted in rem rights in women (Radcliffe-Brown 1965, 32–33). This account of bride service is predicated on the analysis of what men do to get wives: in essence, it holds that services are required of a male in exchange for the bestowal of a female in marriage.

A number of analysts have suggested that bride service is a keystone in the regulation of social order among "tribal" foragers and horticulturalists (Collier and Rosaldo 1981; see also Collier 1988; T. Turner 1979; Kracke 1978, 37, 72; Viveiros de Castro 1992, 118, 376; Rubenstein 2002, 36–37). The themes of control and domination enjoyed a central position within the debates on Amazonian kinship and systems of marriage. For instance, Terence Turner's work (1979) on Gê and Bororo social organization deals explicitly with the structural implications of uxorilocality, which he sees as a critical locus for the emergence of power relations—both intra-generationally and between the sexes. Turner contends that in resource rich Amazonia, males cannot use property to exercise control over their sons-in-law. However, at the intra-familial level of Gê and Bororo social structure, a man's ability to dominate his daughters and sisters does represent a means that can be "manipulated in exchange with other men" (1979, 159). While Turner's model has generated a considerable amount of critical debate in the study of gender and sociality in Amazonia (Rivière 1984; cf. McCallum 2001, 6–8, 87–89; Rival and Whitehead 2002), it falls somewhat short in its general applicability for Amazonia (see Lorrain 2000). Instead of permitting the categories to evolve from the study, Turner's evaluation of Gê and Bororo social organization is problematic precisely because it begins from the postulate that domestic groupings are primordial associations that naturally coincide with the lives of women (Seymour-Smith 1991, 635). In a somewhat different vein, Collier (1988, 1997) links bride service with the establishment and maintenance of a husband's claims on his wife. In this decidedly Hobbesian model of society, goods and services are perpetually tendered by the husband to his wife's kin in order to legitimate his claim to the marriage. For Collier, the most pronounced inequality among men in bride-service societies is between bachelors and married men (1988, 33; see also Lévi-Strauss 1969, 39; Hugh Jones 1988, 111; Gregor 1987, 25–26; Jean Jackson 1992, 8).

In Collier's estimation, the man without a wife must do without "shelter, hearth and sex," or obtain these from his kinswomen or from a lover. Marriage enables men in bride-service societies to initiate political relations through acts of generosity. The married man is an autonomous social actor because he is perceived to have earned his own wife; he owes no debts, nor does he need to incur any to legitimize his marriage. In those societies in which men's claims to women are the "final referent," all women, save the very old and very young, seem to be "taken." This culturally created scarcity of suitable marriage partners implies that those men who make claims on women do so in competition with others. A man who marries declares to other men that his wife is off-limits. A husband's *prestations* and services to his in-laws continue for as long as he is willing to protect his claim to his wife. Bride-service is thus indicative of a male's "willingness and ability to violently defend his claim against the woman's other potential suitors" (Collier 1988, 25).

In sum, Collier links the practice of bride service with the establishment and maintenance of a husband's claims to his wife. But by assuming that men acquire monopolistic rights to their wives' labor power, Collier misinterprets the full significance of marriage (Kelly 1993, 345). While many novel insights have been generated by Collier's bride-service model, they have come at the expense of objectifying women as passive valuables, rather than seeing value as being constituted by desire, a mutually lived experience for both men and women.

I am not alone in expressing reservations regarding the Collier and Rosaldo bride-service model. Seymour-Smith (1991, 646 n. 4) acknowledges that the Jivaroans are a "bride-service society," while insisting that they do not conform to the various attributes described for such societies by Collier and Rosaldo (1981). Likewise, Overing (1986) and Gow (1989, 1991) have registered doubts about the analytical value of Collier and Rosaldo's model for Amazonia. Gow (1989, 581) points out that their bride-service model does not differentiate between initial marriages, which serve as transitions from adolescence to adulthood, and mature marriages, which indicate full adult status.

At varying points in the course of their lives—such as when they are mothers of young children or menopausal widows—women have real stakes in the establishment and maintenance of marriage (see Kelly 1993, 429). This becomes readily evident when one examines the rewards as well as the disadvantages associated with affinity and infidelity. The Collier model suggests that adultery is a corollary of men's competition with one another over their claims to women. One can thus detect a convergence of the bride-service paradigm (á la Collier and Rosaldo) with the compensation perspective; both are concerned with the creation and perpetuation of men's claims to women who are construed as cultural valuables (*caguatua*).

These paradigms misleadingly regard women's matrimonial roles simply as enthrallment, rather than seeing these roles in terms of their potential for active political or social engagement. Before examining the limitations of these perspectives, it will be helpful first to contextualize Urarina marriage by considering it as a component of a broader network of sexual and political relations, themselves determined by "historically specific social processes" (Collier and Yanagisako 1987, 10).

Affinity, Longhouses, and the Politics of Urarina Kinship

The longhouse or *ludéri* is emblematic of Urarina society, itself secured through the union of opposed yet complementary elements, namely men (*kicha*) and women (*ené*) from distinct hearth groups. Characterized by dense marriage alliances, *ludéri* are exogamous social groupings composed of matrilateral extended families or *kaj laitjíra*. Clusters of adjacent *ludéri* within the *deme* appear to be endogamous. Like their rival Achuar neighbors, the Urarina have a pattern of residential atomism counterpoised by a supra-local structure that Descola calls the "endogamous nexus" (Descola 1994) and I have labeled the *deme*. While neither of these formal concepts have any place in either Achuar or Urarina thought, the abstract unity of each is predicated on territory associated with a particular stretch of river, the influence of the local headman, and "the interlacing of ego-focused kindreds" (Descola 1994, 9). An Urarina *deme* comprises roughly a dozen households dispersed over a relatively well-defined territory and consists of members related by ties of consanguinity and affinity.

The term endogamy is used here in the classical anthropological "sense, namely, the rule or practice by which all members of a group marry among themselves" (Goody 1990, 448). Similarly, the term "in-marrying" or "in-marriage" is used to denote marriages "within the group or grouping, however defined." In this sense, one can speak of Urarina *demes* as in-marrying but not endogamous—yet they are clearly not exogamous either. There does not appear to be any general obligation to marry in or out of the *deme*, but there are options and preferences that differ markedly between the sexes and among siblings.

Like the Maku of the Northwest Amazon (Jean Jackson 1983) and the Carib societies of Guiana (Rivière 1984), the Urarina exhibit a propensity for local endogamy and the emphasis of marital alliances in the formation of their settlements and local groups. The Urarinas' preference for local endogamy is conducive to a pattern of marriage uniting persons across generations. I have seen girls as young as ten years old marry men more than thirty years their senior, as well as pubescent boys marrying women twenty years their senior. Age differences between partners are a critical factor determining their respective affinal obligations.

Matrimonial alliances among the Urarina are perhaps best understood as being located in diverse yet interwoven cycles of personal, domestic, and community life. These cycles of social production and reproduction include the oft-mentioned life crisis events, which are of capital import in the validation of Urarina personhood and society. Urarina marriages (*ijtaráriga*) are neither initiated nor instituted by any elaborate nuptial ceremony (see also Holmberg 1969, 216). Like the ripples in the water after a stone plunges to the depths below, the wedding process is not instantaneously enacted. It unfolds over an extended interval of "secular time" (for example, that which is sequential and quantifiable).

The Urarina are inclined to marry non-kin (*ijtaráiñe*) from a nearby matrilateral extended family into which a sibling or first cousin has previously married. This stated and observed preference for local endogamy must be reconciled with the Urarinas' injunction against the marriage of those individuals who are kin (not classed as *ijtaráiñe*). Co-resident, bilateral kindreds practice household exogamy. The manipulation of relationship terminologies is of limited value since children born within the bounds of the same longhouse are always classified as non-marriageable. At the level of the *deme*, however, the avoidance of marriage to persons classified as kin is enhanced by Urarina genealogies of relatively limited depth and through suppressing acknowledgment of collateral relationships (Kramer 1979, 71).

In the selection of a wife, a suitor requests permission from the prospective bride's parents. If the bachelor is young, he is accompanied by his father when seeking his future father-in-law's permission to marry. The prospective wife's parents consult one another about the personal qualities of their potential son-in-law. They ask themselves whether he is a hard worker, a good gardener, and an agile hunter. Notwithstanding the advice of the parents, who can only indicate which suitor is suitable for their daughter, it is the desires of the prospective bride that seem to matter the most. This freedom of marital choice is curtailed in cases where the bride is prepubescent. In such cases, the wishes of the bride's parents figure more prominently, and bride service is virtually obligatory.

At marriage, the groom departs his natal home and goes to reside within his wife's parents' longhouse. The initial period of familiarization between the newlywed couple lasts a few weeks, after which sexual relations begin. Barren marriages are not necessarily grounds for divorce. In some instances, a couple will foster parent the child of a sibling. In other cases of childless marriages, a wife's sister will become a co-wife in the hopes of producing offspring. While in uxorilocal residence (a period of approximately one to two years), the new husband is expected to assist his in-laws with an array of tasks. Husbands will work in their affine's gardens, help their fathers-in-law in the harvesting of lumber, assist in the marketing of petty commodities, and procure food, forest produce, and even barter items. The age of a wife is also a factor influencing patterns of residence. When a wife is younger than ten years old, her parents prefer that the newlyweds reside uxorilocally. At the birth of children, the young couple will usually move to a new house built within the wife's natal community. Neolocality marks attenuation of bonds with the affinal longhouse group and of changing economic factors.

The achievement of the ideal "tranquil marriage" (*rautujiyáka ijtáña*) is a complex process fraught with many difficulties and indeterminacies. As temporally evanescent networks of intermarrying longhouse groups or *kaj laitjíra*, Urarina *demes* are bound eventually to fragment unless they succeed in incorporating eligible marriage partners. The localized longhouse group is faced with two options: 1) induct marriageable males into the *kaj laitjíra*; or 2) resettle on a generational basis to provide unwed members of the *kaj laitjíra* with marriage partners (Kramer 1979, 75). The latter option corresponds with the noted Urarina pattern of frequent local group resettlement.

When members of a longhouse group resettle, they are inclined to do so near those kin with whom alliances of marriage and labor cooperation are possible. Moreover, by fulfilling the wishes of mature adults regarding their ideal place of residence, or the desires of the elderly to return to their natal rivers, individuals who stand in potential relations of conjugality are brought together (Kramer 1979, 76). Analogous to bride service and polygyny, child bestowal (*ranela laujidiniedade*) has particular political and economic importance among the Urarina. In some instances, the unborn sisters of a man's wife can also become his future wives. Urarina men say that a female child is bestowed to another man in "exchange" for provisioning her with forest game and the fruits of his horticultural and scavenging efforts. Adult men will commonly try to acquire adolescent boys as "prospective" husbands for their nubile daughters. The practices of bride service, uxorilocal residence, and child bestowal facilitate the induction of new male members into the local group. These arrangements in turn enhance the productive viability of the longhouse over time.

Headmen, *Bardiguë*, and Unbridled Desire: Interpreting Conjugal Disputes

Quintessentially political in nature, Urarina affinity involves the negotiation of status and the establishment of reciprocal obligation. As the social process conjoining production and reproduction, matrimony is inevitably fraught with competing interests and divergent desires. In spite of the contentiousness of marriage, conflict is minimized through the Urarinas' celebration of an ethos of placidity and self-restraint. In this regard, the Urarina are similar to other native Amazonian societies, such as the Matsigenka, who emphasize the importance of controlling self-centered impulsiveness that threatens collective life. Both the Matsigenka (Johnson 2003) and the Urarina celebrate personal independence and a spirit of self-reliance.

As noted elsewhere in lowland South America (Beckerman and Valentine 2008), the Urarinas' philosophy of social concord is accompanied by a reality of truculence and retaliatory vengeance. In this regard, they resemble the Jivaroan peoples who surround them. Political divisiveness turns on issues of defining group membership and evaluating personal behavior (Seymour-Smith 1991, 646 n.7). In the context of fluid relations of alliance and intense factionalism, direct confrontation often results in the schism of the *deme*, as well as the *kaj laitjíra* or nucleated local longhouse groups. I recall during the 1998 rainy season a bitter personal exchange between two rivals, Majewari and Nudé, that spun out of control at a beer-drinking gathering. Always the peacemaker, the local headman, Kiriná, counseled the disputants to stop casting aspersions on one another and to return to their sleeping platforms. Rather than calming tempers, this enraged the disputatious and wildly drunk Majewari, who fled from the longhouse gathering and began publicly haranguing his competitor. A few junior men loyal to Nudé responded with a show of force, more symbolic than real, which involved mock violence, most notably striking trees with wooden clubs and insulting shouts. This counterresponse humiliated the aggrieved Majewari, who eventually left the Pangayacu River and returned to live with his natal longhouse group on the Río Tigrillo.

Lacking institutional or formalized means of arbitration, Urarina dispute resolution depends upon the initiatives of the contestants and those willing and able to furnish moral and practical support. With the introduction of official, state-sanctioned positions of authority, Urarina mechanisms of self-redress have been undergoing significant changes over the past generation. A number of the Urarina settlements now have civil authorities. Nevertheless, Urarina headmen or *kurana* continue to base their power on their ability to create political alliances through marriage. Becoming a co-resident in the natal longhouse of one's wife signals movement toward political incorporation. Socially skillful headmen have multiple wives with numerous offspring. They rely on sons-in-law as political allies and establish personal obligations among relatives through acts of generosity. Urarina men recognize both the advantages and disadvantages of polygyny. While a plurality of wives assures many children and access to greater surplus production (for example, beer, plantains, scavenged resources), polygynous marriages are fraught with additional problems, such as increased demands in the way of forest game and trade goods, as well as the potential for increased marital tension, particularly when co-wives are not uterine sisters. Those men with one wife often remarked that they preferred this arrangement as it meant they were not poor. In contrast, men with multiple wives downplayed the link between poverty and polygyny, and instead tended to underscore their capacity to maintain numerous households. The most durable polygynous unions unite men with uterine sisters.

On the Chambira, sororal polygyny is widely practiced. Urarina men prefer sororal polygyny because sisters are reputed to "get along better with one another" (Harner 1973, 94). This corresponds with Fox's argument (1971) that sororal polygyny is compatible with uxorilocal residence, whereas general polygyny is not. Logically, the uxorilocal husband in a situation of non-sororal polygyny could go around and "visit" his wives in their various homes. Such is the situation among the Callinago, who have overcome the apparent contradiction between uxorilocality and a pattern of non-sororal polygyny "by wives maintaining separate houses in their own villages while men reside in men's houses" (White 1988, 546). It is, however, more convenient for the uxorilocal, polygynous husband to be married to uterine sisters from the same domestic group, as is the case among the Urarina.

In addition to marital status, a headman's standing is augmented by his possession of strength, hunting prowess, munificence, and knowledge of the natural world and mythological cosmos. With respect to political authority, the Urarina have long grappled with the contradictions associated with the parallelism between traditional modes of authority and those accompanying the expansion of state presence in the area. In the Chambira Basin, the authority of Urarina headmen is bolstered (and in some cases undermined) by the adroit manipulation of the area's nascent civil bureaucracy. For the Urarina, bureaucracy is by no means necessarily expressive of instrumental rationality in the Weberian sense, but rather more akin to Nietzschean self-assertion. In spite of their illiteracy, many mature Urarina men occupy official roles of authority designated by regional state government. These posts are valorized through the possession of written documents and rubber seals issued by the regional authorities. The scribal functions that *ribereños* play in Urarina society warrants considerable attention, particularly in light of the emergence of state-sanctioned civil governance, which is intersected by the limited yet perceptible growth in *mestizo* class differentiation. Literate *ribereños* are responsible for producing the bulk of *oficos* or written legalistic declarations that circulate among *demes*, between communities, and peri-urban and urban officials.

According to my informants, the system of officially recognized local governance appears to have been introduced in the Chambira Basin during the reformist military regime of General Juan Velasco Alvarado (1968–75). While the region saw little at this time in the way of land reform or attempts at restructuring the region's grossly inequitable relations of production (Dean 1994b), the military regime did promote the establishment of local civil hierarchies. This included the creation of the office of the lieutenant governor (*teniente gobernador*), who in addition to representing the community is charged with the arbitration of local disputes. The state's promotion of civil authorities in the Chambira Basin was further emphasized by the efforts of the non-governmental organization CEDIA (Centro de Desarrollo del Indígena Amazónico), which began working in the zone in the mid- to late 1990s. In collaboration with state functionaries, CEDIA implemented the Fujimori government's neoliberal Special Land Titling Project (Proyecto Especial de Titulación de Tierras, PETT).

Not all community lieutenant governors are considered to be the local *kurana*, but many do occupy both roles.[3] The communal governor's authority is strengthened by the existence of the office of police (*policia*), symbolized by the possession of a wooden billy club (*lloque*). To keep the peace and to prevent drunken affrays during beer parties, *policia* patrol the community with hardwood *lloque* clubs in hand. Resistant charges are sometimes struck (*ijtasúaka*) in the upper torso with the clubs or are confined in the community stockade.

The Urarina appreciate the value of captivating and retaining a sizable public following (*adaji cacha sidi*), which is an important part of authenticating their status as influential and authoritative social beings. The context for communal decision making involves the headman calling a community assembly (*asamblea comunal*) attended primarily by adult men. Aspiring headmen visit neighborhood homesteads to inform people of the assembly meeting. Without playing too much to "the gallery" through polemical histrionics, men will speak out against the dissolute behavior of kin and *ribereño* neighbors alike. The persuasiveness of Urarina public oratory lies in the speaker's ability to emphasize proper social conduct through personal example. In general, Urarina community assembly meetings are marked by an ambience of respect and mutualism. In some cases non-Urarina are invited to meetings in the name of the civil authority—the *asamblea comunal* (or community assembly).

Urarina women are completely absent from formal participation in the newly emergent civil hierarchy. While not officially excluded from community assembly meetings, women tend not to accompany their menfolk in attending assembly meetings, particularly when these meetings are held in neighboring longhouse—the metaphorical locus for the decision of community affairs. As a rule, women will not publicly initiate the recruitment process to cajole adult members of the surrounding vicinity to attend a meeting. Nevertheless, as the producers and primary dispensers of cassava beer or *bardiguë*, women have a legitimate arena of action that establishes their symbolic, economic, and political power in this domain. The production and distribution of what can be deemed wealth items of food (*lenuneá*) is fundamental to Urarina social and political life (see also Dean 1994a). Given the importance of cassava beer in ritual and political affairs, those men who are able to rely on a number of large, productive gardens as well as a steady supply of women's labor needed to make beer are at a distinct advantage when it comes to periodically mobilizing the labor power of others. Ample supplies of *bardiguë* ensure popular attendance at communal work parties (*amia niáca*), assembly meetings, and festive gatherings.

Cassava beer production, like other productively charged contexts, such as canoe building, blowgun manufacture, and weaving, is an arena subject to the stipulations of sexual prohibitions. The preparation of *bardiguë* is a very laborious endeavor for women. At least thirty kilos of cassava tubers must be harvested, peeled, and cooked (*tujcurá*). Using wooden pestles, the boiled tubers are then pounded into a paste. To facilitate fermentation, a number of mouthfuls of the mash are masticated and then spat into the vessel used for making the beer (ceramic jars, plastic bins, and on some occasions, wooden canoes). The mixture is left covered for three to five days until it ferments into a beer of low-grade alcohol content (Quintana 1948, 278). Prior to being served, the *bardiguë*'s frothy spume is decanted, and then a drinking vessel made from a gourd is used to scoop up quantities of beer to be consumed. When women serve, they usually do not look directly at the male recipient. Relations among males and females of the same conjugal family are considerably less restrained. The fundamental importance of fermented beverages in lowland South American gender ideologies has not been fully explored. For his part, Viveiros de Castro (1992, 139) contends that the symbol of beer as "female semen" finds parallels in other lowland Amazonian societies. However, when explicitly asked, the Urarina did not express a similar view.

For the Urarina, drinking cassava beer has a supremely diacritical function: it marks off one type of socially sanctioned behavior—sobriety—from another—intoxication (*bariguekᝠajê*). Drunkenness (*ñá ajiyaneu*) is said to result from the cassava's force or spirit (*cuairá*), which a number of my Pangayacu acquaintances described as an "eye." Men and women of different *kaj laitjíra* unite during cassava beer parties, which are the most important venue for the initiation and exposure of illicit relationships. These politically volatile periods of communal life are prone to the corrosive effects of gossip, quarrels, and sometimes violent fighting. Similar to Goldman's (1963) experience among the Cubeo, all of the Urarina cassava beer parties that I have attended were punctuated intermittently by quarrels, many of which revolved around issues of sexual impropriety. Provoked by jealousy or slanderous talk, disputants episodically breach the "peace," resorting to shows of force to dramatize and in some instances to coercively impose their particular points of view. In the context of debauched longhouse drinking festivals—some of which last for days at a time—new offenses invariably revive previous affronts. Squabbles that begin with charges of infidelity or idle talk can quickly escalate to include a convoluted jumble of accusations and countercharges that expose communal fault lines and latent hostilities, many of which have festered for years, if not generations. Open accusations of adultery or misbehavior can then become linked to sorcery (*bajtuhuí*), particularly in the event that one of the disputants falls ill (see Goldman 1963, 216).

In cases of infidelity, there are a number of means at one's disposal to mobilize support, sway public opinion, or admonish behavior. One of the most effective means is resorting to public performance through censure (*ujlerijiyá*). Disputants advance public complaints (*rijkigué kadáu*) either in conference with the headman or in public gatherings. During longhouse assembly meetings, affronted women will actively voice their complaints and accusations, particularly when it involves their own "matriline" in cases of abandonment or sexual misconduct (including gossip and sexual violation or *suayá*). With head bowed to the ground or turned away from the men, clusters of women customarily render grievances in a stylized, high-pitched register. Analogous to men's oratory style, the primary speaker will often be supported by secondary declarations given on her behalf by her female allies, most often sisters and mothers.

Contrary to the Collier and Rosaldo bride-service model, a woman's kin will provide sanctuary and physical protection in those cases in which she is abused or grossly mistreated by her husband. Uxorilocal postnuptial residence and local endogamy provide Urarina women with a significant degree of safety and protection, particularly for younger wives. In cases of virilocal or neo-local postnuptial residence, it is not uncommon for a young woman's kin (especially her mother and grandmother) to assert their prerogatives over her by forcibly repatriating her to her natal longhouse (*dekaj kinamá, ijtasuna*).

Most marital disagreements are resolved by the disputants themselves, without the intervention of the communal assembly, whose involvement signals the expansion of conflict. Communal assembly meetings are occasions for jocular bantering and oral duels, the outcome of which may result in a festive cassava beer party or in temporary confinement (typically twenty-four to forty-eight hours) of the "miscreants" in the communal stockade (*calabozá*). Like many *ribereño* communities, the Urarina distinguish two primary types of confinement in the wooden stockades that resemble North American outhouses: "rigorous punishment" (*castiga de rigor*) and "simple punishment" (*castiga simple*). The first involves confinement in a small stockade, greatly reducing the prisoner's bodily movements. The second form entails imprisonment in a larger stockade with more room for movement, often with a seat and roof to block the sun or the effects of inclement weather. The provision of beverages and food also corresponds to the severity of punishment. In extreme cases, the prisoner is refused all nourishment. In the minds of many Urarina, confinement in the stockade is the supreme form of humiliation. This form of castigation often triggers the fragmentation of matrilateral extended family groups and in some instances the entire *deme*.

A common cause of Urarina marital disputes is adultery (*kasháuki*). From a heterosexual male's point of view, the practices of prescriptive sororal polygyny and child bestowal beget a scarcity of women as wives. As such, adultery is to be expected among the Urarina. Moreover, men's perception of a shortage of nubile partners results in part from the fact that youthful women tend to have the upper hand in selecting their lovers, who must be capable of providing for their domestic needs. From a heterosexual woman's perspective, men as husbands can also be scarce. Demographic contingencies, the proliferation of young bashful fiancés (*ené kuázilla, juejétu*), men's periodic migration to satisfy the labor demands of the region's extractive economy, and accidents and disease are all factors that contribute to women's impression of the chronic scarcity of eligible men.

Public censure (*ujlerijiyá*) is an important means of conflict management. Disputes over material resources, such as land or personal theft (*vasijiaká*), are infrequent points of contention. While the thief (*asijiajtú, kashacurita*) is scorned, the gossiper (*kasáje, idinakáuna*) is reprimanded with relative severity. Punishment for sexual misdeeds and gossip is somewhat less severe for the Urarina than it has been reported to be for their neighbors, the Jivaroan-speaking peoples. The penalty for infidelity among the Jivaroan peoples was vigorously applied since adultery often resulted in the permanent departure of one's wife. Punitive actions included executing the paramour and gashing the wife's head with a machete blade (Newman 1983, 169; Harner 1973, 107, 175).

Urarina husbands (*lana*) will on occasion strike their wives (*kumazái*), and dissatisfied women will at times do likewise, or more commonly they will simply reject an indiscreet or abusive husband. It would be misleading to claim that Urarina women are invariably perceived to be culpable in cases of adultery: every Urarina acknowledges that both men and women have equally voracious sexual appetites. To illustrate this, I turn now to an examination of a case of infidelity. I argue that in spite of the fact that women are discursively portrayed (by men and women) as objects to be exchanged, Urarina women are never actually exchanged. The practice of child bestowal invites provocative questions regarding the "exchange" of people through marital alliance. Nevertheless, as I make clear in the case of Aúdi's infidelity, while people may conceptualize marriage in terms of exchange, in practice individuals are never actually exchanged. This observation underlies my contention that marriage in bride-service societies involves not only the subjective interests of men, but of women as well. This perspective differs from many recent interpretations of marriage in Amazonia. For instance, writing about the Ecuadorian Shuar, Rubenstein asserts that it is "only men's interests . . . [that have] determined social value" (1993, 4).

Infidelity in Practice

During my time among the Urarina, I witnessed firsthand numerous marital disputes, many accounts of which I managed to tape record. The dispute that follows below began in 1991 and involves an ongoing conflict between two competing *kaj laitjíra* located on the Chambira and Pangayacu rivers. Those involved in this marital drama include Aúdi, a mature man living uxorilocally with his co-wives, the uterine sisters Aruba and Lekiná; the sisters' parents, Kajtí and Sumajai; Jarúña, a young unmarried pregnant woman; Jarúña's foster father, Kujkúri, who is a *teniente gobernador* and an aspiring headman; Rurú the Pangayacu's current headman; Mazú, Aúdi's unmarried younger brother; and finally Kaya, the widowed mother of Aúdi and Mazú (all pseudonyms).

For some time prior to the incident of infidelity (*kasháuki*), bad blood existed between Aúdi's affinal longhouse group and his natal longhouse group. Simmering hostilities erupted during a cassava beer party hosted by the Pangayacu's headman, Rurú, and his four wives (two sets of uterine co-wives) for the purpose of opening up new forest gardens. During the *bardiguë* fiesta, Rurú tried to persuade the attendants to return to work before they consumed all of the cassava beer the women of his longhouse had made. However, Sumajai, the mature female head of Kajtí's longhouse group, became drunk and refused to collaborate any further, choosing instead to continue conversing with her husband's sister's daughter (her *mumá*). Angered by what he perceived as women's disruptive gossip, Rurú asked Kajtí to take his wife home. This ejection unleashed a strident verbal reprisal by the inebriated Sumajai.

Later that evening Kajtí retaliated by denouncing Rurú's action toward his wife at a nearby *mestizo* homestead. When Rurú was summoned before the *mestizo teniente gobernador* to defend his actions, Rurú found that the charge had escalated into battery. Enjoying significantly greater personal prestige and political standing in the area, Rurú was able to successfully counter Kajtí's accusations by charging that Kajtí was an untrustworthy rumormonger who should be punished with confinement in the stockade. As a result, Kajtí was sentenced to twenty-four hours in the communal stockade for slanderous, hot talk. At this time, Kajtí's and Rurú's longhouses were at odds over the fate of Mazú, one of the Pangayacu's bashful fiancés who refused to consent to marrying Kajtí's and Sumajai's adolescent daughter. Rurú was convinced that Kajtí's *kaj laitjíra* wanted to punish him for respecting Mazú's decision not to marry Kajtí's daughter. By accusing Rurú of misbehavior, Kajtí was able to reiterate his displeasure over what he perceived as a botched wedding.

When he left the stockade, Kajtí was furious and humiliated. Kajtí's reliance on a non-Urarina audience to censure Rurú is itself indicative of his weak position within the Pangayacu community. Lacking support beyond his own longhouse group, Kajtí was unable to mount a significant riposte. The members of Kajtí's longhouse—composed of five hearth groups, including Aúdi, who was performing bride service for his affines—harvested their gardens and departed precipitously from the Pangayacu River. Under Kajtí's and Sumajai's guidance, a new longhouse and swiddens were established downstream on the Chambira River—near a *mestizo* trader's extractive encampment.

When Aúdi subsequently initiated sexual relations with a nubile woman from the rival longhouse on the Pangayacu tempers inevitably flared. The case of infidelity began when Aúdi told his two co-wives, Aruba and Lekiná, that he was going off to the forest to harvest hard wood house-posts for one of the local river traders (*regatones*). But Aúdi tricked both his co-wives and his in-laws by traveling instead to his natal community on the Pangayacu. Sensing something was amiss, Aúdi's wives and in-laws came in search of him. While making the four-day journey upriver to the Pangayacu community, their suspicions of infidelity were confirmed by rumors circulating about Aúdi's and Jarúña's sexual union (*amijiá*). When they arrived to find Aúdi in the area, the co-wives were prepared to assert their claims to their husband. The sisters, along with Kajtí and Sumajai, retired to their abandoned longhouse and waited for the adult men to return from the forest before publicly denouncing Aúdi's philandering behavior (*enetáujia*). Rather than admitting to his liaison with Jarúña, Aúdi pleaded complete innocence, a response that the residents of the Pangayacu longhouses found hilarious. The following morning, a communal assembly was held in the headman Rurú's longhouse, during which Aúdi was admonished for his behavior.

To fully appreciate the nuanced nature of women's claims to their husbands, and the way they articulate these claims, I turn now to a tape-recorded version of Lekiná's and Aruba's impassioned public censure of Aúdi's adultery. Their angered and terse speech consisted of a staccato presentation of a number of complaints. For the sake of brevity, their dialogue has been condensed.

The Case of Aúdi's Infidelity

In measured, though fiercely determined voices, Aúdi's wives ask, "Why has Jarúña been *ñá tiyeteschá* [bestowed to Aúdi to be deflowered]? She may have been deflowered by Aúdi, but this does not mean that Jarúña is now married to him." The women are livid: "We don't like our husband's *tajédia* [lover]. We are older than Jarúña, but she is still our *kanemai* [mother's sister's daughter, a classificatory aunt who enjoys superior status]." The sisters complain, saying, "Three wives is simply too many. In the past, marriage between non-sisters was uncommon. If our husband marries our *kanemai*, we will not accept him back into the longhouse. Our longhouse was peaceful before all of this trouble; we supported ourselves by hunting whatever we could find. If Aúdi now weds his *kajtanú* [classificatory mother-in-law] it will bring harm upon our children." The sisters worry that their husband will no longer be able to support their six children, commenting that "it is as if Aúdi is not their father." Aruba says, "I am going to return to our parents' longhouse if Aúdi deserts us." Both sisters threaten not to allow him to take away their sons. For her part, Lekiná remarks how she raised her sons, "I am their mother. I will not let their father take my children from me." Lekiná laments, "When we want to *lenune atiyá*—to go out hunting—how will we all be able to go? And how will we be able to chide the youthful Jarúña without Aúdi beating us?" The women continue decrying Aúdi's attempt at forsaking his children, as if what concerned them were solely their children's welfare and not their own emotions. "If he abandons us, we will keep all of his clothes; we want to have justice for our husband who has broken Jarúña." In the assembly meeting, Kujkúri, the local *teniente gobernador*, excoriated

Aúdi for his indecisive behavior in not assuming responsibility for his actions. But as the wives note, "Aúdi was not publicly reproached for neglecting his children. Now we sleep alone . . . it is as if our husband is dead!" The women vehemently oppose Kujkúri's promotion of the marriage of their husband and Jarúña. They conclude by asserting that "the bestowal of Jarúña was contrived to prevent Aúdi from leaving the community. If he does go through with the marriage, he will be dead to us, our children will suffer. If Jarúña comes to live with us, our longhouse will not be tranquil anymore, there will be perpetual discord."

During the unfolding of this case of adultery, it was widely rumored that Kujkúri had impregnated Jarúña, his deceased wife's eldest daughter who was his foster daughter. To dispel the rumors, Kujkúri began promoting the marriage of Jarúña. From Kujkúri's outlook, Jarúña's marriage to Aúdi had the advantage of reincorporating a mature male with many personal assets into the community, and more importantly into Kujkúri's longhouse, where Aúdi would have contributed his labor power through fulfilling bride-service obligations. Kujkúri articulated his sentiments regarding Aúdi's and Jarúña's union when he admonished Aúdi for neglecting his new wife. When it became clear that the trial marriage would fail, Kujkúri changed track by censuring Aúdi for enjoying sexual access to Jarúña without having to assume the responsibility such a relationship necessarily demands. Aúdi the potential son-in-law became Aúdi the philandering nuisance.

Aúdi seems to have initially favored the marriage to Jarúña, not only because Jarúña is considered by many Urarina men to be one of the area's most desirable nubile women, but also because his widowed mother, Kaya, and his unmarried siblings reside on the Pangayacu. Kaya favored the marriage between her son and Jarúña: she would recover her eldest son, a valuable asset, while Jarúña's classificatory father—Kujkúri—would gain another son-in-law, thereby further enhancing his chances of becoming an important headman in his own right. The recent deaths of two adult males in Rurú's longhouse placed a noticeable strain on the headman's ability to feed his large *kaj laitjíra*. Aúdi's initial return to the Pangayacu was greeted by his senior brother-in-law, Rurú, with enthusiasm. Keeping Aúdi nearby would alleviate some of the demands on Rurú's labor power. Rurú's mother-in-law, Kaya, and her hearth group would be able to rely on goods and services provided by Aúdi, rather than exclusively by Rurú.

For her part, Jarúña completely rejected Aúdi's advances by refusing him food and by scratching him repeatedly in the face and thighs during the four nights they slept together under her mosquito netting. Jarúña's behavior is typical of the reluctant female partner in lowland South America (see Nimuendajú 1967, 85). Having a number of suitors herself, Jarúña stood to gain little from becoming a third wife. Moreover, her potential co-wives were extremely hostile to the proposed arrangement. Opposition from Aúdi's co-wives and mother-in-law, all of whom portrayed the proposed wedding in terms of violating affinally appropriate norms, doomed the potential marriage. As an orphan and eldest child without any mature sisters, Jarúña was not in a particularly strong position to have her interests represented by senior kin of her *kaj laitjíra*. Instead, Jarúña was at the mercy of her foster father, who saw her as an asset to be manipulated instrumentally. Jarúña had few options other than resorting to her own wits to assert her desires.

Aúdi's and Jarúña's trial marriage failed because the primary women involved were against its success. Aúdi's co-wives refused to relocate to the Pangayacu; meanwhile, the bride-service obligations Aúdi had with his affines further restricted his options of acceptable action. Residence away from his affinal longhouse group would have been tantamount to divorce. Citing the benefits he derived from membership in his wives' *kaj laitjíra*, Aúdi sheepishly returned with his co-wives to his affine's longhouse downstream. In addition to being able to rely on his wives' productive capacity, they had provided him with children. Marriage to Jarúña would have jeopardized Aúdi's access to his children. This is significant as any aspirations Aúdi had regarding his future status as a *kurana* depended on his access not only to wives, but also to his children. Above all, Aúdi's marriage to Jarúña floundered because Jarúña failed to give her consent. From Aúdi's perspective, Jarúña remained forbidden fruit—an attractive, but unattainable wife.

Among the Urarina, prepubescent and adolescent grooms and brides appear to have little to profit by marriage. The arrangement of their nuptials is managed by senior relatives who inevitably must come to terms with the desires of juniors, including bashful fiancés like Mazú, who vigorously resist the prospects of uxorilocal postnuptial residence. Trial marriages (*tarága*) during adolescence are common, though they seldom result in long-standing conjugal unions. When stable marriages can be formed, offspring soon follow.

In matrimonially precarious situations, such as a relationship with a reluctant or abusive suitor, women who become pregnant will not hesitate to abort their fetuses—as did Jarúña subsequently before marrying Kujkúri's brother's son's son. While this is a sign of women's autonomy over their reproductive capacities, they still have to respond to familial pressures. Urarina acquaintances told me that pregnant women who remain unwed bring shame on their *kaj laitjíra* since they cannot rely on the fathers of the children to lend support. While living with the Urarina on the Pangayacu, I witnessed a number of self-induced abortions (*bedë jituá*).⁴ In two particular incidents, abortion seems to have been precipitated by the impending marriage of the pregnant women to men not recognized as the fetuses' fathers. Along with abortion is the limited though common practice of infanticide (*azé niarebedë*). Congenitally deformed infants (for example, cleft palate, disfigurement of limbs) are seen by the Urarina as non-human creatures, akin to the protean spirits that inhabit the forest (*itará*). These infants are abandoned to perish in the jungle, often near a lupuna tree—the symbolic locus of Ijiá nebá, the mother spirit of the forest who is seen as the baby's spirit guardian.

Following the birth of children, the intergenerational bonds linking hearth groups within the longhouse become somewhat attenuated. Increased demands made on the husband's labor power by his wife or wives and children are accompanied by a gradual decline in affinal bride-service obligations. This corresponds with the eventual maturation of the couple's offspring. It is noteworthy that Aúdi's adultery occurred at the time when his offspring had reached childhood—precisely the period when his affinal bride-service obligations began to wane. The maturation of the domus's children brings with it the possibility—for both mature men and women—of garnering prestige through the successful creation of a matrilateral extended family longhouse group, culminating ultimately in headman relations (*kurana*) linking multiple longhouses groups into a *deme*.

Beyond Compensation: Rethinking Affinity in the Context of Bride Service

While underscoring the fragility of Urarina *kaj laitjíra*, the incident of connubial conflict outlined above also brings into purview men's hymeneal obligations. The episode highlights the competing nature of a man's natal ties with his affinal obligations. Far from being autonomous agents, as the Collier and Rosaldo (1981) model would have it, Urarina men's behavior is conditioned by a philosophy of personal responsibility to affines and consanguines. The study of bride service has privileged a viricentric approach to the analysis of the conjugal rights and obligations necessitated by marriage. Mazú's behavior as the bashful fiancé, as well as Aúdi's reluctance to admit his liaison, point to the limitations of the notion that men appear to "earn" wives in bride-service societies.

Ethnographic accounts of male reluctance to marry in bride-service societies are widespread. Lévi-Strauss, for instance, has written about the Bororo custom of the "bashful fiancé" (1975, 61 n. 12; cf. Firth 1983, 440).

The wife's female kin would have to pressure the young husband to leave the men's house and to take up residence with his wife. To this end, the wife's female relations would forcibly remove his personal belongings. The "'bashful fiancé' would continue residing in the men's house, until he was cured of shame of having become a husband" (Colbacchini and Albisetti, quoted in Lévi-Strauss 1975, 61). Similarly, among the Sherente, a fiancé would appear shy, abashed, and sad at the time of the wedding. The husband's new male affines (the bride's uncle and three related men) would forcibly remove "the weeping and resisting groom to his bride's house" (Nimuendajú 1942, 29). During the first few months of marriage, the husband would not approach his wife for fear of being remonstrated. Throughout this period, a young "wanton" related to the wife shared the husband's bed (Nimuendajú 1942, 29–30). Maybury-Lewis notes (1967) that no newly initiated Xavánte male would take an active part in negotiating his own marriage, which is a matter said to cause him "acute embarrassment and shame." The marriage of the newly initiated age-set is described as a community affair rather than as a process by which individual men appear to "earn" their own wives (Maybury-Lewis 1967, 78–80).

The Maussian exchange model has been ubiquitous in the analysis of Amazonian matrimony and femininity. A commodity-based property analytic is well developed in Kensinger's (1984, 1989, 1995, 1998) works on Cashinahua sexuality. In his estimation, extramarital sex can be understood as "a case of market exchange based on the law of supply and demand . . . a female who makes herself readily available lowers the value of sexuality in the extramarital meat market" (1989, 23). Some analysts have even gone as far as to treat women in horticultural societies as movable property (for example, Friedl 1975, 64–65). Arguably, the chattelization of women in Amazonia, as depicted by "bride- capture," was a concomitant of postcolonial internecine warfare (cf. McLennan 1970, 28, 50; Barnes 1999).

The discussion of bride service as a form of compensation through which wives are exchanged, women are controlled by men, husbands are incorporated by dominating in-laws fails to account adequately for critical components of this social complex, such as the nature, the timing, and the magnitude of duties and privileges transferred through this marriage strategy. Similarly, the essentialist position that marriage is equivalent to the exchange of women by men who dominate them is intimately linked to the belief "that gender is constituted before issues of exchange or control are mobilized" (Gow 1991, 120; Collier and Yanagisako 1987, 7).

Watson-Franke is correct to point out that the anthropological literature on women and property routinely concentrates "on rights in women rather than on rights of women" (1987, 231; cf. Mentore 1987, 514; McCallum 1988; Rivière 1988). McCallum contends (1988) that men in lowland South America do not control women. Rivière (1988, 520) concurs with McCallum but suggests that men in many parts of lowland South America do attempt to control women. Rivière submits that a persistent issue of much of the ethnography of Guiana is the ongoing rivalry for human—in particular—female "resources." In spite of the various means available to ensure male dominance, men invariably fail in their attempts at controlling women (Rivière 1988, 520; 1984, 90–94).

The compensation model of bride service relies on a narrowly focused viricentric model of exchange. Analysis of kinship in small-scale societies confirms that the unreflective use of an occidental logic of proprietorship seriously impedes the study of social formations where such idioms are inappropriate. In indigenous Amazonia, women are never merely the objects of men's desire, nor can they appropriately be seen as valuables or wealth items conceived of as independent variables in bounded systems of exchange (see, for example, Århem 1987, 138; Lizot 1978; cf. Johnson and Johnson 1975, 637). One cannot wrest value from the "symbolic medium" that embodies it in any particular culture. By attributing it to objects, or to the logic by which they circulate, we conceal how value is in fact constituted through the strategic negotiation of interpersonal relationships. Cultural value is deeply embedded in the lived experience of desire, which in turn is created dialectically by both male and female agents. Put simply, the study of marriage must explore not only the calculus of men's desires and interests, but women's as well.

Notwithstanding the linguistic connotation of the term *bride service*, the economic transfers of services and wealth involved are clearly not unilateral. The arrival of a prospective son-in-law places greater demands on women's customary duties. Thus, we should not assume that males are the only ones with labor to transact. Women's generosity will influence whether the prospective groom will stay or not—as was the case with Jarúña's refusal to share her "shelter, hearth, and sexuality" with Aúdi. Furthermore, a prospective son-in-law's labor may be more than reciprocated in terms of his consumption in his wife's natal group (Bossen 1988, 130; see also Basso 1973, 94; Siskind 1977, 75–79; and Da Matta 1982, 46).

Analysis of Amazonian kinship has been overly androgamous: to date, scant consideration has been devoted to understanding how women obtain husbands, or how they gain access to the fruits of male labor. Quite clearly, the case of Aúdi's infidelity illustrates women's interests in the establishment and maintenance of marriage. Informed by the compensation model, the general approach to conjugality in bride-service societies has been to assume that the groom is making an asymmetrical transfer of labor, which can only be recouped when he takes his bride to another residence. This analysis pays little attention to the economic obligations that marriage establishes among the bride, her kin, the groom, and his family (see Kelly 1993, 444–47). Why, for instance, is a son allowed to leave his natal family instead of being compelled to stay and compensate them for his lost services (Bossen 1988, 128–30)?

Declaring that married men in bride-service societies are autonomous social agents obscures both our understanding of the nature of conflicts and how they are resolved. Focusing on the putative autonomy of married men obscures the importance of mutually binding obligations, or what the Urarina deem *amianáñera* or *erenatrónida*. Review of Aúdi's wives' public censure reveals how the discourse of parental and spousal provisioning is directly linked with the Urarinas' perception of affinity and abandonment, which in this society is tantamount to divorce. A bride's parents will rely on a discourse that portrays their actions toward their son-in-law in terms of paternal care and responsibility: coercion is denied both in speech and in behavior. When asked, dependent sons-in-law like Aúdi most often will unequivocally deny that they are in an exploitative relationship. Instead, they discursively conflate the cultural equation of the role of father-in-law with the status of father.

By asserting that the bundle of rights associated with the process of conjugal affiliation is necessarily articulated through the idiom of men "earning" wives, both the compensation model and the Collier and Rosaldo model conceal the interplay of other significant contours of matrimony in the context of bride service. In particular, these models fail to mention one of the most apparent associations between bride service and the ideology of appropriate personal behavior, namely the phenomenon of mother-in-law avoidance (*kurüna*), examples of which abound in the ethnographies of Amazonian bride-service societies.[5] Aruba's and Lekiná's rejection of their husband's trial marriage was framed in terms of their disapproval of Jarúña's status as their husband's *kajtanú*, or classificatory mother-in-law.

Respectful deference denotes one pole of the affinal relationship inscribed in bride service and the practice of uxorilocal postnuptial residence. As Kiriná commented, following marriage a man must "live under the skirt of his mother-in-law." In addition to avoiding speaking directly to his wife's mother (*mitisatanú*), a man will eschew direct communication and interaction with his wife's mother's sisters. Mother-in-law avoidance contrasts sharply with the close if not jocular relationship a man enjoys with his father-in-law. In contrast, the relationship a woman enjoys with her father-in-law is one of discreet circumspection. As beneficiaries of the ideology of respectful deference, or *iriná náiniña*, a bride's parents reciprocate with acts of generosity aimed at forging personal obligations extending beyond their longhouse. This includes the establishment of relations of connubial and labor reciprocity with the groom's kin.

The process of affinal expansion is most often framed in terms of exchange orchestrated by men. When I asked married men why they eventually move away from their in-laws to form their own households, I was often told that wives become the financial obligation of their husbands, much like the way sons-in-law are first incorporated in their new households. In the words of Najlegue-kuktíri as he described his three wives, "Ya se quedan a mi cuenta" (now they are on my bill). Not surprisingly, the female disputants in the case of Aúdi's infidelity depict the incident as one of communal bestowal. In remarking that "the community has bestowed Jarúña to Aúdi," Aruba and Lekiná illustrate the prevalence of the ideology of treating females as entities to be circulated. Having said this, however, all Urarina are aware that no one can be forced into marriage against his or her will.[6] The divergent interests of the various parties involved in managing conjugal arrangements means that successful marriage is tenuous at best. The ties of residence, bonds of affinity, and structures of obligation must be negotiated according to the dictates of personal circumstances and the cultural imperatives of society. To assume that bride service is merely a means by which men assert claims in women is only a partial truth.

Perhaps the most misleading aspect of the negotiation of marriage in bride-service societies is that it is not accomplished through the idiom of property: "things play no mediating role" (Strathern 1985, 197). Consequently, Urarina mechanisms of conflict resolution do not rely on ideas of compensation. Instead, idioms of obligation are cast in terms of appropriate behavior and respect. Urarina dispute resolution relies on a noncompensatory discourse that frames obligations and status recognition against tropes of personal embodiment and social concord. When Aúdi's co-wives threatened to deny him access to his clothes and children, they did not rely on notions of compensation, which are portrayed in terms of how their husband and the Pangayacu community acted inappropriately: theirs is a discourse of obligation and respect, not of compensation.

For the aggrieved women, the incident of infidelity under discussion is indicative of the perils posed to the community by sexual excess, which is synonymous with the denial of obligation and thus with the negation of society. Urarina myth suggests that concupiscence is opposed to the collective interests of the *kaj laitjíra* and ultimately to the cosmos. In their account of the mythic primordium, the Urarina regularly tell how affliction is the flip side of men's uncontrolled sexual appetite. Men are not, however, the sole monopolizers of sexual excess. Sexual desire, or *ijéricha*, is experienced by both Urarina men and women. Urarina cosmology is rife with examples of both male and female sexual surfeit, the consequences of which are mythologically deadly as well as sociologically fatal.

Bride Price in Amazonia?

In a challenging article and a book on Melanesian and Amazonian gender identities, Bruce Knauft (1997; 1999) convincingly demonstrates how the intermeshing of idioms of modernity and aspirations for commodities are key to the elaboration of masculine status and feminine propriety. According to Knauft, the primary difference in each region's gender relations lies in distinctive colonial legacies and differing patterns of kinship. Notwithstanding regional variations, Knauft contends that the political economy of kinship has become increasingly commoditized. Both regions are currently experiencing an intensified "cultural emphasis on bride price—a substantial payment tends to abrogate the necessity of ... bride service.... A large payment legitimates the marriage and effectively compensates the bride's parents for their loss" (Knauft 1997, 248).

Though relevant in many ways, Knauft's analysis of Amazonian marriage is partial, and his emphasis on bride price quite misleading. This shortcoming can be traced to Knauft's uncritical acceptance of the classical "compensatory" interpretation of bride service, which suggests that men serve their in-laws to establish rights in prospective wives. In the anthropological literature, bride price has usually been defined as a payment in the form of a valuable asset (money, goods, property, and so forth) made by—or on behalf of—a prospective husband to the bride's family. Yet, as I have argued, affinity in indigenous Amazonia is largely not valorized through the transfer of rights to resources or through the circulation of gifts.

In Knauft's estimation, senior men's control over the resources of their sons-in-law is diminishing in Amazonia. If older men can no longer "command younger men's cash as they were once able to command their labour" (Knauft 1997, 244), how then can we account for the purported growth in Amazonian bride price in the first place? Moreover, what role do women—themselves "desirous of trade goods" (Knauft 1997, 241)—play in fostering the commoditization of marriage in Amazonia? Knauft is right to emphasize that cash and commodities are increasingly tied to male prestige, yet he fails to explore how they are also important for the establishment and maintenance of female prestige. While Knauft readily acknowledges recent works demonstrating how women's influence over domestic, socioeconomic, and religious affairs "complicates" if not "counteracts" ideologies of masculine control in Amazonia (see, for example, Jean Jackson 1992; Seymour-Smith 1991), he pays little attention to how in fact women actually contest men's efforts at exercising control.

Notwithstanding the occasional report attesting to the incidence of "bride price" in lowland South America (Marcoy 1873, 3: 45; Steinen 1894, 434; Goldman 1963, 145; Rivière 1969, 165; Harner 1973, 199; Dole 1984, 52), it remains to be seen whether the processes underpinning the commodification of social life have in fact led to the widespread appearance of bride-price *prestations* in Amazonia. Bride-wealth transactions are not very common among the Urarina. The occasional item that is exchanged between the groom and his wife's parents stresses circuits of transaction that span beyond Urarina society. These goods include imported fabric, needles, clothes, chickens, batteries, shotgun cartridges, metal cooking utensils, and alcohol. In contrast, women's matrimonial exchanges involve palm-fiber wealth, which emphasizes customary practices and stress continuities to the sacred past. Knauft's point that the arrangement of marriages in Amazonia and Melanesia has lead to the intensification of obligations between newly married couples is well taken (1997, 248; see also Gell 1999). Nevertheless, his use of the term bride price does not effectively capture the transformed "quality of relationships" in Amazonia (Dean 1998a).

Evaluating the Obligations of Marriage

Through an evaluation of the politics of marriage in the context of a bride-service society, this chapter has emphasized the extent to which access to women and the control over their sexuality is deemed problematic. Conjugal disputes in bride-service societies are not just about men fighting over women. Urarina communal relations are informed by a gender hierarchy, which is reinforced by a discourse that portrays women as mere objects of exchange. Yet I have illustrated that this does not prevent women from asserting claims to men as their legitimate partners (see Seymour-Smith 1991, 641).

Rather than interpreting Aúdi's adultery in terms of his competition over access to women, I explored how this incident underscores women's marital interests. Aúdi's infidelity is significant because it illustrates the stakes that women in bride-service societies have in marriage. Review of Urarina ideology and practice demonstrates that women like Aruba and Lekiná are more than willing to "fight" over men to be their husbands. However, this does not preclude women from being discursively portrayed as entities to be exchanged in the course of marriage. This discursive practice is embedded in Urarina headman politicking, which privileges men's role in coordinating alliances among disparate longhouses. But the "events" in the dispute over Aúdi's behavior makes it clear that the orchestration of marriage necessarily collapses the somewhat illusory public/private dichotomy, thus enabling women—to varying degrees—to determine their own fates (see S. Moore 1983, 106).

7

Multiple Regimes of Value

Unequal Exchange and the Circulation of Palm-Fiber Wealth

Turning from the theoretical and practical implications of the objectification of women in marriage, this chapter reviews the cultural significance of women's objective wealth, namely the products of their weaving palm-bast fibers. I examine the creation, circulation, and consumption of women's palm-fiber wealth, or cloth currency, as it accrues value through its circulation within multiple regimes of exchange, ranging from the transmission of inalienable possessions to the quotidian flow of commodities. Woven palm-fiber goods mediate between overlapping spheres of exchange. At times, they can profitably be seen as inalienable possessions: there are specific social contexts when the circulation of palm-bast wealth is restricted to within Urarina descent groups. On other occasions, palm-fiber wealth items occupy the other end of the spectrum of exchangeability: the commodity state. However, Urarina palm-fiber wealth is assessed not simply in terms of ideal types (for example, commodity versus inalienable possession), but rather as exchangeable valuables within specific historical and social milieu. Akin to Thomas's (1991) account of Pacific Islanders' "entangled objects," I highlight the ways in which palm-fiber cloth is socially consequential as it circulates through various regimes of value (see also M. Jamieson 1999). This entails an examination of the ways in which palm-fiber wealth "can, must, or cannot be circulated. This is a matter not just of singularity or uniqueness" Thomas argues, "but of context and narrative" (1991, 100).

Objects—both soft and hard—can enhance personal prestige and the authority of elites. Broadly conceived, cloth encompasses all articles made from fibers, threads, tree bark, and leaves (Weiner 1992, 157). In contemporary Amazonia, this includes, among other things, Yagua cord hammocks, embroidered Shipibo fabric, Tukano bark cloth, and Urarina palm-fiber wealth (for example, cloth, net bags, and plaited palm-leaf mats and roof thatching) (fig. 7.1). In some cultural contexts, cloth serves as the primary medium of exchange, supplanting "hard" valuables such as metal coinage, iron bars, or shells (Weiner 1985). This phenomenon has been well documented for the Andes, where Murra has underscored the importance of textiles in securing Inca state formation (1991, 275–302). In contrast to other regions of Peru, such as the coastal Paracas culture area, little is known about the pre-Columbian, colonial, or postcolonial significance of cloth in Amazonian social life. This is true in spite of the fact that textiles—both indigenous and imported—have functioned for centuries as forms of currency, particularly in the various forms of debt peonage found in the upper Amazon. In terms of the scale of commodification, the circulation of Urarina textiles is still relatively limited. The production of woven palm-fiber wealth in other words has not undergone the definitive shift from "folk art to global commodity" (McGuckin 1997).

The views Spanish colonists in sixteenth-century America held regarding indigenous social status and hierarchies were shaped by their assessment of local apparel, use of precious stones, and personal bodily adornments (MacCormack 1999, 123). Early colonial accounts offer some tantalizing leads regarding the social life of clothing. For example, writing of his expedition to the Ucayali (1557), Salinas de Loyola described the attire of the local inhabitants by saying that "in the ornament of their persons they represent themselves to be lords" (T. Myers 1974, 140; see also T. Myers 1997). I suspect that a comparative analysis of Amazonian exchange of palm-fiber cordage will reveal how it is an elementary form of *cloth* wealth whose value is linked to the production and circulation of ritual vestments.

The extent to which cloth facilitated political hierarchy among the pre-conquest fluvial chiefdoms of Amazonia, such as the Tupí-Guarani-speaking Omagua and Cocama, remains poorly understood. Like the Maina and Záparoan peoples, the ancient Cocama and Omagua fabricated palm-fiber cloth. Men previously donned long cotton tunics (*cushmas*) adorned with painted or woven colored designs. Women's attire consisted of knee-length cotton skirts and on occasion small capes. As with other Tupían peoples, the Cocama and Omagua feather-work were their most conspicuous body adornments. Ligatures, such as waistbands, bracelets, armlets, and anklets, were made of cordage or braided hair. The Cocama exchanged palm-fiber cloth, tunics, and cloaks with their neighbors (Steward and Métraux 1963, 694, 697).

In regions bordering the Chambira Basin, cotton weaving predominated among the Tupían, Cahuapanan, and Panoan peoples of the upper Marañón and middle Huallaga. The Arawakan-speaking Piro and Machiguenga, as well as the Panoan-speaking Conibo and Shipibo, collected wild cotton for weaving their *cushmas*. Along the upper Amazon and its tributaries, cotton

Fig. 7.1. Urarina woman weaving palm fibers with back-strap loom

was less frequently used, while along the Río Negro, it was virtually absent. Cotton was utilized sparingly among the western Tucanoans (Lowie 1963, 24; Steward 1963, 522; Steward and Métraux 1963, 544, 568; Farabee 1922, 9, 57, 82, 97). Similarly, the use of cotton—in comparison with palm fiber—appears quite limited among the Urarina. The nineteenth-century explorer Maw found that cotton, though present throughout the *montaña*, was most plentiful at Lamas, Tarapoto, and Sapo. It was routinely used for making sackcloth (*lienzo*) or *tocuyo* (coarse cotton fabric). According to Maw, the finest and most expensive cotton came from the Ucayali and was "as soft as silk" (1829, 98). In Moyobamba, indigenous peoples used it to pay their tribute (Reyes Flores 1999, 150).

By the 1840s traveling merchants from Chachapoyas, Cajamarca, and Moyobamba were involved in the regional distribution of *tocuyo* cloth, which circulated in exchange for food, labor power, and forest produce, such as sarsaparilla (*Smilax officinorum* or *Esimlax oblicuata*) (Izquierdo Ríos 1976, 64; Roux 1994, 97). The British naval officers Smyth and Lowe confirmed the centrality of cloth in early nineteenth-century commerce in the upper Amazon. At the mission of Sarayacu (founded by the Franciscans in 1791 on the Ucayali River), they noted that the priest "had commenced a trade with Tabatainga and San Pablo, sending cloth woven by the Indians of Sarayacu; and receiving in exchange iron, beads, cottons, and a few trifling luxuries for his own table" (1836, 195; see also Marcoy 1873; T. Myers 1990).

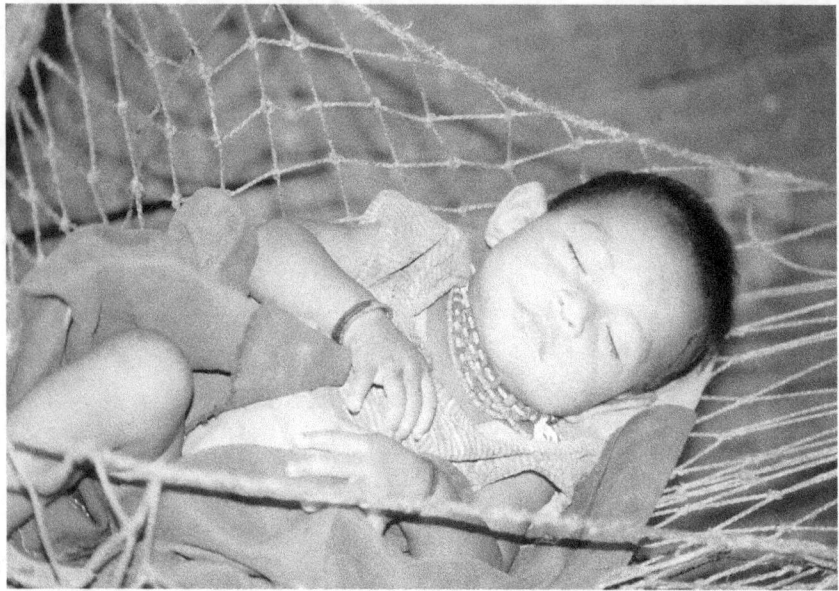

Fig. 7.2. Urarina baby sleeping in hammock

Many of the nineteenth-century explorers of the region commented on how cloth served as a basic form of payment for services rendered, such as oaring and river guiding (Guernsey 1870, 353; Osculati 2000; Litvak 1984, 125 n. 1; Roux 1994, 157–58).

Aguaje palm-bast (*ajlaá, Mauritia flexuosa, Mauritia minor,* or swamp palm) and the frond spears of the Chambira palm (*Astrocaryum chambira, A. munbaca, A. tucuma,* also known as *Cumare* or *Tucum*)[1] have been used for centuries by the Urarina to make cordage, net bags (*siiraá*), and hammocks (*amaá*), and to weave fabric (*ejlá*) (fig. 7.2). In addition to its appearance in the Chambira Basin, reports of the use and widespread circulation of chambira palm-bast cordage have appeared in Amazonia, such as among the contemporary Bora of Peru (Vormisto 2002). Other bast fibers have been botanically important: for instance, pita flora vegetable fibers, from a tropical plant related to the pineapple (*Aechmea magdalenae*) provided the basis for the production of woven cords and accessories. In the Ecuadorian Amazon it was used to pay tribute until the legislature eliminated this practice in 1847 (Osculati 2000, 126). Along the upper Río Tiquié, balls of tough cordage were made and exchanged with other indigenous groups for curare (Lowie 1963, 24). Balls of bast cordage were also an important item of exchange in the Vaupés-Caquetá area (Goldman 1963, 779) and were ritually exchanged among the Nambiquára (see Leví-Strauss 1978b, 303).

Appropriately deemed "a currency of sorts" (Weiner 1992, 3), the production, circulation, and consumption of cloth is essential to the reproduction of all societies. The Urarina are no different in this regard. The elaboration and circulation of palm-fiber wealth immortalizes the past, constitutes the present, and facilitates an imagined future. Palm-fiber goods are symbolically significant for the certification of personal and collective histories. They function as the objectified means for conveying the events of the past into present time. As such, the knowledge surrounding the production of woven palm-fiber goods, and their place within the cosmos, forms an integral part of the Urarinas' stock of inalienable wealth.

Taking intellectual purchase from Mauss's (1967) designation of specific objects as *immeubles* (for example, Samoan fine mats, Maori cloaks, and Northwest Coast Coppers), Weiner (1992) developed the notion of inalienable wealth in an effort to understand those sacred objects that condense historicity into statements about present circumstances (see also Watt 1986 and Liep 1986; Godelier 1999; and Hendon 2000).[2] Items of inalienable wealth are deeply imbued with affective qualities that emphasize the value of keeping them circulating within the family or descent group (Weiner 1985, 224; Folkman Curasi, Price, and Arnould 2004). As Thomas explains, inalienability is an important analytical construct precisely "because it incorporates the sense of singular relations between people and things—in effect between people with respect to things" (1991, 36). As immobile items of value, the goods that constitute palm-fiber wealth emphasize the Urarinas' relationship to the cosmos and historicity. The most extreme form of restricted transmission of palm-fiber wealth is apparent in Urarina mortuary practices.

Notwithstanding their symbolic load emphasizing inalienability, palm-fiber goods are used to expand networks of exchange that span well beyond Urarina society. As such, debt peonage and handicraft production should not be seen as independent spheres of activity but rather as inextricably linked. Palm-fiber goods have long been an important item of exchange between different local Urarina longhouse groups, as well as between linguistic or ethnic groups—such as the neighboring Omurana, Kandozi, Jivaroan, and Tupian peoples (see Requena 1991b, 29–30).

The circulation of woven palm-fiber goods, such as cloth (*cachibanco* or *cachihuango* from Loretano Spanish), net bags (*shigra* from Pastaza Quechua), and hammocks (*hamaca* from Taino), has facilitated the introduction of trade goods in the upper Amazon for well over three hundred years. Since at least the seventeenth-century establishment of the Jesuit missions of Maynas, palm-fiber goods appear to have been significant objects of exchange among the region's indigenous, European, and *mestizo* populations. In 1686, for instance, Samuel Fritz, the renowned Jesuit missionary, encountered Arawakan Manao from the middle Amazon trading among the Yurimagua. The trade consisted of "small plates of gold, vermillion, *yuca* graters, hammocks of *cacivance* [chambira] with various kinds of clubs and shields, that they work very curiously" (Fritz 1922, 62–63; Uriarte 1951, 213). Fritz, the famous curate from Bohemia, was reported to have donned a short cassock made from palm-bast, and his footwear was "hempen" (1922, 80).

Conditioned by the exigencies of the region's various commercial economies, Urarina palm-bast goods have become commodities—objects whose socially relevant characteristic is their condition of exchangeability. The commodity state is never terminal: objects are capable of moving in and out of the commodity condition (Kopytoff 1992, 64–91; see also Levi 1992, 20–21). As Sahlins has argued, "Use-value is not less symbolic or less arbitrary than commodity-value. For 'utility' is not a quality of the object but a significance of the objective qualities" (1991, 281).

The commodity context often brings together people with different beliefs about the value of what is being transacted. Among the Urarina, there are remarkably divergent expectations regarding the nature of transcultural exchange. These discrepancies are perhaps most apparent in the context of what I deem "relations of unequal exchange" (or glossed more broadly as debt peonage). Appadurai's expression—"regimes of value"—is useful here because it suggests that the circulation of palm-fiber goods is not predicated on a complete sharing of cultural assumptions or interests among transactors (1992, 15, 57; cf. F. Myers 2001). Drawing on Georg Simmel's elaboration of the nature of economic value, Appadurai has persuasively assessed the circumstances under which objects circulate through multiple regimes of value. This perspective provides us with a grasp on the various ways "in which desire and demand, reciprocal sacrifice and power interact to create economic value in specific social situations" (Appadurai 1992, 4).

Taken from the producer's vantage point, bast net bags, hammocks, and palm-fiber fabric are infused with deep cosmological import, while from the *mestizo* trader's perspective, these objects' utilitarian potential is foregrounded. Evaluation of Urarina women's handiwork enables me to begin charting the voyage of palm-fiber wealth as it flows through the multiple regimes of value accompanying ritual exchange, bestowal, barter, and commodification.

Women and the Production of Palm-Fiber Wealth

Weaving is a sine qua non of Urarina female identity: the authority of elder women, or *ené biña*, is legitimated through the control of palm-fiber cloth and the technical knowledge necessary for its production. Knowledge of weaving is transmitted matrilineally. Skill in aesthetic elaboration distinguishes women's palm-fiber cloth production. Mastery of this productive activity is critical in discourse regarding rights and obligations among women.

During their rite of menarche (*ña latúa*), pubescent females are taught the processes of harvesting, preparing, and weaving (*jisiñaá*) palm fibers. Menarche includes ritual commemoration (see Guss 1990, 228; Chevalier 1982, 294n.; Fritz 1922, 48), which is achieved through cloistering the novitiate in a menstruation hut (*jatá*), through depilation (*latúa*), and through dietary strictures—all of which are accounted for in stories I heard of the origins of lunation. Acquisition of weaving knowledge is an essential part of female social maturation. The skillful weaver is celebrated in Urarina society as one who fashions objects that bind the living to one another and to the dead as well as objects that can be bartered for trade goods (fig. 7.3).

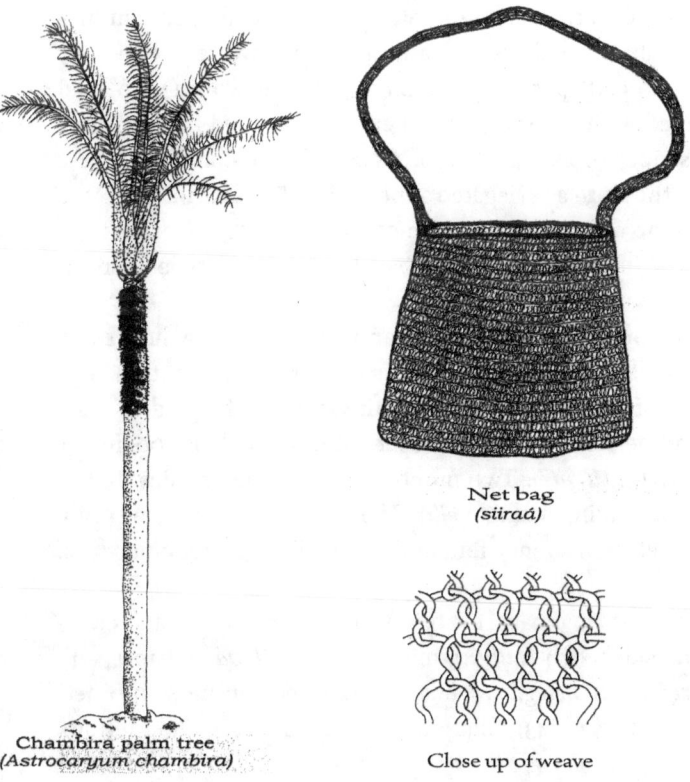

Fig. 7.3. Chambira palm tree and woven net bag

As commodities, Urarina woven palm-fiber goods become valuable through the labor that they "congeal" (Marx and Engels 1978, 307, 316). The production of palm-bast goods demands extraordinary investments of materials and labor power within each female productive unit. Once harvested, the palm frond's soft fibers must be detached from the woody portion of the frond and then dried in the sun. The desiccated strands are painstakingly twisted into fine cordage. Using vegetable dyes (roots, leaves, bark,[3] seeds, and fruits), the strands are either dyed shades of black (*genipa*; or *kutí* in Urarina), red (*Bixa orellana*, better known as *achiote*; *hiáne* in Urarina), or left their natural cream color (Castillo 1958, 14; Kramer 1979, 102–3).

In the regions bordering the eastern Andean slopes, the horizontal loom predominates, the back-strap or belt loom being the most frequent example. One end of the loom is attached to a tree or house post, the other to the weaver's belt (Lowie 1963, 24). With the help of weaving swords, textiles made on the belt-strap loom have an ordinary in-and-out weave (Steward and Métraux 1963, 577). Woven on back-strap looms, palm-bast cloth—known as *ejlá*—consists of unbalanced warp-faced plain weaves. The length of *ejlá* fabric varies between four and ten feet. The width of each section is usually about two and one-half feet. Most palm-bast cloth I collected[4] varied between ten and twelve warps per centimeter and four wefts per centimeter. Fine palm-fiber fabric may have as many as twenty-two to twenty-four warps and six to eight wefts per centimeter. *Ejlá* fabric is woven with dyed palm-fiber warp filled with undyed palm-fiber weft disposed in alternately colored bands or stripes (*dardarárkuaka*). As such, the colored warps are accentuated, giving the cloth a variegated appearance. To make net bags, the weaver will use a "loop and twist" variation of looping (often referred to as knotless netting). The first two rows of the bast bag employ a type of cross-knit looping.

Over a period of a month or two, a woman will spend a few hours at a time weaving a bolt of palm-bast fabric. This occurs in conjunction with ongoing production of other woven goods, cultivation of the gardens, caring for children, and performing other household tasks such as cooking or making cassava beer (*bardiguë*). Two months or more may be devoted to the whole process of making a single *ejlá*. The actual time spent weaving has been estimated between twenty-four and thirty-six hours (Kramer 1979, 103).[5]

The Urarina have used palm-bast fabric to make sleeping mats, cushion covers, women's skirts (*sayá*, *ujuú*), men's trousers (*lebári*), capes, and mosquito nets[6] (*irigarí*, or *hetegáti*, which refers to cotton mosquito net) (see Tessmann 1930, 487, 442–43; Villarejo 1988, 209; Steward and Métraux

1963, 575). Contemporary use of palm fiber is restricted to fabric, net bags, hammocks, and pillows (*binjáu*). Urarina bedding consists of two widths of palm-fiber cloth sewn together. Chambira palm-bast fabric is preferred for children's bedding because urine rots aguaje palm-fiber cloth. Women also make fire fans (*iñarü*) and roof thatching (*ejléle tukunujuí, banaú*). Men's weaving includes hats (*asiyuü*) from *támishi* lianas (*jijchú, Carludovica trigona*) and a variety of baskets (*afuái, amádi*), such as the palm frond basket (*afuái*) used for transporting garden produce (*kiraurí*, or *capillejo* in Spanish; *afuailafuídi*, or *panero* in Spanish). Apart from ligatures, clothing is now made from imported fabric (*kajiú*) or obtained ready-made, often in the form of cast-off or second-hand clothing in various states of decay.

Encoding Value: The Cosmological and Social Import of Palm-Fiber Wealth

Urarina palm-fiber wealth items attain their sacred attributes through cosmological referents, as well as through the special conditions surrounding their production, which include the observance of tabus during manufacture. Palm bast plays a prominent role in many Urarina myths. Chambira fibers (*disíñe*), for instance, were employed by the supreme being Kuánra to fashion the bristles of the first peccaries. The collection of aguaje (*ajlá*) bast and chambira fiber emphasizes gender complementarity: men typically accompany women in their forays to gather these valuable fibers. Their collection is bound to the valorization of geography, in particular, the negative symbolization of the *aguajal*—the palm swamp (*ajláca*). Menstruating and pregnant women are precluded from these spiritually charged spaces. Palm swamps are dangerous loci where spiritual affliction can enter the womb and either deform or cast out nascent life.

The cosmological veracity of Urarina palm-fiber wealth depends in part on color schema and geometric patterning. The colors used are based on the tripartite contrast between black (*ijchuái*), red (*lanajái*), and white (*sumajái*), colors that play an important role in Urarina beliefs and practice.[7] Urarina palm-fiber goods employ patterning that relies on juxtaposing parallel bands of opposed colors. This "parallelism" contrasts with the serpentine or geodesic designs of Urarina ritual ceramic ware (*miráe*) that is used to ingest hallucinogens (*Banisteriopsis caapi* or *iñunú*, and *Brugmansia suaveolens* or *ajcaá*). Symbolic parallelism is evident in other aesthetic realms, such as in women's attire (opposition between red blouses and dark or black wraparound skirts), in the parallel layout of the longhouse's domestic platforms, and in men's ritual arm-scarification, which leaves stratified bands of scar tissue encircling the forearm.

The value of Urarina woven palm-fiber goods is enhanced by these objects' ability to "encode kinship and political histories, making the past valid for successive generations" (Schneider and Weiner 1986, 179). The production of woven palm-fiber goods is imbued with varying degrees of an aesthetic attitude, which draws its authentication from referencing the Urarinas' primordial past. Urarina mythology attests to the centrality of weaving and its role in engendering Urarina society. The myth of postdiluvial creation accords women's weaving knowledge a pivotal role in Urarina social reproduction.

In the Urarinas' creation myth, desire is linked to regeneration, but it is also seen as the cause of affliction, the flipside of rebirth. While urging sexual continence, a motif prevalent in Urarina mythology, the creation myth recounts the acquisition of cultural knowledge, in particular, the ability to weave and to give birth. This knowledge was imparted to women by animals. In the case of weaving, it was transmitted by Ajidi, the hummingbird, and in the case of giving birth, this knowledge was conveyed by Kajtí, the brown capuchin monkey (*Cebus apella*). The narrative's final episode revolves around the denial of sexual reproduction in favor of asexual propagation. Given the transformative power of desire, this is an unworkable solution.

Inverting a prior condition of presumed cultural ignorance, the woman weaves a child from cotton (*ijche*), which is denied paternal recognition. Returning to the metaphor of burial, the woman digs a birthing hole, a prepartum practice that continues to this day. The denial of paternal recognition is followed by sexual intercourse. However, the man's transgression of the post-partum sexual tabu, a belief still practiced, gives rise to fatal immobility.[8] The myth can be read as a commentary on human regeneration and affliction, the result of a failure to curb human desire. Toxic pests and human disease are the consequence of human, and in particular male, shortcomings. As in other myths, like the story of the origin of canoes or food gardens, Urarina hubris brings about affliction and nemesis. This point is of capital importance, for it shows that the recognition of human agency, both in cosmic and in historical terms, is fundamental to Urarina ontology.

The Urarina creation myth recounts how Kuánra, the creator god, dispatches his two daughters to Earth in an astral canoe; the eldest daughter is endowed with cultural knowledge, whereas the younger daughter is designated to be her subordinate helper (Kramer 1979, 106). The position of the two women within the dugout corresponds to the Urarinas' sense of hierarchy: the uncultured and ignorant servant (*cushéra*) is seated in the bow,

Fig. 7.4. Urarina girls and young women in canoe, Pangayacu River

a position associated with women and the less-skilled oarsman (fig. 7.4). Meanwhile, the knowledgeable woman is in the stern, a position associated with the skilled pilot. As a harbinger of her rejection by the male protagonist of the story, the knowledgeable woman is wrapped in palm-fiber cloth, symbolic of the Urarinas' mortuary practice of interring corpses wrapped in this material. Rather than accepting the woman sent him by Kuánra, the primordial man selects the ignorant servant woman. Her subsequent inability to weave palm-fiber cloth, one of the most cherished wealth items produced by women, is paradigmatic of female cultural ignorance (see Dean 1994a). Rejection of the shrouded woman in favor of marriage with the one who lacks the capacity to weave is tantamount to the denial of femininity. Without palm-fiber cloth, Urarina womanhood is culturally inconceivable.

The mythical account of the origin of palm-fiber cloth involves a widowed woman whose son-in-law severs her finger due to her ignorance regarding the skill of transforming Aguaje bast into cordage for weaving. The following version of the origin of palm-fiber cloth represents a combination of Najle-gue-kuktíri's account, which was recorded in August 1991, and Ujkuaizíri's account, which was recorded in May 1996.

The Origin of *Ejlá*

> Long ago, a son-in-law became infuriated after he learned that his mother-in-law was incapable of transforming raw palm-fiber into cordage for weaving—a skill known by all Urarina women. Hence, the son-in-law chopped off his widowed mother-in-law's finger. Crying, the widow began wandering about in a state of despair. Ajidi, the hummingbird, heard the widow's pleas for help. It transformed itself into a beautifully dressed woman. The widow told the "bird-woman" how her son-in-law had chopped off her finger and pleaded to be made whole again. Assuring the widow that she would be cured, Ajidi led the ailing woman to the palm-tree swamp (*ajláca*), where they found a pond full of tadpoles. Ajidi made the widow place her hand missing the finger in the nest of a frog (*dadi*). As a result, the widow's finger was restored to its former condition. The widowed woman asked Ajidi to instruct her how to weave palm-fiber fabric. After all, it was the woman's ignorance of this skill that prompted her son-in-law to chop off her finger and abandon her in the first place. Ajidi responded by telling the widow that weaving is not difficult: "You have to strike your abdomen [with the weaving sword]. . . . And then you will have to teach ten others how to weave." Simulating the sound made by a back-strap loom, the hummingbird-woman began striking the trunk of the Aguaje palm tree. Following this a tremendous bolt of palm-fiber fabric unfurled from the tree. It was from this bolt of palm-fiber cloth that the widow made herself clothing. The woman took the roll of palm-bast fabric back to her longhouse. But the women of the widow's longhouse became *kujtieyah*—very envious. They asked how it was possible for the palm-fiber cloth to have been made so rapidly. However, the widow did not want to reveal what had happened. As a result, the women of the longhouse decided to make cassava beer and to get the widow drunk so that they could ask her about the mysterious *ejlá*. When the widow became drunk, the others asked her how she made the palm-fiber fabric. She told them about Ajidi, at which point her clothing was instantly transformed back into crude aguaje fiber (*champa*), leaving the widow naked.

In the account of the origin of *ejlá*, the woman's bloody stump is rejuvenated when the widow places her mutilated hand in the mud-pool "nests" of the giant South American aquatic frog. The woman makes bands of cloth by striking the aguaje palm with an *ubiñya*, a weaving sword (typically made by men from *cumaceva* wood [*Caesalpinia echinata*?]). A number of Urarina myths describe a widowed weaver's sexual relations with Ajkaguiño—the water boa—an important underworld figure in Urarina cosmology. In the narrative, the widow uses her *ubiñya* to call Ajkaguiño by striking it against the water. In yet another myth, the *cumaceva* weaving sword is transformed into an electric eel, a cosmological analog of the men's ceremonial stave, or *ujtiya*. The weaving sword also figures as the mortal weapon in the Urarinas' mythical account of the death of the jaguar mother and the origins of cannibalism, which is closely associated with the Urarinas' rivals, the Jivaroan-speaking peoples known as the Bajkagá.

Palm-fiber wealth is valuable not only as a marker of the Urarinas' sacred past, but also as an important medium for socially relevant exchanges. The role of exchange in fostering sociality in Amazonia has long been recognized. Echoing Mauss's claim that to trade "man must first lay down the spear" (1967, 80), Lévi-Strauss, for instance, suggested that "when a meeting between two [Nambikwara] groups is conducted peacefully, it leads to reciprocal exchange of gifts; strife is replaced by barter" (1978b, 303; see also Rivière 1984, 81–82).

While I have no evidence suggesting that palm-bast wealth figures in the resolution of conflict, its circulation and the bestowal of palm-fiber goods is integral to the fulfillment of social obligations and duties attendant to the climacteric events of life: birth, menarche, marriage, and death. Certain Urarina rituals that reaffirm individual and collective continuities with the sacred past necessitate the exchange of indigenous fabrics rather than imported ones. Palm-bast goods accentuate sociality, particularly at times of life crises: they authenticate cosmological beginnings, express common ancestry and heritage, and index life histories. Inter- and intra-generational transmission of women's palm-fiber wealth instantitiates Urarina collective identity.

Palm-bast goods are signifiers of social identity: they are emblematic of age, status, and gender. Hammock use is limited to infants (*kananeáma*) and to mature, married men (*kijcháma*). Women do not customarily use hammocks nor do they carry hunting pouches. These small, finely woven bast bags are an important accoutrement of hunting and a symbol of masculinity for socially mature and established men. Made by one's wife, this bag is worn around the neck during the hunt and is used to carry talismans (*talla* or *pusanga*) and the occasional shotgun cartridge (see also Farabee 1922, 83; Lowie 1963, 21; Steward and Métraux 1963, 603). The gendered production and consumption of palm-fiber goods distinguishes men's and women's social identities. This is readily apparent in the establishment of marriage. The bride is expected to weave or provide the newlyweds' palm-bast fabric bedding, as well as her husband's hunting-magic purse and eventually a hammock. Women are also responsible for making cordage for shamanic vesture—shell necklaces and headdresses—as well as items indispensable to the hunt—blow-dart quiver straps—and the ubiquitous woven net bag used to transport food crops.

Large net bags are at once supremely functional and intimately associated with sustenance. This association is acknowledged in Urarina popular mythology, which alludes to the transmogrification of the net-bag into Kiráe, the two-toed sloth (*Choloepus didactylus*)—a reliable, if somewhat tough, source of meat. The most valued and labor-intensive palm-fiber good is *ejlá*, fabric that the Urarina employ to swaddle the young, to blanket lovers, and to shroud the dead. By adumbrating the centrality of palm-fiber fabric in one particular aspect of sociality—death—I will demonstrate the importance that bestowal of palm-fiber goods plays in demarcating social relationships and privileges.

Death and the Circulation of Wealth

Following death, the corpse is sewn up in a palm-fiber shroud and then placed in a coffin hewed from a discarded canoe (fig. 7.5). The sepulchral canoe is interred in a shallow grave within a charnel house. Located in the forest some distance from the longhouse, the cemetery is a miniature replication of the *ludéri* (fig. 7.6). It is only distinguished from the house of the living by its distance from the river and by its weedy overgrowth. Above each burial mound (*ajtane kúbai*), a small rostrum is erected, having been modeled after the sleeping platforms of the longhouse. Here we note the final trajectory in the circulation of Urarina inalienable wealth, which underscores Georges Bataille's observation that "it is only through loss that glory and honour are linked to wealth" (1985, 122).

The deceased's sleeping mat is placed over the mortuary rostrum, along with gender-specific objects: ceramic cooking vessels and firewood for women; and ritual garb—including parrot-feather (*guacamayo*, *Ara* sp.?) headdresses, harpy eagle fans, shell chest bands, and wooden ceremonial staves—for men. Men's inalienable possessions are deposited in a ritual chest or *maleta* (Spanish for suitcase) called a *kamelá* (fig. 7.7). Made from woven shebon palm-bast, this hamper houses shamanic appurtenances: bird feather diadems (*ajleirjíkumaai*); jaguar (*januládi kajtí*) and peccary teeth (*ubana kajtí*) necklaces; shell, nut, and animal claw breast-bands; harpy eagle fans; and sacred ceramics used to consume hallucinogens. In addition to *ejlá*, women's inalienable wealth includes beads (*didiá*), bracelets (*bijiléru*), and necklaces.

Above: Fig. 7.5. Transporting the dead (shrouded in woven palm-fiber fabric)

Left: Fig. 7.6. Urarina cemetery, Chambira River Basin

Ritual chest made from woven
Shebon palm bast
(**Kamelà**)

0   10 cm

Fig. 7.7. Urarina ritual chest

Excavation and burial appear in many Urarina social contexts, including birth, gardening, burial, and rebirth. Adumbrative of loss and regeneration, the motif of burial is prominent in the Urarinas' myth of creation, which begins with the interment of the Creator God's son, Kuánra Kájlaui. The creation story also recounts how the Good Samaritan concealed himself in the ground in anticipation of encountering strangers at an abandoned forest encampment and concludes by recounting how the first Urarina woman dug a birthing hole for her child made from entwined cotton. Interment symbolizes the final leg in the voyage of palm-fiber fabric through the possible trajectories of inalienability and/or commodification. Burial of what can be deemed "personal" *ejlá* fabric defies utilitarian notions of consumption and commodification and supports Bataille's (1985) insistence on linking value to loss and sacrifice. However, at death, certain items of *ejlá* fabric are distributed within the deceased's immediate network, affirming notions of utilitarian and collective consumption and thus solidifying the social bonds that continue to link the living to one another and to the dead.

The Urarina do not have much in the way of heritable property. In general, dispensation of a deceased woman's estate, including most importantly her palm-fiber fabrics and bead necklaces, are administered along matrilines, though secondary (non-sororal) co-wives may also inherit fabrics. Disputes may emerge over counterclaims to the deceased woman's *ejlá* fabrics, as I witnessed on a number of occasions among the Pangayacu longhouses. Nevertheless, certain possessions, such as personal sleeping mats and fire fans (*iñarú*), are so constitutive of the deceased's personhood and identity that they are ultimately inalienable (see Radin 1982, 959ff.). When not interred, sacred inalienable vessels for hallucinogen consumption pass from the deceased male to his son(s). These objects are so intimately bound up with the deceased that they are usually removed from the sphere of exchange and inheritance and rest permanently in the ceremonial longhouse of the dead. Such items contrast with other durable personal goods, such as shotguns, weaving accoutrements, and cooking utensils, which are most often transmitted to the deceased's children, spouse, and/or siblings. On occasion, the disposition of durable goods is the source of bitter conflict.

Even though palm-fiber cloth is regularly removed from circulation through mortuary rites, Urarina palm-fiber wealth is neither completely inalienable nor fungible since it is a fundamental medium for the expression of labor and exchange. The circulation of palm-fiber wealth stabilizes a host of social relationships, ranging from marriage and fictive kinship (*compadrazco*, spiritual compeership) to perpetuating relationships with the deceased. While it is important to emphasize how palm-fiber goods circulate according to customary patterns of domestic production and consumption, this only partially captures the social life of palm-fiber wealth. By exploring the interstices of labor and exchange relations through the mediation of palm-bast goods, we see the ways in which palm-fiber wealth figures in networks of exchange that stretch beyond Urarina society.

Cloth and Commerce in Amazonia

Review of the historical role fabric has played in mobilizing labor power is helpful in discerning how palm-fiber wealth items have migrated through commoditized circuits of exchange. *Ejlá* cloth, hammocks (for adults), and bast net bags are produced by Urarina women for the acquisition of quotidian goods necessary for domestic reproduction. Urarina men and women have historically expressed desires for cultural equivalents in exchange for their hand-woven goods.

One of the most culturally significant trade items introduced by stouthearted missionaries, intrepid explorers, and extractive entrepreneurs has been imported cloth (*kajiúne*). Textiles—both indigenous and ready-made—have long served as forms of currency in the various systems of peonage characteristic of upper Amazonia. Urarina petty-commodity and handicraft production are best regarded not as separate spheres of activity but rather as intermeshed domains of activity. While an extensive survey of trade and commoditization of women's palm-fiber wealth is beyond the reach of this chapter, I historicize the interstices of labor and exchange relations as expressed through the medium of fabric. This enables me to convey a sense of the importance that both imported cloth and palm-fiber wealth have played in exchange relations over the centuries.

In small-scale Amazonian societies, like the Urarina, artistic and ritualized production and exchange of woven palm- bast goods can be assessed as enclaved economic zones, "where the spirit of the commodity enters only under conditions of massive cultural change" (Appadurai 1992, 22). In some regions of Amazonia, the "spirit" of the commodity plays a primary role in handicraft production for external markets. In Central Brazil, for instance, plaitwork is marketed among the Karajá, Xavante, Xerente, Timbira, and Kayapó. Likewise, among the Tembé of Brazil, handicraft production is a significant economic activity (Mitchell 2000). In the northern Amazon, the Tukúna sell painted bark cloth as well as hammocks and purses made of *tucum*. The Yanomami, Waiwai, Wayâna-Aparai, Waiâpi, and the upper Negro River groups market basketry. In the upper Negro region, there were two indigenous cooperatives that marketed handicrafts (Ribeiro 1989).[9]

Indigenous handicrafts have a long history in the fronts of colonial and postcolonial expansion. Palm-bast hammocks are an excellent case in point. Hammocks have been exchanged for a number of centuries among indigenous, *ribereño*, and national networks of exchange. In 1879, Orton reported that the Záparo were making their living by marketing hammocks for twenty-five cents each (1879, 171). The Záparo received iron knives for the hammocks, which were swapped with more geographically isolated peoples (Steward and Métraux 1963, 644; Figueroa 1904, 151). Yagua and Tukuna hammock trade with Europeans began in the eighteenth century during the Jesuits' presence in the region. Following national independence and the mid-nineteenth century "internationalization" of Amazonia, the commerce in hammocks increased. Hammocks were sent from the ports of Loreto, Pebas, and Tabatinga downriver to Manaus and Pará and upriver to Moyobamba. In 1851, a standard hammock fetched US$1.50 at the Peruvian-Brazilian frontier, an elaborate one was worth US$4, and hammocks with feather fringes were being sold for as much as US$30 (Seiler-Baldinger 1988, 290; Avé-Lallemant 1860 1, 114; Herndon 1952, 226). One and a half centuries later, hammocks continue to find their way into both the regional and specialized tourist markets. Throughout the lower Marañón Basin, hammocks are still an important barter item, in spite of the popularity of cloth hammocks purchased in Iquitos, Nauta, or Yurimaguas. During the 1990s, palm-bast hammocks retailed in Iquitos's artisanal markets for US$6–US$12.

Compared with other areas of Amazonia, the commodification of palm-fiber wealth among the Urarina has been considerably less pronounced. In fact, the economic importance of palm-bast woven goods has apparently declined among the Urarina (Kramer 1979, 102). Undoubtedly, this has been a result of the widespread introduction of ready-made cloth and cast-off clothing, which has rendered imported fabric a major substitute for palm-fiber clothing and mosquito nets. Nevertheless, palm-fiber wealth continues to represent an important component in the Urarinas' stock of alienable wealth, as it has for hundreds of years (cf. Quintana 1948).

In the Maynas missions (1636–1767), locally produced palm-bast mosquito nets were used by the Jesuits (Golob 1982, 42). Indigenous goods, including *lona* cloth, were regularly sent to Quito in exchange for religious paraphernalia, including paintings and communion vessels. During the eighteenth century, locally produced woven goods in the Maynas missions were varied. Among other items of trade were woven goods from the mission of Santiago de la Laguna; palm-bast net bags from Santo de Tomas in Andoas; woven and dyed fabrics from La Limpia Concepción de Cahuapanas; painted cloaks from San Joaquín de los Omaguas; hammocks, sleeping mats, and palm-bast cloth from Roamainas, San Xavier de Urarinas, San Joseph de Pinches, and San Pablo de Napeanos; woven and painted mantles (sold for four pesos each) and clothes from the Upper Marañón; and hammocks (valued at one peso each) from the Napo River (Golob 1982, 304; Magnin 1988, 481; see also Reyes Flores 1999, 151–52). At the missions, palm-fiber fabric fetched different prices according to its provenance. A yard (or *vara*) of palm-bast cloth made by the Mainas was worth two reales, Roamainas cloth was valued at three reales, and palm-bast cloth made elsewhere was valued at only one-half real (Golob 1982, 233). As recently as the 1940s, Catholic priests visiting the Urarina were presented with "heaps" of palm-fiber cloth. The surplus production of palm-fiber cloth probably antecedes the Spanish conquest, when an elaborate trade network circulated fine cotton and palm-fiber fabrics, ceramics, blowguns, venom, and salt throughout Amazonia (Kramer 1979, 102).

The Urarinas' historical reliance on trade goods finds expression in their sartorial desires. The lure of manufactured fabric has drawn Urarina men, women, and children into exchange relations with outsiders whose behavior is animated by entrepreneurial motives to profit from indigenous surplus production and forest extraction. Throughout the nineteenth century, explorers of Amazonia reported that cloth was regularly circulated by traders in return for indigenous labor power and produce. *Tocuyo* cloth served as a general equivalent or medium of barter transactions between Amazonian peoples and traders until well after the introduction of steam navigation (1850s) augmented trade and the rubber bonanza further diversified commercial exchanges in the region (Muratorio 1991, 33, 156; Scazzocchio 1978, 42; Oberem 1974, 353; Simson 1878, 507–8; Orton 1879, 176; Herndon 1952, 160; Castelnau 1850–59, 458; Smyth and Lowe 1836, 149; Maw 1829, 157). Once in the hands of local consumers, *tocuyo* was used to make garments (the customary use of which had been forced upon many by the missions and by the old system of *repartimiento de mercancías* or *repartos*) and as medium of exchange for other transactions.

In the upper Amazon, the system of *repartos* continued throughout the nineteenth century. *Repartos* involved the forced transfer of goods like manufactured cotton fabric and salt to indigenous peoples who were then required to return a fixed quantity of their produce within a stipulated time period (see Oberem 1974, 356; Orton 1879, 195). Herndon's report of the sinking of a Lagunas river boat, filled with salt and cotton cloth, as it passed the Río Tigre is an indication of mid-nineteenth century importance of cloth and salt in the commerce of Amazonia (1952, 11).

Historical reliance on imported cloth, like other commodities, such as tools, guns, and fuel, has left indigenous Amazonian societies in a quandary. Acceptance of imported cloth leads to a decline in domestic production of palm-fiber fabric for quotidian use as mosquito netting and clothing, as we see among the Shuar, Quijo, and Canelo (Harner 1973, 208; Oberem 1974, 352–53; Broseghini 1983, 93–95). This in turn has reinforced local demand for manufactured cloth, thus increasing Urarina reliance on *mestizo* intermediaries who advance cloth (and other goods) against debts.

The circulation of woven palm-bast goods is a mark of sociality, and as such it figures as a strategic point of engagement with the region's supra-local commercial economies. Differential access to cloth—both imported and locally produced—has exacerbated hierarchical tendencies within Urarina society. Civility and the possession of clothes are intimately associated in Urarina thought. Similarly, salt is conceptualized as paradigmatic of civilization, culture, and domesticity (see Hirschkind 2000). An Urarina person without adequate clothing is not merely poor, but is seen as a "savage" (*salvaje*), likened to one who consumes unsalted food.[10] This pre-social condition is referred to in the local vernacular with the highly derisive ethnonym Shimaco. In those instances involving interaction with outsiders—such as at a soccer match or communal assembly attended by neighboring *mestizo* settlers and *patrones*—the Urarina esteem imported fabric for its capacity to communicate prestige and urbane worldliness. When out visiting, *ribereño* women are usually bedizened in their Sunday finest; some in bright polyester dresses or faded cottons of various stages of deterioration. These clothes contrast sharply with the carmine colored blouses or black skirts that Urarina women typically wore throughout the 1990s.

Manufactured clothing—especially trousers—are donned by men to convey to observers that "these have been earned through hard work and expert bargaining." Similarly, women's cloth and beads, particularly the highly coveted small black, cobalt blue, and carmine glass beads, denote female prestige garnered through their associations with high-status male negotiators. In the eyes of Urarina women, cloth and beads are the ultimate status symbols. These objects convey to onlookers that their owners are allied with producers of surplus who are able to trade not only for necessities, but also for extravagant or non-utilitarian items.

Once in the hands of the Urarina, clothes are distributed according to gerontocratic criteria that favor senior men and women. Most Urarina do not have more than one or two sets or changes of clothes. Young Urarina children have very limited clothing. Given both the symbolic import and overall scarcity of ready-made garments and manufactured cloth, it is not surprising that clothes are donned until they are literally spent (*ña sejtegá kajiuné*)—worn until they are no more than threadbare rags, which are then recycled for bedding and patchwork.

A concomitant of the trade in fabric is the circulation of needles, thread, and scissors. For many households, scissors (or *terázu* from the Spanish *tijera*) are lifetime purchases and thus very important to those women who wield control over them. They typically remain in the hands of the materfamilias, who apportions bolts of cloth to junior wives, daughters, and widows according to necessity and the legitimacy of internally generated claims. Indeed, the senior women's discretionary allocation of cloth parallels the patterned circulation of clothing I have just described.

When generational and affiliative claims to cloth distribution are clear, or are at least—on the surface—meritocratic, the authority of senior women to apportion cloth is unchallenged. However, the situation becomes more complicated when women are dissatisfied with their remuneration, particularly when there are not enough consumer items to meet the demands of all those whose goods were part of the calculus of exchange. Internal dynamics of distribution inevitably break down in the event of scarcity, leading to fierce competition between aggrieved coeval women. Nevertheless, given the restraints on women in transcultural commercial negotiations, they are forced to seek alternative arrangements with men to represent their interests.

Urarina women's labor power and the commoditization of their woven palm-bast goods cannot be seen as economic isolates. The wealth items that women produce move strategically between persons and come to represent or embody the claims and relationships that link them. Women's control over the production and dispensation of palm-fiber wealth provides them with a degree of autonomy that is ultimately restricted by their total reliance on men in barter relations with non-Urarina groups and individuals (men do have a hand in the regulation of Urarina cloth currency). The commoditization of women's handicraft production has reinforced Urarina patterns of inequality, particularly with regard to gerontocratic impulses and male dominance. Reliance on mature men to manage the commercial exchange of palm-fiber wealth restricts both women's and junior men's spheres of autonomous action. Patterns of social inequality—both internally and externally generated—are mutually replicated through the circulation of handicrafts within the context of unequal exchange.

8

Mitayo, Myth, and Meaning

Alienation and the Circulation of Urarina Forest Game

This chapter examines the exchange of Urarina bushmeats (*iniñú*) or feral game commonly called *mitayo* in Peruvian Amazonia. Throughout the neotropics, indigenous societies have long exchanged vegetable produce, live animals, forest game, pelts, and feathers for other forms of wealth. In the pre-Columbian era, for example, anacondas and caiman were transported from the tropical lowlands up to the Andean city of Cuzco for use in the royal Inca menageries (Lathrap 1973). More recently, the Bará Makú of the Vaupés watershed have been reported to barter smoked forest game and wild fruits with "river Indians" in exchange for peppers, manioc bread, and tobacco (Moran 1991, 369; Silverwood-Cope 1990, 70–71; Hugh-Jones 1992, 61; see also Harner 1973, 206; Århem 1981, 53; Stearman and Redford 1992, 235–44). Subsistence-oriented and commercial-based hunting occurs concurrently among the Urarina, who regularly procure trade goods in exchange for game animals. The circulatory trajectory of Urarina forest game goes well beyond domestic consumption, terminating in some instances as pelts or as comestible goods destined for urban markets (Ferrúa Carrasco et al. 1980, 68).

By exploring the circulation of Urarina forest game within the context of peonage, this chapter highlights the conflictual tension between unfree relations of production and the exchange of goods, labor power, and knowledge, particularly hunting or *ayahuasca* shamanism. On the Chambira, hunted game is ritually, socially, and economically consequential as "true food" (Hugh-Jones 1992, 62) because it is shared within and sometimes between Urarina longhouses. Food, as Malthus pointed out, "is necessary to the existence of man" (1970, 70). But food is not simply a utilitarian necessity—for like all "things" it has symbolically charged biographies shaped by cross-cutting production, distribution, and consumption logics (see Kopytoff 1992).

Material exchanges are inherently social transactions, but material exchanges of food are unique. In "social terms," food is unlike anything else: "Food is life-giving, urgent, ordinarily symbolic of hearth and home. . . . By comparison with other stuff, food is more readily, or more necessarily, shared" (Sahlins 1972, 215; see also Lévi-Strauss 1969, 33). Instead of having narrowly conceived material natures—as in the "cost-benefit" approach of current optimal-foraging theorists who rely on outputs of labor or energy as a gauge of value—forest game animals are seen within the full social context of their total relational dimensions. To this end, I illustrate how bushmeat circulation involves "a relation of internal and external" (namely longhouse versus *mestizo*) corresponding to what Thomas has called "the entanglement of a kinship economy and petty commodity production" (1993, 134; 1991; see also Hugh-Jones 1992, 51).

As food objects whose distribution and consumption have potent implications for human socialization, hunted game is idealized by the Urarina in ways comparable to the attitudes they hold toward inalienable possessions. Like all possessions, inalienable wealth items do eventually enter the marketplace—yet their hegemony is never more than "partial and limited" (Wiener 1994, 401). Indeed, forest game is regularly exchanged with *mestizo* traders and labor bosses, or *anazairi*, as the Urarina designate them. Bushmeats are traded for objects the Urarina say are *niya cahuatua*—"things of value."

Personhood, Society and the Exchange of Forest Game

The circulation of forest game facilitates the construction of Urarina personal identity (hunter/shaman, distributor, and consumer) and fosters the collective reproduction of society. Hunters, hosts, and consumers of game are reciprocally defined through their mutual implication in the exchange, display, and consumption of forest game. The exchange of bushmeats is epitomized by strategic action informed by cultural conceptions of reciprocal food sharing (*siya lenunejké*), social precedence, and consumerism. Many Urarina life cycle ceremonies include stringent dietary regulations regarding the consumption of forest game. Pubescent females refrain from eating forest game during their menarchial rites of cloistering, whereas men undergoing rituals intended to enhance the efficacy of their blowguns and the potency of their darts tipped with curare (*virádi*) are prohibited from eating anything but the game they have personally bagged.

In the conventional system of *mitayo*, people on the Chambira are involved in hunting and production relationships with *patrones* and traders. These relations of labor exploitation or *patronazco* are embedded in durable familial and affinal ties centering on the domus. Because of the defaunation accompanying the episodic boom and bust pattern of petty-commodity extraction,[1] Urarina hunting and food sharing have been transformed: household circulation and consumption of relatively "scarce" goods like bushmeats have undergone a series of internal contradictions. One of the ways the Urarina resist the alienation accompanying the commoditization of social life is by ideologically discouraging trade in culturally prized forest game and fish. The Urarinas' creation story can be read as indicative of the perils of exchange, especially corresponding to the refusal to recognize the social imperatives accompanying *prestation*. In this regard, Hill provides a provocative explanation of the symbolic importance of Wakuénai mythical narratives recounting poisoning, which he views as "a disturbance of the horizontal dimension of exchange relations between groups of people that results from a failure to mediate between 'we people here' and 'those other (i.e., fish) people there'" (1993a, 189). Clearly, fish-poisoning expeditions involve collective efforts, and their orchestration elicits vexing questions regarding the distribution of the catch. In the Urarinas' creation story, this issue is circumvented by Kuánra Kájlaui's use of a technology—*sudiríji* or the spear—that stresses individual effort and expertise.

Mauss held that exchange relations are inherently moral relations: things transacted stand synecdochially for a part of the self. In *Essai sur le don, forme archäique de l'echange* [1923–24] Mauss noted that the native peoples of Samoa and New Zealand believe that *prestations*, especially of forest game, embody a spirit like the *mana* of humans, which they call *hau* (1967, 8). For Mauss, the existence of a spirit in the *thing* was what compelled the recipient to return it. In rejecting the total break between *persons* and *things*, Mauss challenged the object-subject division implicit in classical liberal economic theory. As a result, Mauss's phenomenological approach to exchange is well suited for understanding Urarina beliefs about the transubstantiation of people into animals and animals into people.

Reliance on hunted game is a characteristic distinguishing the Urarina from the neighboring Cocama and *ribereño* peoples, among whom fishing predominates (Quintana 1948, 280). For the Urarina, hunting is an essential aspect of all forest-based pursuits, including fishing, lumbering, and scavenging for medicinal and utilitarian plants. Hunting figures as a prominent feature of everyday talk. The Urarinas' imagery of alienation is refracted through elaborate hunting narratives. In some contexts, these narratives can be "read" as indigenous commentaries on the malevolence and perils associated with the commodification of social life. Local resistance to the commoditization of forest game finds expression in Urarina bestiaries, particularly those tales dealing with hunting game animals, which are revered as venerable "gifts" from the demiurge Kuánra (see also Århem 1981, 197).

Comprising a magnificent corpus of moralizing tales about real and mythical creatures,[2] Urarina bestiaries reveal a clear injunction against avarice and *mestizo* "poaching." The Urarina say the following items were created by the *mestizo* God Anazairi Kuánra for *mestizo* consumption: pigs, ducks, rice, squash, apples, bananas, potatoes, chickens, and beans. In contrast, Urarina demiurgic creation included cassava, plantains, sugar cane, tapir, peccary, paca, monkeys, and capybara exclusively for the subsistence of the Kachá—the Urarina people.

Animals such as peccaries and hound dogs are primal creatures with human attributes. They are salient for our analysis not only because of their totemic qualities (for example, their formal suitability in symbolizing aspects of Urarina social life), but because they are capable of metaphorically representing the alienation of human consciousness through misrepresenting social phenomena as natural. As domestic cohabitants dogs participate in Urarina society in the capacity as subjects: they are deemed inedible, they have proper names, and they are part of elaborate ritual action. In contrast, comestible "pets," such as peccaries, have the status of objects to Urarina subjects, "living their own lives apart, neither the direct complement nor the working instrument of human activities. . . . They are anonymous . . ." (Sahlins 1991, 284).

Study of Urarina oral narratives and their relationship to social practice enables us to explore the interminable passage of Urarina people and things from "nature to culture." Lest it be misunderstood, I am not here positing a prediscursive, autonomous realm of "nature": nature is an ideological construct composed of socially and historically inscribed folk taxonomies whose stability is merely an artifice of our own imagination. This brings us to one of the problems with structuralist analysis—namely its universalizing tendency to reduce the multiplicity of cultural configurations of "nature" down to the nature/culture dichotomy. As Butler notes, this "prediscursive" approach to nature makes it impossible to determine what is *natural* within a given cultural context (1990, 37; cf. Lévi-Strauss 1966, 94f.).

Symbolizing Virility: The Accoutrements of Hunting

Pursuing and killing large game is men's work. Women participate in fishing and in the chase and capture of smaller game. Wives accompany their husbands on multiple-day hunting forays and fishing trips and assist them in the butchering, field dressing, and curing of game animals and fishes. Bushmeats are transported in string-net game bags, or in the case of larger game, slung over one's shoulder. The Urarina rely on a number of hunting instruments, such as rifles, blowguns, machetes, and spears. They employ flashlights and kerosene lamps during night hunting and use a number of snares. These include tapir traps (*bijtuhúa*) made from wood and *tamishi* cordage and armed with a spear, and what the Urarina call armadillo snares (*üjhaya*), which are used for capturing armadillos and the highly prized paca or *ichá*. Previously, blowguns (*jijchana*) were the primary hunting devices, while the bow and arrow were utilized for fishing the well-stocked rivers and rivulets (Tessmann 1987, 55). Today, the Urarina affix spent machete blades onto wooden shafts that are six to eight feet long. These are then used as either lances or harpoons. Given their association with exotic figurations of Amazonia (Slater 2002), a number of these items regularly make their way into the tourist market in Iquitos, and some even find their way to internet marketing.

As in many areas of Amazonia (Chaumeil 2002; Erikson 2002), blowgun preparation is not a generalized skill but more appropriately designated a specialized art known only to a select number of Urarina men. Made from cashapona (*Iriartea* sp.) or *Puca quiro* (*Aspidosperma cylindrocarpon*?) wood, blowguns typically last for ten to fifteen years and range in size from 1.3 to 2.2 meters. These hunting implements are prepared under strict dietary restrictions and the tabu of sexual relations. Failure to comply with these strictures results in a blowgun that only shoots darts that follow crooked paths. If *ejlá* fabric is paradigmatic of femininity, curare dart quivers (*jadé*) are paradigmatic of Urarina virility (fig. 8.1).

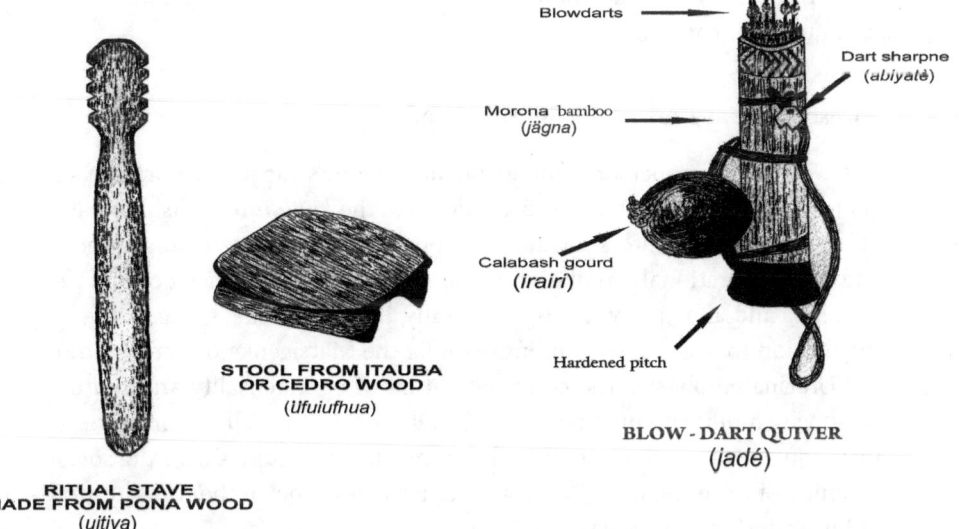

Fig. 8.1. Urarina ritual stave, stool, and blow-dart quiver

A brief description of the phallomorphically structured *jadé* or quiver will help to make this clear. *Jadé* are made by men from the hollow shaft of marona bamboo (*jägna, Bambusa guadua*). The blow-dart quiver's base is coated by a hardened pitch (*miräné*)[3] from the *Leche Caspi* tree (*arési, Couma macrocarpa*). A globular calabash gourd (*iráiri*) (*Crescentia cujete*?) housing the fiber used for the blow-dart plugs is attached to the base of the bamboo shaft. The silky hairs that surround the seeds of the fruit of the *Huimba* tree (*ijché, Bombax* sp.) are used to fashion dart plugs. *Tamishi* wood (*jijchú ajkísi, Carludovica palmate*) and string made from the Chambira palm fasten the gourd to the bamboo shaft.

The petioles of the Maripa Palm (*Maximiliana* sp. or *ajcuashí, inayuca*) and *Shebón* Palm (*ejlelé, Scheelea tessmannii*?) are used to make darts, which average about thirty centimeters long. The darts are wrapped in a skirt of finely woven *piasaba* fibers (*ajcodí, Leopolidnia piassaba*) made by women and then housed vertically in the bamboo shaft. A thin, delicately woven Chambira fiber strap is attached to the top of the shaft. Stylized, linear notched incisions are made in the bamboo shaft's lip as ornamentation. A dart sharpener (*abiyaté*, made from either the dried razor-sharp teeth or jaw of *piraña* fish, or a metal strip from a discarded battery casing) is tied to the quiver's strap and used to incise the darts. Small cuts are made in the dart's shaft so that when it enters the prey it breaks off at the point where it was notched (usually four centimeters from the dart tip, just at the edge of the curare poison). In some instances, a narrow bone whistle (*anahué cujtíara*) made from the Saddleback tamarin is also attached to the strap and is used to simulate simian calls.

Forest Game as *Prestation*: Sharing Food

The Urarina gauge personal independence by one's capacity to bring back game to be shared among the co-residents of the *kaj laitjíra*. Bushmeat exchange connects hunters, hosts, and consumers. In Amazonia, gendered and intergenerational circulation of forest game distinguishes donors, recipients, and the uninvited by culturally inscribing the space between them. Akin to Rosengren's findings among the Matsigenka of Peru (2006), the Urarina emphasize the convivial nature of commensality and mutual trust, which mitigate hierarchial tendencies within the *deme*. Commensality is equivalent to community, and thus misunderstandings over the social meaning of the exchange of food are perhaps inevitable in the transcultural "ethnoscape" of Amazonia.

A central dynamic of Urarina society is the continuous circulation of

Fig. 8.2. Urarina hunter with the head of a tapir

"true food" among co-residents of the longhouse. Urarina household division and consumption of forest game is regulated by conventionalized patterns of behavior, which respond to the pressures of "demand sharing" and more recently to the "extractive" dictates of the regional market in forest bushmeats and pelts. Credit for bagging game is given to the hunter, and in cases involving firearms, to the owner of the gun and ammunition. In this way the "owner" of the firearm or ammunition gains rights to bushmeat for distribution. Depending upon the size and quantity of game animals slain, the hunter responsible for bagging bushmeat, or *ininú*, plays the role of host in welcoming other co-residents of his longhouse to join him in eating forest game prepared by his wife or wives. All of the co-residents of the hunter's longhouse are entitled to partake in the distribution of large game, such as tapir (*aránla*)[4] and peccary (fig. 8.2).

In December 1990, Kujkurí—the Pangayacu River's aspiring headman—acquired five shotgun shells and three kilos of salt from a river merchant as an "advance." After five days of hunting for game with the assistance of two of his three co-wives and four of their male children, Kujkurí killed a very large tapir, the eleventh of his hunting career. All of the *deme*'s three primary longhouses shared in portions of the tapir's meat. The quantity of meat apportioned to each hearth group or individual longhouse is an open affair liable to the vagaries of interpersonal negotiation and to entailments

Fig. 8.3. Boat, Chambira River Basin

corresponding to the Urarinas' gerontocratic prestige hierarchy. The tapir's head (greatly esteemed) and other choice parts like the backbone were given to Kujkurí's wives' parents. The division of the tapir meat signaled Kujkurí's ongoing affinal obligations, particularly toward his father-in-law, the Pangayacu's most important headman. Parts of the tapir flesh were then boiled and the fat was skimmed off and placed in bottles to be used latter. Tapir viscera are eaten, but they are not seen as savory fare and hence provide food for the hungry and lowly. The majority of the tapir meat was roasted (*ajiyu*)—a process that took two days to complete and was accompanied by festive cassava beer drinking and episodic outbreaks of drunkenness. Upon his downstream, return voyage the trader who had advanced the ammunition and salt received approximately one quarter of the roasted tapir meat (fig. 8.3).

Distribution of bushmeats from smaller-sized game does privilege one's own children and their mother's hearth group(s). On a typical daylong hunting trip in 1998, Kujkurí returned to his longhouse with a night monkey, a two-toed sloth, a three-toed sloth, and a kinkajou (*igneé*, *Potos flavus*). This bushmeat was consumed exclusively among the three hearth groups respectively headed by each of Kujkurí's three sororal co-wives. Given that the quantity of meat (*iniñú*) in this instance was not very much (approximately eight to ten kilos of undressed forest game divided among two dozen people), it was not shared beyond Kujkurí's longhouse, nor did any of the other primary or ancillary longhouses expect it to be.

Initial bushmeat distribution can be a site for contention, especially among disgruntled co-wives who commonly jockey for choice cuts of forest game. It is not uncommon to hear grumblings from the *deme*'s men and women over the size of their "fair" share of the daily catch. After distribution, bushmeats are prepared for immediate consumption or cured for exchange or future consumption by smoking, salting, or drying. At the hearth, lambent tongues of fire singe the fur from the game animal destined for the cooking pot. For larger game, such as the tapir, Urarina women will prepare sausages by using a cooking technique that combines salting, roasting, and drying. Women clean and fillet (*cujlaá*) fish and game in large wooden platters called *bajtilla* or *rudiyá*. Forest game is prepared (*jarekí*) in a variety of ways: boiled, smoked, salted, dried, and roasted in the embers of the hearth fire. Often forest game is simply barbecued on a skewer (*vasijchú*) placed over a raised frame of sticks (*anaá*).

All of the co-residents of the *kaj laitjíra* share in eating a portion of the daily catch of fish or hunted forest game. Bushmeats are regularly prepared as a large communal stew served with parboiled (*rí-naná*) or roasted plantains (*ajíñu, asichu*) and cassava. A hunter's wife plays the part of hostess—she is in charge of apportioning the cooked forest game, starch, and beverages. The hostess serves the stewed bushmeat from a big clay pot or tureen (*darue senjua*) placed in the middle of her domestic platform. The hosting hunter then signals to the other men of the longhouse to join him in partaking of a meal. The adult men settle near the communal serving pot, orienting themselves toward the longhouse's central "passageway" (*inacajtái*). The hostess periodically replenishes the serving pot and metes out cooked cassava and plantains.

When intra-demic consumption of forest game does occur, it is regulated by formalized etiquette. During these infrequent moments of collective food consumption, only one serving container is used, a practice that operates to accent publicly the donor-recipient statuses. Visitors to longhouse feasts are served in order of age and social standing. Senior men are attended to prior to any of the women and children. Hunks of stewed meat, bones, and dollops of gravy or broth are dished out with calabash gourds into a smaller ceramic, metal, or plastic receptacle and then distributed among the longhouse's hearth groups according to the number of its respective members. The host's children act as public emissaries, separately delivering portions of the oleaginous bushmeat stew to each of the longhouse's hearth groups. The hearth group's focal female accepts the serving bowl and empties its contents into her own clay or metal container. The empty serving container is then brought quickly back to the host, at which point it is filled for allocation to the other hearth groups. Each hearth group's mature females prepare the plantains and cassava that the group consumes during the course of the meal. While eating, women and their children sit in a semicircle on a side of their domestic platform facing away from the centrally located male housespace.

Prestations of forest game both within and between longhouse groups valorize social relationships and serve in a number of critical contexts, such as marriage, and in communal work parties (*mingas*) to actually help institute them. The ethic of sharing is well developed among the Urarina, who emphatically claim that their generosity distinguishes them from the neighboring riparian *mestizos*. In contrast to the *ribereños*, who are said to restrict the distribution of forest game to within their own immediate "nuclear" kin group, the Urarina ethic of demand sharing dictates that one must share food (*siya lenunejké*) with all those present—kin or not.

Following Sahlin's (1972, 188) distinction between redistribution and reciprocity, Urarina bushmeat distribution can be considered redistributive in the sense that game and fish are pooled from all able-bodied adult members of the longhouse and redistributed in acts of hearth group commensality. Bushmeat redistribution tends to emphasize reciprocal relationships among co-residents of the *kaj laitjíra*, rather than relations between the longhouse groups of a *deme*. This helps explain why ceremonial *prestations* of food—aside from fermented beverages—play relatively insignificant roles in Urarina social life (cf. Hill 1987, 183ff., 1993a, 43–5; Hugh-Jones 1992, 61; Maybury-Lewis 1967, 42, 80, 201). Except for cassava beer festivals, alimentary reciprocity at the intra-demic level is extremely restricted. The Urarina, like the Tupian Araweté, do not rely on any elaborate system of food exchanges to distinguish social roles or activate interpersonal or group relations. Both the Urarinas' and the Arawetés' ideologies of reciprocity typically take the form of repetition: "eating the same thing from house to house—prevails over any metaphorical complementarity" (Viveiros de Castro 1992, 107).[5]

Largess and generosity in the allocation of forest game within longhouse groups does distinguish individual personas, giving them the edge in localized hierarchies of prestige. The same may also be said of the exchange of forest game with *mestizo* traders. A skilled hunter who manages to barter meat for domestic consumer goods can parlay his successful exchange into a reputation of worldliness. This symbolic capital suggests to the others of his group that he is qualified to be the *deme*'s interlocutor with *mestizo* labor bosses and merchants. Bringing back sufficient game to satisfy domestic demand as well as to discharge the longhouse's outstanding consumer debts to traders is a difficult task. The ability to complete a transaction, that is, the "payment" of *mitayo* to traders and *patrones*, valorizes chiefly prerogatives. Urarina men of renown rely on their abilities to manage petty-commodity relations with *mestizo* traders and labor bosses. Typically, Urarina headmen will assert, "Yo sabe trabajar, yo sabe negociar" (I know how to work, I know how to negotiate), a shorthand verbal expression of one's capacity to participate in relations of petty-commodity peonage.

Notwithstanding its instrumental, political value, bushmeat circulation is circumscribed by notions of mutual obligation and entailments, expressed in generalized reciprocity and "demand sharing." Urarina notions of generosity and reciprocity are implicated in relations of mutual "demand sharing." It is always appropriate to ask for the things one wants from those friends (*ámiu*) or family who possess them. Demand sharing means that the things asked for from the donor must be dispensed immediately. The language that relays demand sharing "is not polite, but insistent" (Guddemi 1992, 307; see also Murphy 1978, 145). In the field of "noncontractual relationships," demand sharing is a way in which Urarina individuals can guarantee the acknowledgment of their standing, influence, and interests (Peterson 1993, 870). In spite of their insistent claims of personal candor and forthrightness, Urarina are socialized from an early age to become "masters of secrecy" (MacClancy 1992, 103). Where food or *lenuneë* is to be widely shared, individuals shrewdly conceal consumption of victuals so that they can eat without being constantly badgered by ravenous onlookers. Reluctance to share and hoarding are equated with necromancy. Stinginess elicits sanctions of disapproval, evidenced by slanderous talk, the rejection of exchange, ostracism, and ultimately death. When it comes to demand sharing powerful shamans are said to fear no one since those who refuse to share are liable to fatal spirit attacks.

In the domain of narrative, the Urarina resemble the Tukano since "gluttony, improvidence, aggressiveness and all forms of overindulgence are punished by the superior forces" (Reichel-Dolmatoff 1976b, 311; see also Goldman 1963, 80). The Urarina culture hero Kuánra discourages excess in behavior, especially when it comes to satiating personal self-centered impulses. Demand sharing is thus tempered by mythological prerogatives discouraging material or bodily engorgement. However, this attitude is inverted in the Urarinas' account of the animal leader of the forest—the howler monkey or Rurú. Kuánra originally designated the black spider monkey or Ajláu to act as the forest's chief monkey. As a test, Kuánra asked all of the monkeys to swallow some very large tree fruit. However, Ajláu's mouth was too small to ingest the fruit. Being the only one to gulp down the large fruit, the big-mouthed howler gained the right to be chief. When howler monkeys are slain, Urarina hunters claim other animals of the forest go silent in deference to the death of their chief.

Preserved bushmeats do not stay in the longhouse for much time. The compulsion to share (*lerigá*)—often among multiple hearth groups, and on occasion even among multiple longhouses—precludes the extended availability of forest game within the community at any given time. Examination of the inter-ethnic circulation of bushmeats between the Urarina and the *anazairi* or *mestizos* features the ambivalence embedded in this practical aspect of the replication of the domus. This contradiction finds expression in the Urarina account of Rimae Santú, a narrative that urges the restriction of the circulation of forest game.[6] Certainly, the inter-ethnic exchange of bushmeats between the Urarina and the *mestizos* is a point of considerable ideological concern. The ambiguity noted in Urarina bushmeat circulation points to the impartial nature of the gift/commodity polarity as presented in many theories of exchange and society.

Rimae Santú

> Long ago during the time of ignorance and slavery, a Urarina man paddling his canoe upstream (*majkuí kigá*) encountered the house of Rimae Santú—the Dog Spirits.[7] They are the *mestizos*—anazairi—but we call them dogs (*rimáe*). Well, the Urarina man went ashore and exclaimed "Pucha!" Meat was stock piled. The Dog Spirits had all sorts of bushmeats: Collared peccary meat, tapir, deer, paca... all different types of *mitayo* were stockpiled there. Wanting to be well received, the man asked the Rimae Santú for shelter. The Dog Spirits respond-

ed, "Collect together these bones." The Urarina man did as he was told and collected up the bones. "Your food shall come from these bones," said Rimae Santú. "What am I going to do with these bones? " asked the Urarina man. "Eat them, because when my *paisanos* [brethren] are in your territory that's what you feed them . . . and my *paisanos* suffer. Let's see you eat the bones." The man began eating the bones, and his body then changed from its human form to that of a dog. The Rimae Santú wanted to attack him. But the "man-dog" embarked in his canoe and managed to escape.

The narrative of Rimae Santú carries considerable allegorical weight. In the narrative the *mestizos'* stockpile of forest game is emblematic of surplus or hoarding—an activity that is coterminous with avidity, and hence asociality.[8] When the *mestizo* Dog Spirits balk at circulating meat as a comestible item, the protagonist is forced to eat the bone refuse of the bushmeats created specifically for the Urarina people by Kuánra. The asociality associated with the act of refusing to feed others "is equivalent to debarring oneself from much of the ordinary day-to-day life" (MacClancy 1992, 103).

Clearly then, the story of Rimae Santú is a parable about the morality of food sharing, which warns of the peril of divesting forest game beyond the circuits of sociable exchange. Here the denial of exchange is equivalent to social death and is echoed in quotidian life with the aphorism "The death of a dog warrants no funeral." Similarly, when only a few kith or kin attend one's funeral, the Urarina will say, "It's like the death of a dog . . . no one cares."

The negation of commune effects the man's transformation into a canine—an animal whose ambivalence makes it particularly fitting for the metaphorical expression of the ambiguities attending the commoditization of forest game. Located at a juncture between "nature and culture," the equivocal evaluation of dogs—domesticated versus feral—makes them an appropriate medium for the expression of a kind of wild ferocity that people have "redirected to social ends" (Descola 1994, 230).

The narrative of Rimae Santú recounts the story of an ancient Urarina man's fateful encounter with the Dog Spirits who symbolize the avaricious *mestizo* trader. In practice, hound dogs are integral complements to Urarina hunting. They are regularly acquired through *mestizo* traders and *patrones*.[9] Urarina demand for dogs as scavenging and hunting companions has given the traders strategic access to a crucial productive resource. As a result of their position along the chain of commodity peonage, river merchants are able to tap into a bountiful supply of tortoises and forest game.

The domestication of the Urarinas' carnivorous rival in the narrative of Rimae Santú binds dogs and *mestizos*. The practical relationships the Urarina have with their dogs reflect their attitudes toward *mestizo* traders. Both dyadic relationships entail competitive interdependence. In the case of the *ribereños* and the Urarina, the former enjoys the upper hand, whereas for dogs and the Urarina, the latter is the dominant party. Though a necessary part of securing forest game, dogs stand in direct competition with the Urarina for the consumption of the kill. Similarly, because *mestizos* are purveyors of hounds, shotgun shells, and curare, Urarina trade relationships with *mestizos* ensure the procurement of forest game, but *mestizos* also represent a predatory group who are a perpetual drain on the total amount of game bagged.

When there is no shotgun ammunition, fishing implements, or dart poison, dogs are a dependable last resort for procuring *mitayo*. The Urarina benefit from dogs' expertise in discerning, trailing, and trapping game. The Urarina, like the Siona-Secoya, devote significant time to the selection, training, and curing of their hunting dogs, which "are among a man's most valued possessions" (Vickers 1989a, 52; 1989b). Hounds regularly assist in the hunt by tracking agoutis, paca, collared peccaries, anteaters, and coati (*anái, Nasua nasua*). Dogs are also trained to forage for tortoises and armadillos. It is not uncommon for dogs to be maimed or killed when hunting more aggressive, bigger game, such as white-lipped peccaries, whose large social herds number fifty to three hundred or more (Emmons 1990, 159). The death of a highly esteemed dog provokes visible consternation and tears, even among those men who pride themselves on their stoical reputations (cf. R. Rosaldo 1989, 27).

Hierarchy between humans and dogs is evident when scanning the confines of the Urarina longhouse. Invariably, one sees a wide assortment of dogs, from well-kept hunting hounds to mangy whelps that are ostracized with kicks and shouts from the warmth of the domestic hearths. Some dogs are coddled, well fed, and generally overindulged. Others are significantly less fortunate and suffer as a result in both appearance and in demeanor. Boiled cassava, kitchen scraps, bones of game kills, and some discarded offal provide proficient hunting dogs with food, while the inept are liable to starve (see Harner 1973, 63, 86; Maybury-Lewis 1967, 37 n.1; Crocker 1985, 32).

The Urarina are more than capable of converting commodities such as shotguns and dogs into singularized possessions by endowing them with a personal identity. For firearms, this is achieved through carving scrollwork on the shotgun's buttstock. Urarina dogs are personalized by instating them with descriptive or metaphorical terms like *abaríti* (cane alcohol), *sumajai* (white), and *rimae biña* (old dog) (cf. Lévi-Strauss 1966, 181f., 205; 1985, 155; Sahlins 1991, 288 n. 6). Lévi-Strauss contends that when the relation between humans and animals (dogs) is "socially conceived as metaphorical," the nomenclature system assumes a metonymical character (1966, 205). The Urarina case only lends partial support to this provocative assertion. However, in naming their hound dogs the Urarina do conform to what Sahlins calls a "general rule . . . named/unnamed: inedible/edible" (1991, 288 n. 6).

Hunting Magic

To be successful in the pursuit of game, it is not enough simply to be a master ethologist, an expert reader of spoors, or a skilled distinguisher of animal sounds and birdcalls. In addition to stamina, perseverance, and ethological knowledge, hunting proficiency entails the necessary magical skills to ensure the productive collaboration of tutelary spirit helpers (*madres*) (see Luna 1992a, 232; 1992b; Brown 1984; Chaumeil 1999).

All full-fledged hunters must eventually endure stringent sequences of ritualized preparations or "seasonings," which include the acquisition of esoteric arcanum, the consumption of purgative narcotics, celibacy, and culinary and tactile prohibitions. Disregard for ritual prohibitions results in sickness and bad luck when stalking game animals. Hunters avoid the impurity of menstrual effluvia (*nejlacdiá*), contact with which is said to strike men by turning their hearts and stomachs sour with "vinegar" (*yája náfa, ij tiya jáuna*). Urarina men told me that in severe cases this can result in fatal bouts of vomiting blood. In August 1998, one of the prominent junior men of the Pangayacu complained to me of his suffering from vinegar of the heart. The young hunter claimed drinking cassava beer prepared by a menstruating woman of his longhouse caused this affliction. To rid himself of the vinegar afflicting his heart, the hunter sought the shamanic assistance of his father-in-law, a prominent local *ayahuasca* shaman.

To enhance their hunting abilities, the Urarina rely on a wide pharmacopoeia of narcotic herbal magic for themselves and their hunting dogs.[10] The Urarina use the leaves of *Brunfelsia grandiflora* (*yinánja*)[11] and *Heisteria* sp. (*eneasüjí*) to "fortify" their bodies, such fortification being achieved through vision quests accompanied by stylized incantations and songs. Consumption of these fortifying narcotics is closely associated with elaborate prohibitions on the consumption of foods and sexual intercourse. My Pangayacu acquaintances recounted that *makusayári* or *pucuna uchu* (*Capsicum annuum*) and *Uchu sananco* (in Quechua, "pepper" *sananco*) are also used in an undisclosed manner for the preparation of noviate blowgun users and for "curing" blowguns.

Yinánja is consumed by men to ensure that their blow-darts follow a direct path toward their targets. As Townsley (1993) suggests for the Yaminahua, the reference to path (*berú* in Urarina) is apropos of hunting shamanism. Like the Yaminahua, Urarina hunting paths radiate out like starbursts from the cluster of longhouses making up a *deme*. These paths are part of a broader geo-cosmographic topography. During the ecstatic use of narcotics and while actually stalking game, the hunter/shaman traverses the *berú* much like a curare dart in search of forest game.

When consuming *yinánja*, men abstain from sexual relations for a period of a few days up to a few weeks. During this time they are prohibited from eating banana mash, salt, and cassava beer and consume only what they are able to hunt with their blowguns and curare darts. Three "straight" rather than "crooked" *yinánja* roots are pulverized into a pulpy fluid that is drunk, causing the huntsman to be intoxicated for ten to twenty hours. When the hunter subsequently uses his blowgun the curare tipped darts are thought to follow a "straight" trajectory or path.

Neophyte hunting dogs are also forced to swallow the juice of *yinánja*. Akin to the upper Amazonian practice of administering pepper and tobacco juice to the eyes of hunters and their dogs (Wilbert 1987, 166; see also Rojas Zolezzi 1992, 205; Rosengren 1987, 32), the consumption of *yinánja* is a requisite for tracking game animals. The forced consumption of *yinánja* is said to make a dog an agile hunter or *atiyá* by helping it to "scent" prey (see Alarco de Zadra 1988, 111). When a dog shows signs of failure at tracking animals, it is given a repeat dose of *yinánja*.

Dogs are tightly bound to a roughly hewn wooden frame and then suspended upside down with their bellies facing the sky. Their mouths are pried open with sticks while the *yinánja* juice is methodically dripped down their throats by way of a leaf-funnel. The dogs react immediately as if fighting a cataleptic fit: they lapse into wild contortions, accompanied by defecation, foaming of the muzzle, and howling cries of displeasure. After all of the juice is administered, the "cured" dogs are released and left to run about wildly in a total drunken and agitated state that lasts the best part of a day. Arguably, the Urarinas' customary administration of narcotics to their dogs indicates the most extreme form of the social impulse aimed at the total domestication of naturally feral creatures.

Urarina hunting magic appears to be much more prominent than gardening magic. The materiality of hunting magic centers on the possession of herbal talismans (these plants are called *tallá* and have provisionally been identified as *Caladium* sp.), which are kept in the hunter's finely woven Chambira hunting sachet. When hunters encounter fresh footprints of game animals, they will rub some of the imprinted soil on the herbal charm. A small amount of this "hunting poultice" is then rubbed onto the barrel of the shotgun, where it is said to direct the bullet toward its target. It seems it

Fig. 8.4. Urarina boy and necklace

is in this sense that *tallá* are referred to by the Urarina as *pushana/pusanga*, a term that among the Quechua speakers of the Pastaza and Chachapoyas-Lamas regions denotes the act of "guiding" animals or people (Landerman 1973, 40; G. Taylor 1979, 144; see also A. Fuentes 1988, 79). The *tallá* guides the ammunition along a straight path to the stalked prey.

Necklaces for infants and collars for shamans are fetishlike embodiments of culturally important creatures. Raptor talons and the teeth of peccaries and felines are especially valued for their use as infant and shamanic amulets. Resembling bandoliers, shaman breast bands (*rijkuguí, majadi*) are made from giant snail shells, white-lipped peccary teeth, various bone fragments, and *huairuro* (*irilé*) seeds whose black and red coloration the Urarina equate with women's garb (that is, red blouses and black/blue skirts). Animal teeth, bones, and claws are worn apotropaically as neckwear by children, men, and women, or displayed as trophies (particularly peccary mandibles) and put on view in the sloping eaves of the longhouse's palm-thatch. These fetishlike objects are valued simultaneously as talismans against threats of evil and as public insignia of a hunter's and a shaman's consecrated virtue (see also Guallart Martínez 1989, 38; Holmberg 1969, 240). Regardless of bushmeat's final destination—as *prestation* or as commodity—game animal's "hard" wealth (teeth [*cajte*]; bones [*ebüíjki*]; claws, and shells) are coveted by the Urarina as fetishized objects (fig. 8.4).

Insect body parts, such as rhinoceros beetle horns (*Megasoma elephas*?) and the body casings of Hercules beetles (*Dynastes Hercules*), as well as the luminescent portions of a number of unidentified beetles, should also be classified as "hard" forms of animal wealth. They are used by the Urarina in headdress and necklace ornamentation. While the Urarina do not participate as suppliers, there is a small market for such items in Iquitos, where they are made into jewelry for the tourist market (particularly earrings and broaches), or included in small glass-cased collections of insects, spiders, and butterflies sold to tourists. Seldom is this "hard" wealth the explicit object of commercial exchange, though inevitably a considerable amount of it is in fact alienated along with comestible forest game in the form of *mitayo*. To see how bushmeats circulate beyond the domus in supra-local orbits of exchange, I turn now to a further exploration of the intimate relationship between Urarina hunting patterns and commodity peonage on the Chambira.

The Commodification of Forest Game

Hunting feral animals provides the Urarina with a marketable stock of goods. Men process feline (*januladilájadi*) and peccary pelts (*ajcadí*) and then exchange these items for trade goods. In the past the barter in pelts included the skins of caiman (*yajcarí*) and nutria (*aruba, Lutra Incarum?/ Lutria longicauda*?) (Castillo 1958, 25; Kramer 1979, 89; Ferrúa Carrasco et al. 1980, 68). Much of the contemporary market for Amazonian skins is for luxury consumer goods, such as handbags, footwear, gloves, and jackets. The principal animals hunted for this market are collared and white-lipped peccaries, capybara, otters (giant and river), different types of edible chelonians, and felines. In the two decades following the end of the Second World War, Iquitos exported 2.8 million peccary skins; 22,644 giant otter skins; 90,574 river otter skins; 12,704 jaguar skins; and 138,102 ocelot skins (Redford 1992; see also Rumrril and Zutter 1976). Throughout the 1990s the Urarina continued to trade salted, smoked, and freshly slaughtered forest game, as well as pelts for barter goods—ammunition figuring prominently among the items animating the circuits of exchange.

Smoked (*ahumado*) or salted bushmeats are coveted wealth items esteemed greatly by Amazonian peoples—both rural and urban. *Mestizo* consumption of smoked bushmeat (*carne de monte*) and salted fish includes simple home-fare such as *caldo de carne* (flesh broth), *chupé* (creamy soups), *aycha kusnishqa* (smoked forest game), *patarashqa* (roasted fish wrapped in *bijao* leaves), *paichipango* (cassava and *paiche* fish soup), *sarapatera* or *menudo de charapa* (turtle soup), and regional culinary delicacies such as *inchicapi* (peanut and poultry stew), *juanes* (poultry and rice ball wrapped in *bijao*), and the Loretano specialty platter *picadillo de majaz* (capybara stew).[12] Traders seeking to capitalize on the growing urban demand for forest game, particularly at times of *fiesta*, provide the Urarina with hounds, shotgun shells, and dart poisons to ensure their continued access to a steady supply of marketable food products. The direct exchange of forest game for ammunition and other items (namely dogs and dart poison) simultaneously reproduces the means of subsistence production and contributes to the continuation of commodity peonage.

In the system of *mitayo*, the hierarchical ordering of objects valorizes the ranking of persons—Urarina, *ribereño*, and *mestizo*. Symbolically dense (Weiner 1994) items, such as ammunition, hounds, and dart poison, are politically and economically conspicuous; regulating their exchange both demarcates and intensifies the difference between the *patrón* and the covetous Urarina hunter/consumer. Just as the Urarina are cognizant of what is being exchanged, they are keenly aware of what is not being transacted—of which prior requests made to *patrones* for specific trade goods (*pedidos*) were completed and which ones were disregarded. Similarly, *mestizo* traders are intensely interested in the productive fruits of Urarina hunting and foraging expeditions. Weiner contends that the apparently linear dimensions of this mutual "give-and-take" amount to overt efforts at capturing that which resists circulation (1994, 395)—in this case, forest game.

Since at least the turbulent rubber boom, transformations in Urarina hunting techniques have modified game procurement. The introduction of firearms has altered Urarina patterns of hunting, but they have not replaced the dog, blowpipe, machete, or spear (*kuaderno* and *rejon* in Loretano Spanish) as the principal armaments of the hunt. In addition to shotguns, imported tools and implements include machetes (*sabré* from *sable*, Spanish for saber), knives (*anújua* from *navaja*, Spanish for clasp-knife, folding knife), saws (*cerruchú* from *cerrucho*, Spanish), needles (*ejcú*), fishing hooks (*kajtaí*), metal cooking pots (*guadárjui*), and kerosene lanterns, which have completely replaced beeswax candles referred to by Kramer (1979, 8).

Game birds, monkeys, and a number of small rodents are still killed by single or paired hunters with their blowguns, which have a firing range of about forty meters.[13] Shotguns, however, are preferred when hunting larger animals such as peccary or tapir, which are also captured with spring traps. Fleet or burrowing game such as deer (*ujkuái*) or the neotropic's largest rodents—pacas (*ichá*)—are stalked by a group of hunters and their dogs and then slain with the aid of machete, spear, or rifle. Continued reliance on muzzle-loading firearms and rifles (discharging either single slug or multiple pellet loads) reveals the Urarinas' lasting dependency on commodity peonage. Blowgun use requires dart poison, which most Urarina do not know how to concoct—in spite of the fact that many are master artisans at making blowguns. The primary headman along the Pangayacu regularly repairs *ribereño* blowguns, sometimes in exchange for rock salt traded from the Alto Marañón.

Indigenous trade routes previously ensured the widespread distribution of curare. This has now given way to merchant control of the long-distance trade in dart poisons (see Guernsey 1870, 353; Marcoy 1873, 3: 37 n.1; Cipolleti 1988; Descola 1994, 227; Reeve 1994, 125–30). When curare is absent, the Urarina supplement hunting by procuring shotgun shells and the basic components for making ammunition (shell casings, primer, powder charge, and buckshot), which are both costly and comparatively scarce. Traders use their virtual monopoly over the distribution of these critical means of subsistence production to further increase their leverage in the system of commodity peonage. In the early 1960s, the cost of one round of ammunition was reported to be equivalent to one day of work. This compared with twenty days of work in return for about two meters of cloth (which is the amount needed to make one blouse). By 1976, Kramer indicated that the Urarina were receiving "comparatively large quantities of goods or expensive merchandise, such as bolts of cloth, boxes of shotgun shells or batteries, aluminum pots, barrels of kerosene, shotguns and sewing machines" (1979, 111). My own experience in the mid- to late 1990s suggests that one day's labor was equivalent to approximately two shotgun shells. The costly trade items reported for the mid-1970s had all but completely dried up by the early 1990s. The advantages of shotgun use are many, but the risks of wasting costly ammunition often outweigh the benefits. The Urarina acquire ammunition in large part from traders and *patrones*, but more commonly on credit (Kramer 1979, 88). Among the neighboring Achuar peoples of Ecuador, Descola reports that one 16–caliber cartridge is bartered for each peccary hide: "the cartridge just pays for itself" (1994, 228; for a similar account, see Warren 1992, 102). *Patrones* and traders routinely charge the Urarina for their hunting excursions, regardless of whether these forays yield bushmeats or not.

The practice of *mitayo* dictates that sizeable portions of slain animals are apportioned to the "owner" of the ammunition; rates range from a quarter to one half of the slain game animal. The ammunition is "loaned" by the *patrón* or trader to the hunter, who is obliged to "pay" for it through the provision of forest game. Styles of bargaining between the *patrones* and the Urarina assume a number of postures, which all exhibit scorn or indifference to lucre.

Bargaining, as Steiner notes, is a means to deal with the "indeterminacy in a transcultural economic exchange" (1994, 68). When seen from the inside, bargaining between the traders and the Urarina denotes sociability since it intimates reciprocity (Herzfeld 1991, 164). Indeed, as many have noted, bartering is in itself "a mark and device of sociability" (Hugh-Jones 1992, 61). Nevertheless, the bargaining implicit in the system of *mitayo* also provides a way for the Urarina to exhibit cunning and skill. Urarina huntsmen try to maximize the number of cartridges they are loaned while minimizing the amount of bushmeats they provide the owner of the ammunition. This is achieved by concealing the total number of animals killed or by providing the owner of the ammunition with animals many *mestizo* traders find unsavory, such as sloth or anteater.

Urarina and *mestizo* acquaintances recounted that one of the Chambira's primary *patrón* family operations was responsible for the extraction of tens of thousands of pelts during the export boom in pelts (1950s–1975).[14] It was not until 1976 that the government licensed the collection of peccary and deer hides, as well as the collection of turtles, tortoises, and their highly coveted eggs, apparently leading to a diminution in the market demand for these items (Kramer 1979, 131). However, by the late 1980s and the early 1990s, demand had once again picked up—though not to former levels with respect to the market in pelts. Trade in forest game with *patrones* and traveling merchants jeopardizes generalized meat distribution within the longhouse, but when exchanged for the instruments necessary for subsistence—curare, dogs, and ammunition—it promises to yield additional marketable produce. This productive potential can be manipulated as the basis upon which to mobilize a communal hunting excursion, which itself holds the future prospect of securing significantly greater quantities of forest game, that is of course until game scarcity becomes a problem.

Peccaries, Putrification, and Shamanism: Ideological Interpretations of Game Depletion

In spite of its apparent plentitude, game depletion does appear to have influenced the Urarinas' culinary repertoire. Today, formerly tabu foods such as red brocket deer and caiman (Castillo 1958; Kramer 1979, 88) are salted by men and then boiled by women as they would any other comestible meat. Tabu animals include serpents (*ainú*) and frogs (*dadí*). The Urarina leave tapir meat to putrefy in their spring traps. The Achual of the Río Corrientes contend that this is a purificatory technique that permits the tapir's life essence to withdraw to the netherworld (Kramer 1979, 101).

The Urarinas' reliance on putrification and their sporadic access to salt as a preservative give credence to their renown among neighboring *ribereño* and indigenous populations as consumers of unfit grovel (cf. Viveiros de Castro 1992, 289). The Urarina do consume rancid meats and fish in varying stages of putrification. Indeed, putrification is an important theme that pervades their account of the origin of peccaries, a narrative that delineates the sociological bounds of hunting and eating. According to the Urarina, from time immemorial social life has been predicated on the sharing of food, which began with the collective consumption of the toucan (*iñüdií?*). Moreover, the Urarinas' peccary creation narrative[15] reveals the close connection made between hunting success, shamanic (*kanikuichára*) capabilities, and an apocalyptic eschatology.

Raána: The Creation of Peccaries

During the "time of the grandfathers"—a time of ignorance, Kuánra came to the Chambira before going to live in the sky. At that time, there were no white-lipped peccaries—*raána*—nor any forest animals, only the toucan. Therefore, a man climbed a tree and blow-darted a toucan. After being hit by just one blow-dart, it fell to the ground. The bird was cooked in a large clay pot and eaten by many Urarina who later gave thanks to God. Hearing their gratitude, Kuánra decided to create peccaries—food for all of the people suffering from hunger. Kuánra invited a group of Urarina to cultivate peanuts. To produce collared peccaries (*ubana*), Kuánra sent two men to the edge of the forest clearing, and to make white-lipped peccary, he sent a group of people to the other edge. They were told to sing and laugh while they planted peanuts. Kuánra then transformed his fishing spear into a bow and arrow. Kuánra coated an arrow with salt and shot it at the people, causing them all to race into the forest. The people were then transformed into collared and white-lipped peccaries. The remaining Urarina people wanted to hunt the peccaries, but the newly created white-lipped peccaries still had human limbs. So Kuánra sent Chambira palm fronds, which the Urarina worked into yarns. These were used for the peccaries' bristles. When the Urarina went again to hunt the peccaries they had completely changed into animals. The peccaries multiplied rapidly and soon threatened to take over the forest. When the Urarina slew the peccaries, they left their carcasses in the forest to putrefy. The smell of rotting white-lipped peccary flesh displeased Kuánra so much that he decided to send the peccaries to dwell in the sky. That is why it is difficult to encounter peccaries around here. Datura (*toé*) drinkers can ask God to send white-lipped peccaries here to be hunted. But today there are only a few white-lipped peccaries found on the Chambira. This is because only a small number of people still know how to ingest hallucinogens and to communicate with Kuánra. The trembling that occurs after ingesting datura is what transports a person to God's side. The shamans will always be able to eat white-lipped peccary—until the end of time.

In the Urarinas' origin myth of peccaries, horticultural pursuits precede hunting: the communal planting of peanuts is a prelude to the bountiful food source in the form of peccary meat. This origin tale exemplifies transformative processes that endow forest game such as white-lipped and collared peccary with vital social values. Lévi-Strauss maintains that the paired contrast between white-lipped and collared peccaries is well suited to relate symbolically the mediation between humanness and bestiality. He argues that peccaries are animals through the forfeiture of their original human nature, to which they were untrue through asocial conduct: "The ancestors of the peccaries were human beings who showed themselves to be 'inhuman'" (Lévi-Strauss 1975, 86; see also Jara 1986, 167–90; Siskind 1977, 91–93; Viveiros de Castro 1992, 65, 343 n. 16; cf. Whitten 1988, 299). While there is no indication of the peccaries' asociality in the Urarina account, what is clear is that the peccaries' ancestors were once human.

The Urarina recognize two types of peccaries (*Tayassuidae*): the white-lipped peccary (*Tayassu pecari*) or *huangana* called *raána*, and the collared peccary (*Tayassu tajacu*) or *sajíno* called *ubana*. Resembling wild pigs, peccaries are even-toed ungulates. They have a dorsal scent gland that exudes a strong musky odor, which provides them with a means for recognition and herd solidarity. *Raána* have white bands of bristly hair between their neck and shoulder. Compared with *ubana*, they are smaller (approximately fifty to sixty-five pounds). The ashen colored circles of hair around their mouths distinguish *raána*. They assemble in large herds, are potentially more dangerous than *ubana*, and have even been known to charge humans (Kricher 1989, 289; Spruce 1970, 10).

Ubana herds are significantly smaller than *raána* herds (usually six to nine, compared with fifty to three hundred for *raána*). This suggests why Kuánra sent only two men to become *ubana*, but an entire group to make *raána*. As related in myth, the reproductive potential of the peccary is extraordinary. Gestation lasts approximately 148 days, producing litters of four. In the absence of predation, peccaries have the capacity to over run their territory quickly (Sponsel 1989, 43). To control the proliferation of peccaries, the Urarina turn to predation, which yields a ready supply of raw bushmeats.

The Urarinas' transformation of slain game animals into "true food" is a process accentuating the "deculturation" of forest game. The natural process of putrification renders raw meats edible—in the case of slain peccary, decomposition "dehumanizes" the flesh. However, Kuánra disapproves of this procedure, a change of heart it would appear prompted by the peccaries' putrescent miasma. In response to the rotting stench, Kuánra dispatches the peccary herds into the sky. Salt (*tevé*), an important preservative, condiment, and item of commerce, is used by Kuánra to enact the transformation of humans into animals. Salinization leads to human death and stands in direct opposition to mephitic putrification that results in spiritual death. This symbolic dyad—salinization/putrification—frames the Urarinas' gustatory circuit dictating their food preferences and tastes.

Reminiscent of the communicative function of peccaries' dorsal scent glands, strong, putrid smells provide a means of communication between the mundane terrestrial sphere of existence and the transcendental domain of the Creator God. Ontological transition is effected not through smells but through hallucinogenic trance. Consumption of datura (*Brugmansia suaveolens* or *ajcaá*) enables the skilled shaman to petition Kuánra to send peccary herds to pass through Chambira territory. In this regard, the peccary origin narrative reflects the Urarinas' conception of their own agency in determining game density. The depletion of game is tied to failures in the social production of knowledge and ritual praxis rather than to any externally generated pressures, such as the rural extractive economy. By denying the intrusive presence of "market" relations in the system of *mitayo*, the mythical account of the creation of peccaries is tantamount to an ideological rejection of the regional extractive economy.

The account of the origin of peccaries is indicative of the Urarinas' generalized understanding that forest game were all produced by Kuánra for their benefit. This contrasts with pigs, chickens, and cows, which the *mestizo* creator deity made for "his people." During a rare trading expedition to Iquitos during the dry season of 1991, Kiriná explained this to me in the following way:

> *Cumpá* [*Compadre*], they say before Kuánra was here, the Peruvians were all evil. They say the Peruvians were very evil. To this day, some are still evil. When Kuánra was here, the Peruvians would punish him. They say they would punish him, sometimes by burying him, sometimes by throwing him into the water, sometimes tying his wrists together and then throwing him in the water. That is how the Peruvians were before. Before there were native peoples (*nativos*), there were Peruvians. God then made us. "Eat among yourselves," said God. That is why there are now pigs. That's right, that's why there are now pigs and chickens. It didn't have to turn out this way. If those Peruvians had behaved differently, our God would still be here among us.

Kiriná's explanation for the different alimentary regimes distinguishing the neo-Peruvians and the Urarina plays directly on the Urarinas' myth of creation. In Kiriná's account, Peruvians have been assimilated into the category of "evil people" and are held responsible for the persecution of Kuánra. This hostility gives rise to separate food domains between the Urarina and the *mestizo* Peruvians. Doubtless, these and other "imaginary schemes" have been shaped by the Urarinas' long history of engagement with various "fronts of national expansion" (Dean 1990).

Understanding the Alienation of *Mitayo*

While Thomas (1991, 34) has skillfully written against the discourse of radical alterity registered in ethnographic primitivizations of the "other," he does not fully explicate the "indigenous conceptual structures through which alienation is figured and produced" (Lattas 1993, 105). Similarly, my portrayal of Urarina social life "makes no attempt to grasp indigenous constructions of exchange and is obviously inaccurate insofar as those constructions actually give transactions their meaning and logic" (Thomas 1991, 32). Instead, my aim has been an effort at imparting to economic anthropological analysis a sense of the alienation inscribed in Urarina cultural constructions of exchange. The links of "labour, ownership and contact" (H. Moore 1993, 129) through which things and people are connected have become attenuated on the Chambira. But alienation is not in itself enough to distinguish "commodity" transactions from "gift" exchanges, which can also be alienated (Hugh-Jones 1992, 54; see also Tambiah 1985). Like palm-fiber wealth, bushmeats are most profitably viewed as occupying positions along a mutable spectrum spanning "from industrial, completely alienated commodities at one pole to completely 'singularized' possessions at the other" (Liep 1993, 23).

Alienation in the realm of bushmeat circulation denotes a social process whereby the basic distinction between the sociocultural and the world of nature has become blurred. The Urarina experience alienation when their control over their own possessions, forest game, and productive activities like hunting is limited (Carrier 1992b, 540). In the system of *mitayo*, *patrones* and traders have a hand in regulating the duration and periodicity of hunting. As a result, the Urarina have forfeited control over certain aspects of hunting. Alienated through mercantile exchanges, bushmeats have become disembodied from the hunter. Commercial traffic in forest game is inimical to Urarina participation in hunting shamanism. By participation, I have in mind Tambiah's use of the term to refer to the process whereby "persons, groups, animals, places, and natural phenomena are in a relation of contiguity" that renders "existential immediacy . . . contact and shared affinities" (1990, 107).

Alienation in the domain of hunting can only be said to be partial among the Urarina. While they have in fact surrendered control over some aspects of the production process—such as reliance on imported raw materials and tools, and the selection of product (that is, venison or paca as opposed to sloth)—the Urarina retain control over the tempo, duration, and timing of productive hunting. Indeed, the organization of production continues to be deeply embedded in the household structure of the Urarinas' *kaj laitjíra*.

Forest game exhibits profound instability, both as food objects of social exchange and as commoditized items sold in the markets stalls of Nauta and Iquitos. From the vantage point of debt peonage, bushmeats embody objectifications of the hunter's labor power while simultaneously standing as a sign of ongoing relations of debt. "Ownership" of bushmeats is derived from the act of bagging the game. Nevertheless, circulation of forest game continues to communicate a diverse set of values whose axis of meaning revolves around shamanic beliefs, gendered acts of reciprocity, and "demand sharing"—now tempered by alternative distribution and consumption logics made possible through the expansion of regional and national markets.

Several factors, such as the twentieth-century introduction of guns, the increased market for game products in growing urban markets, and the logic of commercial economies, have all conjoined to accelerate the demand for bushmeats on the Chambira. While the exigent demands of debt peonage have diversified Urarina property rights and commodity production, the very embeddedness of forest game in the cosmological and practical spheres of Urarina social life has meant that the cultural construction of *mitayo* has been fraught with contradictory practical and symbolic evaluations. The Urarina typically cast the circulation of forest game as ethnically inalienable in their mythopoeic discourse; yet, forest game continues to provide the Urarina with an important though scarce medium for the establishment of reciprocal relations, and for the ongoing mediation of the localized hierarchies of prestige.

During times of flooding along the fertile banks of the Marañón, *ribereños* make their way to the Chambira Basin, as they did in December 1990 and September 1993 (reported to be the most severe flooding in over a decade). *Ribereños* come in search of forest game and garden produce, which is exchanged for *farinha*, salt, dried fish, and limited quantities of trade goods (matches, batteries, soap, and so forth). Urarina and *ribereños* exchange not only goods, but labor power as well. Unlike reports about the decline of *min-*

gas or communal labor exchanges among *ribereño* communities (Hiraoka 1985, 225, 230), Urarina and Chambira *ribereños* continue the practice of reciprocal labor exchanges. Victuals are closely intertwined with the circuit of labor assistance. The circulation of forest game and the sharing of cassava beer are significant media of exchange through which inter-ethnic reciprocity in the form of labor parties (gardening, house building), sanctuary, and sport can be actualized.

Among the Urarina, the memory of an idealized system of distribution providing for all the members of the longhouse has been supplanted by external economic demands accompanying labor contracts for trade goods. In their procurement of trade goods, the Urarina have submitted to unequal terms of exchange decided largely by commercial agents. The circulation and division of food in the form of bushmeats, however, is conduct that continues to be tightly bound by the requisites of etiquette. In spite of the ambivalence the Urarina express in terms of the commodification of hunted forest game, food sharing continues to be a ritualized succession of acts ensuring the gendered interdependence of all members of the longhouse.

9

Chanting Rivers, Fiery Tongue

Ayahuasca Shamanism and Resistance in Amazonia

In this concluding chapter I illustrate how *ayahuasca* shamanism is integral to Urarina hunting and healing—two arenas of social life at the margins of both the kinship and market economies. In exploring what I characterize as the Urarinas' "messianic" impulse, I examine the Urarinas' ideological conception of the circulation of commodities by comparing the prohibition on the commoditization of meat with the increasing commoditization of produce and wealth items traded for Western consumer goods. Discussion of the Urarinas' apocalyptic cosmology situates the contradiction between the commensality of bushmeat circulation and the commercial transactions that circulate trade goods. For the Urarina, the triumphalism of technological advance in the guise of guns, chain saws, and boat motors conceals an uncertain vision of humanity's future.

While this book has tried to link multiple levels of analysis, I have not emphasized the Urarinas' cultural displays or political mobilization for outsiders, as has been done elsewhere in lowland South America. Recently, Laura Graham has demonstrated the Xavantes' multiple and multifaceted perceptions of political instrumentalities and objectives, especially when it comes to indigenous cultural displays intended primarily for non-indigenous audiences (2005). Among the Urarina I came to know, local political objectives were complex, yet they were neither particularly abstract nor overly concerned with public "image" or what Graham has aptly described as "existential recognition" (2005). Instead, it is through the optic of shamanism that I offer insight into the ways in which the Urarina have ambivalently dealt with the outside world.

Shamanism and the Apocalypse

Since the time of initial contact in 1653, the Urarina peoples of the Chambira Basin have challenged Occidental civilizing stratagems and modes of appropriating nature. The region as a whole has been susceptible to discursive excess in the form of utopian fictions as well as "dystopian visions" of brutalizing savagery and ineffable terror. The Urarina have vigorously reacted to the presence of non-Amerindian outsiders who have been propelling themselves—often violently—into their midst for centuries. Urarina responses to these colonial intrusions have encompassed a number of strategies ranging from hostile resistance to accommodative incorporation. This chapter focuses on one particular response that the Urarina have developed to interpret and deal with the encroaching "outside world"—namely *ayahuasca* shamanism.

Urarina shamanism occurs in tandem with "the millennial dream"—the belief that the conditions of scarcity and human affliction will terminate in well-being and splendorous abundance in the way of trade goods and game animals (see Brown and Fernández 1991, 3). Indeed, in the context of the Urarinas' historical struggles with the systematic exploitation of their labor power, coupled with the demographic disasters unleashed by virulent epidemics, and the influence of Christian millenarian beliefs, shamanism has assumed a messianic character.[1] For Christianity, millennial ideas and practices emerged out of customary eschatology derived from both the Mediterranean world and medieval Europe. In this context, St. Augustine viewed the millennial epoch in present-day terms: those living in faith on Earth bravely waiting for the final end and a return to the true home, the City of God.

Perhaps the millenarian movements best known to anthropology are the cargo cults of Melanesia. As Worsley describes (1970), cargo-cult adherents construct airstrips, docks, and warehouses in anticipation of the arrival of manufactured goods from the industrial world. In more extreme instances of these millenarian movements, adherents have even destroyed their own tools and crops to make way for the novel Western goods. While cargo-cult tendencies have been found in lowland South America, there has been relatively less interest in trade goods than in Melanesia (see Brown 1991, 404; Hugh-Jones 1994, 69). Indeed, in Amazonia, native peoples like the Urarina have historically been less concerned with commandeering the source of all wealth than with terminating the abusive labor conditions under which they are compelled to toil in exchange for trade goods. In those societies structured primarily by the bonds of kinship, phenomena as diverse and contradictory as cargo cults, witchcraft, cannibalism, head taking, and millenarianism more broadly can all be interpreted as radical responses to profound and far-reaching social crisis. Millenarian beliefs can give rise to political action; in extreme cases people see themselves as representing instruments in a divine plan and willingly participate in a "cosmic war."

Amazonian millenarian impulses are mobilized by the great disparity in the distribution of knowledge and by asymmetry in positions of power and decision making. Amazonian millenarianism is ostensibly linked to economic and cultural dispossession, geographic dislocation, and ultimately human alienation.[2] In his seminal account of the Asháninka of Peruvian Amazonia, Varese (2002) notes how "heroic shamanism," myth, and millenarian inclinations emphasize solidarity and cosmic interdependence (Dean 2006b, 466), as illustrated by Apu Inca, or Juan Santos Atahualpa, who claimed that he was heir to the Spanish crown and called for the creation of an empire east of the Andes. Yet as Varese points out, the beliefs animating Juan Santos Atahualpa's eighteenth-century messianic movement were "those of a religious renewer rather than those of a social revolutionary in search of worldly power" (2002, 465). Millenarian theologies of salvation, prophetic narratives, and apocalyptic eschatologies are all part of broader indigenous efforts at adapting to perpetually changing sociopolitical circumstances, efforts that involve an ongoing process of resisting and incorporating rival political and cultural claims.

Turning to the study of pre-Columbian Amazonian history, a number of scholars have argued persuasively against the notion that millenarianism was "sparked [simply] by the arrival of Europeans" (Brown 1991, 390; cf. Barabas 1986, 540; Hugh-Jones 1994, 34). Clearly, such causal and reductive associations cannot account for the multiplex beliefs associated with apocalyptic ideologies. Rather, the incidence of apocalyptic ideologies and social movements are a response not only to external pressures, but also to indigenous societies' own internal fields of conflict. In Amazonia, millenarian movements reflect the interminable tension between egalitarian and hierarchal social formations.

Given the similar characteristics that prevail in millenarian groups, it is generally held that the prophetic impulse that inspires millenarian sects may remain dormant for long stretches of time, as demonstrated among the Asháninka (Varese 2002). When utopian renewal movements do emerge, they question received political authority and orthodox ritual wisdom; they represent a rupture with the past, a self-reflective and often unflattering probing of contemporary social formations and relational structures bounding social fields of action. The iconoclastic and rebellious impulses associated with utopian and millennial ideologies can perhaps best be thought of as a denial of the prevailing system of exploitation and status devaluation (Scott 1985, 332). In Amazonia, millenarianism has historically involved a constellation of features that have emerged during periods of turmoil and heightened reflexivity. Biblical ideas of redemption and reckoning abound, which reflect preconversion processes and worldviews.

Millenarianism champions fundamental changes in the allocation of power, wealth, and knowledge. On the Chambira, this is tantamount to a direct threat both to the indigenous and postcolonial status quos. The Urarinas' penchant for a nativistic ideology, their proclivity to retreat from relations with *mestizos*, and their periodic repudiation of debt all challenge the authority of extractive mercantilism. This nativist attitude has been noted elsewhere in Amazonia, often in the context of utopian renewal movements and the ideological resistance to extractive mercantilism. For example, the millenarian and messianic heritage of the Cocama, Yagua, and Tikuna finds expression in the Crusader Order (Orden Cruzada or Hermanadad de la Cruz) lead by the Brazilian visionary José Francisco da Cruz who toured Peruvian Amazonia from 1969 to 1972 (Regan 1983, 1988; Brown 1991, 399). An eclectic group influenced by the Catholic, evangelic, and apostolic churches, the Crusader Order actively promotes disengagement with *mestizo* traders and labor bosses. Members of this millenarian group contend that their founder is the reincarnation of Jesús, who will lead them to the edenic "land without evil."

The Urarina likewise embrace an eschatology with definite apocalyptic undertones. Human behavior, I was often told by my Urarina friends, must be understood in light of the fact that from time immemorial there have always been both *good* and *evil* people. A person's wrongdoings are typically represented not in terms of lapses from reasonable standards of integrity, but as corresponding to immutable moral qualities ascribed to them from birth. Arguably, this Manichaeanism alludes to a kind of dualistic epistemology that "offers the reassurance of cosmic harmony" (Maybury-Lewis 1989, 14). Whatever its philosophical status, dualism is integral to Urarina cosmogony, which is epitomized by the perpetual struggle of good and evil, by the tension between knowledge and ignorance, and by oscillating cycles of cultural order versus apocalyptic chaos. The Urarinas' prophetic visions of the bountiful society are found in allusions to biblical themes of equality, deliverance, justice, and the struggle for human liberation in a new social order. Their oral culture draws freely on millenaristic concerns, as exhibited in their extensive myths of world destruction, and in their acts of mythic praxis such as trance, fasting, and sexual asceticism associated with *ayahuasca* shamanism. *Ayahuasca* shamanism and the elaborate mythological corpus attesting to its efficacy recognize the value of the individual—in terms of both perdurable and historical time.

History for the Urarina is coursing inevitably toward final consummation, marked by cataclysmic destruction and total cultural annihilation. Their cosmic eschatology asserts a clear distinction between human essence

Fig. 9.1. Urarina shaman, Chambira River

and human existence, which they think will eventually collapse into oblivion at the end of the world. But by participating in *ayahuasca* shamanism, the Urarina not only deify humanity, they defy history. Indeed, they believe that their salvation lies beyond modernist conceptions of history (fig. 9.1).[3]

The Urarinas' shamanic complex is associated with the ecstatic consumption of entheogens and the use of parrot feather headdresses, giant snail-shell breast bands, harpy eagle feather fans, and elaborate oral performances (tales, incantations, songs) influenced by narcotic visions and dreams. These phenomena and objects are Urarina *sacra*. They all intermingle in helping to canalize the processes of disengagement, transmutation, and equivalence attending to the emergent commoditization of Urarina society.

In Amazonia, many rituals—both indigenous and "folk"—are fashioned after myths (Suárez-Araúz 2004). They can be categorized as imitative for they replicate key aspects of myth. Shamanic rites are imitative because they dramatize a repetition of the creative act of the gods and reflect the termination of cultural time. According to the people of the Río Pangayacu, the deaths of all hallucinogen consumers—who in Amazonia are the shamans par excellence (see Bellier 1986, 132)—are equivalent to the Urarinas' own *Götterdämmerung*—the twilight of the Urarina creator god Kuánra and the world he fashioned. This is made clear in the poignant account of the forthcoming apocalypse by one prominent headman (Calísto).

Ayahuasqueros and the End of Time

> They say when all of the shamans—the *ayahuasqueros*—of the jungle disappear the world will come to an end. All of the Peruvians will die. It is the shamans who now maintain this world, but when they are all gone, *pucha, pucha* [explicatives]!! The world will come to an end . . . the world will come to an end. Even though they [the Peruvians] deny this, when the shamans all die, our world will end. All of the land we walk on will be gone. When all of those who know how to drink *ayahuasca* are gone, this world will end—it will boil. However, before this happens, before we all die, the things [we trade for] have to be inexpensive. When the shamans are all gone it will be pitch dark, our world will boil, and then it is going to be dark. Water, water will cover all of the forest, it will cover the entire world. But before this happens, Señor Gringo, the things [we have to trade for] have to be cheap; they have to be inexpensive so that at least we can clothe ourselves. Then our Kuánra will receive us in the sky; there will be total darkness—that's what I am waiting for, the end of time. (Calísto, Pangayacu, September 1992)

Arguably, this account is an illustration of what a number of anthropologists, including Sahlins (1985, 54–55), have dubbed *mythopraxis*—to wit, the conjuring up of a mythic vision in an effort to frame conceptually the experience of current events (see also Ram and Sabar-Friedman 1996). Analogical correspondences between myth and social life are invariably used by the Urarina "to make any myth relevant to new experience and daily issues" (Hugh-Jones 1988, 148). Myth shapes native Amazonia's cultural possibilities. In this respect, mythopoesis shapes both the Urarinas' social history and their understanding of it. This is also demonstrated by Wright (1998), who has skillfully revealed how the Baniwas' elaborate mythology of destruction and renewal has made them more receptive to both Catholic and Protestant missionaries. Above all, mythopoeic discourse derives its power from its capacity to pervade multiple contexts—to hold and as such to influence people's imaginations.

Familiar accounts of indigenous annihilation, survival, or resistance often fail to encompass adequately the "specific ambivalence of life," particularly for indigenous peoples like the Urarina, who in the face of ever encroaching fronts of national expansion have weathered centuries of conflict, political negotiation, and cultural innovation. Dieken (1998) defines ambivalence through the lens of modernity conceived of as an "ordering project." Rather than simply pitting tradition against modernity Dieken deftly argues that the dichotomous theorizing about tradition and (post)modernity is predicated on a chronological view of time and is not some sort of monolithic construct in which the one is hermetically sealed off from the other. While modernity and civilization held the promise of making life understandable and open to control (Bauman 1991), this never occurred in the Chambira, and few Urarina people I know think it ever will. The Urarinas' ostensibly (post)modern sensibility urges us to pay closer attention to the ways in which society deals with ambivalence in an incurably ambiguous world.

Calísto's narrative draws upon conceptions of utopian renewal, which he discursively contrasts with negative characterizations of Peruvians, who personify stinginess. Framed as a plea for the partial inversion of mercantilism, Calísto's monologue envisages a transformation of the *mestizo* social universe to more closely reflect Urarina ideas of reciprocal sharing, which itself is an ideal not borne out by ethnographic observation. Indeed, relative to the distribution of beer and "true food," the Urarina are egoistic when it comes to apportioning trade goods among themselves.

The narrative's "reflexive symbolism" predicts a pre-apocalyptic utopia of abundant—that is inexpensive—material goods. This is not, however, equivalent to "a society of brotherhood" intimated in other peasant millenarian movements (see Scott 1985, 332). As I have demonstrated throughout this book, there is no neutral medium of value among the Urarina. Everyone knows that trade goods "cost" money, but cash is virtually absent from their networks of exchange. Barter goods are apportioned relative to considerations of labor and prestige hierarchies. There is no ideal of sharing between coevals, but there is an idea of bestowal between unequally situated persons, an ideal ideologically naturalized when people construe it as relationships of complementarity. Calísto's narrative insists that the knowledge of ritual experience (in the form of *ayahuasca* shamanism) is something to be circulated, shared, and expended widely among the natal and affinal longhouses. While the power of *ayahuasca* shamanism is invested in individual persons, this hierarchal impulse is mitigated by the cultural obligation to circulate the benefits (bushmeats and healing) among co-residents of the longhouse.

Assurances of copious amounts of trade items seem altogether fitting when it comes to revelatory visions of apocalyptic change and to promises of social renewal and equity. But I do not want to imply that the Urarina desire or crave (*jerich*) manufactured goods solely for their utility. Rather, I want to suggest that these items of exchange have "defined a semiotic field much larger than immediate material needs" (Brown and Fernández 1991, 136–37). An ambivalent stance toward powerful outsiders can profitably be read in terms of indigenous socio-cosmological notions of otherness. Lepri has confirmed (2006) the ambivalent attitude the Ese Ejja of Bolivia exhibit toward outsiders, which reflects the contextual, fluid, and relational aspects of social identity. Similarly, the Urarina feel deeply ambivalent about labor bosses and traders. On the one hand, traders are the source of valuable consumer goods and tools necessary for subsistence production, while on the other hand, they are the purveyors of illness, violent social discord, and death. Ambivalent exchange relationships are described by self-abasement on the part of the Urarina. This is partially due to historical, economic, and political factors, yet this is also consistent with their strategy of shunning confrontation with dangerous beings.

Drawing on insights gleaned from the notion of ambivalence,[4] I have argued that traders and *patrones* have subjected the Urarina to a world for which their domestic experiences and corpus of myths have often proven inadequate to regulate commercial transactions. This has not prevented the Urarina from mobilizing their oral performative genres as a means of coping with the changes wrought by outsiders and the world they represent. Through the expressive tropes of irony, metaphor, surreal juxtaposition, and metonymy, the Urarina regularly reassign meaning to dominant and emergent cultural symbols. Indeed, by way of subversive bricolage, the Urarina have sought not only to depict "empirical social realities, but to control and change them" (Hill 1993b, 48). In the same way, Kensinger has argued persuasively that the Cashinahua of central Peru employ Inka myths as a way of not only comprehending the identity of non-native traders, but also for associating with them (1995, 259).[5] Likewise, stories about mythical animals— the "extra-human prototype of the Other," to paraphrase Viveiros de Castro (1998, 3)—and diabolic *patrones* enable Urarina male leaders to negotiate intellectually the presence of merchants and labor bosses from the "outside." As Montag and Bastien's interpretation (1996) of the Cashinahuas' foundational myth demonstrates, indigenous explanations of antagonism and conflict are primary concerns of Amazonian cosmologies. In both the Cashinahua and Urarina cases of narrativized violence, one encounters rhetoric of brutality animated by a historical context of real aggression. Yet, violence, as Pareto noted, "is not to be confused with force" (1966, 135). Aggression is clearly a significant aspect of sociality, especially for societies like the Urarina and their historical adversaries, the Jivaroans, whose social life some analysts claim "is structured by endemic warfare and intertribal warfare" (A. Taylor 1996, 4; see also Clastres 1994 cf. Overing 1989).

Instead of hiving off the cultural or performative dimensions of violence from the instrumental domain of power, violence is interpreted here "as a narrated form of symbolic exchange" (George 1996, 2). Like feuding, I contend that the dramatization of violence is itself part of a broader category of communicative exchange. Urarina stories of violence are a mode of exchange between persons who convey and receive reciprocal messages of hostility and theatricalized brutality. The foundational discourses to which *patronazco* narratives belong emphasize the dialectical interplay between relations of violence, aggressive domination, and those characterized by community and relations of reciprocity. Violent inter-ethnic conflict figures prominently in the Urarina story of the Bajkagá, which stands as a testament to the dangers associated with the condition of alterity. But alterity is central to Urarina notions about the reproduction of the social body. From the Urarinas' perspective, the Bajkagá are alien beings who are necessary for all of those purposes, such as trade, "in which the symbolic and material interpenetrate" (Henley 1996, 235).

The circulation of trade goods stands in a metonymic relationship to the world of the *mestizo* outsiders and the power it has over the Urarina. This point is particularly resonant among the Asháninka, whose mythology holds that critical items of exchange underwriting social reproduction, such as cloth and metal tools, were at one time monopolized by the Inka. After surfacing from the underworld's abyss, the Inka and their trade goods were abducted by malevolent "whites." The Asháninka prophesize that they will regain control over the production and circulation of trade goods when the abusive system of labor relations and inequitable distribution of material wealth currently holding sway is finally smashed by their culture-hero (Brown and Fernández 1991, 136–37; see also Urton 1999, 73; Varese 2002).

Messianic narratives like the Asháninkas' and Calísto's apocalyptic account of the end of the world elaborate fundamental reversals in the unequal relations binding indigenous and *mestizo* society. For the Urarina, this reversal is facilitated by the practice and belief in *ayahuasca* shamanism, which is portrayed in opposition to their understanding of the relationships within *mestizo* society. The possession of this cultural knowledge sustains the world as the Urarina know it and establishes an irreducible distinction between themselves and the non-Urarina social universe. As Najlogue kuktíri put it rather cogently: "Those who consume *ayahuasca* and *toé* [datura], they are the ones who are resisting the end of the world . . . they are sustaining our lives, and when the end does arrive, those who do not know Kuánra are going to remain behind. . . . Damn it! There are those *mestizos* who just want to boss people around, but one day the end of the world will arrive, and then there won't be anybody here left to command" (Pangayacu, October 1991).

The Urarinas' entanglement in relations of debt peonage and petty-commodity production has heightened their own awareness of the social implications of possessing power through possessing things. Arguably this is an epistemological stance at considerable odds with their own conceptions of demand sharing, mutual reciprocity, and the constitution of sociality. For the Urarina, sociality is realized through the circulation of knowledge in the form of words, sung meta-language (in the form of chants and songs), as opposed to the exchange of commodities according to the dictates of debt peonage and the logic of market relations.

When discussing equitable rates of exchange, the Urarina will often speak as Ujkuaizíri did to me and say that *patrones* are entitled to *la mitad* or one-half of commodity production. This ambiguous scale of measure refers to the formal distribution of butchered game in the system of *mitayo*. In the words of Ujkuaizíri, "If the *regatones* spend money for fuel, they should earn a little for their journey. Yet, they want to earn *everything* for some little thing they bring us. . . . Why don't they just earn 'half' (*la mitad*)?" (Pangayacu, October 1998).

When asked to elaborate, Ujkuaizíri remarked that unequal exchange is short-sighted behavior in the face of impending apocalyptic destruction. Insisting on the inherent *substantive* equality of the Urarina and *mestizo* peoples, Ujkuaizíri ruminates on the negative character of inter-ethnic exchange:

> When the world ends, what will they do with their things? What will they do with all of their money (*plata*)? We are all equal. Our God and their Cristo are equal. Why don't the *mestizos* say we are all from the same blood? Why don't they give us some gifts, some little thing? When they bring batteries or ammunition they say they are worth so much . . . they want to fuck over the natives (*nativos*) to earn their *plata*. But when the world ends they won't be able to bring their things with them. We have to change everything, we are now living peacefully . . . we don't live to earn. What happens if you earn a huge sum and the world ends? (Pangayacu, October 1998)

Personhood, Hunting, and Shamanism

The affirmation of Urarina cultural values and prerogatives comes from their knowledge of *ayahuasca* shamanism. The Urarina believe that it is the *ayahuasca* shamans, or *kuichá*, who chant and sing the world into being (see also Hill 1993a; Olsen 1996). Urarina cosmology is delineated not by the four cardinal directions, but rather by fluvial references to the ebb and flow of rivers that are said to continue coursing because of the valiant efforts of *kuichá*. Shamanic chanting is central to communal life and to the social production of the person. It accompanies rituals of childbirth, initiation, healing, and hunting magic (fig. 9.2).

Throughout Amazonia, shamanism is expressed in ritualized elaborations of nature, society, and the body (see Chaumeil 1999; Fausto 2001). Shamanism is manifest among the Urarina in their elaborate ideologies of

Fig. 9.2. Headman playing music, Pangayacu River

hunting and is reflected in their socially traumatic experience of inter-ethnic violence. Versed in the techniques and experiences of the ecstatic condition, Urarina shamans are distinguished from others by their possession and manipulation of cosmic forces. Through mastery of trance (*ajená*), chanting (*bagniñá*), and dreaming (*siniñucá*), shamans mediate between mortal and supra-human domains. Because dreams are believed to result from the travels of one's spirit (*siíji*) during sleep, the analyses of dreams (*siní*) are taken very seriously since they are interpreted as omens of the future. For example, dreaming about encountering numerous turtles is thought to signal the death of a family member. Dreams about canoe construction are said to be portents of hunting tapir. Dreams of sexual relations are linked to hunting peccary, and dreams associated with fishing hooks are seen as a sign of an impending snakebite. Urarina *kuichá* are liminal figures who are once both powerful and dangerous. Their power legitimizes diverse roles within Urarina society: healer, hunter, and headman.

Among the Urarina *ayahuasca* is called *iñunö/iñunú*; *dedé iñunú* means "heavenly" *ayahuasca*; *ajláidi iñunú* means "parrot *ayahuasca*." Datura or *toé* is called *ajcaá*; there is "white" *toé* and *safuarájcaa* or "yellow" *toé*. It is mixed with the leaves of an unidentified plant of a similar size called *abené* (*hoja purga*). Both are then pulverized ("seven times" according to one acquaintance) in a ceramic vessel called a *miráe* or *baiyaje* and then boiled. The ornate clay *ayahuasca* vessels are made by women, who are required to abstain from sexual intercourse during their manufacture (approximately six days) so that the vessels will not crack while being fired. These vessels are inalienable wealth items. At death they either go to the grave with their owner or are transmitted patrilineally. *Paujil* (*yajtari*) bird feathers are used to remove what the Urarina call the *piojos* ("lice" in Spanish) or impurities (insects or unwanted flora matter) from the boiled *ayahuasca*.

In their account of the mythical creation of the underworld, the Urarina say that Lumaí, the daughter of the master of *ayahuasca*, was brought from the celestial abode of the deities down to Earth to attend a cassava beer festival. During the celebration, the woman's suitor refused to let her go and urinate, insisting instead that they continue dancing. As a result, the woman's urine drowned all the festival participants, giving rise to the chthonic world of spirits and creatures. Said to have occurred at a place the Urarina call Banuctrí—the whirlpool below the mouth of the Tigrillo River—the flood of Lumaí's urine produced dolphins from those who drowned. Conversely, water tortoises were transformed into wooden stools (*üfuiufhua*) and the land turtles became wooden vats the Urarina use to prepare food. The account of the origination of the underworld converges with the epic of Kuánra kajlaui and the universal deluge: both narratives illustrate how men's insatiable desire leads to ontological transformation and ultimately affliction—be it corporeal or spiritual. Liquids and their movement are potent signifiers of the changes accompanying social life and mythic practice. The flow of cassava beer into a thirsty open mouth, followed by the urge to urinate, symbolizes festive satiation. Bodily liquids, as in the onset of menarche or the passage of amniotic fluid, signal generational movement from one life stage to another, while drug-induced emetic purgation and defecation marks the openness of the body and in turn effects physical and mental transition from one mode of consciousness to another.

In addition to the consumption of narcotic beverages, the Urarinas' shamanic complex (*kuichára*) includes elaborate incantations (*bagniñá* or in Spanish *icaro*), dream quests, tactile healing (*datáa*), and curative tobacco smoke "blowing" (*enuatá jidirichakña*). Oneiric and narcotic visions are portals of shamanic power: they provide the skilled *kuichá* with a vortex to transcendental existence. Hallucinogenic phantasmagorias—dreamlike scenes induced by the release of massive quantities of tryptamine in the cerebral cortex—-are proof of the vitality of transcendental realities, glossed here as *dedé*. As Maybury-Lewis writes regarding the spiritual efficacy of Cashinahua narcotic shamanic experience, "Taking yage [*ayahuasca*] is like spiritual coitus. It allows them to experience the union that they believe to be the true reality, instead of discrete entities of the apparent reality in which they live their everyday lives" (1992, 223).

Urarina shamanism is informed by notions of personhood that revolve around a bifurcated bodily essence, itself tethered to a dualistic spiritual incorporeality—distinguished as *siíji* and *anekai* (cf. Tessmann 1987, 63). Urarina notions of the person hint at what has been called the "partibility" of personhood (see Beckerman and Valentine 2002). Like the spatial position of a tree's duramen, *siíji* usually inhabit the middle of one's body. *Siíji* are equated with a person's cognitive capacities. During episodes of dreaming or narcotic trance, *siíji* temporarily depart the body's center. At death, *siíji* migrate permanently to the firmament, while the deceased's corpse remains behind to rot in the longhouse of the dead (*ajtánabana*). After a corpse has been interred, the deceased's significant female relatives (wife, sister, and daughter) light a small fire at the foot of the funerary dais. The fire is said to keep the *siíji* warm and is kept ablaze for a few weeks following the death of important persons. In preparation for the *siíji*'s afterlife, gender specific items are displayed on the burial platform: shamanic accoutrements and domestic ceramic ware.

In contrast to *siíji*, *anekai*[6] are ghouls who do not journey to the celestial realm, but linger instead on Earth (see Ferrúa Carrasco et al. 1980, 42). These revenant spirits eventually return to their natal community and wander about in a state of loneliness, spending their time trying to entice living relatives (especially the young and infirm) to join them in the land of the dead. As visible specters of disembodied spirits, morpho butterflies (family Morphidae, genus *Morpho*, called *ijiatáuri anekai*) are equated with ghoulish *anekai*.

The Urarina believe that the tops of *anekai* headdresses can be seen in the form of the blue morpho butterfly. When boys and young men spot these butterflies in a garden clearing or see them flying near the homestead, they will not hesitate to chase away these majestic butterflies as feared harbingers of evil. The appearance of shimmering blue morphos near a receptacle of cassava beer (*barigué*) is cause for even greater agitation because people think that this is evidence of the *anekai*-butterfly trying to pollute the beer with its urine.

The Urarinas' animistic ontology contends that the natural worlds of the skies, waters, and earth are all suffused with vital life forces, many of which are conceptualized as feminized animate essences (colloquially called *madres* in Loreto). Knowledge of these animate life essences—both benevolent and demonic—is constitutive of Urarina shamanism. Spirits influenced through shamanic chants embody all fauna and flora. The Panoan-speaking Yamináwa (Yaminahua) have a comparable notion of "spirit or animate essence" that they call *yoshi* and see as the ultimate source of all shamanic power. As "paths" [*wai*] into the spirit world, origin myths are indexed by the Yamináwa and the Urarina when they recast them into the elliptical speech of shamanic chants (Townsley 1993, 452–53). Iconic and indexical signs mediate the world in distinctive ways, yet there are similar patterns that span the far reaches of the upper Amazon. Like the Urarina, the Quechua-speaking Runa of Ecuador maintain conceptions of nature that emphasize obtaining and sharing iconically and indexically loaded modes of communicating experience of ecological knowledge, rather than engaging in the traffic of this local knowledge (Kohn 2005).

Among the Urarina, all plants are thought to have their "mothers" (*néba*), which are believed to be responsible for floral conception and maturation. Important mother spirits are associated with subsistence crops, such as cassava (*lanebá*) and plantains (*juanaranéba*). One of the most potent floral spirits is Ijiá néba (Lupuna mother), said to be the mother spirit of the forest capable of killing infants. The mother spirit of the rivers or Yacumama (Quechua) is similarly a potent life-taker known as Ajkaig néba. The Urarina also speak of animal "mothers" and liken them to "celestial gamekeepers," a generalized belief in the region, as among the Cahuapanan-speaking Chayahuita (A. Fuentes 1988, 78) or the Makuna of the Colombian Vaupés (Århem 1998, 104).

Animate *essences* are omnipresent in terrestrial zones such as palm swamps and the forest's interior (*ajtanecájtai*). In the symbolically charged intersection between the terrestrial firmament and the aquatic realm reside *aguajal* spirits called *jirijána amuenánaja*. Numerous fiendish forest apparitions, goblins, and gnomes (*Taibiña kuitikichí, Chuyacháki, Sañatúa dijiái, Bainí*) lurk in these spiritually charged spaces and frighten people by becoming animals or by assuming anthropomorphic shapes. Some of the more malevolent spirits (*shapshico* in Quechua) have the power to abduct unsuspecting individuals as they journey through the jungle. Typical of such accounts is the one told to me in July 1991 by Calísto about Aséij, a forest demon.

Aséij the Demon

A man went out hunting with his blowgun in search of monkeys to eat. He went very far, all the way to the center of the forest where a menacing demon—Aséij—waited. Night fell while the man was still listening for animals. Having killed a number of monkeys, the man sheltered himself in the pyramidal buttress of a large tree. The hunter had a net bag full of monkeys—*ruru* [red howler], *ajláu* [black spider monkey], and *adähuata* [common wooly monkey] which he placed by his side. There at the base of the tree he stayed sleeping in the cold. The man heard the demon knocking against the tree's buttress: "tan—tan—tan. " "It's coming . . . Pucha . . . ! What am I going to do. . . ? The demon will kill me!" The man grabbed his machete and waited for the demon. From the pitch darkness came, "Hello, *paisano*." The man replied, "Hello." "What are you doing sitting here?" asked the demon. After he told him, the demon then said, "Ah . . . I too am looking for *mitayo*. Why don't you take out your liver for me to eat?" So the man removed the liver from an *adähuata* and said, "Here is my liver." The demon ate the liver and then said, "I am still hungry. Give me your leg." The man removed the *adähuata*'s leg and gave it to the demon. "You can feed me well!" responded the demon. "Yes, luckily I have a lot. Pucha! I also want to eat your liver. Remove it for me," said the man to the forest demon. The demon split open his abdomen. "Taalán . . ." the demon fell dead. "Pucha!" cried the man. After he had sat for a long time, daylight finally appeared. The man could now see the demon stretched out on the ground. He wore black trousers and a black shirt. The man took hold of his machete and struck the demon's teeth, which were identical to jaguar teeth. The demon sat bolt upright and asked, "What are you doing?" "I am hitting you in the teeth so that you will awaken," said the man. The demon responded, "Thank you. Fortunately you have woken me. Since you have come to my aid I will do you a favor." "How are you going to help me?" the man asked. "I am going to give you bow and arrows so that you can hunt white-lipped peccary, tapir, and deer," said the demon. "How am I to hunt with them?" asked the man. "When white-lipped peccary, tapir, and deer are fleeing, take aim and fire. The animals will fall, and when you go to them you will see that they are dead" (fig. 9.3).

Like many other Urarina legends, the narrative's protagonist is celebrated as a trickster, a universal archetype that permeates cultures across the globe. Ambivalence is manifest in the playful/malevolent dualities of the trickster (Spinks 2001). The huntsman's own cunning releases him from what the Urarina consider the ultimate in negative commensality—cannibalism—or what some analysts have called "ontological predation."[7] Under the cover of darkness, the protagonist circulates "true food" in the form of bushmeats from slain monkeys. The demon, however, is tricked into killing himself, a death that stands as a cautionary illustration of the hazards of anthropophagy, which the Urarina equate with their Jivaroan archrivals, the Bajkagá. While the narrative's mention of the bow and arrow is significant, given the fact that these implements are no longer used by the Urarina (see Tessmann 1987, 55), the teeth of the predatory demon, described as resembling those of the jaguar, warrant greater attention. Contact with these adamantine objects of hard wealth discursively engenders life, as evidenced by the demon's revivification after being struck in the teeth. At the level of symbolic praxis, use of feline teeth as neckwear facilitates Urarina hunting shamanism—an intricate corpus of knowledge and ritual action whose objectives are aimed at neutralizing evil while ensuring a bountiful catch. In the Urarinas' estima-

Fig. 9.3. Urarina boy and peccary "pet"

tion, the evil effects of the forest's wicked vitalities are mitigated by tutelary animal spirits responsible for revealing useful knowledge to *kuichá*—such as the practical techniques necessary for everyday living, including methods of healing, weaving, cooking, gardening, and the procurement of forest game.

An integral aspect of Urarina hunting shamanism is detailed descriptions of celestial travels—mythical as well as prosaic encounters and symbolic exchanges between humans, animals, and supernatural entities (see Hamayon 1994, 78–81). For many Amazonian peoples, access to forest game is ensured through the shamanic disembodiment, which occurs during narcotic trance and dreaming (Vickers 1989b, 135ff.; Kracke 1992, 130; Luna 1992a, 223; Holmberg 1969, 241). Whenever game animals become sparse, Urarina hunting shamans smoke tobacco and imbibe hallucinogens, which enable their *siíji* to journey the arduous path to *dedé*—the abode of the animal spirits. With the assistance of the tutelary mother spirit of *ayahuasca* (known as *réi cuaé*), which enters the body, *kuichá* attempt to procure the release of additional game animals and according to some Urarina trade goods as well. *Réi cuaé* are held to be matriarchal spirits because as one acquaintance stated in 1994, "Everyone knows that mothers always have more force than fathers" (see also Luna 1992a, 232; Kamppinen 1988, 146; A. Fuentes 1988, 168–70).

In indigenous Amazonia nature is not ontologically detached from the realm of humanity but rather is part of a broader domain of human sociality and bodily intersubjectivity. This distinctive worldview has been called perspectivism by a number of theorists. Perspectivism emphasizes the multifaceted subjectivities found in indigenous Amazonian notions of corporeal processes, ties of kinship, and cosmology (Vilaca 2002; Uzendoski et al. 2005). According to Rival (2005), Huaorani perspectivism expresses the point of view of the prey rather than the predator and connects the soul with masculinity and predation, which are opposed to the body, femininity, and resisting victimhood.

My interest in the idea of perspectivism is to underscore the transformative capacity of the body and highlight the Urarinas' belief—like that of many native Amazonians—that all living creatures have spirits that flow in an animistic way (Descola 1994; Vilaca 2002). Vilaca (2002, 351) spells it out: "What enables the permutability of the body is precisely the equivalence of spirits: all are equally human, equally subjects. By modifying the body alimentation, change in habits, and the establishment of social relations with other subjects, another point of view is acquired: the world is now seen in the same way as the new companions, that is, the members of the other species."

In Amazonia the body assumes centrality in ideas about social reproduction and cultural survival and hence it must constantly be refashioned. *Ayahuasca* shamanism facilitates the embodiment of spirits, humans, and other creatures, which constantly mutate, and in the process these entities assume new subjectivities and relational perspectives. Among the Urarina, the location of game animals and birds is also divulged by "celestial gamekeepers" in dreams. The Pangayacu's huntsmen regularly have fatidic dreams about encounters with game animals. On one particular occasion in July 1992 a local headman told me and the others of his longhouse about an elaborate dream he had that night, which culminated with his stalking and killing a paca. In the afternoon, the headman returned to the longhouse glowing with pride for he had managed to bag a very large and plump paca with his blowgun—ten kilos of which he promptly exchanged for half-spent flashlight batteries with the *patrón* of a local *fundo* on the middle Chambira (at the site called Tropezón).

Linguistically the verb *bajtuhuí*—the action of using a blowgun to kill game—is equivalent to the term used to describe a witch's magical dart or thorn. Urarina witchcraft or *venané* is closely associated with the process known colloquially in Loretano Spanish as *chontear*. This term refers to the sorcerer's action of sucking *chonta* palm spines (*Guilielma gasipaes*) and then maliciously projecting them at victims. Urarina witches or *ñasatiyá* are dart spitters: they ingest the thorny spines of the peach palm or *pejibaye* (*Bactris gasipaes* or *Guilielma gasipaes*), sting-ray barbs, or fish spines and then magically hurl them at unsuspecting scapegoats, causing them illness and misfortune (*bajtuhuiñá kachá sátiya najän*).

To counteract these deadly projectiles, *kuichá* imbibe hallucinogens that enable them to see the invisible darts afflicting the body. With a harpy eagle fan the shaman circulates air around the "patient's" body (*shajtigá ujídi itaruké*) and then begins chanting and singing. A shaman will beseech the spiritual pathogens and magical darts to "leave the body." Then the *kuichá* will attempt to literally suck the dart pathogens out of the sufferer (*tujtujuídi kuiché*), a vigorous procedure that leaves bruises and small hematomas on the patient's body.

Ayahuasca shamans also loom large in times of scarcity in bushmeat procurement. The precarious situation regarding access to trade goods, coupled with the fact that the Urarina have to work so diligently to be able to secure game means that bushmeat scarcity is a constant preoccupation. So there should be no surprise that the alienation of forest game—because of whatever factors (such as rising demand for *carne del monte* in the city or the market in pelts)—has rendered it into a commodity, and this is profoundly troubling to the Urarina.[8]

Myth, Meat, and the Morality of Commodities

All societies have inalienable possessions: wealth items that ideally should be kept outside of impersonalized exchange networks. Among the Urarina, this includes shamanic appurtenances, woven palm-fiber wealth, and hunted bushmeats. As a class of things, these wealth items are "loaned rather than sold and ceded" (Mauss 1967, 42; see also Sahlins 1972, 217–19). Moral peril awaits any effort at transforming food items of wealth into pure transactional objects (Parry 1989, 88). This Maussian insight gives meaning to the Urarina belief that thunder (*arára*) and lightning (*marimarí*) are the result of the creator god Kuánra clapping his hands in displeasure with wayward hunters who have exchanged forest game with *mestizo patrones*. The onset of rain and lightning is a focus of deep concern for the Urarina, particularly as noted in their mythical expression of the primordial flood. Their story of worldly creation exemplifies one of the most widely dispersed narratives known to humankind—the deluge myth. This fear also finds life in their story of the competition between the jaguar and rain to see who could frighten the Urarina more. Jaguar spirit was unsuccessful and was chased off by gun-wielding Urarina. Rain spirit, however, unleashed a tremendous storm with lightning and was successful in frightening the Urarina. The Urarina contend that barter of bushmeats between themselves and *mestizo* traders is prohibited by Kuánra, who uses fire to boil their *siíji* or corporeal "spiritual cores."

The ashes of burnt *siíji* are then transformed into electric eels, which are a cosmological analogue of men's ceremonial staves (*ujtiya*) used for *ayahuasca* shamanism, as well as women's wooden *cumaceva* weaving swords (*ubiñya*). Made by men from pona wood (*ajanahé, Iriartea deltiodea*), *ujtiya* are used exclusively for imbibing *ayahuasca*. The ceremonial stave is used percussively as well as for balancing while vomiting or urinating during a hallucinogenic session. *Ujtiya* are never used as war clubs (see Tessmann 1987, 62). When men talk in Spanish about their *siíji* or *süjhe* they refer to them as *shungos*, which in the vernacular Quechua of the region denotes liver or heart (Landerman 1973, 48; G. Taylor 1979, 167). In spoken Urarina, heart is rendered as *inajári*, and viscera (for example, intestines) are called *ijkiasi*.

The Urarina are fully cognizant of the fact that their inalienable appurtenances are systematically being appropriated. Urarina understandings of unequal exchange are routinely refracted through their graphic accounts of commodity flows. Like other marginalized groups, the Urarina elaborate fabulous mythologies because they are largely alienated from the supra-local circulation and consumption logics of the commodities they both produce and consume (see also Oostra 1991, 37f.; T. Turner 1988, 263f.; cf. O. Harris 1989, 241, 253; Carrier 1992a, 189). Regarding the origins of trade goods and money, a local Pangayacu headman explained them to me rather cryptically late one evening during the rainy season of 1998: "Kane Kuánra—the artificer of our world—sent the Anazairi [*mestizos*] in canoes to give trade goods and silver coins [*plata*] to us. 'Go and deliver these things to the Kachá—the Urarina people' commanded Kuánra. But the Anazairi refused to heed his command. They kept the trade goods instead of giving them to the Urarina; they robbed like a *regatón* [river merchant]. Because the Anazairi refused to give the Urarina their trade goods, today they have everything—they tricked our ancestors."

In this instance, this myth mimics reality by caricaturing the egoistic behavior of the nefarious *patrón*, of whom there are many real life models from which to draw. A tone of retaliatory vengeance shapes many narrative accounts of *patrón* relations with the Urarina. Particularly common are the Urarinas' vivid accounts of the poisoning of omnivorous *patrones* with deadly toxins, such as *ajá* (*Hura crepitans*), which is mixed furtively into libations of cassava beer. In the eyes of the Urarina, the inhumane and acquisitive behavior of the *mestizo* labor bosses aligns them with the undomesticated Dog Spirits and the likes of cannibalistic forest Demons that all refuse to share—a failure that subverts the moral economy of Urarina society.

The ethnographic record is replete with many instances in which indigenous peoples like the Urarina resort to "irony, mockery, humor, dissimulation, and protest to talk down the patrons or the authorities" (Muratorio 1991, 211). By way of subversive bricolage, Urarina headmen have sought to depict not only "empirical social realities, but to control and change them" (Hill 1993b, 48). The discursive formations associated with *habilitación* give the Urarina a means for apprehending the past and a way for coping with an ever changing world—particularly the commodification of social life (see Knauft 1997; cf. Dean 1998a). Reference to Urarina oral narratives describing shamanism, labor bosses, peonage, and trade goods helps situate our understanding of economic and sociocultural production.

The economic determinations of society are largely absent from the Urarinas' ideological representations of themselves and their relations of production. As I have made clear in previous chapters, the overt connections between petty-commodity production and the Urarinas' familiar forms of oral representation (myths, aphorisms, songs, and so forth) are obfuscated. Representations of debt peonage are routinely naturalized as part of the Urarinas' common-sense view of the world. This process is evident in Urarina daily conversations about work where qualifying adjectives are dropped, such as *mestizo* from *patrón* or unequal from exchange. Quite clearly we are dealing here with an ex-nominating process, the assumption being that *patrones* are naturally *mestizo* and petty-commodity exchange is naturally inequitable.

Mythology is of particular interest because it provides the Urarina with the intellectual space for the articulation of countervailing tendencies, namely, the ineluctable pull of *immeubles* valuables and the forces of impersonal chattelization characteristic of petty-commodity production and peonage. The latter tendency, which imperils the ties that connect the living to both the remembered past and the envisioned future, is nullified in the domain of myth, which celebrates the reciprocity of gifting while denouncing the commoditized relations of mercantile exchange (Dean 1994b). Unlike taxes or extortion, genuine gifts are characterized by the absence of "calculation," not by the absence of obligations (Godelier 1999, 5, 14).

This model of mythopoeis—positing the dichotomy of *immeubles* valuables versus impersonal chattelization—parallels the oft-cited distinction between personalized gift and alienated commodity (see Herrmann 1997; Ledeneva 1996–97). While the gift/commodity dualism is a convenient heuristic, its analytical essentialism becomes obvious when it is used to understand the cultural practices of bushmeat procurement, distribution, and consumption. An obdurate and essentialized distinction between gift and commodity systems of exchange and sociality has lately held sway in anthropology, dominating the terms of debate in a number of subfields, such as the ethnology of Melanesia and even to some degree the ethnology of Amazonia (Chevalier 1982). In contrast to the dichotomous tendency implicit in the polemic over the social implications of commoditized versus gift exchanges, a number of analysts have advocated viewing exchange as "a processual field of practices" (Liep 1993, 23; see also Carrier 1990, 703; Strathern 2002; H. Moore 1993, 127; Weiner 1994; Satherm 2002; Foster 2002; Hughes 2004).

Carrier's description (1992a; 1992b) of Ponam exchange, for instance, challenges Strathern's (1988; 1993) designation of Melanesian transactions as pertaining to a gift economy. Carrier argues that the classification of transactions as "gifts" or "commodities" falters when trying to account for the inherent ambiguity and contention in all systems of exchange (1992a, 185). In a somewhat related way, Weiner (1994) has argued that objects should be arranged according to their symbolic densities. At one polar extreme are inalienable items of wealth—things that must be retained within the confines of the family or local group. Resembling commodities, items at the other polar extreme lack "symbolic density"; their interchangeability is predicated on the ease by which they are replaced (Weiner 1994, 394).

Hunted bushmeats are symbolically dense—for the Urarina they are so thick with cultural significance that traders and labor bosses have trouble wresting these items from their "owners." Urarina huntsmen regularly conceal the total kill-number from the *patrones*. In addition to their economic value, bushmeats' symbolic density is a function of their metaphorical associations, their proclivity to be socially concealed, and their intimate connection with a hunter's prestige, as well as a host's reputation for generosity. Rather than a simple act of conservation or sustainable development (Beckerman et al. 2001; Posey and Balick 2006), it is this symbolic density that accounts in large part for the Urarinas' ideological resistance to the mercantilization of their forest game. Hunted bushmeats are indexical signs of shamanism—a practice itself at the nexus of inter-ethnic conflict. As Najlegue-kuktíri explained by reference to hunting shamanism:

> Our God Kuánra was here in this place before the evil *mestizos*. Our God was here, but he went to the sky with the *huangana* [collared peccaries]. Now our God says: "Only those who know how to drink *ayahuasca* and who can thus see me are able to ask me to send *huangana* to appear on Earth. Those who know how to take *ayahuasca* and who become dizzy with visions of me and knowledge of who I am—they can ask for *huangana*." God will aid them by sending *huangana* to them. If you don't know how to take *ayahuasca* and to ask our God for them, then *huangana* do not come here. *Huangana* wander about like *sajino* [white-lipped peccary] ... they wander into ugly and dangerous areas like *aguajales* [palm swamps], but eventually they arrive where God is. This is why when we take *ayahuasca* we chant: "Ada ada ge-ge-ge ge-ge-geé ijchiterá lumai terá lumai terá nijkukajgé ijchiterá aiterá lumai jarrá...." (Chambira River, July 1992)

This chapter has examined one particular strategy—shamanism—as a response to those external pressures shaping the Urarina people's lives: namely the lure of consumer goods, predacious labor practices, and epidemics. I have used ethnographic examples of *ayahuasca* shamanism in an attempt to show how the Urarina deal with affliction and invest the rights to deal effectively with the sources of affliction in one person—the shaman. As I have illustrated, their use of *ayahuasca* shamanism often coincides with messianic messages because the common causes of affliction are seen by the

Urarina as emanating from the outside. In this regard, one cannot separate the external pressures of extractive mercantilism from the Urarinas' own ambivalent interpretations of their relations of unequal exchange with outsiders.

Mythogenesis and Social Trauma in Amazonia

Indigenous societies throughout lowland South America are intensely conscious of the historical transformations and the struggle to achieve hegemony. Nonetheless, the Urarina insist on the timeless nature of their worldview, while at the same time struggling very hard to protect it from the onslaught of a hostile Peruvian national society. It is in this sense that the Urarina can be considered as a cold society—not because they lack historical consciousness, but rather because they seek to preserve the timeless cosmos underwriting the social order as they know it. Like other Amazonian peoples (Rubenstein 2002, 31), it is the Urarinas' own intimate understanding of the supernatural that valorizes the social order. Claude Lévi-Strauss's monumental *Mythologiques* (for example, 1975, 1978a) successfully revealed how South American mythic narratives are not random; there is in fact "a definite logical coherence to them, that elements which remain un-explained in one myth become clear in the analysis of other contrasting myths from the same or neighboring tribes" (Yalman 1967, 75). The Urarinas' mythic universe is a narrative domain framed by a series of contrasts and inversions based in part on binary oppositions implicit in analogical reasoning. Literally, anything can happen in this cosmic discourse, but it does not. Yet Urarina myth has no elemental code or underlying private language to be elucidated or decoded.

Post-structural and deconstructionist perspectives have problematized the concept of binary opposition. The notion of binary opposition represents an imposition of order or "centering" that essentializes the analysis of myth: analogical oppositions oversimplify the diffuse signification of a myth, which is never singular or stable, but rather is characterized by its pluri-signification (Derrida 1970). Like any art form, Urarina myth resists translation but invites contextualization. Throughout Amazonia, mythogenesis is inflicted by colonial and postcolonial experiences of social trauma. The Urarina are no different for their sense of the lived world and the past is mythicized. They believe that the primordial cosmic paradise gave birth to the social order of everyday existence. But in the face of both abusive and alluring market relations with *mestizo* representatives of Peruvian national society, some Urarina see their social order as fraught with instability, teetering on the brink of collapse.

Many of the novel insights emerging from the ethnology of indigenous Amazonia have resulted from the synergistic interaction between structural and historical approaches that privilege a dialectical appreciation of the interrelationship between society and nature (Viveiros de Castro 1996, 179–201). The articulation of the social and metaphysical is highly developed in lowland South America (Maybury-Lewis 1992; A. Taylor 1996; Fausto 2001; Rival and Whitehead 2002; N. Whitehead 2002). Indigenous peoples in Amazonia emphasize ritual and the cosmos rather than institutional politics driven by acquisitive economies oriented toward the consumption of surpluses. By interpreting sacred narratives as collective representations (à la Durkheim), I have illustrated some of the ways in which Urarina rhetorical practices and ritual performances are not only informed by the cosmos, but are deeply embedded within the flux of social experience (see Oakdale 2005, 173). This included highlighting the sometimes subtle but always complex interplay between social practice and cosmology as expressed in Urarina verbal arts. It entailed demonstrating how the Urarinas' narratives "layer, conjoin and linger" (Feld 1998, 446). Review of Urarina cosmogonic discourse provides insight into our understanding of how significance is conveyed through the intervocality of oral genres. The Urarinas' elaborate creation story, and its emphasis on deluge and rebirth, reveals a multiplicity of meanings typical of mythopoeic discourse (Dean 1994b; Olawsky 2002, 70–122). Like all primal myths, the Urarinas' creation story provides a series of answers to implied questions of fundamental import: how the earth came into being; how humankind began; and why death and suffering entered the world. A full appreciation of the historicity of Urarina mythopoeic discourse calls for a detailed analysis of the ways in which Urarina myths not only "incorporate historical realities" (Guss 1981), but also integrate the stuff that makes up the narratives of the unrecorded lives of ordinary people and seemingly insignificant events. Urarina personal histories are integral to what Renato Rosaldo has called the "broader collective fabric of shared residence and the common experience of wider events" (1980, 56).

For many indigenous South American societies, history is as Hill argues "understood in relation to a few 'peak', or critical periods of rapid change, rather than a smoothly flowing progression. The periods most frequently selected in Amazonian societies are the rubber boom and times of abrupt, violent change forced upon indigenous peoples from outside and above" (1988, 7). Writing against the romanticized, literary traditions of Western naturalism, Raffles (2002) emphasizes Euro-American interests in the Amazon but does not present the vast region as a singular or homogenous construct. Rather, he presents it as a dynamic and heterogeneous web of places and relations configured by various human-driven historical projects. Shuttling back and forth between various sites and scales of analysis, Raffles (2002) reviews a number of human engagements through which the very nature of the "Amazon" has been constructed—exploratory voyages, natural history expeditions, ecological experimentations, practices of colonization, development, and literary imageries (see also Suárez-Araúz 2004). Likewise, this book has chronicled some of the critical historical peaks or periods of rapid and in some cases profound social change that have characterized Urarina relations with the various fronts of colonial and national expansion.

Based on his work among the Kayapó of central Brazil, Terence Turner (1993) has argued that portrayals of native Amazonian peoples' encounters with national society and the forces of transnational capital have often come at the expense of not paying significant attention to indigenous cultural forms. In Amazonia, societal stress invariably conditions sorcery beliefs and efforts at discursively representing the rapidity of social transformations. This is amply illustrated in the Matsigenka case of Peru, where the expressions of feelings of envy associated with accelerated socioeconomic change have been noted accompanying the forces of colonization (Izquierdo and Johnson 2007).

Similarly, semiotic and structuralist studies of Amazonia's prodigious sociocultural variation have often excluded from analysis issues of political economy as well as the cultural realities of transcultural conflict and interdependencies (Pineda Camacho 2003). Both the Urarina and the Kayapó cases clearly indicate the need for "more sociologically, historically and materially grounded forms of cultural analysis" (T. Turner 1993, 1; see also Whitehead and Wright 2004; Heckenberger 2004). As Alcida Ramos asserts, "History"—either derived from ethnological inquiry or from an indigenous peoples' own perspective—should strive to erase the myth "of the big demographic void the Amazon allegedly represents, a fallacy created to loot the region" (2002, 8).

To this end, this work is a sociocultural analysis of Urarina responses to colonial and postcolonial intrusions, which have encompassed a number of strategies, including entheogenic transcendence, hostile resistance, and accommodative incorporation. Well over a century of academic anthropology has revealed that the amazing variety of humanity is linked to historical patterns that "shape perceptions of cultural events, while the collective sum of human experience is itself constitutive of the very stuff of cultural life"

(Dean 2006c, 1). Urarina valuables—entities and relational structures—are intimately entangled in Urarina exchange and hence they yield "imaginary schemes" (Lattas 1993, 105) for figuring the alienation accompanying the processes of commodification. Here I have in mind tangible and intangible items of wealth—phenomena and things as diverse as narcotic trance, snail shell and peccary teeth breast bands, myths, shamanic wizardry, harpy eagle quill feather fans, palm-bast cloth, and hunted forest game.

Urarina imaginary worlds—their narratives, oral traditions, songs, and public memories—are routinely performed or deployed in one way or another to mediate the internal contradictions accompanying the intrusion of market relations into the Chambira Basin. The Urarinas' conflict among disparate discourses, definitions, and meanings of cultural value is at once a battle within signification itself: it entails a contest over control of the sign, which permeates even the most prosaic and routine arenas of social life.

Notes

Introduction

1. This idea is elaborated in *Streams of Cultural Capital*, the provocative title of the collection of essays edited by David Palumbo-Liu and Hans Ulrich Gumbrecht (1997).

2. Coercive relations of labor and the social dislocations accompanying the Amazonian rubber boom are well documented (Taussig 1987; Barham and Coomes 1994; Ochoa Siguas 1999; and Stanfield 1998).

3. As Maybury-Lewis puts it, "In traditional societies the motto is 'seller beware,' for a person who gouges or shortchanges will become a moral outcast, excluded from social interaction with other people. He will end up dying alone under a tree" (1992, 85). A burgeoning moral economy literature supports this perspective; "classic" moral economy perspectives are given by Scott (1985) and Roseberry (1993).

4. Speaking the Loretano dialect of Spanish is referred to as *charapeando*, a term derived from the word *charapa* (water tortoise), a euphemism for residents of Loreto (Castonguay 1990; Alvarez Vita 1990; and Tovar 1996).

5. This awe was dampened after the eventual shattering of the lamp's cylindrical glass covering after it came into repeated contact with the "blood" of countless insects and moths whose lives were sacrificed in their quest for light.

6. The issue of female silence or "mutedness" in the context of ethnographic "fieldwork" is addressed by Ardner (1989, 72–85). For an exemplary account of an intergenerational approach addressing indigenous women's life histories and socioeconomic change in the Upper Napo region of Amazonia, see Muratorio 1998.

7. The fourteen linguistic familias are Arawak, Cahuapano, Harakmbet, Jíbaro, Pano, Peba-Yagua, Quechua, Tacano, Ticuna, Tucano, Tupí, Urarina, Witoto, and Záparo.

8. On the structure and history of peonage in Amazonia, see Villanueva 1902, 136–37; Rumrrill and Zutter 1976, 71ff.; Chevalier 1982, 198ff.; Stocks 1983, 87; Barclay Rey de Castro et al. 1991; Santos Granero and Barclay 2000. For the Chambira-Urituyacu region, see Domville-Fife 1924, 201. For a list of early twentieth-century *patrones* and traders of the region along the Río Pastaza, to west of the Chambira Basin, see Jáuregui 1943, 481.

9. My use of the concept of hegemony follows Gramsci 1971. For similar elaborations, see William's (1977) idea of "oppositional, emergent and residual cultures"; Foucault's (1980) concept of "subjugated knowledges"; or Bourdieu's description of (1986) "symbolic domination."

10. On the recent growth and appeal of indigenism, see Perry 1996; Gomes 2000; Niezen 2003; Maybury-Lewis, ed. 2002; Warren and Jackson 2003; Dean and Levi 2003; Dean 2000, 2004a.

Chapter 1. The "People from Downstream"

1. The meaning of the term *montaña* varies. For instance, in David Adamson's account of Colonel Pedro Portillo's Amazonian "expedition" of 1900, *montaña* is "freely

translated as unoccupied or waste land and forests" (1904, 14 n.). In Bolivia, the equivalent term for *montaña* is *yungas*, while in Ecuador the term is *oriente* (Moran 1982, 30 n. 12).

2. This paired opposition appears elsewhere as riverine and interfluve habitat (Lathrap 1970) or tropical forest and flood plain (Roosevelt 1999).

3. The greenish-brown, umber, and sienna shades of blackwater rivers stem from their humic and fulvic acid loads. Tannins leached from tree bark and peat turn the water its characteristic tea color (Gragson 1992b, 429; see also Moran 1991, 364–65; 1995).

4. I use the term *regatón* to signify an itinerant, fluvial trader and his boat—a veritable "floating shop" as Cressy-Marks noted (1932). Historically those boatmen who have plied primary river ways, such as the Ucayali and Marañón, have been expert navigators as well as traders. When they pull into port, they regularly open their floating store "and do a brisk trade" (Cressy-Marcks 1932, 148). The Urarina refer to small-scale traders as *regatoncillo* in Loretano Spanish, and *regatonlauyi* in spoken Urarina.

5. This genre includes atlases, monographs, and various descriptive surveys of Amazonia. Among these many figurations, see Raimondi 1863; Farabee 1922; Coriat 1943; Girard 1958; Chirif and Mora 1977; Ravines and de Matos 1988; Brack Egg 1997; and Peisa 2003, 35.

6. When pushed on the origin of outsiders such as myself (*gringos*), Urarina acquaintances responded by saying they come from downstream—from somewhere "below Iquitos" (and according to one, "below Lima and the endless sea that stretches beyond"). On Cocama identity formation and the historical impact of migration, see Petesch's recent figuration (2003).

7. In addition to me, the only other people on the Chambira referred to as *gringos* during the time I did my primary fieldwork in the late 1980s and 1990s were Ron and Phyllis Manus, missionaries for the Summer Institute of Linguistics (SIL) who worked sporadically in the region for four decades (Manus and Manus 1973, 1976, 1990, 1996). In daily conversation, categories such as *gringo* and *blanco* are rarely used.

8. The term *deme* comes from the Greek word *demos*. In ancient Greece, *demos* signified a rural district or village, as distinct from a *polis*, or city-state. Like the Latin *plebs*, *demos* also denoted the common people. The *demes* of Attica were local corporations with their own property, cults, and officials.

9. I collected the following eight "clan" names during my fieldwork: Lumai, Maña, Yayé, Teguidi, Itucuaidi, Cutirití, Bajaudiadá, and Ujídi. Of particular interest were descriptions I heard of Ujídi and Lumai. Ujídi is associated with the harpy eagle, whereas Lumai is said to have been the Creator God's "peon" who was responsible for introducing darkness, which enabled the first Urarina peoples to sleep at night.

10. In January 2002 fares between Nauta and Iquitos were seven soles via river boat (*lancha*) and between eighty-nine and one hundred soles for the overland bus fare, both of which are beyond the modest means of most Urarina. Similarly, the fare for the passage aboard a 120-horsepower diesel river ferry (*lancha*) for the twenty-five-hour journey between Nauta and Intuto on the Río Tigre was twenty-five soles.

11. For many indigenous Amazonian peoples, like the Wari of Brazil, blood is the primary element shaping health and social identity (Conklin 2001, 115).

12. For instance, Nudé—with his prominent aquiline nose and spiked hair—received his name in recognition of his strange visage, which many said made him appear like a paca. Rinirá ("stubby") was given her name in recognition of her short stature and stout build, while Tontoó ("drum") received his sobriquet in acknowledgment of his abdominous characteristics. The social import of systems of naming—noted elsewhere in Amazonia (Hugh-Jones 2002), lies well beyond the scope of this book.

Chapter 2. Ninichú

1. Unfortunately, Tessmann makes only passing remarks on these issues (1987, 63). It is unclear why Tessmann translated Oxpwá diosi as Grandfather God, rather than Father God, as elsewhere Oxpwá is rendered by Tessmann as "my father" (1987, 73,77), whereas grandfather is Kadínjaha (1987, 76). Both Kramer's findings (1979, 66) and my own indicate that Oxpwá (Ofwa) is the vocative term for father. Diosi is derived from the Spanish term for God, Díos. My Urarina acquaintances seldom spoke of Diosi, but instead referred to Kuánra (God, Kanu Kuánra; Kane Kuáinidia, my God). Father God is called Kana Najca (*yaka*) and Mother God is referred to as Kana Nebá. Kuánra is rendered in Summer Institute of Linguistic's publications as Coaunera (ILV 1993; see Dean 1994b, 37 n. 10).

2. This account of Rurú is drawn from a number of versions of the same myth recounted by Najlegue-kuktíri (1990, 1991, 1998). All were recorded on the Pangayacu in Urarina and in Loretano Spanish.

3. The black spider monkey (*Ateles paniscus chamek*) is known colloquially by its name in Quechua—Maquisapa.

4. Maquisapa's mobility finds further emphasis in other popular accounts. In the words of Najlegue-kuktíri: "Chosna once had an apron to hold its children while it moved about. Maquisapa stole this skirt. Now that's why *chosna* must carry its offspring in its mouth, and *maquisapa* has a waistline pouch."

5. This contrasts sharply with the Aguarunas' elaborate system of garden magic (Brown and Van Bolt 1980; Brown 1986).

6. The version presented here is a synthesis of three accounts of the same myth recounted by Ujkuaizíri and Najlegue-kuktíri and recorded on the Pangayacu in 1991, 1992, and 1996.

7. The primary types of soil identified by the Urarina include fertile black soils (*ajtané jichújuai*), red earth from the high ground (*ajtané lanájai*), relatively barren yellow soils (*ajtané sumára*), and infertile sandy earth (*vajillakua*). Barren soils are referred to as *ajtané chátua*.

8. A highly variable species, the edible root crop cassava (manioc or *yuca*; *Manihot esculenta*) was most likely first cultivated in the Yucatán peninsula by the Maya. The cyanide-producing sugar derivative (hydrocyanic acid) that occurs in varying quantities in most types of cassava is removed through the process of grating, pressing, and heating.

9. The Urarina recognize the following plantains: *Musa paradisiaca* or *juanara*; *maduro* (*juanara cájta*); *Isleño*, also known as *plátano de la Isla* or *juanara lanajai*, lit. "red banana"; *mamaluca*, a variety of banana characterized by its thin fruits; *ajlaubijí*; *capirona, afanárä; bellaco*, a type of plantain not particularly esteemed by Loretaños; *juanára tabáne*, lit. "large plantain"; *seda/sedillo; kamerenáti; tosquino* (*kajtebíji*); *manzano* (*manzanaá*); *viejilla* (*juanara biña*, lit. "old plantain"); and, *gunicha*, a type of small "honey banana."

10. The Urarina refer to this waterway as *lanaá*—or red—in recognition of the crimson brown earthen high grounds that border the Pucayacu, a tributary of the middle Chambira River.

11. For an excellent description of communal work parties among Peruvian *ribereño* communities, see Chibnik and de Jong 1992.

12. Members of the Morphinae do not visit flowers, but instead feed entirely upon the succuss of decomposing fruits or fungi (DeVries 1987, 237).

13. Common throughout Loreto, *panero* are baskets made from *tamishi* palm bast, and they are used for transporting garden produce, such as cassava and corn.

14. The combined districts of Tigre, Trompeteros, and Urarinas in the Province of Loreto average well under 0.5 persons per square kilometer (Odicio Egovail 1992, 14).

15. I write Achuar with some degree of uncertainty; the Urarina spoke to me of the Murato and Bakagá synonymously. Inter-ethnic relations along the "peripheral" frontiers of the Chambira Basin are little understood.

16. I too was subjected to similar treatment during the initial leg of fieldwork when my boat was temporarily detained by a group of drunken Urarina men from a community located along the lower Chambira. After threats of my drowning, I quickly conceded to paying a "toll" in the form of batteries and shotgun shells.

17. For a recent overview of land demarcation in indigenous Peruvian Amazonia, see Chirif and García Hierro 2007.

18. Financed by international lending agencies, Belaunde's government continued with an ambitious Amazonian highway construction project (La Carretera Marginal de la Selva) and launched a series of top-down mega-development schemes, such as the Pichis-Palcazu Special Project.

19. Founded by Abimael Guzmán Reynoso in 1970 as an offshoot of the Peruvian Communist Party, Sendero Luminoso (SL) was a major player in the civil war that raged in Peru throughout the 1980s and 1990s. In response to the insurgent threat, Alberto Fujimori's government (1990–2000) declared martial law and implemented a savage counterinsurgency campaign that eventually led to the capture and incarceration of Guzmán and key members of the SL's central committee. This in turn has diminished the organization's operational capacity. Collective memory, social discourse, and the military campaign against the SL are explored in Theidon 2000, 2001; Degregori 1991, 2000; and Manrique 1993. Local responses to the war are covered in numerous works, including essays in Starn 1997 for the Andes, and Fabián 1995 for the Amazonia.

20. This point is supported by Pearson's observation during the height of the rubber bonanza that the Peruvian state "has been exceedingly generous with those taking up

lands and has voted many valuable concessions to the companies that have constructed roads" (1911, 160).

Chapter 3. Historicizing Amazonia

1. On the antiquity of Upper Amazonian cultures and the highland-lowland interface, see Lathrap 1970; P. Porras 1975, 75–134; Camino 1977; Dávila Herrera 1980; DeBoer 1981; Lyon 1981; T. Myers 1983, 1988b; Salomon 1986, 98, 102–3, 115 n. 2; Barletti Pasqual 2000, 23–24. In addition to the pre-Columbian trade in goods between the inter-Andean highlands and the humid, tropical lowlands, there are many indications of both contemporary and historic exchange of items of value over longer and shorter distances within Amazonia itself (Colson 1973; T. Myers 1981, 1983, 1992a). Hornborg (2005) has advocated for the import of interregional exchange networks in producing the complex distributions of ethno-linguistic identities noted in pre-Columbian Amazonia, where ethnic identities, social hierarchy, economy, and ecology were all intertwined.

2. Archaeological data from the Urituyacu is provided by Ravines 1998. Upper Amazonian floodplain migration in historical perspective is provided by Pärssinen, Salo, and Räsänen's study (1996).

3. The Jesuit fathers decided punishments in the missions, which were generally lashes or the pillory (Regan 1983, 50; Chantre y Herrera 1901, 594, 597–601; Fritz 1922, 110; Smyth and Lowe 1836, 219; Marcoy 1873, 3: 112).

4. The significance of the Upper Amazon's extensive salt trade networks are addressed in Raimondi 1942, 98f.; Orton 1879, 196; Tibesar 1950; Steward and Métraux 1963, 644, 654; Smyth and Lowe 1836, 260, 263; Reyes Flores 1999, 152.

5. Consecrated in 1807 in Quitos, Maynas' first bishop was Father Hipólito Sánchez Rangel, who was responsible for conducting the first census of the province (Villarejo 2000, 17; Quecedo 1942).

6. The *ribereño/mestizo* population of Peruvian Amazonia has received very limited attention in the literature (see Hiraoka 1985, 1989; Padoch and de Jong 1987; Chibnik 1991, 1994).

7. Quintana refers to non-Urarina inhabitants of the Chambira as *ribereños* (1948, 278).

8. Reyes Flores gives a description of the five primary colonial routes into the Marañón Basin (1999, 133). Depending on the route, these paths included passage through Quito, Ambato, Jaén de Bracamoros, Moyobamba/Lamas, and Chachapoyas.

9. Infrastructure that was needed to facilitate transport between the Amazon and the coast has been the focus of many works (B. Arana 1896; Torres Lara 1898; Villanueva 1902; Habich 1903; Maúrtua 1911, 4, 19; Coronel Zegarra 1914; Davalos y Lisson 1930, 171–80).

10. On Brazil's expansionist tendencies, see Cunha, Sousa, and Sá 2006.

11. For detailed lists of baptisms, confirmations, and marriages conducted among the Urarina (Shimacos) and Omurano peoples of the Bajo Marañón (Nauta and Parinari), as well as the Romainas peoples of Río Tigre, see Villarejo 1942, 33–35.

12. On the nature of unequal exchange and extractive economies in Brazilian Amazonia, see Ross 1978, 206ff.; and Bunker 1988, 12–18.

Chapter 4. Localizing Webs of Power in the Chambira Basin

1. In Quintana's (1948) estimation, the Urarina were the laziest indigenous group he had ever encountered. In the account of his evangelical crusade in the Chambira Basin Quintana remarks that the forced work for the *patrones* was having the desired effect of countering the Urarinas' innate "laziness" (*haraganeria*) (1948, 279).

2. In the past, the Urarina used the non-elastic rubber obtained from the latex of the *balata* tree (*Manilkara bidentata*) for waterproofing fabrics. It has been used commercially in the fabrication of machine belts and casings for baseballs and golf balls. *Balata* trees are typically found growing in high-ground regions of the Chambira River drainage, such as the headwaters of the Pucayacu.

3. García Jordán's foundational historical account (2001) emphasizes the close alliance between the Catholic Church and extractive entrepreneurs, particularly rubber barons.

4. In my conversations with the last generation of Ocampos to work in the Chambira Basin I was struck by their expressions of marked allegiance to Loreto's ancien régime of exclusiveness based on economic privilege and restriction of access to symbolic capital.

5. Ronald and Phyllis Manus are now near retirement and spend most of the year away from the Chambira. A full study of the effects of SIL presence among the Urarina is unfortunately beyond the scope of this work.

6. *Tagua* nuts (marfil or vegetable ivory) were gathered for their value as a cheap replacement for ivory in the manufacture of buttons, decorations, and chess pieces.

7. Note, for example, the declaration in 1841 by the bishop of Maynas prohibiting non-priests from performing baptisms (except in the case of impending death) (see Regan 1983, 76; Izaguirre 1925, 9: 199).

8. Uncured tobacco cigarettes are known in Loreto as *mapacho*. In addition to smoking *mapacho* cigarettes, the Urarina continue to grow their own tobacco (*enuata*).

9. The issue of alcoholism on the Chambira is a complex issue worthy of further study. Morey Alejo and Sotil García assert that alcoholism accompanied the demise of the Jesuit missions and the introduction of Brazilian cane alcohol (*cachaza*) as a medium of petty-commodity exchange (2000, 150). The consumption of commercially produced alcohol is widespread in western Amazonia (Siskind 1977, 173; Oberem 1980, 117; cf. Muratorio 1991, 151).

10. By the Great Depression, lumber had become the most important commodity exported from the Peruvian Amazon (Coomes 1995, 111). La Torre estimates that since commercial logging's inception, almost seven million hectares of territory have been deforested. Overharvesting has resulted in the virtual extinction of some species, particularly in their natural high-jungle habitat (La Torre López 1998, 26–27).

11. In a somewhat "benign" analysis of Sironó economy, Stearman and Redford have suggested that "for the time being at least, they [the Sironó] balance the scales of social indebtedness by allowing the traders their profits" (1992, 242).

12. This is made amply clear in Conklin's review of the "pacification" (1956–62) of the Wari of Brazil. Colonizers consciously tried to conceal or refigure data about Wari cannibalism in ways that "affirmed the humanity of the cannibals themselves" (Conklin 1997, 76). Conklin's ethnographic portrayal (2001) of Wari conceptions of person, body, and spirit is one of the most authoritative accounts of funerary cannibalism in lowland South America.

Chapter 5. "When There Were No Women"

1. A safeguard against environmental disaster, namely flooding, periodic visiting promotes alliances, which facilitate continued access to food supply in times of shortages (T. Myers 1992a, 92).

2. *Adánah*, domestic platforms (*tarima* in Loretano Spanish), are made from the water-resistant *huacrapona* palm (*ajkeydaná, Iriartea* sp) and are supported by *huacapu* posts (*anesíyu, Vonacapona Americana*) embedded in the ground.

3. Siskind reports that Sharanahua have sexual relations with *patrones* for trade items such as cloth and kerosene (1977, 179; cf. Kensinger 1984; 1998, 53). As far as I could determine, exchange of sexual favors for trade goods seems to be a relatively rare occurrence among Urarina women. However, those few Urarina women who do have *mestizo* husbands tend to have had close contact with *patrones*, often as their servants or concubines. Urarina men often commented that once women had experienced the *hullo* (penis) of a *mestizo* man they were "hooked."

4. For reports of forced conscription in Peruvian Amazonia, see Gray 1997, 68 and Bergman 1990, 216.

5. This is based on an account by Kiriná that was recorded in June 1991 in Iquitos and supplemented by details from a version told to me by Ujkuaizíri that was recorded in May 1996 in the Pangayacu community. For an excellent collection of oral accounts chronicling the Napu-Runas' (Kichwa from the Río Napo) painful experience with *patrones*, see Mercier (1979, 259–66).

6. This is echoed by what I was often told in Spanish by my Urarina friends: "A la fuerza no se hace communidad" (coercion does not create community).

7. Similarly, as Basso notes among the Kalapalo of Brazil, "In warrior biographies, a contrast is first developed between the hero's local community and some nearby hostile group, variously called . . . ferocious" (1995, 20).

8. Within the rubric of debt peonage, payment of cash for future produce (*habilitar con dinero*) is referred to as *kurkitiyá*.

9. As Hugh-Jones notes, failure to acknowledge this fact "has led to an underestimation of the role and significance of Indian 'chiefs' and other brokers or middlemen in alliance with . . . traders" (1992, 44; see also Lévi-Strauss 1978b; Goldman 1963, 68–69). On the Chambira, the traders' principal clients become creditors in their own right to other Urarina individuals within their immediate spheres of influence.

10. For the Wakuénai, the anaconda is linked to the idea of forbidden, adulterous sexuality (Hill and Wright 1988, 95). The Gorotire, a Kayapó group of Central Brazil, think of themselves as the offspring of an illicit union between a married woman and a serpent (T. Turner 1988, 206). The Arapaco, an Eastern Tukanoan people of Colombia,

say that they are the grandchildren of the anaconda. Many of the other language groups of the Vaupés share a similar cosmogonic myth, portraying the first people emerging "from a primordial anaconda who swam up the Río Negro to the Vaupés with the rising waters" (Chernela 1988, 37; see also Reichel-Dolmatoff 1971, 26–27). The examples could easily be multiplied: a mythological motif linking snakes and humans through sexual relationships is dispersed throughout South America (among others, see Gregor 1987, 53–54; Goldman 1963, 147–48; Guss 1990, 40).

11. Framed psychoanalytically, Gregor writes that in the dream of one Mehinaku woman the anaconda is a "symbol of a phallus" (1987).

12. Guss notes, however, that in the account of her genesis, "Wiyu is clearly portrayed as a woman—Wanadi's [God's] lover as well as the sister of the Moon, whose attempted rape of her leads to her flight below the water. It is there that she assumes her permanent form as the feathered serpent and the mistress (arache) of the water and all that inhabits it" (1990, 228).

13. From accounts recorded in 1994, 1996, and 1998.

14. This mythologically important fish has a long, laterally compact body composed of numerous spines (Espinosa Perez 1955, 521). Lisa are comestible fish that the Urarina do not particularly prize since they have many bones and not very much meat (Fisostomos Abdominales order, Cobitodos family, *Cobitis Gunth* genus, *Cobitis taenia* L. sp.?/ *Leporinus* sp.).

15. Bushmasters (*Lachesis muta*) are a species of pit viper related to rattlesnakes. Measuring up to twelve feet long, *jergon* are the New World's largest venomous snake.

16. In this context, Derrida's critique of the phenomenologist's approach to "pure essences" is persuasive precisely because it demonstrates the inadequacy of arguments deploying the atemporal and precultural as unconditionally valid (Fuss 1989, 13–15).

17. See Bunker's study of "inappropriate modernity" in the Brazilian Amazon (1988).

18. Some of these logics can be dubbed hegemonic, while others are quite clearly subversive and counterhegemonic, while still others resist the simple categorization of anesthetizing versus challenging.

19. The Urarina myth of the creation of women is similar to a Yanomami version that describes the homosexual conception of the first girl, who was born from a man's leg after another had ejaculated into it (Chagnon 1968, 48).

20. For myths of inversion "explaining" male domination, see among others Goldman 1963, 193; Gregor 1987; Jean Jackson 1992; Hugh-Jones 1988, 263–66; Wilbert and Simoneau 1992, 28; cf. Lévi-Strauss 1975, 112–13.

21. To reinforce the grave consequences of breaking the ten-month post-partum tabu on sex, Ujkuaizíri told me how Najlegue-kuktíri's child died because of its parents continued sexual activity.

22. In other areas of lowland South America, such as among the Zapára of Ecuador, linguistic politics have shaped the character of the indigenous movement (Viatoria 2007).

23. Emphasizing the consciousness of the colonizers and the role of terror in shaping social life, Taussig (1987) describes the process whereby a culture of torture was

produced and sustained in the upper Amazon based on the rubber barron's awareness of impending danger and their fears of the forest, indigenous savagery, cannibalism, witchcraft, and violent revolt. Ethnographic reports did little to dispel the exotic and ferocious characterizations of the local inhabitants (see, for instance, Brinton's essay dispelling the existence of a tribe of Amazonian dwarves, 1898).

24. Calls for reform peaked in 1992 with COICA's general congress ratifying a series of structural reforms aimed at decentralizing power and enhancing organizational accountability—both political and economic (see Inoash 1997, 71). In spite of concerted efforts to address problems surrounding the lack of equal participation and direct representation, the movement has been slow to respond to the voices at the margins.

25. Commentators have noted that Amazonia's pan-ethnic movement suffers from an organizational incapacity to represent the region's diverse constituencies (Varese 1996b). Moreover, the pan-ethnic federation movement needs to ensure a much greater degree of grass-roots community participation (Varese 1996a, 1996b; Leon 1987).

26. Hence, mythology or current social practices cannot be seen as completely determinative of women's ability to assert themselves in novel contexts. While impossible to escape the socializing effects of the discursive forces that give rise to human subjectivity, conscious subjects can countermand if not subvert the ways in which discourse constitutes, valorizes, and undermines social life. The introduction of intercultural bilingual education is perhaps the best example of this in Peruvian Amazonia (Dean 1999; Aikman 1999; Trapnell 2003).

Chapter 6. Forbidden Fruit

1. Bride-service and bride-wealth models frame discussions of kinship in many global regions. See, for instance, Fricke, Thornton, and Dahal 1998; Hagen 1999; Gose 2000; Helliwell 2000; and M. Jamieson 2003.

2. Patterns of uxorilocal postmarital residence, as well as the practice of temporary or prolonged bride service, have been widely reported for Amazonia (among others, see Arevolo-Jiménez 1971, 104; Dumont 1978, 75; Harner 1973, 79–80; Hill and Moran 1983, 124–25; Holmberg 1969, 217; Kracke 1976; Maybury-Lewis 1979, 9; Murphy 1956; Renshaw 2002, 186ff.; Rivière 1984, 40f.; Siskind 1977, 79–81; T. Turner 1979, 159–60).

3. According to Morey Alejo and Sotil García, the local administrative role of the *teniente gobernadores* dates to the start of republican Peru (2000, 204).

4. Common abortifacients include the latex of the fast growing *cético* tree (*cuinëjä*, *Cecropia latifolia*), or the sap from the Sangre de Grado tree (*ajiñará*).

5. See, for instance, Da Matta's account (1982) of the Apinayé, where the uxorilocal son-in-law customarily avoids his wife's parents. Da Matta asserts that this avoidance behavior (*piam*) "is a mechanism for controlling certain contradictory tendencies that result from the rule of uxorilocal residence" (1982, 47; see also Basso 1973, 92ff.; cf. Lubbock 1978, 84).

6. For comparable observations elsewhere in lowland South America, see Nimuendajú 1967, 78; Goldman 1963, 143; Johnson and Johnson 1975; Jean Jackson 1992, 6; and McCallum 1990, 419. A counterperspective is developed in Centitagoya's ethno-

graphic description of the Machiguenga, which highlights the apparent powerlessness of daughters to select their future spouses (1943, 172–74; cf. Johnson 2003).

Chapter 7. Multiple Regimes of Value

1. For the ethnobotany, economic importance, and religious significance of palms in the neotropics, see Balick 1984, 9–23; Bodley and Benson 1979; Bates 1989, 57f.; Schultes 1974; Schultes and Raffauf 1990; Jones 1995, 47–65; Vormisto 2002.

2. The social implications of inalienability have been explored by a number of scholars, including Komter (2001, 59–75) and Ferry (2002). For a provocative critique of Weiner's theory of inalienable possessions and her thoughts about "keeping-while-giving," see Mosko (2000).

3. Bark dyes include the reddish-brown crabwood (called *jaiyá* in Urarina and known colloquially in Loreto as *andiroba* or *carapa*), and the softwood mahogany *aguano*, which produces a dark brown hue.

4. During the course of fieldwork, I made a number of material culture collections for museums, including the Peabody Museum of Anthropology and Archeology at Harvard University, the University of Kansas Museum of Anthropology, the Museo Nacional de Arqueología, Antropología e Historia del Perú (Lima), the Museo de la Amazonia (Iquitos), and the Museo del Alto Amazonas (Yurimaguas).

5. Seiler-Baldinger's study (1988, 287) of Yagua weaving found that between forty-three and forty-six hours of labor is required for a hammock, which includes preparing some 1,500 meters of cordage.

6. Densely woven palm-bast mosquito netting, or tents, were utilized by the Panoans, Tupí, Western Tucano, Yameo, Záparoans, and perhaps by the indigenous peoples of the central Huallaga (Steward 1963, 520).

7. On color symbolism in lowland South America, see Maybury-Lewis 1967, 251–52 and Reichel-Dolmatoff 1971, 122–23. On the importance of the color red as a dye, see Schneider 1987, 427. The relationship between the Urarinas' ritual clan system and transmission of patterns and color schemes is unclear.

8. Compare this motif with the Urarina practice of using cotton cord (*ijché*) ligatures around the calves (*pijia sedí*) as well as the belly to "fatten up" infants and the young. In both instances, binding is thought to heighten human vitality.

9. On the production and marketing of chambira palm-fiber bags and hammocks among the Bora of Peru, see Vormisto 2002.

10. In Father Quintana's estimation, the Urarina did not use salt (1948, 280). Quintana noted how salt had to be forced into the mouths of Urarina during the rites of baptism he conducted during the two months he spent in the Chambira Basin in 1947.

Chapter 8. Mitayo, Myth, and Meaning

1. The number of game animals killed in Amazonia each year has been estimated in the tens of millions (Redford 1992). A survey of Iquitos-based commerce in game animals indicated the marketing of two dozen species of game animals, including six species of primates (Castro, Revilla, and Neville 1975–76).

2. For representative examples from this oral genre, see Ministerio de Educación Pública and Instituto Lingüístico de Verano 1981.

3. Men also obtain *miräné* from beehives. Smoke is first used to "intoxicate" the bees so that the hive can be removed safely. The hive is then boiled and mixed with water to make the pitch.

4. In addition to Brazilian tapir (*Tapirus terrestris*), the Urarina also deem Baird's tapir (*pirus bairdii*) *aránla*.

5. In contrast to Melanesian societies, Urarina activation of hierarchy relies less on the circulation of foodstuffs. In her portrayal of hierarchy and value on the island of Gawa, Munn (1992) asserts that the primary hierarchizing act is the *prestation* of food. The same can certainly not be said for the Urarina.

6. The narrative I detail here represents a condensed version of the myth told on various occasions (1991, 1992, 1996, and 1998) in the Chambira Basin.

7. In his 1996 account of this popular story, Ujkuaizíri went to great lengths to note that the Rimae Santú appeared as "*cristianos*," that is as *mestizos*.

8. See N. Smith for comparative case material from Brazil on great white dog stories that "warn people of the consequences of murder and abusing alcohol" (1996, 151).

9. Study of pre-Columbian and colonial regional exchange of dogs has gone largely unexplored in the scholarly literature. Ethnographic accounts hint at the significance of dogs in regional networks of exchange (for example, Harner 1973, 64; Descola 1994, 231); nevertheless, the comparative cynology of Amazonia remains in its infancy.

10. On the issue of the employment of herbal magic for dogs in indigenous Amazonia, among others, see Guallart Martínez 1989, 98–103; Guss 1990, 62; Harner 1973, 73, 13f.; Schultes and Raffauf 1990, 77, 85, 42f.; and Rodway 1917, 498.

11. I have tentatively identified *yinánja* as either *Tabernaemontana* sp. or *Brunfelsia* sp. In Quechua *Brunfelsia grandiflora* is *Chiric sanango*, which means cold (*sanango*).

12. On the diverse regional culinary traditions of the upper Amazon, see, among others, Mora de Jaramillo 1985, 237–43 and Naar Ruiz's comprehensive studies (1989, 95–285, 1999).

13. In 1998, during a competition I staged on the Pangayacu to determine the blow-dart range of various hunters, I determined that the men of the area had firing ranges from about thirty-nine to roughly forty-four meters.

14. The Urarina hunt a number of animals for their pelts, primarily feline and peccary species. In the past, they also pursued caiman and hunted nutria for their skins. On the commoditization of pelts in western Amazonia, see Dourojeanni 1990, 287f.; Chirif 1983, 64f.; Mora de Jaramillo 1985, 142f.; and Zutter 1976, 56–59.

15. The following version represents a composite of three accounts, one rendered by Najlegue-kuktíri (1991) and the other two by Ujkuaizíri (1996, 1998).

Chapter 9. Chanting Rivers, Fiery Tongue

1. Shamanism has assumed a messianic character among many indigenous peoples of Amazonia, including the Tupi-Guaraní, Tucuna, Arawakan, and Tukanoan societies of Northwest Amazonia (among others, see Regan 1988; Brown 1991; Brown and

Fernández 1991; Clastres 1987, 158; Goldman 1963, 16; Hugh-Jones 1994; Métraux 1963a, 93f.; 1963c, 131; Nimuendajú 1963, 725; T. Turner 1988, 263; Varese 2002).

2. Examples of millenarianism abound: in addition to Worsley 1970, see Cohn 1970, 1995; Chaumeil 1997; Wright and Hill 1992; and Agüero 1994.

3. On indigenous Amazonian conceptualizations of temporality and social change, see Fausto and Heckenberger 2007.

4. The relevance of the notion of ambiguity stretches beyond social anthropology. In the arena of archaeology Breglia (2006) recounts the "monumental ambivalence" that arises from contentious claims to cultural patrimony.

5. On Inka myths as being reflective of Asháninka relations with outsiders and new technologies, see Rojas Zolezzi 1994, 61ff. For a similar case among the Shipibo, see Roe 1982.

6. When speaking Loretano Spanish, the Urarina deem *anekai* as *tunchi*. In Loretano Spanish, *tunchi* signifies evil spirits as well as a type of bird called *supay* or "devil" in Pastaza Quechua. This bird's nocturnal call is considered an omen of evil. On the Pastaza River, the word *supay* also refers to shamans (Alvarez Vita 1990, 528; Landerman 1973, 46, 100).

7. Viveiros de Castro has elaborated the notion of "ontological predation" to refer to the Amazonian phenomenon whereby personhood and collective empowerment are based on the practice of killing and consuming those deemed external to the self (Conklin 2001, 154). The broader implications of commensality and cannibalism in Amazonia are explored by Fausto 2002; 2007.

8. The alienation of forest game is cause for concern elsewhere in the world. For instance, see Mauss 1967, 64 on his discussion of the prevalence of customs in France designed to "detach" animals from those who sell them.

Bibliography

Abu-Lughod, Lila. 1993. *Writing Women's Worlds: Bedouin Stories*. Berkeley: University of California Press.

Adamson, David. 1904. "Col. Pedro Portillo's Expedition: The Rivers Apurímac, Mantaro, Ené, Perené, Tambo, and Upper Ucayali (Peru)." *Liverpool Geographical Society* 12(12): 14–23.

Agüero, Oscar. 1994. *El milenio de la Amazonía Peruana: Mito utopía tupí-cocama o la subversión del orden simbólico*. Lima: Abya Yala.

Aikman, Sheila. 1999. *Intercultural Education and Literacy: An Ethnographic Study of Indigenous Knowledge and Learning in the Peruvian Amazon*. Amsterdam: John Benjamins.

Alarco de Zadra, Adriana. 1988. *Perú, el libro de las plantas mágicas: Compendio de farmacopea popular*. Lima: Consejo Nacional de Ciencia y Tecnología.

Alayza y Paz Soldán, Francisco. 1910. "Decreto contra la explotación de los indios." In *Mi país, algo de la Amazonía Peruana*, ed. L. Alayza y Paz Soldán, 115–17. Lima: Libería e Imprenta Gil., 1960.

Albert, Bruce. 1988. "Fumée du metal: Histoire et représentations du contact chez les Yanomami (Brésil)." *L'Homme* 28(106–7): 87–119.

Albo, Xavier. 1996. "Making the Leap from Local Mobilization to National Politics." *NACLA Report on the Americas* 29(5): 15–21.

Alvarez Vita, Juan. 1990. *Diccionario de peruanismos*. Lima: Librería Studium Ediciones.

Amich, José. 1883. *Historia de las misiones de fieles é infieles del Colegio de Propaganda Fide de Santa Rosa de Ocopa, por los pp. misioneros del mismo colegio*. Barcelona: Impr. Peninsular.

———. 1975. *Historia de las misiones del Convento de Santa Rosa de Ocopa*, ed. and notes J. Heras. Lima: Editorial Milla Batres.

Anda Aguirre, Alfonso. 1995 [1955]. *Primeros gobernadores de Mainas: Los generales Vaca de Vega*. Quito: Abya-Yala.

Anderson, Benedict. 1987. *Imagined Communities: Reflections on the Origin and Spread of Nationalism*. London: Verso Press.

———. 1992. "The New World Disorder." *New Left Review* 193: 39–113.

———. 2000. *The Spectre of Comparisons: Nationalism, Southeast Asia, and the World*. London: Verso Press.

———. 2003. "Nationalism and Cultural Survival in Our time: A Sketch." In *At the Risk of Being Heard: Identity, Indigenous Rights, and Postcolonial States*, ed. Bartholomew Dean and Jerome Levi, 165–90. Ann Arbor: University of Michigan Press.

Anderson, Robin. 1999. *Colonization as Exploitation in the Amazon Rain Forest, 1758–1911*. Gainesville: University Press of Florida.

Appadurai, Arjun. 1992 [1986]. "Introduction: Commodities and the Politics of Value."

In *The Social Life of Things: Commodities in Cultural Perspective*, ed. A. Appadurai, 3–63. Cambridge: Cambridge University Press.

———. 2000. "Grassroots Globalization and the Research Imagination." *Public Culture* 12(2) 1: 1–19.

Arana, Benito. 1896. *De Lima al Amazonas vía Mayro: Colección de las opiniones más competentes y autorizadas en favor de esta vía*. Lima: Imprenta y Librería de San Pablo.

Arana, Julio César. 1913. *Las cuestiones del Putumayo*. Barcelona: Impr. Viuda de L. Tasso.

Ardito Vega, Wilfredo. 1992. "La estructura de las reducciones de Maynas." *Amazonía Peruana* 11(22): 93–124.

Ardner, Edwin. 1989. "Belief and the Problem of Women." In *The Voice of Prophecy and Other Essays*, ed. M. Chapman, 72–85. Oxford: Basil Blackwell.

Århem, K. 1981. *Makuna Social Organization*. Stockholm: Almqvist and Wiksell International.

———. 1987. "Wives for Sisters: The Management of Marriage Exchange in Northwest Amazonia." In *Natives and Neighbors in South America*, ed. H. Skar and F. Salomon, 130–77. Goteborg: Goteborgs Etnografiska Museum.

———. 1998. *Makuna: Portrait of an Amazonian People*. Washington: Smithsonian Institution Press.

Arevolo Jiménez, Nelly. 1971. *Political Relations in a Tribal Society: A Study of the Ye'cuana Indians of Venezuela*. Ithaca, N.Y.: Cornell University Press.

Assies, Willem. 2002. "From Rubber Estate to Simple Commodity Production: Agrarian Struggles in the Northern Bolivian Amazon." *Journal of Peasant Studies* 29(3/4): 83–130.

Avé-Lallemant, Robert. 1860. *Reise dürch Nord-Brasilien im Jahre 1859*. Leipzig: Brockhaus.

Aza, José Pio. 1922. "De las tribus salvajes del Amazonas." *Boletín de la Sociedad Geográfica de Lima* 39: 263–74.

Balée, William. 1993. "Indigenous Transformation of Amazonian Forests: An Example from Maranhão, Brazil." *L'Homme* 33(126–28): 231–54.

———. 1994. *Footprints of the Forest: Ka'apor Ethnobotany; The Historical Ecology of Plant Utilization by an Amazonian People*. New York: Columbia University Press.

Balée, W., and C. Erickson, eds. 2006. *Time and Complexity in Historical Ecology Studies in the Neotropical Lowlands*. New York: Columbia University Press.

Balick, M. J. 1984. "Ethnobotany of Palms in the Neotropics." In *Ethnobotany in the Neotropics*, ed. G. Prance and J. Kallunki, 9–23. Bronx: The New York Botanical Garden.

Ballón Landa, Alberto. 1917. "Los hombres de la selva: Apuntes para un ensayo de sociología aplicada." Tesis doctoral, Universidad Mayor de San Marcos. Lima: Oficina tipográfica "La opinión nacional."

Barabas, Alicia. 1986. "Movimientos étnicos religiosos y seculares en América Latina: Una aproximación a la construcción de la utopía india." *América Indígena* 46(3): 497–529.

Barclay Rey de Castro, Frederica, et al., eds. 1991. *Amazonía 1940–1990: El extravío de una ilusión*. Lima: Terra Nuova—CISEPA/PUCP.

Barham, B., and O. Coomes. 1994. "Reinterpreting the Amazon Rubber Boom: Investment and the Role of the State." *Latin American Research Review* 29(2): 73–109.

———. 1996. *Prosperity's Promise: The Amazon Rubber Boom and Distorted Development*. Boulder, Colo.: Westview Press.

Barletti Pascual, José. 1992. *Los pueblos amazónicos en tiempos de la llegada de Orellana*. Iquitos: Gobierno Regional de Loreto.

Barnes, R. H. 1999. "Marriage by Capture." *Journal of the Royal Anthropological Institute*, n.s., 5: 57–73.

Basso, Ellen. 1973. *The Kalapalo Indians of Central Brazil*. New York: Holt, Rinehart and Winston.

———. 1995. *The Last Cannibals: A South American Oral History*. Austin: University of Texas Press.

Bataille, Georges. 1985. *Visions of Excess: Selected Writings, 1927–1939*. Minneapolis: University of Minnesota Press.

Bates, Henry Walter. 1989 [1863]. *The Naturalist on the River Amazons*. New York: Penguin Books.

Battaglia, Debbora. 1997. "Ambiguating Agency: The Case of Malinowski's Ghost." *American Anthropologist* 99(3): 505–10.

Bauman, Zygmunt. 1991. *Modernity and Ambivalence*. Ithaca, N.Y.: Cornell University Press.

Beattie, Peter M. 2001. *The Tribute of Blood: Army, Honor, Race, and Nation in Brazil, 1864–1945*. Durham, N.C.: Duke University Press.

Beckerman, Stephen, et al. 2001. "Conservation and Native Amazonians: Why Some Do and Some Don't." *Antropológica* 96: 31–51.

Beckerman, Stephen, and Paul Valentine, eds. 2002. *Cultures of Multiple Fathers: The Theory and Practice of Partible Paternity in Lowland South America*. Gainesville: University Press of Florida.

———. 2008. *Revenge in the Cultures of Lowland South America*. Gainesville: University Press of Florida.

Bedoya Garland, Eduardo. 1991. *Las causas de la deforestación en la Amazonía Peruana: Un problema estructural*. Lima: Centro de Investigación y Promoción Amazónica.

Behrens, Clifford. 1989. "The Scientific Basis for Shipibo Soil Classification and Land Use: Changes in Soil-Plant Associations with Cash Cropping." *American Anthropologist* 1(91): 83–100.

Belaunde, Luisa Elvira, et al. 2005. *Ciudadanía y cultura política entre los awajún, asháninka y shipibo-konibo de la Amazonía Peruana*. Lima: CAAAP.

Bellier, Irene. 1986. "Los cantos Mai Huna del Yaje (Amazonia Peruana)." *América Indígena* 46(1): 129 45.

Bennet Ross, J. 1984. "Effects of Contact on Revenge Hostilities among the Achuara Jivaro." In *Warfare, Culture, and Environment*, ed. R. Ferguson, 83–109 (Orlando, Fla.: Academic Press).

Bergman, Roland. 1990. *Economía amazónica: Estrategias de subsistencia en las riberas del Ucayali en el Perú*. Lima: CAAAP.
Bodley, John, and Foley Benson. 1979. "Cultural Ecology of Amazonian Palms." *Reports of Investigation* 56. Pullman: Washington State University Laboratory of Anthropology.
Boehm, Christopher. 1989. "Ambivalence and Compromise in Human Nature." *American Anthropologist* 91(4): 921–37.
Booth, George. 1910. Introduction to *An Amazon Andes Tour*, by Margaret Booth. London: Edward Arnold (published for the authors for private circulation).
Booth, Margaret. 1910. *An Amazon Andes Tour*. London: Edward Arnold (published for the authors for private circulation).
Bossen, L. 1988. "Toward a Theory of Marriage: The Economic Anthropology of Marriage Transactions." *Ethnology* 27: 127–44.
Bourdieu, Pierre. 1984. *Distinction: A Social Critique of the Judgment of Taste*. Cambridge, Mass.: Harvard University Press.
———. 1986. *Outline of a Theory of Practice*. Cambridge: Cambridge University Press.
Bouroncle Carrion, Alfonso. 1973. "Idiomas, lenguas y dialectos en el Perú." *America Indígena* 33(2): 375–403.
Bowman, Isaiah. 1916. *The Andes of Southern Peru*. New York: Henry Holt and Co.
Brack Egg, Antonio, ed. 1997. *Amazonía Peruana: Comunidades indígenas, conocimientos y tierras tituladas; Atlas y baso de datos*. Lima: GRF, PNUD, and UNOPS.
Braun, Robert. 1982. "The Formative as Seen from the Southern Ecuadorian Highlands." In *Primer Simposio de Correlaciones Antropológicas Andino-Mesoamericanas*, ed., J. G. Marcos and P. Norton, 41–100. Guayaquil: ESPOL.
Breglia, Lisa. 2006. *Monumental Ambivalence: The Politics of Heritage*. Austin: University of Texas Press.
Brentano, Carlos. 1922. "State of the Mission of the Omaguas and Jurimaguas after the Year 1715." In *Journal of the Travels and Labours of Father Samuel Fritz in the River of the Amazons between 1686–1723*, trans. and ed. G. Edmundson, 138–42. London: Hakluyt Society.
Brinton, Daniel. 1898. "The Dwarf Tribe of the Upper Amazon." *American Anthropologist* 11: 277–79.
Broseghini, Silvio. 1983. *Cuatro siglos de misiones entre los Shuar*. Quito: Mundo Shuar.
Browder, John, and Brian Godfrey. 1997. *Rainforest Cities*. New York: Columbia University Press.
Brown, Michael. 1984. "The Role of Words in Aguaruna Hunting Magic." *American Ethnologist* 3(11): 545–58.
———. 1986. *Tsewa's Gift: Magic and Meaning in an Amazonian Society*. Washington: D.C.: Smithsonian Institution Press.
———. 1991. "Beyond Resistance: A Comparative Study of Utopian Renewal in Amazonia." *Ethnohistory* 38(4): 388–413.
———. 1996. "On Resisting Resistance." *American Anthropologist* 98(4): 729–35.
Brown, Michael, and Eduardo Fernández. 1991. *War of Shadows: The Struggle for Utopia in the Peruvian Amazon*. Berkeley: University of California Press.

Brown, Michael, and Margaret Van Bolt. 1980. "Aguaruna Jívaro Gardening Magic in the Alto Río Mayo, Perú." *Ethnology* 19: 169–90.

Bruhns, Karen Olsen, James Burton, and George R. Miller. 1990. "Excavations at Pirincay in the Paute Valley of Southern Ecuador, 1985–1988." *Antiquity* 64(243): 221–33.

Brysk, Alison. 2000. *From Tribal Village to Global Village: Indian Rights and International Relations in Latin America*. Stanford, Calif.: Stanford University Press.

Bunker, Stephen. 1988. *Underdeveloping the Amazon: Extraction, Unequal Exchange, and the Failure of the Modern State*. Chicago: University of Chicago Press.

Burga Cabrera, Elena, et al. 2005. *Estudios sobre la Amazonía*. Lima: Fondo Editorial de la Facultad de Ciencias Sociales, UNMSM.

Butler, Judith. 1990. *Gender Trouble: Feminism and the Subversion of Identity*. New York: Routledge.

———. 1993. *Bodies That Matter: On the Discursive Limits of "Sex."* New York: Routledge.

Cajas Rojas, Judith, et al. 1987. *Bibliografía etnolingüística urarina*. Lima: Instituto De Lingüística Aplicada, Universidad Nacional Mayor de San Marcos.

Callahan, Robey. 1999. "The Liberty Bell: From Commodity to Sacred Object." *Journal of Material Culture* 4(1): 57–78.

Camino, Alejandro. 1977. "Trueque, correrías e intercambios entre los quechuas andinos y los piro y machiguenga de la montaña Peruana." *Amazonía Peruana* 1(2): 122–40.

Carneiro, Robert L. 1993. "Factors Favoring the Development of Political Leadership in Amazonia." In *Leadership in Lowland South America*, ed. W. Kracke. South American Indian Studies 1: 4–8. Bennington, Vt.: Bennington College.

Carrasco, Francisco. 1901. "Principales palabras de las cuatro tribus infieles que siguen: Antis, piros, conibos, sipibos." *Boletín de la Sociedad de Geografía de Lima* 11: 205–11.

Carrier, James. 1990. "The Symbolism of Possession in Commodity Advertising." *MAN*, n.s., 25(4): 693–706.

———. 1992a. "The Gift in Theory and Practice in Melanesia: A Note on the Centrality of Gift Exchange." *Ethnology* 31(2): 185–93.

———. 1992b. "Emerging Alienation in Production: A Maussian History." *MAN*, n.s., 27(3): 539–58.

———. 1994. "Alienating Objects: The Emergence of Alienation in Retail Trade." *MAN*, n.s., 29(2): 359–80.

Carsten, Janet, and Stephen Hugh-Jones. 1995. Introduction to *About the House: Lévi-Strauss and Beyond*, ed. J. Carsten and S. Hugh-Jones, 1–46. Cambridge: Cambridge University Press.

Casement, Roger. 1912–13. "Correspondence Respecting the Treatment of British Colonial Subjects and Native Indians Employed in the Collection of Rubber in the Putumayo District." *The House of Commons Sessional Papers. Accounts and Papers* 68: 7–52, 154–59.

Castelnau, Francis comte de. 1850–59. *Expédition dans les parties centrales de l'Amérique du Sud, de Rio de Janeiro à Lima, et de Lima au Para*. Paris: Bertrand.

Castillo, G. 1958. "Los shimacos." *Peru Indígena* 16–17: 23–28.

———. 1961. "La medicina primitiva entre los shimacos." *Peru Indígena* 20–21: 3–94.

Castonguay, Luis. 1990. *Vocabulario regional del Oriente Peruano*. Iquitos: Centro de Estudios Teológicos de la Amazonía.

Castro, N., J. Revilla, and M. Neville. 1975–76. "Carne de monte como una fuente de proteinas en Iquitos, con referencia especial a monos." *Revista Forestal del Peru* 6: 19–32.

Castrucci da Vernazza, Giuseppe Emanuele. 1854. *Viaggio da Lima ad alcune tribù barbare del Perù e lungo il fiume delle Amazzoni*. Genova: Stabilimento tipografico Ponthenier.

Cavero-Egusquiza, Ricardo. 1941. *La Amazonía Peruana*. Lima: Imprenta Torres Aguirre.

CEDIA. 1996a. "Primer Congreso de Comunidades Nativas de la Cuenca del Río Chambira: Resultados de la discusión de los grupos de trabajo." Lima: Centro para el Desarollo del Indígena Amazónico.

———. 1996b. "Reglamento del Primer Congresso de Comunidades Nativas Urarina del Rio Chambira." Lima: Centro para el Desarollo del Indígena Amazónico.

———. 1996c. "La comunidad nativa y sus autoridades." Lima: Centro para el Desarollo del Indígena Amazónico.

Centitagoya, Vicente. 1943. *Los machiguengas*. Lima: Sanmarti y Cia. S.A.

Chagnon, Napoleon. 1968. *Yanomamö: The Fierce People*. New York: Holt, Rinehart and Winston.

Chango, Alfonso, Dorothea Scott Whitten, and Norman E. Whitten. 1997. "Return of the Yumbo: The Indigenous Caminata from Amazonia to Andean Quito." *American Ethnologist* 24(2): 355–92.

Chantre y Herrera, J. 1901. *Historia de las Misiones de la Compañía de Jesús en el Marañón español 1637–1767*. Madrid: Imprenta de A. Avrial.

Chaumeil, Jean Pierre. 1984. *Between Zoo and Slavery: The Yagua of Eastern Peru in Their Present Situation*. Copenhagen: International Work Group for Indigenous Affairs.

———. 1997. "Retour a la terre promise: Colonisation des frontieres et mouvement israelita dans la foret peruvienne." *Cahiers des Ameriques latines* 23(60): 158–76.

———. 1999. *Ver, saber, poder: El chamanismo de los yagua de la Amazonía Peruana*. Lima: CAAAP.

———. 2002. "The Blowpipe Indians: Variations on the Theme of Blowpipe and Tube among the Yagua Indians of the Peruvian Amazon." In *Beyond the Visible and the Material: The Amerindianization of Society in the Work of Peter Riviere*, ed. L. Rival and N. Whitehead, 81–100. Oxford: Oxford University Press.

Chernela, Janet. 1988. "Gender, Language, and 'Placement' in Uanano Songs and Litanies." *Journal of Latin American Lore* 14(2): 193–206.

———. 2003. "Language Ideology and Women's Speech: Talking Community in the Northwest Amazon." *American Anthropologist* 105(4): 794–806.

Chevalier, J. 1982. *Civilization and the Stolen Gift: Capital, Kin, and Cult in Eastern Peru*. Toronto: University of Toronto Press.

Chibnik, Michael. 1991. "Quasi-Ethnic Groups in Amazonia." *Ethnology* 30(2): 167–82.

———. 1994. *Risky Rivers: The Economics and Politics of Floodplain Farming in Amazonia*. Tucson: University of Arizona Press.
Chibnik, Michael, and Wil de Jong. 1992. "Organización de la mano de obra agrícola en las comunidades ribereños de la Amazonía Peruana." *Amazonía Peruana* 11(21): 181–215.
Chirif, Alberto. 1980. "Internal Colonization in a Colonized Country: The Case of the Peruvian Amazon." In *Land, People, and Planning in Contemporary Amazonia*. Centre of Latin American Studies Occasional Publication 3: 185–92. Cambridge: Cambridge University.
———. 1983. "El colonialismo interno en un país colonizado: El caso de la Amazonía Peruana." In *Saqueo Amazónico*, ed. A. Chirif, 47–80. Iquitos: CETA.
Chirif, Alberto, and Pedro García Hierro. 2007. *Marcando territorio: Progresos y limitaciones de la titulación de territorios indígenas en la Amazonía*. Lima: TAREA Asociación Gráfica Educativa.
Chirif, Alberto, and Carlos Mora. 1977. *Atlas de comunidades nativas*. SINAMOS. Lima: Ministerio de Guerra.
Cipolletti, María Susana. 1988. "El tráfico de *curare* en la cuenca amazónica (Siglos XVIII y XIX)." *Anthropos* 83: 527–40.
Clark, Leonard. 1953. *The Rivers Ran East*. New York: Funk and Wagnalls.
Clastres, Pierre. 1987 [1974]. *Society against the State: Essays in Political Anthropology*. New York: Zone Books.
———. 1994. *Archeology of Violence*. Cambridge, Mass.: MIT Press.
Cleary, David. 2001. "Towards an Environmental History of the Amazon: From Prehistory to the Nineteenth Century." *Latin American Research Review* 36(2): 65–96.
Clifford, James. 1986. "Introduction: Partial Truths." In *Writing Culture: The Poetics and Politics of Ethnography*, ed. J. Clifford and G. Marcus, 1–26. Berkeley: University of California Press.
Cohn, Norman. 1970 [1957]. *The Pursuit of the Millennium: Revolutionary Millenarians and Mystical Anarchists of the Middle Ages*. New York: Oxford University Press.
———. 1995. *Cosmos, Chaos, and the World to Come: The Ancient Roots of Apocalyptic Faith*. New Haven, Conn.: Yale University Press.
Collier, Jane. 1988. *Marriage and Inequality in Classless Societies*. Stanford, Calif.: Stanford University Press.
———. 1997. "Response to Bell's 'Defining Marriage and Legitimacy.'" *Current Anthropology* 38(2): 237–55.
Collier, Jane, and Michelle Rosaldo. 1981. "Politics and Gender in Simple Societies." In *Sexual Meanings*, ed. S. Ortner and H. Whitehead, 275–329. New York: Cambridge University Press.
Collier, J., and S. Yanagisako. 1987. Introduction to *Gender and Kinship: Essays toward a Unified Analysis*, ed. J. Collier and S. Yanagisako, 14–52. Stanford, Calif.: Stanford University Press.
Colson, Audrey Butt. 1973. "Inter-tribal Trade in the Guiana Highlands." *Antropológica* (Venezuela) 34: 1–69.
Conklin, Beth. 1997. "Consuming Images: Representations of Cannibalism on the Amazonian Frontier." *Anthropological Quarterly* 70(2): 68–78.

———. 2001. *Consuming Grief: Compassionate Cannibalism in an Amazonian Society*. Austin: University of Texas Press.

Coomes, Oliver. 1992. "Blackwater Rivers, Adaptation, and Environmental Heterogeneity in Amazonia." *American Anthropologist* 94(3): 699–701.

———. 1995. "A Century of Rain Forest Use in Western Amazonia: Lessons for Extraction-Based Conservation of Tropical Resources." *Forest and Conservation History* 39(3): 108–20.

Cooper, Frederick. 1993. "Africa and the World Economy." In *Confronting Historical Paradigms: Peasants, Labor, and the Capitalist World System in Africa and Latin America*, ed. F. Cooper et al., 84–204. Madison: University of Wisconsin Press.

Coriat, Juan E. 1943. *El hombre del Amazonas y ensayo monográfico de Loreto*. Lima: Librería Coriat Imprenta.

Coronel Zegarra, Enrique. 1914. *Ferrocarril de Paita al Marañón: Artículos referentes a importante proyecto*. Lima: La Opinión Nacional.

Corrales Caraval, Socorro. 2005. "Rutas narrativas de mujeres indígenas en el Cauca: Territorio, tradición, re(presensión)." *Convergencia* 37: 59–83.

Costa, Alberto, Conrad Kottak, and Rosanne Prado. 1997. "The Sociopolitical Context of Participatory Development in Northeastern Brazil." *Human Organization* 56(2): 138–46.

Cressy-Marcks, Violet O. 1932. *Up the Amazon and over the Andes*. London: Hodder and Stoughton.

Crocker, Jon Christopher. 1985. *Vital Souls: Bororo Cosmology, Natural Symbolism, and Shamanism*. Tucson: University of Arizona Press.

Crosby, Alfred. 1972. *The Columbian Exchange: Biological and Cultural Consequences of 1492*. Westport, Conn.: Greenwood Publishers.

———. 1986. *Ecological Imperialism: The Biological Expansion of Europe, 900–1900*. Cambridge: Cambridge University Press.

———. 1994. *Germs, Seeds and Animals: Studies in Ecological History*. Armonk, N.Y.: M. E. Sharpe.

Cunha, Euclides da, Ronald Sousa, and Lucía Sá. 2006. *The Amazon: Land without History*. Oxford: Oxford University Press.

Da Matta, Roberto. 1982. *A Divided World: Apinayé Social Structure*. Cambridge, Mass.: Harvard University Press.

———. 1991. *Carnivals, Rogues, and Heroes: An Interpretation of the Brazilian Dilemma*. Notre Dame, Ind.: University of Notre Dame Press.

Davalos y Lisson, Pedro. 1930. *Diez años de historia contemporánea del Peru, 1899–1908: Gobiernos de Piérola, Calderón y Pardo*. Lima: Librería e Imprenta Gil, S.A.

Davies, Thomas. 1974. *Indian Integration in Peru: A Half-Century of Experience, 1900–1948*. Lincoln: University of Nebraska Press.

Dávila Herrera, Carlos. 1980. *Prehistoria y Amazonía*. Lima: Ediciones "Panorama Amazónico" SEAS/UNMSM.

Dávila Herrera, Carlos, and Angel Corbera Mori. 1982. *Lingüística en la Amazonía Peruana*. Lima: SEAS-UNMSM.

Davis, John. 1992. *Exchange*. Buckingham, U.K.: Open University Press.

Dean, Bartholomew. 1990. "The State and the Aguaruna: Frontier Expansion in the Upper Amazon, 1541–1990." M.A. thesis, Harvard University.

———. 1992. "Informe socio-económico para la inscripción de la comunidad nativa-urarina: Santa Beatríz del Pangayacu." Report presented to the Gobierno Regional de Loreto, Secretaria Regional de Asuntos Sociales, Iquitos, Peru (Ley No. 24656–Decreto Supremo No. 008–91 TR).

———. 1994a. "Multiple Regimes of Value: Unequal Exchange and the Circulation of Urarina Palm-Fiber Wealth." *Museum Anthropology* 18(1): 3–18.

———. 1994b. "The Poetics of Creation: Urarina Cosmogony and Historical Consciousness." *Latin American Indian Literatures Journal* 10(1): 22–45.

———. 1995. "Forbidden Fruit: Infidelity, Affinity, and Brideservice among the Urarina of Peruvian Amazonia." *Journal of the Royal Anthropological Institute* 1(1): 87–110.

———. 1996. "From the Fat of Their Being: Vampires and Andean Modernity." Review of *Gods and Vampires: Return to Chipaya*. *Cultural Dynamics* 9(1): 111–13.

———. 1998a. "Brideprice in Amazonia?" *The Journal of the Royal Anthropological Institute* 4(2): 345–48.

———. 1998b. Review of *Amazonian Caboclo Society: An Essay on Invisibility and Peasant Economy*. *American Ethnologist* 25(1): 58–59.

———. 1999. "Language, Culture, and Power: Intercultural Bilingual Education among the Urarina of Peruvian Amazonia." In "Reversing Language Shift in Indigenous America," ed. L. Watahomigie, T. McCarty, and A. Yamamoto, special issue, *Practicing Anthropology* 20(2): 39–43.

———. 2000. "Respecto a los derechos de los pueblos indígenas: Maybury-Lewis y la diversidad cultural." *El Comercio*, August 4, A20.

———. 2001. "Review: *Peasant Resistance*." *American Ethnologist* 28(1): 263–64.

———. 2002a. "Critical Re-vision: Clastres' *Chronicle* and the Optic of Primitivism." In *Best of Anthropology Today, 1974–2000*, ed. J. Benthall, with a preface by M. Sahlins, 66–71. London: Routledge.

———. 2002b. "State Power and Indigenous Peoples in Peruvian Amazonia: A Lost Decade, 1990–2000." In *The Politics of Ethnicity: Indigenous Peoples in Latin American States*, ed. D. Maybury-Lewis, 199–238. Cambridge, Mass.: Harvard University Press.

———. 2003. "At the Margins of Power: Gender Hierarchy and the Politics of Ethnic Mobilization among the Urarina." In *At the Risk of Being Heard: Indigenous Rights, Identity, and Postcolonial States*, ed. Bartholomew Dean and Jerome Levi, 217–54. Ann Arbor: University of Michigan Press.

———. 2004a. "Digital Vibes and Radio Waves in Indigenous Peru." In *Indigenous Intellectual Property Rights: Legal Obstacles and Innovative Solutions*, ed. M. Riley, 27–53. New York: Altamira Press.

———. 2004b. "El Dr. Máxime Kuczynski-Godard y la medicina social en la Amazonía Peruana." In *La vida en la Amazonía Peruana: Observaciones de un médico*, by Máxime Kuczynski-Godard, 17–20. Lima: Fondo Editorial de la Universidad Nacional Mayor de San Marcos.

———. 2004c. "Ambivalent Exchanges: The Violence of *Patronazgo* in the Upper Amazon." In *Cultural Construction of Violence: Victimization, Escalation, Response*, ed. M. Anderson, 214–26. West Lafayette, Ind.: Purdue University.

———. 2004d. "Indigenous Education and the Prospects for Cultural Survival." *Cultural Survival Quarterly* 27(4): 14–18.

———. 2005. "The Ethics of Spying." *Anthropology Today* 21(4): 19–21.

———. 2006a. "Ethnology Section: Lowland South America." In *Handbook of Latin American Studies* 61 (Social Sciences, Prepared by a Number of Scholars for the Hispanic Division of the Library of Congress), 96–109. Austin: University of Texas Press.

———. 2006b. Review of Stefano Varese's *Salt of the Mountain: Campa Ashaninka History and Resistance in the Peruvian Jungle*. *The Americas* 62(3): 464–66.

———. 2006c. Introduction to *The Varieties of Human Experience: An Anthropological Reader*, ed. N. Erickson Lamar, B. Dean, and H. Meiers, 1. 1st ed. Dubuque, Iowa: Kendall/Hunt Publishing.

———. 2007. "Commentary on Cristina Alacalde's 'Why Would You Marry a Serrana? Women's Experiences of Identity-Based Violence in the Intimacy of Their Homes in Lima.'" *Journal of Latin American and Caribbean Anthropology* 12(1): 29–32.

Dean, Bartholomew, et al. 1999. "The Amazonian Peoples' Resources Initiative: Promoting Reproductive Rights and Community Development in the Peruvian Amazon." *Health and Human Rights: An International Journal* 4(2): 3–10.

Dean, Bartholomew, and Jerome M. Levi, eds. 2003. *At the Risk of Being Heard: Identity, Indigenous Rights, and Postcolonial States*. Ann Arbor: University of Michigan Press.

Dean, Bartholomew, and Michelle McKinley. 1997. "Building Partnerships in Health, Education, and Social Justice." *Cultural Survival Quarterly* 21(3): 14–15.

DeBoer, Warren. 1981. "The Machete and the Cross: Conibo Trade in the Late Seventeenth Century." In *Networks of the Past*, ed. P. Francis and P. Duke, 31–48. Calgary: Archaeological Association of the University of Calgary.

———. 1986. "Pillage and Production in the Amazon: A View through the Conibo of the Ucayali Basin, Eastern Peru." *World Archaeology* 18(2): 231–46.

Degregori, Carlos Iván. 1991. "How Difficult It Is to Be God: Ideology and Political Violence in Sendero Luminoso." *Critique of Anthropology* 11(3): 233–50.

———. 2000. "Shining Path's Discourse and Political Violence." *Bulletin de l'Institut Francais d'Etudes andines* 29(3): 493–513.

———, ed. 2000. *No hay país más diverso: Compendio de antropología peruana*. Lima: Red para el Desarrollo de las Ciencias Sociales en el Perú.

Denevan, William. 1996. "A Bluff Model of Riverine Settlement in Prehistoric Amazonia." *Annals of the Association of American Geographers* 86(4): 654–81.

Derrida, Jacques. 1970. "Structure, Sign, and Play in the Discourse of the Human Sciences." In *The Language of Criticism and the Sciences of Man*, ed. R. Macksey and E. Donato, 499–501. Baltimore: Johns Hopkins University Press.

Descola, Philippe. 1982. "Territorial Adjustments among the Achuar of Ecuador." *Social Science Information* 21(2): 301–20.

———. 1994. *In the Society of Nature: A Native Ecology in Amazonia*. Cambridge: Cambridge University Press.

Descola, Philippe, and Anne-Christine Taylor. 1981. "El Conjunto Jívaro en los comienzos de la conquista española del Alto Amazonas." *Bulletin del Institut Français d'Etudes Andines* 10(3–4): 7–54.

DeVries, Philip. 1987. *The Butterflies of Costa Rica and Their Natural History*. Princeton, N.J.: Princeton University Press.

Díaz Barba, Armando. 1987. "La Chawa chacra urarina: Una técnica tradicional de agricultura amazónica." *Boletín de Lima* 49: 65–72.

Dieken, Bülent. 1998. *Strangers, Ambivalence, and Social Theory*. Brookfield, Vt.: Ashgate Publishing.

Dole, Gertrude. 1984. "The Structure of Kuikuru Marriage." In *Marriage Practices in Lowland South America*, ed. K. Kensinger, 45–62. Urbana: University of Illinois Press.

Dollfus, Oliver. 1986. "The Tropical Andes: A Changing Mosaic." In *Anthropological History of Andean Polities*, ed. John Murra, Nathan Watchel, and Jacques Revel, 11–22. Cambridge: Cambridge University Press.

Dominguez, Camilo, and Augusto Gómez. 1990. *La económia extractiza en la Amazonia Colombiana*. Bogotá: COA.

Domville-Fife, Charles William. 1924. *Among Wild Tribes of the Amazons*. London: Seeley, Service and Co. Ltd.

Dourojeanni, Marc. 1990. *Amazonia: Que Hacer?* Iquitos: CETA.

Dumont, J.-P. 1978. *The Headman and I*. Austin: University of Texas Press.

Dundes, Alan. 1988. Introduction to *The Flood Myth*, ed. A. Dundes, i–vi. Berkeley: University of California Press.

Early, John, and John Peters. 2000. *The Xilixana Yanomami of the Amazon: History, Social Structure, and Population Dynamics*. Gainesville: University Press of Florida.

Eichenberger, Ralph. 1961. "Nacimiento, vida y muerto en la selva." *Perú Indígena* 9(20–21): 51–65.

Ember, M. 1973. "Taxonomy in Comparative Studies." In *A Handbook of Method in Cultural Anthropology*, ed. R. Naroll and R. Cohen, 697–706. Garden City, N.Y.: Natural History Press.

Emmons, Louise. 1990. *Neotropical Rainforest Mammals: A Field Guide*. Chicago: University of Chicago Press.

Erickson, Lamar, Nancy and Bartholomew Dean, and Heather Meiers, eds. 2006. *The Varieties of Human Experience: An Anthropological Reader*. Dubuque, Iowa: Kendall/Hunt Publishing.

Erikson, Philippe. 2002. "Myth and Material Culture: Matis Blowguns, Palm Trees, and Ancestors." In *Beyond the Visible and the Material: The Amerindianization of Society in the Work of Peter Rivière*, ed. Laura M. Rival and Neil L. Whitehead, 101–22. Oxford: Oxford University Press.

Espinosa Perez, Lucas. 1955. *Contribuciones lingüísticas y etnográficas sobre algunos pueblos indígenas del Amazonas Peruano*. Tomo I. Madrid: Consejo Superior de Investigaciones Científicas, Instituto Bernardino de Sahagun.

Espinoza Galarza, Max. 1979. *Toponimos quechuas del Perú*. Lima: Talleres Gráficos de Imprenta Noriega.

Fabián, Beatriz. 1995. "Cambios culturales en los asháninka desplazados." *Amazonía Peruana* 12(25): 159–76.

Fabian, Johannes. 1983. *Time and the Other: How Anthropology Makes Its Object*. New York: Columbia University Press.

Fachín Terán, Augusto. 1992. "Desove y uso de playas para nidificación de Taricaya (*Podocnemis Unifilis*) en el Río Samiria, Loreto-Peru." *Boletín de Lima* 79: 65–75.

Farabee, William Curtis. 1922. *Indian Tribes of Eastern Peru*. Papers of the Peabody Museum of Archaeology and Ethnology, Harvard University, vol. 10. Cambridge, Mass.: Harvard University Press.

Faura Gaig, Guillermo S. 1964. *Los ríos de la Amazonía Peruana*. Lima, Callao: Imp. Colegio Militar Leocio Prado.

Fausto, Carlos. 2001. *Inimigos fiéis: História, guerra e xamanismo na Amazônia*. São Paulo: Edusp.

———. 2002. "Commensality and Cannibalism in Amazonia." *Mana* 8(2): 7–44.

———. 2007. "Feasting on People: Eating Animals and Humans in Amazonia." *Current Anthropology* 48(4): 497–530.

Fausto, Carlos, and Michael Heckenberger, eds. 2007. *Time and Memory in Indigenous Amazonia: Anthropological Perspectives*. Gainesville: University Press of Florida

Fejos, Pál. 1943. *Ethnography of the Yagua*. Viking Fund Publications in Anthropology 1. New York: The Viking Fund.

Feld, Steven. 1998. "They Repeatedly Lick Their Own." *Critical Inquiry* 24: 445–72.

Feldman, Allan. 1991. *Formations of Violence: The Narrative of the Body and Political Terror in Northern Ireland*. Chicago: University of Chicago Press.

Femeninas, Blenda. 2004. *Gender and the Boundaries of Dress in Contemporary Peru: Gender, Clothing, and Representation in Contemporary Peru*. Austin: University of Texas Press.

Ferguson, Brian. 1990. "Blood of the Leviathan: Western Contact and Warfare in Amazonia." *American Ethnologist* 17(2): 237–57.

Ferguson, James. 1992. "The Cultural Topography of Wealth: Commodity Paths and the Structure of Property in Rural Lesotho." *American Anthropologist* 94(1): 55–73.

Fernández, Eduardo. 1986. *Para que nuestra historia no se pierda: Testimonios de los asháninca y nomatsiguenga sobre la colonización de la región Satipo-Pangoa*. Lima: CIPA.

Ferrúa Carrasco, Freddy, et al. 1980. *La sociedad urarina*. Iquitos: Organismo Regional de Desarrollo de Loreto (ORDELORETO).

Ferry, Elizabeth Emma. 2002. "Inalienable Commodities: The Production and Circulation of Silver and Patrimony in a Mexican Mining Cooperative." *Cultural Anthropology* 17(3): 331–58.

Figueroa, Francisco de. 1904 [1661]. *Relación de las misiones de la Compañía de Jesús en el país de los Maynas*. Madrid: Librería General de Victoriano Suárez.

Firth, R. 1983 [1936]. *We, the Tikopia: A Sociological Study of Kinship in Primitive Polynesia*. Stanford, Calif.: Stanford University Press.

Flores Mariín, Joseí. 1977. *La explotacioìn del caucho en el Peruì*. Lima: Universidad Nacional Mayor de San Marcos (Seminario de Historia Rural Andina).

Flores Paitán, Salvador. 1987. "Old Managed Fallows at Brillo Nuevo." In *Swidden-Fal-*

low Agroforestry in the Peruvian Amazon, ed. W. Denevan and C. Padoch, 53–66. New York: New York Botanical Gardens.

Folkman Curasi, Carolyn, Linda Price, and Eric Arnould. 2004. "How Individuals' Cherished Possessions Become Families' Inalienable Wealth." *Journal of Consumer Research* 31(3): 609–22.

Foster, Robert. 2002. *Materializing the Nation: Commodities, Consumption, and Media in Papua*. Bloomington: Indiana University Press.

Foucault, Michel. 1979. *Discipline and Punish: The Birth of the Prison*. New York: Vintage Books.

———. 1980. *Power/Knowledge: Selected Interviews and Other Writings*, ed. Colin Gordon. New York: Pantheon.

Fox, R. 1971. *Kinship and Marriage*. Harmondsworth, Middlesex: Penguin Books.

Fraile Tejedor, Senén. 1927. *Breve reseña histórica de la Misión Agustiniana de San Léon del Amazonas*. El Escorial: Imprenta del Monasterio del El Escorial.

Frazer, J. G. 1919. *Folklore in the Old Testament*. 3 vols. London: MacMillan.

Fricke, T., A. Thornton, and D. Dahal. 1998. "Netting in Nepal: Social Change, the Life Course, and Brideservice in Sangila." *Human Ecology* 26(2): 213–37.

Friedl, E. 1975. *Women and Men*. New York: Holt, Rinehart and Winston.

Fritz, Samuel. 1922 [1686–1723]. *Journal of the Travels and Labours of Father Samuel Fritz in the River of Amazons between 1686 and 1723*. Trans. and ed. G. Edmundson. London: The Hakluyt Society.

Fuentes, Aldo. 1988. *¿Por qué, las piedras no mueren? Historia, sociedad y ritos de los chayahuitas del Alto Amazonas*. Lima: CAAAP.

Fuentes, Hildebrando. 1908. *Loreto: Apuntes geográficos, históricos, estadísticos, políticos y sociales*. Lima: Imprenta de La Revista.

Fuss, Diana. 1989. *Essentially Speaking: Feminism, Nature, and Difference*. New York: Routledge.

Gamarra, Agustín. 2000 [1832]. "Address before Peruvian Congress, November 21." In *Panorama histórico de la Amazonía Peruana*, ed. H. Morey Alejo and G. Sotil García, 174–75. Iquitos: Municipalidad Provincial de Maynas.

García, Joaquín. 2000. "La Prefectura Apostólica de San León del Amazonas." *Kanatari* 17(850).

Garcia, Maria Elena. 2005. *Making Indigenous Citizens: Identities, Education, and Multicultural Development in Peru*. Stanford, Calif.: Stanford University Press.

García Canclini, Néstor. 1993. *Transforming Modernity: Popular Culture in Mexico*. Austin: University of Texas Press.

———. 2001. *Consumers and Citizens: Globalization and Multicultural Conflicts*. Trans. G. Yúdice. Minneapolis: University of Minnesota Press.

García Hierro, Pedro, Søren Hvalkof, and Andrew Gray. 1998. *Liberation Through Land Rights in the Peruvian Amazon*. Copenhagen: International Work Group for Indigenous Affairs.

García Jordán, Pilar. 1997. "Vías de penetración y métodos de conquista del territorio e indígenas amazónicos." *Boletín Americanista* 47: 127–41.

———. 2000. "Régimen eclesiástico de principios de siglo en la Amazonía Peruana." *Kanatari* 17(850).

———. 2001. *Cruz y arado, fusiles y discursos: La construcción de los Orientes en el Perú y Bolivia, 1820–1940*. Lima: Institut français d'études andines/Instituto de estudios peruanos.

Gasche, Jurg. 1997–98. "Un programme interculturel de formation d'instituteurs en Amazonie peruvienne." *Ethnies* 12(22–3): 155–77.

Gell, Alfred. 1999. *The Art of Anthropology: Essays and Diagrams*, ed. Eric Hirsch. London: Athlone Press.

Gelles, Paul H. 2000. *Water and Power in Highland Peru: The Cultural Politics of Irrigation and Development*. New Brunswick, N.J.: Rutgers University Press.

George, Kenneth M. 1996. *Showing Signs of Violence: The Cultural Politics of a Twentieth-Century Headhunting Ritual*. Berkeley: University of California Press.

Germaná, César. 1995. *El "Socialismo Indo-americano" de José Carlos Mariátegui: Proyecto de reconstitución del sentido histórico de la sociedad peruana*. Lima: Editora Amauta.

Gheerbrant, Alain. 1992. *The Amazon: Past, Present, and Future*. New York: Harry N. Abrahams.

Gibbon, Lardner. 1854. *Exploration of the Valley of the Amazon. Made Under the Direction of the Navy Department*. Washington D.C.: Government Printing Office.

Gill, Lesley. 1994. *Precarious Dependencies: Gender, Class, and Domestic Service in Bolivia*. New York: Columbia University Press.

Girard, R. 1958. *Indios selvaticos de la Amazonía Peruana*. Mexico D.F.: Libro Mex.

Godelier, Maurice. 1999. *The Enigma of the Gift*. Chicago: University of Chicago Press.

Godoy, Ricardo. 2001. *Indians, Markets, and Rainforests: Theory, Methods, Analysis*. New York: Columbia University Press.

Goehring, Herman. 1877. *Informe al Supremo Gobierno del Peru sobre la expedición a los valles de Paucartambo en 1873, al mando del Coronel D. Balthazar la Torre*. Lima: Imprenta del Estado.

Goldman, I. 1963. *The Cubeo: Indians of the Northwest Amazon*. Urbana: University of Illinois Press.

Golob, Ann. 1982. "The Upper Amazon in Historical Perspective." Ph.D. diss., City University of New York.

Gomes, Mercio Pereira. 2000. *The Indians and Brazil*. Gainesville: University Press of Florida.

González, Gisela. 2003. "El resurgimiento de las identidades étnicas en América Latina." *Iberoamericana* 25(1): 1–16.

González-Cueva, Eduardo. 2000. "Conscription and Violence in Peru." *Latin American Perspectives* 27(3): 88–102.

Gonzaìlez Prada, Manuel. 1966. *Paìginas libres*. Lima: Ediciones Paìginas de Oro del Peruì.

González Suárez, Federico. 1913. *Estudio historico sobre la cédula del 15 de julio de 1802*. Quito: Imprenta del Clero.

Goody, Jack. 1973. "Bridewealth and Dowry in Africa and Eurasia." In *Bridewealth and Dowry*, ed. J. Goody and S. J. Tambiah, 1–58. Cambridge: Cambridge University Press.

———. 1990. *The Oriental, the Ancient, and the Primitive: Systems of Marriage and the Family in Pre-industrial Societies of Eurasia*. Cambridge: Cambridge University Press.

Gootenberg, Paul. 1991. "Population and Ethnicity in Early Republican Peru: Some Revisions." *Latin American Research Review* 26(3): 109–57.

Gose, Peter. 2000. "The State as a Chosen Woman: Brideservice and the Feeding of Tributaries in the Inka Empire." *American Anthropologist* 102(1): 84–97.

Gow, Peter. 1989. "The Perverse Child: Desire in a Native Amazonian Subsistence Economy." *MAN*, n.s., 24: 567–82.

———. 1991. *Of Mixed Blood: Kinship and History in Peruvian Amazonia*. Oxford: Clarendon Press.

———. 1993. "Gringos and Wild Indians: Images of History in Western Amazonian Cultures." *L'Homme* 33(126–28): 327–47.

———. 2001. *An Amazonian Myth and Its History*. Oxford: Oxford University Press.

Gragson, Ted. 1992a. "Strategic Procurement of Fish by the Pumé: A South American Fishing Culture." *Human Ecology* 20(1): 109–30.

———. 1992b. "Fishing the Waters of Amazonia: Native Subsistence Economies in a Tropical Rain Forest." *American Anthropologist* 94(2): 428–40.

Graham, Laura. 2005. "Image and Instrumentality in a Xavante Politics of Existential Recognition: The Public Outreach Work of Etenhiritipa Pimentel Barbosa." *American Ethnologist* 32(4): 622–41.

Graham, Richard. 1972. *Independence in Latin America: A Comparative Approach*. New York: Alfred A. Knopf.

Gramsci, Antonio. 1971. *Selection from Prison Notebooks*. London: Lawrence and Wishart.

Gray, Andrew. 1997. *Indigenous Rights and Development: Self-Determination in an Amazonian Community*. Oxford: Berghan Books.

Great Britain, Foreign Office. 1913. *Report by His Majesty's Consul at Iquitos on His Tour in the Putumayo District*. (George B. Michell, consul at Iquitos.) London: H. M. Stationery office, printed by Harrison and Sons.

Greenberg, Joseph H. 1960. "The General Classification of Central and South American Languages." In *Men and Cultures*, ed. A. F. C. Wallace, 791–94. Philadelphia: University of Philadelphia Press.

Gregor, Thomas. 1987. *Anxious Pleasures: The Sexual Lives of an Amazonian People*. Chicago: University of Chicago Press.

Gregor, Thomas, and Donald Tuzin, eds. 2001. *Gender in Amazonia and Melanesia: An Exploration of the Comparative Method*. Berkeley: University of California Press.

Gregorio y Alonso, B. 1951. "Acción Misionera de los PP. Agustinos en Loreto bajo su triple aspecto, religioso, cultural y científico." In *Misiones Agustinianas: Album Recordatorio del Cincuentenario de la llegada de los Padres Agustinos a Loreto*, 11–164. Lima: Editorial Antonio Lulli.

Gregory, C. A. 1980. "Gifts to Men and Gifts to God: Gift Exchange and Capital Accumulation in Contemporary Paupa." *MAN*, n.s., 15: 626–52.

Grohs-Paul, Waltraud. 1974. "Los indios del Alto Amazonas del siglo XVI al siglo XVIII: Poblaciones y migraciones en la antigua provincia de Maynas." *Bonner amerikanistische Studien* 2: 1–133.

Guallart Martínez, José María. 1976. "Peces, pescadores y pesqueras entre los aguaruna del Alto Marañón." *Biota* 10: 372–96.

———. 1989. *El mundo mágico de los aguarunas*. Lima: CAAAP.

Guddemi, Philip. 1992. "When Horticulturalists Are Like Hunter-Gatherers: The Sawiyanö of Paupa New Guinea." *Ethnology* 31(4): 303–14.

Gudeman, Stephen, and Alberto Rivera. 1995. "From Car to House (Del Coche a la Casa)." *American Anthropologist* 97(2): 242–50.

Guernsey, A. H. 1870. "The Andes and the Amazon." Review of James Orton's Text. *Harper's New Monthly Magazine* 240(40): 344–58.

Guillaume, Herbert. 1894. *The Amazon Provinces of Peru as a Field for European Emigration*. London: Wyman and Sons.

Guss, David M. 1981. "Historical Incorporation among the Makiritare: From Legend to Myth." *Journal of Latin American Lore* 7(1): 23–35.

———. 1990. *To Weave and Sing: Art, Symbol, and Narrative in the South American Rain Forest*. Berkeley: University of California Press.

Habich, Eduardo. 1903. "El camino de Eten a Bellavista y exploración de Bellavista al pongo de Manseriche el Río Marañón." In *Vías del Pacífico al Marañón*, Publicación de la Junta Vías Fluviales, 3–34. Lima: Imprenta La Industria.

Hagen, James. 1999. "The Good behind the Gift: Morality and Exchange among the Maneo of Eastern Indonesia." *Journal of the Royal Anthropological Institute*, n.s., 5(3): 361–76.

Hamayon, Roberte. 1994. "Shamanism in Siberia: From Partnership in Supernature to Counter-Power in Society." In *Shamanism, History, and the State*, ed. N. Thomas and C. Humphrey, 76–89. Ann Arbor: University of Michigan Press.

Haraway, Donna. 1989. *Primate Visions: Gender, Race, and Nature in the World of Modern Science*. New York: Routledge.

Hardenburg, Walter Ernest. 1912. *The Putumayo: The Devil's Paradise*. London: T. Fisher Unwin.

Haring, M. 1986. *Boomtown aan de Amazone: Een historisch-sociologische studie over de Peruaanse Amazoneregio en de stad Iquitos, met nadruk op de periode 1880–1980*. Utrecht: Instituut voor Culturele Antropologie, Rijksuniversiteit Utrecht.

Harner, Michael. 1973. *The Jívaro: People of the Sacred Waterfalls*. Garden City, N.Y.: Anchor Press, Doubleday Books.

Harris, Mark. 2001. *Life on the Amazon: The Anthropology of a Brazilian Peasant Village*. London: British Academy.

Harris, Olivia. 1989. "The Earth and the State: The Sources and Meanings of Money in Northern Potosí, Bolivia." In *Money and the Morality of Exchange*, ed. J. Parry and M. Bloch, 232–68. Cambridge: Cambridge University Press.

Hebdige, Dick. 1979. *Subculture: The Meaning of Style*. London: Methuen.

Heckenberger, M. 2004. *The Ecology of Power: Culture, Place, and Personhood in the Southern Amazon, A.D. 1000–2000*. New York: Routledge.

Heise Mondino, María, Lilian Landeo del Pino, and Astrid Bant. 1999. *Relaciones de género en la Amazonía Peruana*. Lima: CAAAP.

Helliwell, Christine. 2000. "Restoring the Balance: 'Marriage Exchange' in a Borneo Community." *Asia and Pacific Journal of Anthropology* 1(1): 37–53.

Hendon, Julia. 2000. "Having and Holding: Storage, Memory, Knowledge, and Social Relations." *American Anthropologist* 102: 42–53.

Henley, Paul. 1982. *The Panare, Tradition, and Change on the Amazonian Frontier.* New Haven, Conn.: Yale University Press.

———. 1996. "Recent Themes in the Anthropology of Amazonia: History, Exchange, Alterity." *Bulletin of Latin American Research Review* 15(2): 231–45.

Hernández, Toribio. 1946. *Historia de la fundación del pueblo de Tamshiyacu provincia de Maynas departmento de Loreto, 1906–1924.* N.p.

Herndon, William Lewis. 1952 [1854]. *Exploration of the Valley of the Amazon.* Ed. H. Basso. New York: McGraw-Hill.

Herrera, José Fermín. 1905. "Estado comercial de la región peruana del Amazonas el año 1872, por. . . ." In *Colección de leyes, decretos, resoluciones i otros documentos oficiales referentes al departmento de Loreto,* ed. C. Larrabure i Correa, 16: 104–38. Lima: La Opinión Nacional.

Herrmann, Gretchen. 1997. "Gift or Commodity: What Changes Hands in the U.S. Garage Sale?" *American Ethnologist* 24(4): 910–30.

Herzfeld, Michael. 1991. *A Place in History: Social and Monumental Time in a Cretan Town.* Princeton, N.J.: Princeton University Press.

Hill, Jonathan. 1987. "Wakuénai Ceremonial Exchange in the Venezuelan Northwest Amazon." *Journal of Latin American Lore* 13(2): 183–224.

———. 1988. "Introduction: Myth and History." In *Rethinking History and Myth: Indigenous South American Perspectives on the Past,* ed. J. Hill, 1–17. Urbana: University of Illinois Press.

———. 1993a. *Keepers of the Scared Chants: The Poetics of Ritual Power in an Amazonian Society.* Tucson: University of Arizona Press.

———. 1993b. "Cosmology and Situation of Contact." In *Cosmology, Value, and Interethnic Contact in South America,* ed. T. Turner. South American Indian Studies 9: 46–55. Bennington, Vt.: Bennington College.

Hill, Jonathan D., and Robin Wright. 1988. "Time, Narrative, and Ritual: Historical Interpretations from an Amazonian Society." In *Rethinking History and Myth: Indigenous South American Perspectives on the Past,* ed. Jonathan Hill, 78–105. Urbana: University of Illinois Press.

Hill, K., and E. Moran. 1983. "Adaptive Strategies of Wakuenai Peoples to the Oligotrophic Rain Forest of the Rio Negro Basin." In *Adaptive Responses of Native Amazonians,* ed. R. Hames and W. Vickers, 113–35. New York: Academic Press.

Hiraoka, Mário. 1985. "Cash Cropping, Wage Labor, and Urbanward Migrations: Changing Floodplain Subsistence in the Peruvian Amazon." *Studies in Third World Societies* (32): 199–242.

———. 1989. "Patrones de subsistencia mestiza en las zonas ribereñas de la Amazonía Peruana." *Amazonía Indígena* 9(15): 17–25.

Hirsch, N. 1990. "From Bones to Betelnuts: Processes of Ritual Transformation and the Development of 'National Culture' in Paupa New Guinea." *MAN,* n.s., 25: 18–34.

Hirschkind, Lynn. 2000. "Sal/Manteca/Panela: Ethnoveterinary Practice in Highland Ecuador." *American Anthropologist* 102(2): 290–302.

Holmberg, Allan. 1969 [1950]. *Nomads of the Long Bow: The Siriono of Eastern Bolivia*. Prospect Heights, Ill.: Waveland Press.

Hornborg Alf. 2005. "Ethnogenesis, Regional Integration, and Ecology in Prehistoric Amazonia: Toward a System Perspective." *Current Anthropology* 46(4): 589–620.

Huertas Castillo, Beatriz. 2005. *Indigenous Peoples in Isolation in the Peruvian Amazon: Their Struggle for Survival and Freedom*. Copenhagen: IWGIA.

Hughes, Alex, ed. 2004. *Geographies of Commodity Chains*. New York: Routledge.

Hugh-Jones, Stephen. 1977. "Amazonian Smoked Fish and Meat—A Technique from the Barasana Indians of the Vaupés Region of Colombia." In *The Anthropologists' Cookbook*, ed. Jessica Kuper, n.p. London: Routledge and Kegan Paul.

———. 1988 [1979]. *The Palm and the Pleiades: Initiation and Cosmology in Northwest Amazonia*. Cambridge: Cambridge University Press.

———. 1992. "Yesterday's Luxuries, Tomorrow's Necessities: Business and Barter in Northwest Amazonia." In *Barter, Exchange, and Value*, ed. C. Humphrey and S. Hugh-Jones, 42–74. Cambridge: Cambridge University Press.

———. 1994. "Shamans, Prophets, Priests, and Pastors." In *Shamanism, History, and the State*, ed. N. Thomas and C. Humphrey, 32–75. Ann Arbor: University of Michigan Press.

———. 1995. "Inside-Out and Back-to-Front: The Androgynous House in Northwest Amazonia." In *About the House: Lévi-Strauss and Beyond*, ed. J. Carsten and S. Hugh-Jones, 226–52. Cambridge: Cambridge University Press.

———. 2002. "Nomes secretos e riqueza visible: Nominação no noroeste Amazônico." *Mana* 8(2): 45–68.

ILV. 1993. "1994 Calendar: Urarina del Río Chambira, Loreto, Perú." N.p.: David C. Cook Foundation.

Inoash, Gil. 1997. "Perspectivas generales de la situación indígena." In *Desarrollo y participación de las Comunidades Nativas: Retos y posibilidades*, 65–73 Lima: Defensoría del Pueblo/CAAAP.

Intrator, Kira. 2006. "For the Love of Furniture." *Cultural Survival Quarterly* 30(4): 26–31.

Izaguirre, B. 1925. *Historia de las misiones Franciscanas y narración de los progresos de la geografía en el Oriente del Peru*. Lima: Talleres Tipográficos de la Penitenciaría.

Izquierdo, Carolina, and Allen Johnson. 2007. "Desire, Envy, and Punishment: A Matsigenka Emotion Schema in Illness Narratives and Folk Stories." *Culture, Medicine, and Psychiatry* 31(4): 419–44.

Izquierdo Ríos, Hildebrando. 1976. *Comandancia General de Mainas: Aspectos de Mainas Libre*. Lima: Editorial Imprenta "Ultra."

Jackson, Jean. 1983. *The Fish People: Linguistic Exogamy and Tukanoan Identity in Northwest Amazonia*. Cambridge: Cambridge University Press.

———. 1992. "The Meaning and Message of Symbolic Sexual Violence in Tukanoan Ritual." *Anthropological Quarterly* 65: 1–18.

Jackson, Joe. 2008. *The Thief at the End of the World: Rubber, Power, and the Seeds of Empire*. New York: Viking Publishing

Jacobsen, Nils. 1993. *Mirages of Transition: The Peruvian Altiplano, 1780–1930*. Berkeley: University of California Press.

Jamieson, Mark. 1999. "The Place of Counterfeits in Regimes of Value: An Anthropological Approach." *Journal of the Royal Anthropological Institute*, n.s., 5(1): 1–11.

———. 2003. "Miskitu or Creole? Ethnic Identity and the Moral Economy in a Nicaraguan Miskitu Village." *Journal of the Royal Anthropological Institute*, n.s., 9(2): 201–22.

Jamieson, Ross. 2001. "The Essence of Commodification: Caffeine Dependencies in the Early Modern World." *Journal of Social History* 35(2): 269–94.

Jara, Fabiola. 1986. "Implicaciones del mito de origen de los cerdos salvajes la etnoetnología Kaliña." In *Myth and the Imaginary in the New World*, ed. E. Magaña and P. Mason, 167–90. Amsterdam: CEDLA.

Jáuregui, Atanasio. 1943. "Cuestionario censal de la población salvaje." In *Misiones pasionistas del Oriente Peruano*, 480–81. Lima: Empresa Grafica T. Scheuch S.A.

Johnson, A., and O. Johnson. 1975. "Male/Female Relations and the Organization of Work in a Machiguenga Community." *American Ethnologist* 2: 634–48.

Johnson, Allen. 2003. *Families of the Forest: The Matsigenka Indians of the Peruvian Amazon*. Berkeley: University of California Press.

Jones, David. 1995. *Palms throughout the World*. Washington, D.C.: Smithsonian Institution Press.

Junquera Rubio, Carlos. 1999. "Impactos causados y producidos por la búsqueda de oro en la selva amazónica peruana." *Revista Española de Antropología Americana* 29: 283–307.

Junta Fluvial (Peru). 1907. *Ultimas exploraciones ordenadas por la junta de viajes fluviales en el Ucayali, Madre de Dios, Paucartambo, y Urubamba: Informes de los señores Stiglich, Von Hassel, Olivera, Ontaneda*. Lima: Tipográfica La Opinión Nacional.

Kalliola, Risto, and Salvador Flores Paitán, eds. 1998. *Geoecología y desarrollo amazónico: Estudio integrado en la zona de Iquitos, Perú*. Annales Universitatis Turkuensis, Ser. A II, Tom. 114. Turku: Turun Yliopsito Julkaisuja.

Kamppinen, Matti. 1988. "Espíritus Incorporados: The Roles of Plants and Animals in the Amazonian Mestizo Folklore." *Journal of Ethnobiology* 8(2): 141–48.

Karsten, Rafael. 1923. *Blood Revenge, War, and Victory Feasts among the Jibaro Indians of Eastern Ecuador*. Washington, D.C.: Government Printing Office.

Katz, Fredrich. 1990. "Debt Peonage in Tulancingo." In *Circumpacifica. Band I: Mittel- und Südamerika*, ed. B. Illius and M. Laubshcer, 239–48. Frankfurt: Peter Lang.

Kearney, Michael. 1996. "Indigenous Ethnicity and Mobilization in Latin America." *Latin American Perspectives* 23(2): 5–17.

Kelly, Raymond. 1993. *Constructing Inequality: The Fabrication of a Hierarchy of Virtue among the Etoro*. Ann Arbor: University of Michigan Press.

Kensinger, Kenneth. 1984. "Sex and Food: Reciprocity in Cashinahua Society?" In *Sexual Ideologies in Lowland South America*. Working Papers on South American Indians 5: 1–3. Bennington, Vt.: Bennington College.

———. 1989. "Hunting and Male Domination in Cashinahua Society." In *Farmers as Hunters*, ed. S. Kent, 118–26. Cambridge: Cambridge University Press.

———. 1995. *How Real People Ought to Live: The Cashinahua of Eastern Peru*. Prospect Heights, Ill.: Waveland Press.

———. 1998. "Los Cashinahua." In *Guía etnográfica de la Alta Amazonía*, ed. F. Santos and F. Barclay, 3: 1–124. Quitos: Abya-Yala/STRI.

Kerbey, J. Orton. 1906. *The Land of Tomorrow: A Newspaper Exploration up the Amazon and over the Andes to the California of South America*. New York: W. F. Brainard.

Klarén, Peter. 2000. *Peru: Society and Nationhood in the Andes*. New York: Oxford University Press.

Knauft, Bruce. 1997. "Gender Identity, Political Economy and Modernity in Melanesia and Amazonia." *Journal of the Royal Anthropological Institute*, n.s., 3: 233–59.

———. 1999. *From Primitive to Postcolonial in Melanesia and Anthropology*. Ann Arbor: University of Michigan Press.

Kohn, Eduardo. 2005. "Runa Realism: Upper Amazonian Attitudes to Nature Knowing." *Ethnos* 70(2): 171–96.

Komter, Aafke. 2001. "Heirlooms, Nikes, and Bribes: Towards a Sociology of Things." *Sociology* 35(1): 59–75.

Kopytoff, Igor. 1992. "The Cultural Biography of Things: Commoditization as Process." In *The Social Life of Things: Commodities in Cultural Perspective*, ed. A. Appadurai, 69–91. Cambridge: Cambridge University Press.

Kracke, Waud. 1976. "Uxorilocality in Patriliny: Kagwahiv Filial Separation." *Ethos* 4: 295–310.

———. 1978. *Force and Persuasion: Leadership in an Amazonian Society*. Chicago: University of Chicago Press.

———. 1992. "He Who Dreams: The Nocturnal Source of Transforming Power in Kagwahiv Shamanism." In *Portals of Power: Shamanism In South America*, ed. E. J. Langdon and G. Baer, 127–48. Albuquerque: University of New Mexico Press.

Kramer, B.-J. 1977. "Las implicaciones ecológicas de la agricultura de los urarina." *Amazonía Peruana* 1: 75–86.

———. 1979. "Urarina Economy and Society: Tradition and Change." Ph.D. diss., Columbia University.

Kricher, John. 1989. *A Neotropical Companion: An Introduction to the Animals, Plants, and Ecosystems of the New World Tropics*. Princeton, N.J.: Princeton University Press.

Kuczynski Godard, Máxime H. 1943. "Civilización del Indio Silvícola." *América Indígena* 3: 313–22.

———. 2004 [1944]. *La vida en la Amazonía Peruana: Observaciones de un médico*. Lima: Fondo Editorial de la Universidad Nacional Mayor de San Marcos.

La Condamine, Charles-Marie. 1986 [1745]. *Viaje a la América Meridional por el río de las Amazonas*. Barcelona: Editorial Alta Fulla "Mundo Científico."

Lagos, Ovidio. 2005. *Arana, rey del caucho: Terror y atrocidades en el Alto Amazonas*. Buenos Aires: Emecé.

Landerman, Peter. 1973. *Vocabulario quechua del Pastaza*. Serie Lingüistica Peruana 8.Yarinacocha, Perú: Instituto Lingüistico de Verano.

Langer, Erick. 1986. "Debt Peonage and Paternalism in Latin America." *Peasant Studies* 13(2): 121–27.

Larrabure i Correa, Carlos. 1903. Preface to *Vías del Pacífico al Marañón*. Publicación de la Junta Vías Fluviales. Lima: Imprenta La Industria.

———. 1905–9. *Colección de leyes, decretos, resoluciones i otros documentos oficiales referentes al departmento de Loreto (1777–1908) formada de orden supreme*. Lima: La Opinión Nacional.

Las Casas, Bartolomé de. 1992 [1542]. *A Short Account of the Destruction of the Indies*. Ed. and trans. N. Griffin. Intro. A. Pagden. London: Penguin Books.

Lathrap, Donald. 1970. *The Upper Amazon*. London: Thames and Hudson.

———. 1973. "The Antiquity and Importance of Long-Distance Trade Relationships in the Moist Tropics of Pre-Columbian South America." *World Archaeology* 5(2): 170–86.

La Torre López, Lily. 1998. *Sólo queremos vivir en paz!: Experiencias petroleras en territorios indígenas de la Amazonía Peruana*. Copenhagen: IWGIA; Lima: Grupo de Trabajo Racimos de Ungurahui.

Lattas, Andrew. 1993. "Gifts, Commodities, and the Problem of Alienation." *Social Analysis* 34: 102–18.

Lea, Vanessa. 2002. "The Composition of Me Bengokre (Kayapo) Households in Central Brazil." In *Beyond the Visible and the Material: The Amerindianization of Society in the Work of Peter Riviere*, ed. L. Rival and N. Whitehead, 157–76. Oxford: Oxford University Press.

Leach, Edmund. 1961. *Rethinking Anthropology*. London: Athlone Press.

Ledeneva, Alena. 1996–97. "Between Gift and Commodity: The Phenomenon of Blat." *Cambridge Anthropology* 19(3): 43–66.

Lehm Ardaya, Zulema. 1992. "Efectos de las reducciones jesuíticas en las poblaciones indígenas de Maynas y Mojos." In *Opresión colonial y resistencia indígena en la Alta Amazonía*, ed. F. Santos Granero, 135–64. Quito: FLACSO.

Leon, Lydia. 1987. "AIDESP: The Inter-Ethnic Development Association of the Peruvian Jungle." *Cultural Survival Quarterly* 4: 70.

Lepri, Isabella. 2005. "The Meanings of Kinship among the Ese Ejja of Northern Bolivia." *Journal of the Royal Anthropological Institute* 11(4): 703–24.

———. 2006. "Identity and Otherness among the Ese Ejja of Northern Bolivia." *Ethnos* 71(1): 67–86.

Léry, Jean de. 1990 [1578]. *History of a Voyage to the Land of Brazil*. Berkeley: University of California Press.

Levi, Jerome M. 1992. "Commoditizing the Vessels of Identity: Transnational Trade and the Reconstruction of Rarámuri Ethnicity." *Museum Anthropology* 16(3): 7–24.

Lévi-Strauss, Claude. 1966. *The Savage Mind*. Chicago: University of Chicago Press.

———. 1969 [1949]. *The Elementary Structures of Kinship*, ed. R. Needham, trans. J. Bell and J. Sturmer. Boston: Beacon Press.

———. 1975 [1964]. *The Raw and the Cooked: Introduction to a Science of Mythology*. Vol. 1. Trans. J. and D. Weightman. New York: Harper Colophon.

———. 1978a [1968]. *The Origin of Table Manners: Introduction to a Science of Mythology*. Vol. 3. Trans. J. and D. Weightman. New York: Harper Colophon.

———. 1978b [1955]. *Tristes Tropiques*. Trans. J. and D. Weightman. New York: Atheneum.

———. 1985. *A View from Afar*. Trans. J. Neugroschell and P. Hoss. New York: Basic Books.
Liep, John. 1986. "Further Comments on "Inalienable Wealth."" *American Ethnologist* 13: 158–59.
———. 1993. "Entangled Concepts: The Mutual Implications of Commodity and Gift in Melanesia." *Suomen Antropologi* 4: 18–29.
Little, Paul. 2002. *Amazonia: Territorial Struggles on Perennial Frontiers*. Baltimore: Johns Hopkins University Press.
Litvak, Lily. 1984. "Estudio preliminar: La Comisión Científica del Pacífico, 1862–1865." In *La Comisión Científica del Pacífico, viaje por sudamérica y recorrido del Amazonas, 1862–1866*, by Manuel Almagro, iii–iv. Barcelona: Alertes.
Lizot, J. 1978. *Tales of the Yanomami*. Cambridge: Cambridge University Press.
Llanos Vargas, Hector, and Roberto Pineda Camacho. 1982. *Etnohistoria del Gran Caqueta (Siglos XVI–XIX)*. Bogotá: Banco de la República (Fundación de investigaciones arqueológicas nacionales).
López Alfonso, Francisco José, ed. 1995. *Indigenismo y propuestas culturales: Belaúnde, Mariátegui y Basadre*. Alicante: Instituto de Cultura Juan Gil-Albert.
Lorrain, Claire. 2000. "Cosmic Reproduction, Economics, and Politics among the Kulina of Southwest Amazonia." *Journal of the Royal Anthropological Institute*, n.s., 6(2): 293–310.
———. 2002. "The Hierarchy Bias and the Equality Bias: Epistemological Considerations on the Analysis of Gender." In *Beyond the Visible and the Material: The Amerindianization of Society in the Work of Peter Riviere*, ed. L. Rival and N. Whitehead, 263–72. Oxford: Oxford University Press.
Loukotka, Cestmír. 1968. *Classification of South American Indian Languages*. Vol. 7. Los Angeles: UCLA Latin American Center.
Lovera Vásquez, Armando Jesús. 2000. "Llegada de los agustinos a la Prefectura de San León del Amazonas." *Kanatari* 17(850).
Lowie, Robert H. 1963 [1948]. "The Tropical Forests: An Introduction." In *Handbook of South American Indians*, ed. J. Steward, 3(4): 1–56. New York: Cooper Square Publishing.
Lu, Flora. 2007. "Integration into the Market among Indigenous Peoples: A Cross-Cultural Perspective from the Ecuadorian Amazon." *Current Anthropology* 48(4): 593–602.
Lubbock, J. 1978 [1870]. *The Origins of Civilization and the Primitive Condition of Man*, ed. P. Rivière. Chicago: University of Chicago Press.
Luna, Luis Eduardo. 1992a. "Icaros: Magic Melodies among the Mestizo Shamans of the Peruvian Amazon. In *Portals of Power: Shamanism in South America*, ed. E. J. Langdon and G. Baer, 231–53. Albuquerque: University of New Mexico Press.
———. 1992b. "Therapeutic Imagery in Amazonian Shamanism: Some Observations." *Scripta Ethnologic* 14: 19–25.
Lyon, Patricia, ed. 1981 [1974]. *Native South Americans: Ethnology of the Least Known Continent*. Prospect Heights, Ill.: Waveland Press.
Lyotard, Jean-François. 1997. *Jean-Francois Lyotard: Collected Writings on Art*. London: Academy Editions.

MacClancy, Jeremy. 1992. *Consuming Culture*. London: Chapmans.
MacCormack, Sabine. 1999. "Ethnography in South America: The First Two Hundred Years." In *The Cambridge History of the Native Peoples of the Americas*, ed. Frank Salomon and Stuart Schwartz, 3(1): 96–187. Cambridge: Cambridge University Press.
———. 2006. *On the Wings of Time: Rome, the Incas, Spain, and Peru*. Princeton, N.J.: Princeton University Press.
Magnin, Juan. 1988 [1740]. "Breve descripción de la Provincia de Quito, en la América Meridional. . . ." In *Noticias auténticas del famoso Río Marañón*, ed. J. P. Chaumeil. Monumenta Amazonica B4. Iquitos: IIAP and CETA.
Mallon, Florencia. 1995. *Peasant and Nation: The Making of Postcolonial Mexico and Peru*. Berkeley: University of California Press.
Malthus, Thomas R. 1970 [1798]. *An Essay on the Principle of Population: In an Essay on the Principle of Population and a Summary View of the Principle of Population*. New York: Penguin.
Manrique, Nelson. 1993. "Violencia en el Perú: El caso de Sendero Luminoso." *Antropología* 6: 5–35.
Manus, Ronald, and Phyllis Manus. 1973. *I Timoteo, II Timoteo: 1a y 2a Carta a Timoteo* [The Epistles of Paul to Timothy in Urarina]. Yarinacocha, Perú: Editorial Sagradas Escrituras Para Todos.
———. 1976. *Filipoo nenacauru rai, I Tesalonecau nenacauru rai, II Tesalonecau nenacauru rai* [The Epistles of Paul to the Philippians and Thessalonians in Urarina]. Yarinacocha, Perú: Liga bíblica mundial del hogar [World Home Bible League].
———. 1990. *Ichanohichuru: Los Hechos de los Apóstoles* [The Acts of the Apostles in Urarina]. Yarinacocha, Perú: Liga bíblica [Bible League, South Holland, Ill.].
———. 1996. *Cana necoaauna nunuhe* [Genesis in Urarina]. Yarinacocha, Perú: Liga bíblica [Bible League, South Holland, Ill.].
Marcoy, Paul. 1873. *A Journey across South America, from the Pacific Ocean to the Atlantic Ocean*. London: Blackie.
Mariátegui, José Carlos. 1969. *Ideología y política*. Lima: Biblioteca Amauta.
———. 1988 [1928]. *Seven Interpretive Essays on Peruvian Reality*. Trans. M. Urquidi. Intro. J. Basadre. Austin: University of Texas Press.
Markham, Clements R., trans. and ed. 1963 [1859]. *Expeditions into the Valley of the Amazons, 1539, 1540, 1639*. New York: Burt Franklin.
Maroni, Pablo. 1889–92 [1738]. "Noticias auténticas del famoso Río Marañón, y misión apostólica de la Compañía de Jesús en los dilatados bosques de dicho río." *Boletín de la Sociedad Geográfica de Madrid* 26–33: n.p. [See also the edition published in Iquitos in 1988 by IIAP-CETA, 1–565.]
Martínez Riaza, Ascensión. 1998. "La incorporación de Loreto al Estado-Nación Peruanao: El discurso modernizador de la Sociedad Geográfica de Lima (1891–1919)." In *La nacionalización de la Amazonía*, ed. Pilar García Jordán and Núria Sala I Vila, 99–126. Barcelona: Publicacions Universitat de Barcelona.
Martín Rubio, María del Carmen. 1991. *Historia de Maynas, un paraíso perdido en el Amazonas; descripción de Francisco Requena*. Madrid: Ediciones Atlas.
Marx, Karl, and Fredrich Engels. 1978. *The Marx-Engels Reader*. Ed. R. Tucker. New York: Norton.

Marzal, Manuel. 1984. "Las reducciones indígenas en la Amazonía Peruana." *Amazonía Peruana* 5(10): 7–45.

Mathews, Edward. 1879. *Up the Amazon and Madeira Rivers, through Bolivia and Peru.* London: Sampson Low, Marston, Searle and Rivington.

Maúrtua, Aníbal. 1911. *Geografía económica del Departmento de Loreto.* Lima: Litografía Tip. Carlos Fabbri.

Mauss, Marcel. 1967 [1925]. *The Gift: Forms and Functions of Exchange in Archaic Society.* New York: W. W. Norton and Comp.

Maw, Henry Lister. 1829. *Journal of a Passage from the Pacific to the Atlantic, Crossing the Andes in the Northern Provinces of Peru, and Descending the River Marañon, or Amazon.* London: John Murray.

May, Peter H. 1999. *Natural Resource Valuation and Policy in Brazil.* New York: Columbia University Press.

Maybury-Lewis, David. 1967. *Akwê-Shavante Society.* Oxford: Clarendon Press.

———. 1979. "Conclusion: Kinship, Ideology, and Culture." In *Dialectical Societies: The Gê and Bororo of Central Brazil*, ed. D. Maybury-Lewis, 301–12. Cambridge, Mass.: Harvard University Press.

———. 1984. "Age and Kinship: A Structural View." In *Age and Anthropological Theory*, ed. D. Kertzer and J. Keith, 123–40. Ithaca, N.Y.: Cornell University Press.

———. 1989. "The Quest for Harmony." In *The Attraction of Opposites: Thought and Society in the Dualistic Mode*, ed. D. Maybury-Lewis and U. Almagor, 1–17. Ann Arbor: University of Michigan Press.

———. 1992. *Millennium: Tribal Wisdom and the Modern World.* New York: Viking Press.

———. 1997. *Indigenous Peoples, Ethnic Groups, and the State.* Boston: Allyn and Bacon.

———. 2003. "From Elimination to an Uncertain Future: Changing Policies toward Indigenous Peoples." In *At the Risk of Being Heard: Indigenous Rights, Identity, and Postcolonial States*, ed. Bartholomew Dean and Jerome Levi, 324–34. Ann Arbor: University of Michigan Press.

———, ed. 1984. *The Prospects for Plural Societies.* Washington, D.C.: American Ethnological Society.

———, ed. 2002. *The Politics of Ethnicity: Indigenous Peoples in Latin American States.* Cambridge, Mass.: Harvard University Press.

McCallum, Cecilia. 1988. "The Ventriloquist's Dummy?" *MAN*, n.s., 23: 560–61.

———. 1990. "Language, Kinship, and Politics in Amazonia." *MAN*, n.s., 25: 412–33.

———. 1996. "The Body That Knows: From Cashinahua Epistemology to a Medical Anthropology of Lowland South America." *Medical Anthropology Quarterly* 10(3): 347–72.

———. 2001. *Gender and Sociality in Amazonia: How Real People Are Made.* Oxford: Berg.

McCormack, C., and M. Strathern, eds. 1980. *Nature, Culture, and Gender.* New York: Cambridge University Press.

McGuckin, Eric. 1997. "Tibetan Carpets: From Folk Art to Global Commodity." *Journal of Material Culture* 2(3): 291–310.

McKinnon, Susan. 1993. "On Entangled Asymmetries in Entangled Objects." *Social Analysis* 34: 119–31.

McLennan, J. F. 1970 [1865]. *Primitive Marriage: An Inquiry into the Origin of the Form of Capture in Marriage Ceremonies*, ed. P. Rivière. Chicago: University of Chicago.

McSweeny, Kendra, and Shahna Arps. 2005. "A 'Demographic Turnaround': The Rapid Growth of Indigenous Populations in Lowland Latin America." *Latin American Research Review* 40(1): 3–29.

Meggers, Betty. 1971. *Amazonia: Man and Culture in a Counterfeit Paradise*. Chicago: Aldine.

———. 1994. "Pre-Columbian Amazonia." *National Geographic Research and Exploration* 10(4): 398–421.

Mentore, G. P. 1987. "Waiwai Women: The Basis of Wealth and Power." *MAN*, n.s., 22: 511–27.

Mercier, Juan Marcos. 1974. *Amazonía: ¿Liberación o esclavitud?* Lima: Libería San Pablo.

———. 1979. *Nosotros los Napu-Runas, Napu Runapa Rimay: Mitos e historia*. Iquitos: CETA.

Métraux, Alfred. 1963a [1948]. "The Guaraní." In *Handbook of South American Indians*, ed. J. Steward, 3(4): 69–94. New York: Cooper Square Publishing.

———. 1963b [1948]. "Tribes of the Middle and Upper Amazon River." In *Handbook of South American Indians*, ed. J. Steward, 3(4): 687–712. New York: Cooper Square Publishing.

———. 1963c [1948]. "The Tupinamba." In *Handbook of South American Indians*, ed. J. Steward, 3(4): 95–133. New York: Cooper Square Publishing.

Meunier, Jacques, and A. M. Savarin. 1994. *Amazonian Chronicles*. San Francisco: Mercury House.

Mignolo, Walter D. 1995. *The Darker Side of the Renaissance: Literacy, Territoriality, and Colonization*. Ann Arbor: University of Michigan Press.

Ministerio de Educación Pública and Instituto Lingüístico de Verano. 1981. *Icha, Majás (y otros cuentos de animales)*. Colección literaria urarina, libro 1. Lima: Ministerio de Educación, Educación Bilingüe de la Selva.

Ministerio de Relaciones Exteriores. 1913. *Reconstitución del Obispado de Maynas*. Documentos Oficiales. Lima: Imprenta del Estado.

Mitchell, Halley. 2000. *Commercial Handicraft Production by the Tembé People of Brazil*. Belém: NAEA.

Molina, Enrique. 1906. "El Jebe." Tesis que para optar el grado de Doctor en Ciencias Naturales, Universidad Mayor de San Marcos. Lima: Tip. De "El Lucero."

Montag, Richard, and Joseph W. Bastien. 1996. "A Cashinahua Creation Story." *Journal of Latin American Lore* 19(1–2): 85–100.

Montoya Rojas, Rodrigo. 1998. *Multiculturalidad y política: Derechos indígenas, ciudadanos y humanos*. Lima: Sur Casa de Estudios de Socialismo.

Moore, Henrietta. 1993. "Things Ain't What They Seem." *Social Analysis* 34: 126–31.

Moore, Sally Falk. 1983. *Law as Process: An Anthropological Approach*. London: Routledge and Kegan Paul.

———. 1986. *Social Facts and Fabrications: "Customary" Law on Kilimanjaro, 1880–1980*. New York: Cambridge University Press.
———. 1994. *Anthropology and Africa: Changing Perspectives on a Changing Scene*. Charlottesville: University Press of Virginia.
Mora, Carlos. 1995. "Una revisión del concepto de cholo en la Amazonía Peruana." *Amazonía Peruana* 12(25): 145–58.
Mora de Jaramillo, Yolanda. 1985. *Alimentación y cultura en el Amazonas*. Bogotá: Ediciones Fondo Cultura Cafetero.
Morales Chocano, Daniel. 1998. "Chambira: Una cultura de sabana árida en la Amazonía Peruana." *Investigaciones Sociales* 2(2): 61–75.
Moran, Emilio. 1982. "Ecological, Anthropological, and Agronomic Research in the Amazon Basin." *Latin American Research Review* 17(1): 3–41.
———. 1991. "Human Adaptive Strategies in Amazonian Blackwater Ecosystems." *American Anthropologist* 93(2): 361–82.
———. 1995. "Disaggregating Amazonia." In *Indigenous Peoples and the Future of Amazonia: An Ecological Anthropology of an Endangered World*, ed. L. Sponsel, 72–95. Tucson: University of Arizona Press.
Morey Alejo, Humberto, and Gabel Daniel Sotil García. 2000. *Panorama histórico de la Amazonía Peruana: Una visión desde la Amazonía*. Iquitos: Municipalidad Provincial de Maynas.
Mosko, Mark. 2000. "Inalienable Ethnography: Keeping-While-Giving and the Trobriand Case." *Journal of the Royal Anthropological Institute*, n.s., 6: 377–96.
Mukhopadhyay, C., and P. Higgins. 1988. "Anthropological Studies of Women's Status Revisited: 1977–1987." In *Annual Review of Anthropology*, ed. B. Siegel, 461–95. Palo Alto, Calif.: Annual Reviews.
Munn, Nancy. 1992. *The Fame of Gawa: A Symbolic Study of Value Transformation in a Massim (Paupa New Guinea) Society*. Durham, N.C.: Duke University Press.
Muratorio, Blanca. 1991. *The Life and Times of Grandfather Alonso: Culture and History in the Upper Amazon*. New Brunswick, N.J.: Rutgers University Press.
———. 1998. "Indigenous Women's Identities and the Politics of Cultural Reproduction in the Ecuadorian Amazon." *American Anthropologist* 100(2): 409–20.
Murdock, George P. 1949. *Social Structure*. New York: MacMillan.
Murphy, Robert. 1956. "Matrilocality and Patrilineality in Mundurucu Society." *American Anthropologist* 58: 414–34.
———. 1978 [1960]. *Headhunter's Heritage: Social and Economic Change among the Mundurucú Indians*. New York: Octagon Books.
Murra, John. 1991 [1962]. "Cloth and Its Function in the Inka State." In *Cloth and Human Experience*, ed. A. Weiner and J. Schneider, 275–302. Washington, D.C.: Smithsonian Institute Press.
Myers, Fred, ed. 2001. *The Empire of Things: Regimes of Value and Material Culture*. Oxford: James Currey.
Myers, Thomas. 1974. "Spanish Contacts and Social Change on the Ucayali River, Peru." *Ethnohistory* 21(2): 135–57.
———. 1981. "Aboriginal Trade Networks in Amazonia." In *Networks of the Past: Regional Interaction in Archaeology*, ed. P. Francis, F. Kense, and P. Duke, 19–30. Al-

berta: Proceedings of the Twelfth Annual Conference of the Archaeological Association of the University of Calgary.

———. 1983. "Redes de intercambio tempranas en la hoya amazónica." *Amazonía Peruana* 8: 61–75.

———. 1988a. "El efecto de las pestes sobre las poblaciones de la Amazonía Alta." *Amazonía Peruana* 8(15): 61–81.

———. 1988b. "Visión de la prehistoria de la Amazonía Superior." In *I Seminario de investigaciones sociales en la Amazonía*, ed. F. Santos, 37–81. Iquitos: CETA.

———. 1990. *Sarayacu: Ethnohistorical and Archaeological Investigations at a 19th-Century Mission Site in the Peruvian Montaña*. Lincoln: University of Nebraska Press.

———. 1992a. Agricultural Limitations of the Amazon in Theory and Practice. *World Archaeology* 24(1): 82–97.

———. 1992b. "Expansion and Collapse of the Omagua." *Steward Journal of Anthropology* 20(1/2): 129–52.

———. 1997. "Conservatism in Ucayali Dress and Ornamentation." In *Resistencia y adaptación nativa en las tierras bajas latinoamericanas*, ed. by M. S. Cipolletti, 123–56. Quito: Abya-Yala.

Myers, Thomas, and Bartholomew Dean. 1999. "Cerámica prehispánica del Río Chambira, Loreto." *Amazonía Peruana* 13(26): 255–88.

Naar Ruiz, Casilda. 1989. *Tradición alimentaria aborigen y aspectos medicinales de la Amazonía Peruana*. Lima: CONCYTEC.

———. 1999. *Amazonía: Cocinas regionales peruanas*. Lima: Universidad San Martín de Porres.

Nash, June. 1994. "Global Integration and Subsistence Insecurity." *American Anthropologist* 96(1): 7–30.

Newman, K. 1983. *Law and Economic Organization: A Comparative Study of Preindustrial Societies*. Cambridge: Cambridge University Press.

Niezen, Ronald. 2003. *The Origins of Indigenism: Human Rights and the Politics of Identity*. Berkeley: University of California Press.

Nimuendajú, Curt. 1942. *The Serente*. Los Angeles: The Southwest Museum.

———. 1963 [1948]. "The Tucuna." In *Handbook of South American Indians*, ed. J. Steward, 3(4): 713–25. New York: Cooper Square Publishing.

———. 1967 [1939]. *The Apinaye*. Trans. R. Lowie. Oosterhout N.B., The Netherlands: Anthropological Publications.

Norberg-Schulz, Christian. 1980. *Genius Loci: Towards a Phenomenology of Architecture*. New York: Rizzoli International Publications.

Nugent, David. 1994. "Building the State, Making the Nation: The Bases and Limits of State Centralization in 'Modern' Peru." *American Anthropologist* 96(2): 333–69.

———. 1997. *Modernity at the Edge of Empire: State, Individual, and Nation in the Northern Peruvian Andes, 1885–1935*. Stanford, Calif.: Stanford University Press.

Nugent, Stephen. 1981. "Amazonia: Ecosystem and Social System." *MAN*, n.s., 16(1): 62–74.

———. 1990. *Big Mouth: The Amazon Speaks*. London: Fourth Estate.

———. 1993. *Amazonian Caboclo Society: An Essay on Invisibility and Peasant Economy*. Oxford: Berg.

Nugent, Stephen, and Mark Harris, eds. 2004. *Some Other Amazonians: Perspectives on Modern Amazonia*. London: Institute for the Study of the Americas, University of London.

Oakdale, Suzanne. 2005. *I Foresee My Life: The Ritual Performance of Autobiography in an Amazonian Community*. Lincoln: University of Nebraska Press.

Oberem, Udo. 1974. "Trade and Trade Goods in the Ecuadorian Montaña." In *Native South Americans: Ethnology of the Least Known Continent*, ed. P. Lyon, 346–57. Boston: Little, Brown.

———. 1980. *Los Quijos: Historia de la transculturación de un grupo indígena en el Oriente Ecuatoriano*. Otavalo: Instituto Otavaleño de Antropología.

Oberg, Kalervo. 1965. "The Marginal Peasant in Rural Brazil." *American Anthropologist* 67(6): 1417–27.

Ochoa Siguas, Nancy. 1999. *Niimúhe: Tradición oral de los Bora de la Amazonía Peruana*. Lima: CAAAP and Banco Central de Reserva del Perú.

Odicio Egoavil, Elmer. 1992. *Perfil demográfico de la región Loreto*. Documento Técnico 1 Iquitos: Instituto de Investigaciones de la Amazonía Peruana.

Olawsky, Knut. 2002. *Urarina Texts*. Languages of the World/Text Collections 17. Muenchen: LINCOM EUROPA.

Oliart, Patricia. 1998. "Alberto Fujimori: 'The Man Peru Needed?'" In *Shining and Other Paths: War and Society in Peru, 1980–1995*, ed. S. Stern, 411–24. Durham, N.C.: Duke University Press.

Olsen, Dale. 1996. *Music of the Warao of Venezuela: Song People of the Rain Forest*. Gainesville: University Press of Florida.

Oostra, Menno. 1991. "El Blanco en la tradición oral: Historia e ideología de contacto en el Mirití-Paraná." In *Etnohistoria del Amazonas*, 29–43. Colección 500 Años 36 Quito: ABYA-YALA and MLAL.

Ortner, Sherry. 1990. "Gender Hegemonies." *Cultural Critique* 14: 35–80.

Orton, James. 1879 [1870]. *The Andes and the Amazon*. New York: Harper and Brothers.

Osculati, Gaetano. 2000 [1854]. *Exploraciones de las regiones ecuatoriales a traves del Napo y de los ríos de las Amazonas: Fragmento de un viaje por las dos Américas en los años 1846–1848*. Trans. V. de Vela. Quito: Abya-Yala.

Otero, Joseì G. 1929. *Desde el mar hasta la selva, con motivo del II Congreso sud-americano de turismo*. Lima: Imprenta T. Aguirre.

Otterbein, Keith. 1999. "A History of Research on Warfare in Anthropology." *American Anthropologist* 101(4): 794–805.

Overing, J. 1986. "Men Control Women? The 'Catch 22' in the Analysis of Gender." *International Journal of Moral and Social Studies* 1: 135–56.

———. 1989. "Styles of Manhood: An Amazonian Contrast in Tranquility and Violence." In *Societies at Peace: Anthropological Perspectives*, ed. S. Howell and R. Willis, 79–99. London: Routledge.

Padoch, Christine, and Wil de Jong. 1987. "Traditional Agroforestry Practices of Native and Ribereño Farmers in the Lowland Peruvian Amazon." In *Agroforestry: Realities, Possibilities, and Potentials*, ed. H. L. Gholz, 179–94. Dordrecht: Martinus Nijhoff.

Pagden, Anthony. 1986. *The Fall of Natural Man: The American Indian and the Origins of Comparative Ethnology*. Cambridge: Cambridge University Press.

———. 1993. *European Encounters with the New World*. New Haven, Conn.: Yale University Press.

Palumbo-Liu, David. 1997. "Introduction: Unhabituated Habituses." In *Streams of Cultural Capital*, ed. D. Palumbo-Liu and H. Ulrich Gumbrecht, 1–21. Stanford, Calif.: Stanford University Press.

Palumbo-Liu, David, and Hans Ulrich Gumbrecht, eds. 1997. *Streams of Cultural Capital*. Stanford, Calif.: Stanford University Press.

Pareto, Vilfredo. 1966. "Les systèmes socialistes." In *Sociological Writing*, 107–224. New York: Praeger.

Parker, Eugene, ed. 1985. *The Amazon Caboclo: Historical and Contemporary Perspectives*. Studies in Third World Societies 32. Williamsburg, Va.: College of William and Mary.

Parry, Jonathan. 1989. "On the Moral Perils of Exchange." In *Money and the Morality of Exchange*, ed. J. Parry and M. Bloch, 64–93. Cambridge: Cambridge University Press.

Pärssinen, Martti, Jukka S. Salo, and Matti Räsänen. 1996. "River Floodplain Relocations and the Abandonment of Aborigine Settlements in the Upper Amazon Basin: A Historical Case Study of San Miguel de Cunibos at the Middle Ucayali River." *Geoarchaeology* 11(4): 345–59.

Pearson, Henry C. 1911. *The Rubber Country of the Amazon*. New York: India Rubber World.

Peisa. 2003. *Atlas Departmental del Perú: Imagen, geográfica, estadística, histórica y cultura*. Tomo 12. Loreto/San Martín. Lima: Ediciones Peisa S.A.C.

Peloso, Vincent. 1999. *Peasants on Plantations: Subaltern Strategies of Labor and Resistance in the Pisco Valley, Peru*. Durham, N.C.: Duke University Press.

Pennano, Guido. 1988. *La economía del Caucho*. Iquitos: CETA.

Perrin, Michel. 1988. "Du mythe au quotidien, penser la nouveauté." *L'Homme* 28(106–7): 120–37.

Perry, Richard. 1996. *From Time Immemorial: Indigenous Peoples and State Systems*. Austin: University of Texas Press.

Peterson, Nicolas. 1993. "Demand Sharing: Reciprocity and the Pressure for Generosity among Foragers." *American Anthropologist* 95(4): 860–74.

Petesch, Natalie. 2003. "Los Cocama nacen en el Perú: Migración y problemas de identitad entre los Cocama del Río Amazonas." *Antropológica* 21: 99–116.

Pineda Camacho, Roberto. 2003. "La metamorfosis de la historia en la Amazonía." *Boletín de historia y antigüedades* 90(822): 459–85.

Pollock, D. 1992. "Culina Shamanism: Gender, Power, and Knowledge. In *Portals of Power: Shamanism in South America*, ed. J. Langdon and G. Baer, 25–40. Albuquerque: University of New Mexico.

Porras, Pedro. 1975. "Fase Pastaza: El formativo en el Oriente Ecuatoriano." *Revista de la Universidad Católica* 3(10): 75–134.

Porras P., María Elena. 1987. *Gobernación y obispado de Mainas: Siglos XVII y XVIII*. Quito: ABYA-YALA.

Posey, D. A., and M. J. Balick, eds. 2006. *Human Impacts on Amazonia: The Role of Traditional Ecological Knowledge in Conservation and Development*. New York: Columbia University Press.

Pozzi-Escot, Inés. 1998. *El multilingüismo en el Perú*. Biblioteca de la tradición oral Andina 17. Cuzco: CBC and PROEIB.

Prado, Manuel. 1943. "El Excmo. Sr. Presidente de la República visita nuestro Vicariato Apostólico." In *Boletín de la Junta de Bienhechores de las Misiones Agustinianas de San Leon del Amazonas* (Iquitos) 2(1944): 49.

Pratt, Mary Louise. 1992. *Imperial Eyes: Travel Writing and Transculturation*. New York: Routledge.

Quecedo, Francisco. 1942. *El ilustrísimo fray Hipólito Sánchez Rangel, primer obispo de Maynas*. Buenos Aires: Coni.

Quintana, José. 1948. "Viaje al Río Chambira." *Boletín de la Junta de Bienhechores de las Misiones Agustinianas de San Leon del Amazonas* 6: 276–80.

Radcliffe-Brown, A. R. 1965 [1952]. *Structure and Function in Primitive Society*. New York: The Free Press.

———. 1987 [1950]. Introduction to *African Systems of Kinship and Marriage*, ed. A. R. Radcliffe-Brown and D. Forde, 1–85. London: KPI Ltd.

Radding, Cynthia. 2005. *Landscapes of Power and Identity: Comparative Histories in the Sonoran Desert and the Forests of Amazonia from Colony to Republic*. Durham, N.C.: Duke University Press.

Radin, Margaret Jane. 1982. "Property and Personhood." *Stanford Law Review* 34: 957–1015.

Raffles, Hugh. 2002. *In Amazonia: A Natural History*. Princeton, N.J.: Princeton University Press.

Raimondi, Antonio. 1863. "On the Indian Tribes of the Great District of Loreto, in Northern Peru." *Anthropological Review* 1: 33–43.

———. 1874. *El Perú*. Tomo I. Parte Preliminar. Lima: Imprenta del Estado.

———. 1929 [1863–69]. *El Perú: Itinerarios de viajes*. (Versión literal de la libretas originales). Lima: Imprenta Torres Aguirre.

———. 1942 [1862]. *Apuntes sobre la provincia litoral de Loreto*. Iquitos: El Oriente.

Ram, Haggay, and Galia Sabar-Friedman. 1996. "The Political Significance of Myth: The Case of Iran and Kenya in a Comparative Perspective." *Cultural Dynamics* 8(1): 51–78.

Ramos, Alcida. 2002. "Bridging Troubled Waters: Brazilian Anthropologists and Their Subjects." Série Antropología 324. Brasília: Departmento de Antropología, Universidade de Brasília.

Rausch, Jane. 1999. *Colombia: Territorial Rule and the Llanos Frontier*. Gainesville: University Press of Florida.

Ravines, Rogger. 1998. "Cerámica antigua del Río Urituyacu, provincia y departamento de Loreto." *Boletín de Lima* 20(112): 49–70.

Ravines, Rogger, and Rosalía de Matos. 1988. *Atlas etnolingüístico del Perú*. Lima: Instituto Andino de Artes Populares del Convenio Andrés Bello Comisión Nacional del Perú.

Redford, Kent. 1992. "The Empty Forest." *BioScience* 42(6): 412–22.

Reeve, Mary-Elizabeth. 1994. "Regional Interaction in the Western Amazon: The Early Colonial Encounter and the Jesuit Years: 1538–1767." *Ethnohistory* 41(1): 106–38.

Regan, Jaime. 1983. *Hacia la tierra sin mal: Estudio sobre la religiosidad del pueblo en la Amazonía*. Iquitos: CETA.

———. 1988. "Mesianismo Cocama: Un movimiento de resistencia en la Amazonía Peruana." *América Indígena* 48(1): 127–38.

———. 2000. "La misión de los jesuitas en Maynas: 1638–1767." *Kanatari* 17(850).

Reichel-Dolmatoff, Gerardo. 1971. *Amazonian Cosmos: The Sexual and Religious Symbolism of the Tukano Indians*. Chicago: University of Chicago Press.

———. 1976a. *Amazonian Cosmos: The Sexual and Religious Symbolism of the Tukano Indians*. Chicago: University of Chicago Press.

———. 1976b. "Cosmology as Ecological Analysis: A View from the Rain Forest." *MAN*, n.s., 11(3): 307–18.

Renshaw, John. 2002. *The Indians of the Paraguayan Chaco: Identity and Economy*. Lincoln: University of Nebraska Press.

Requena, Francisco. 1991a [1782]. *Ilustrados y bárbaros: Diario de la exploración de límites al Amazonas*. Ed., introduction, and notes by Manuel Lucena Giraldo. Madrid: Alianza Editorial.

———. 1991b [1784]. "Descripción del gobierno de Maynas." In *Historia de Maynas*, ed. M. Martín Rubio. Madrid: Ediciones Atlas.

Rey de Castro, Carlos. 1913. *Los escándalos del Putumayo: Carta abierta dirigida a Mr. Geo B. Michell, cónsul de S. M. B.; acompañada de diversos documentos, datos estadísticos y reproducciones fotográficas*. Barcelona: Impr. Viuda de L. Tasso.

Reyes Flores, Alejandro. 1999. *Hacendados y comerciantes: Piura-Chachapoyas-Moyobamba-Lamas-Maynas (1770–1820)*. Lima: Juan Brito.

Ribeiro, Berta. 1989. *Arte indígena, linguagem visual*. Sao Paulo: Editora da Universidade de Sao Paulo.

Rijke, Els. 2000. "Ya no es como antes ... Een antropologisch onderzoek naar de gevolgen van oliewinning in Chambira, Peru." Doctoraalscriptie Culturele Antropologie, Universiteit Utrecht.

Ríos Zañartu, Mario. 1995. *Historia de la Amazonia Peruana*. Iquitos: Editorial El Matutino S.A.

———. 2000. "La sociedad civil de Loreto a la llegada de los agustinos." *Kanatari* 17(850).

Rival, Laura. 1993. "The Growth of Family Trees: Understanding Huaorani Perceptions of the Forest." *MAN*, n.s., 28: 635–52.

———. 1998. "Androgynous Parents and Guest Children: The Huaorani Couvades." *Journal of the Royal Anthropological Institute*, n.s., 4: 619–42.

———. 2002. *Trekking Through History: The Huaorani of Amazonian Ecuador*. New York: Columbia University Press.

———. 2005. "The Attachment of the Soul to the Body among the Huaorani of Amazonian Ecuador." *Ethnos* 70(3): 285–310.

Rival, Laura, and Neil Whitehead. 2002. "Forty Years of Amazonian Anthropology: The Contribution of Peter Rivière." In *Beyond the Visible and the Material: The Amerindianization of Society in the Work of Peter Riviere*, ed. L. Rival and N. Whitehead, 1–18. Oxford: Oxford University Press.

Rivière, Peter. 1969. *Marriage among the Trio: A Principle of Social Organization*. Oxford: Clarendon Press.

———. 1977. "Some Problems in the Comparative Study of Carib Societies." In *Carib-Speaking Indians, Culture, Society, and Language*, ed. E. Basso, 39–42. Tucson: University of Arizona Press.

———. 1984. *Individual and Society in Guiana*. Cambridge: Cambridge University Press.

———. 1988. "Men and Women in Lowland South America." *MAN*, n.s., 24: 520–21.

Rodriguez, Manuel. 1684. *El Marañon y Amazonas: Historia de los descubrimientos, entradas, y reducción de naciones, trabajos malogrados de algunos conquistadores y dichosos de otros, assi temporales como espirituales*. Madrid: Imprenta de Antonio Gonçalez de Reyes.

Rodríguez Achung, Martha. 2000. "Iquitos: Ciudad Intercultural." *Iquitos: Memoria de 100 años. Kanatari* (edición extra) 17(799–800): 9–14.

Rodríguez Rodríguez, Isacio, and Jesús Álvarez Fernández. 2001. "Prólogo." *Monumenta historico-augustiniana de Iquitos*. Volumen primero 1894–1902. Centro de Estudios Teológicos de la Amazonía. Valladolid: Ediciones Monte Casino.

Rodway, James. 1917. "Indian Charms." In *Tropical Wild Life in British Guiana*. Zoological Contributions from the Tropical Research Station of the New York Zoological Society 1: 488–99. New York: New York Zoological Society.

Roe, Peter. 1982. *The Cosmic Zygote: Cosmology in the Amazon Basin*. New Brunswick, N.J.: Rutgers University Press.

Rojas Zolezzi, Enrique. 1992. "Concepciones sobre la relación entre generos: Mito, ritual y organización del trabajo en la unidad doméstica campa-asháninka." *Amazonía Peruana* 11(22): 175–223.

———. 1994. *Los ashaninka: Un pueblo tras el bosque*. Lima: Pontifica Universidad Católica del Perú.

Romanoff, Steven. 1992. "Food and Debt among Rubber Tappers in the Bolivian Amazon." *Human Organization* 51(2): 122–35.

Romero, Fernando. 1964. "Hace un siglo: Notas para una historia de la Marina Fluvial de Guerra." In *Anales de la semana Loretana: Centenario de la fundación del puerto fluvial de Iquitos*, 36–49. Iquitos: Talleres Graficos Imprenta de la Marina.

———. 1983. *Iquitos y la Fuerza Naval de la Amazonía, 1830–1933*. Lima: Dirección General de Interes Marítimos, Ministerio de Marina.

Roosevelt, Anna. 1999. "Maritime, Highland, Forest Dynamic." In *The Cambridge History of the Native Peoples of the Americas*, ed. Frank Salomon and Stuart Schwartz, 3(1): 264–49. Cambridge: Cambridge University Press.

Rosaldo, Michelle Z. 1980. "The Use and Abuse of Anthropology: Reflections on Feminism and Cross-cultural Understanding." *Signs: Journal of Women in Culture and Society* 5: 389–417.

Rosaldo, Renato. 1980. *Ilongot Headhunting 1883–1974: A Study in Society and History.* Stanford, Calif.: Stanford University Press.

———. 1989. *Culture and Truth: The Remaking of Social Analysis.* Boston: Beacon Press.

Rose, C. 1988. "Crystals and Mud in Property Law." *Stanford Law Review* (40): 577.

Roseberry, William. 1993. "Beyond the Agrarian Question in Latin America." In *Confronting Historical Paradigms: Peasants, Labor, and the Capitalist World System in Africa and Latin America*, ed. F. Cooper et al., 318–70. Madison: University of Wisconsin Press.

Rosenberg, Tina. 1991. "Time of Cholera: Peru Battles an Epidemic." *The New Republic* 205(5): 10–12.

Rosengren, D. 1987. *In the Eyes of the Beholder: Leadership and the Social Construction of Power and Dominance among the Matsigenka of the Peruvian Amazon.* Goteborg: Goteborgs Etnografiska Museum.

———. 2006. "Transdimensional Relations: On Human-Spirit Interaction in the Amazon." *Journal of the Royal Anthropological Institute* 12(4): 803–16.

Ross, Eric. 1978. "The Evolution of the Amazon Peasantry." *Journal of Latin American Studies* 10(2): 193–218.

Roux, Jean-Claude. 1994. *L'Amazonie Péruvienne: Un Eldorado dévoré par la forêt, 1821–1910.* Paris: Editions L'Harmattan.

Rubenstein, Steven. 1993. "Chain Marriage among the Shuar." *Latin American Anthropology Review* 5(1): 3–9.

———. 2002. *Alejandro Tsakimp: A Shuar Healer in the Margins of History.* Lincoln: University of Nebraska Press.

———. 2007. "Circulation, Accumulation, and the Power of Shuar Shrunken Heads." *Cultural Anthropology* 22(3): 357–99.

Rumrrill, Roìger. 1982. *Amazonìa hoy: Croìnicas de emergencia.* Iquitos: CETA/CAAAP.

Rumrrill, Roìger, and Pierre de Zutter. 1976. *Los condenados de la selva: Amazonía y capitalismo.* Lima: Editorial Horizonte.

Sabate, R. P. Luis. 1887. *Viaje de los padres misioneros del Convento de Cuzco a las tribus salvajes de los campas, piros, cunibos y sipibos en el año de 1874.* Lima: Tipografía de "la Sociedad."

Sahlins, Marshall. 1972. *Stone Age Economics.* New York: Aldine Publishing Company.

———. 1985. *Islands of History.* Chicago: University of Chicago Press.

———. 1991. "La Pensée Bourgeoise: Western Society as Culture." In *Rethinking Popular Culture: Contemporary Perspectives in Cultural Studies*, ed. C. Mukerji and M. Schudson, 278–90. Berkeley: University of California Press.

Salomon, Frank. 1986. "Vertical Politics on the Inka Frontier." In *Anthropological History of Andean Polities*, ed. John Murra, Nathan Watchel, and Jacques Revel, 89–117. Cambridge: Cambridge University Press.

San Román, Jesús Victor. 1975. *Perfiles históricos de la Amazonía Peruana.* Lima: Ediciones Paulinas.

———. 1986. "Mitos de los huitoto." *Amazonía Peruana* 7(13): 113–18.

Santos Granero, Fernando, and Frederica Barclay. 1999. *Tamed Frontiers: Economy, Society, and Civil Rights in Upper Amazonia*. Boulder, Colo.: Westview Press.

Satherm, Clifford. 2002. "Commodity Trade, Gift Exchange, and the History of Maritime Nomadism in Southeastern Sabah." *Nomadic peoples* 6(2): 20–44.

Saussure, F. D. 1966 [1916]. *Course in General Linguistics*. Trans W. Baskin. New York: McGraw-Hill.

Scazzocchio, Francoise Barbira. 1978. "Curare Kills, Cures, and Binds: Change and Persistence of Indian Trade in Response to the Contact Situation in the North-western Montaña." *Cambridge Anthropology* 4(3): 30–57.

Schindler Catalao, Rosa Alejandra. 2002. *Ensayo de una bibliografía de los augustinos del Vicariato Apostólico de Iquitos*. Iquitos: CETA.

Schmink, Marianne, and Charles Wood. 1984. *Frontier Expansion in Amazonia*. Gainesville: University Press of Florida.

Schneider, Jane. 1987. "The Anthropology of Cloth." *Annual Review of Anthropology* 16: 409–48.

Schneider, Jane, and Annette Weiner. 1986. "Cloth and the Organization of Human Experience." *Current Anthropology* 27(2): 178–84.

Schultes, Richard Evans. 1974. "Palms and Religion in the Northwest Amazon." *Principles Journal of the Palm Society* 18: 3–21.

———. 1984. "Amazonian Cultigens and Their Northward and Westward Migration in Pre-Columbian Times." In *Pre-Columbian Plant Migration*, ed. D. Stone. Papers of the Peabody Museum 76: 19–37. Cambridge, Mass.: Harvard University Press.

Schultes, Richard Evans, and Robert F. Raffauf. 1990. *The Healing Forest: Medicinal and Toxic Plants of the Northwest Amazonia*. Portland, Me.: Dioscorides Press.

Scott, James. 1985. *Weapons of the Weak: Everyday Forms of Peasant Resistance*. New Haven, Conn.: Yale University Press.

Segal, Ariel. 1999. *Jews of the Amazon: Self-exile in Earthly Paradise*. Philadelphia: Jewish Publication Society.

Seiler-Baldinger, Annemarie. 1988. "Yagua and Tukuna Hammocks: Female Dignity and Cultural Identity." In *Identidad y transformación de las Américas*. 45 Anual Congreso Internacional de Americanistas. Bogotá: Ediciones Uniandes.

Sepúlveda, Juan Ginés de. 1987 [1550]. *Tratado sobre las justas causas de la guerra contra los indios*. Mexico D.F.: Fondo de Cultura Económica.

Seymour-Smith, C. 1988. *SHIWAR: Identidad étnica y cambio en el Río Corrientes*. Lima: CAAAP.

———. 1991. "Women Have No Affines and Men No Kin: The Politics of the Jivaroan Gender Relation." *MAN*, n.s., 26: 629–49.

Shell R., Olive, and Mary Wise. 1971. *Grupos idiomáticos del Perú*. Lima: Universidad Nacional Mayor de San Marcos and Instituto Linguistico Verano.

Silverblatt, Irene. 2004. *Modern Inquisitions: Peru and the Colonial Origins of the Civilized World*. Durham, N.C.: Duke University Press.

Silverwood-Cope, Peter. 1990. *Os Makú: Povo cacador do Noroeste da Amazonia*. Brasília: Editora Universidade de Brasília.

Simson, Alfred. 1878. "Notes on the Záparos." *Journal of the Royal Anthropological Institute of Great Britain and Ireland* 7: 502–10.

Siskind, Janet. 1977 [1973]. *To Hunt in the Morning*. New York: Oxford University Press.
Slater, Candice. 2002. *Entangled Edens: Visions of the Amazon*. Berkeley: University of California Press.
Smith, Gavin. 1989. *Livelihood and Resistance: Peasants and the Politics of Land in Peru*. Berkeley: University of California Press.
Smith, Nigel. 1996. *The Enchanted Amazon Rain Forest: Stories from a Vanishing World*. Gainesville: University Press of Florida.
———. 1999. *The Amazon River Forest: A Natural History of Plants, Animals, and People*. Oxford: Oxford University Press.
Smith, Richard Chase. 1985. "A Search for Unity within Diversity: Peasant Unions, Ethnic Federations, and Indian Movements in the Andean Republics." In *Native Peoples and Economic Development: Six Case Studies from Latin America*, vol. 16, ed. T. Macdonald. Cambridge, Mass.: Cultural Survival.
———. 1996. "Las políticas de la diversidad: COICA y las Federaciones Etnicas de la Amazonia." In *Pueblos indios, soberanía y globalismo*, ed. Stefano Varese, 81–125. Quito: Abya-Yala.
Smith, Richard Chase, and Danny Pinedo. 2003. "Comunidades y áreas naturales protegidas en la Amazonía Peruana." *Debate Agrario* 36: 15–37.
Smole, William. 1976. *The Yanoama Indians: A Cultural Geography*. Austin: University of Texas Press.
Smyth, William, and Frederick Lowe. 1836. *Narrative of a Journey from Lima to Para, Across the Andes and Down the Amazon: Undertaken with a View of Ascertaining the Practicability of a Navigable Communication with the Atlantic, by the Rivers Pachitea, Ucayali, and Amazon*. London: J. Murray.
Solís Fonseca, Gustavo. 2003. *Lenguas en la Amazonía Peruana*. Lima: Visual Services S.R.L.
Soria Casaverde, María Belén. 1997. *Administración eclesiástica amazónica, siglo XIX*. Lima: Universidad Nacional Mayor de San Marcos, Seminario de Historia Rural Andina.
Spinks C. W. 2001. *Trickster and Ambivalence: The Dance of Differentiation*. Madison, Wisc.: Atwood Publishing.
Sponsel, Leslie. 1989. "Farming and Foraging: A Necessary Complementarity in Amazonia?" In *Farmers as Hunters: The Implications of Sedentism*, ed. S. Kent, 37–45. Cambridge: Cambridge University Press.
Spruce, Richard. 1970 [1908]. *Notes of a Botanist on the Amazon and Andes*. Ed. A. R. Wallace. New York: Johnson Reprint Corporation.
Stanfield, Michael Edward. 1998. *Red Rubber, Bleeding Trees: Violence, Slavery, and Empire in the Upper Amazon, 1850–1933*. Albuquerque: University of New Mexico Press.
Starn, Orin. 1997. "Villagers at Arms: War and Counterrevolution in Peru's Andes." In *Between Resistance and Revolution: Cultural Politics and Social Protest*, ed. R. Fox and O. Starn, 223–49. New Brunswick, N.J.: Rutgers University Press.
Stearman, Allyn, and Kent Redford. 1992. "Commercial Hunting by Subsistence Hunt-

ers: Sironó Indians and Paraguayan Caiman in Lowland Bolivia." *Human Organization* 51(3): 235–44.
Steel, Daniel. 1999. "Trade Goods and Jívaro Warfare: The Shuar 1850–1957, and the Achuar, 1940–1978." *Ethnohistory* 46(4): 745–76.
Steinen, Karl Von Den. 1894. *Unter den Naturvölkern Zentral-Brasiliens: Reiseschilderung und Ergebnisse der Zweiten Schingú-Expedition 1887–1888*. Berlin: Geographische Verlagsbuchhandlung von Dietrich Reimer.
Steiner, Christopher. 1994. *African Art in Transit*. Cambridge: Cambridge University Press.
Stern, Steve. 1987. *Peru's Indian Peoples and the Challenge of Spanish Conquest*. Madison: University of Wisconsin Press.
Steward, Julian. 1963 [1948]. "Tribes of the Montaña." In *Handbook of South American Indians*, ed. J. Steward, 3(4): 507–33. New York: Cooper Square Publishing.
Steward, Julian, and Alfred Métraux. 1963 [1948]. "Tribes of the Peruvian and Ecuadorian Moñtana." In *Handbook of South American Indians*, ed. J. Steward, 3(4): 535–656. New York: Cooper Square Publishing.
Stiglich Alvarez, Germán. 1922. *Diccionario geográfico del Perú*. Lima: Imprenta Torres Aguirre.
Stirling, Matthew. 1938. *Historical and Ethnographical Material on the Jivaro Indians*. Washington, D.C.: Government Printing Office.
Stocks, Anthony. 1983. "Native Enclaves in the Upper Amazon: A Case of Regional Non-Integration." *Ethnohistory* 30(2): 77–92.
Strathern, Marilyn. 1985. "Kinship and Economy: Constitutive Orders of a Provisional Kind." *American Ethnologist* 12: 191–209.
———. 1988. *The Gender of the Gift: Problems with Women and Problems with Society in Melanesia*. Berkeley: University of California Press.
———. 1993. "Entangled Objects: Detached Metaphors." *Social Analysis* 34: 88–98.
———. 1996. "Cutting the Network." *Journal of the Royal Anthropological Institute*, n.s., 2: 517–35.
———. 2002. "Afterword." *Social Analysis* 46(1): 90–91.
Suárez-Araúz, Nicomedes. 2004. *Literary Amazonia: Modern Writing by Amazonian Authors*. Gainesville: University Press of Florida.
Sullivan, Lawrence. 1988. *Icanchu's Drum: An Orientation to Meaning in South American Religions*. New York: Macmillan Publishing Company.
Szyszlo, Vitold de. 1947. "La agricultura y la colonización en Loreto." *Boletín de la Sociedad Geográfica de Lima* 64(1–2): 63–69.
Tambiah, Stanley J. 1985. *Culture, Thought, and Social Action: An Anthropological Perspective*. Cambridge, Mass.: Harvard University Press.
———. 1990. *Magic, Science, Religion, and the Scope of Rationality*. Cambridge: Cambridge University Press.
Taussig, Michael. 1987. *Shamanism, Colonialism, and the Wild Man*. Chicago: University of Chicago Press.
Taylor, Anne-Christine. 1981. "God-Wealth: The Achuar and the Missions." In *Cultural Transformations and Ethnicity in Modern Ecuador*, ed. N. Whitten, 647–76. Urbana: University of Illinois Press.

———. 1993. "Remembering to Forget: Identity, Mourning, and Memory among the Jivaro." *MAN*, n.s., 28: 653–78.

———. 1996. "The Soul's Body and Its States: An Amazonian Perspective on the Nature of Being Human." *Journal of the Royal Anthropological Institute* 2(2): 201–16.

Taylor, Gerald. 1979. *Diccionario normalizado y comparativo quechua: Chachapoyas-Lamas*. Paris: L'Harmattan.

Tessmann, Gunther. 1930. *Die Indianer Nordost-Perus: Grundlegende Forschungen fur eine systematische Kulturkunde*. Hamburg: Friederichsen, de Gruyter, and Co.

———. 1987. "Los Simacos." Partial translation of *Die Indianer Nordost-Perus*. In *Bibliografía etnolinguistica urarina*. Lima: Instituto de Lingüistica Aplicada (CILA), Universidad Nacional Mayor de San Marcos.

Theidon, Kimberly. 2000. "How We Learned to Kill Our Brother: Memory, Morality, and Reconciliation." *Bulletin de l'Institut Francais d'Etudes andines* 29(3): 539–54.

———. 2001. "Terror's Talk: Fieldwork and War." *Dialectical Anthropology* 26(1): 19–35.

Thiele, Graham. 1995. "The Displacement of Peasant Settlers in the Amazon: The Case of Santa Cruz, Bolivia." *Human Organization* 54(3): 273–82.

Thomas, Nicholas. 1991. *Entangled Objects: Exchange, Material Culture, and Colonialism in the Pacific*. Cambridge, Mass.: Harvard University Press.

———. 1993. "Related Things." *Social Analysis* 34: 132–41.

Thurner, Mark. 1997. *From Two Republics to One Divided: Contradictions of Postcolonial Nationmaking in Andean Peru*. Durham, N.C.: Duke University Press.

Tibesar, Antonine. 1950. "The Salt Trade among the Montaña Indians of the Tarma Area of Eastern Peru." *Primitive Man* 23(3): 103–7.

Todorov, Tzvetan. 1982. *La conquête de l'Ameìrique: La question de l'autre*. Paris: Seuil.

Torres Lara, J. T. 1898. *Las mariposas blancas: Episodios de la expedición á Iquitos*. Lima: n/p.

Tournon, Jacques. 2002. *La merma mágica: Vida e historia de los shipibo-conibo del Ucayali*. Lima: CAAAP.

Tovar, Enrique. 1996. *Vocabulario del Oriente Peruano*. Lima: UNSM.

Townsley, Graham. 1993. "Song Paths: The Ways and Means of Yaminahua Shamanic Knowledge." *L'Homme* 33(126–28): 449–68.

Trapnell, Lucy. 2003. "Some Key Issues in Intercultural Bilingual Education Teacher Training Programmes—As Seen from a Teacher Training Programme in the Peruvian Amazon Basin." *Comparative Education* 39(2): 165–83.

Tsing, Anna Lowenhaupt. 1993. *In the Realm of the Diamond Queen: Marginality in an Out-of-the-Way Place*. Princeton N.J.: Princeton University Press.

Turner, Frederick Jackson. 1893. "The Significance of the Frontier in American History." Speech delivered to the American Historical Association's World's Columbian Exposition in Chicago.

Turner, Terence. 1979. "The Gê and Bororo Societies as Dialectical Systems: A General Model." In *Dialectical Societies: The Gê and Bororo of Central Brazil*, ed. D. Maybury-Lewis, 147–78. Cambridge, Mass.: Harvard University Press.

———. 1988. "History, Myth, and Social Consciousness among the Kayapó of Central

Brazil." In *Rethinking History and Myth: Indigenous South American Perspectives on the Past*, ed. J. Hill, 195–213. Urbana: University of Illinois Press.

———. 1993. "From Cosmology to Ideology: Resistance, Adaptation, and Social Consciousness among the Kayapo." In *Cosmology, Values, and Inter-ethnic Contact in South America*. South American Indian Studies 2: 1–13. Bennington, Vt.: Bennington College.

———. 1996. "Brazil Indigenous Rights vs. Neoliberalism." *Dissent* 43(3): 67–70.

Tylor, E. B. 1937. *Anthropology*. London:ÊWatts and Company.

Up de Graff, F. W. 1923. *Head Hunters of the Amazon: Seven Years of Exploration and Adventure*. New York: Duffield and Company.

Uriarte, Manuel. 1952 [1771–74]. *Diario de un misionero de Mainas*. Madrid: Instituto Santo Toribio de Mogrovejo, Ediciones Jura.

Urton, Gary. 1999. *Inca Myths*. Avon, U.K.: British Museum Press and University of Texas Press.

Uzendoski, Michael, et al. 2005. "The Phenomenology of Perspectivism: Aesthetics, Sound, and Power in Women's Songs from Amazonian Ecuador." *Current Anthropology* 46(4): 656–61.

Van Gennep, Arnold. 1960 [1908]. *The Rites of Passage*. Trans. M. Vizedom and G. Caffee. Chicago: University of Chicago Press.

Varallanos, Joseì. 1959. *Historia del Huanuco: Introduccioìn para el estudio de la vida social de una regioìn del Peruì, desde la era prehistoìrica a nuestros diìas*. Buenos Aires: Impr. Loìpez.

Varese, Stefano. 1968. *La sal de los cerros*. Lima: Universidad Peruana de Ciencias y Tecnologías.

———. 1996a. "The Ethnopolitics of Indian Resistance in Latin America." *Latin American Perspectives* 23(2): 58–72.

———. 1996b. "The New Environmentalist Movement of Latin American Indigenous People." In *Valuing Local Knowledge: Indigenous People and Intellectual Property Rights*, ed. S. Brush and D. Stabinsky, 122–42. Washington D.C.: Island Press.

———. 2002. *Salt of the Mountain: Campa Asháninka History and Resistance in the Peruvian Jungle*. Trans. S. Giersbach Rascón. Foreword by Darcy Ribeiro. Norman: University of Oklahoma Press.

Varese, Stefano, and Cesar Terrientes. 1982. "Restoring Multiplicity: Indianities and the Civilizing Project in Latin America." *Latin American Perspectives* 9: 29–41.

Verber, Haanne. 1998. "The Salt of the Montaña: Interpreting Indigenous Activism in the Rain Forest." *Cultural Anthropology* 13(3): 382–413.

Velasco, Juan de. 1960 [1841–44]. *Historia del reino de Quito en la América Méridional*. Segunda Parte, *La Colonia y la República*. Puebla, Mexico: Editorial Jungle.

Viatori, Maximilian. 2007. "Zápara Leaders and Identity Construction in Ecuador: The Complexities of Indigenous Self-Representation." *Journal of Latin American and Caribbean Anthropology* 12(1): 104–33.

Vickers, William. 1989a. "Patterns of Foraging and Gardening in a Semi-Sedentary Amazonian Community." In *Farmers as Hunters: The Implications of Sedentism*, ed. S. Kent, 46–59. Cambridge: Cambridge University Press.

———. 1989b. *Los sionas y secoyas: Su adaptación al ambiente amazónico.* Quito: AB-YA-YALA and MLAL.
Vilaca, Aparecida. 2002. "Making Kin out of Others in Amazonia." *Journal of the Royal Anthropological Institute* 8: 347–66.
Villanueva, Manuel Pablo. 1902. *Fronteras de Loreto.* Lima: Imprenta y Librería de San Pedro.
Villarejo, Avencio. 1942. *Heraldos de la fe: Homenaje de los Agustinos del Perú a Mons. José García Pulgar.* Lima: n.p.
———. 1965. *Los agustinos en el Perú.* Lima: Editorial Ausonia.
———. 1988 [1943]. *Así es la selva.* Iquitos: CETA.
———. 2000. "Un iterregno eclesiástico: Desde los jesuitas (1767) a los agustinnos (1901)." *Kanatari* 17(850).
Viveiros de Castro, Eduardo. 1992. *From the Enemy's Point of View: Humanity and Divinity in an Amazonian Society.* Chicago: University of Chicago Press.
———. 1996. "Images of Nature and Society in Amazonian Ethnology." *Annual Review of Anthropology* 25: 179–201.
———. 1998. "Cosmological Deixis and Amerindian Perspectivism." *Journal of the Royal Anthropological Institute* 4(3): 469–89.
Vormisto, Jaana. 2002. "Making and Marketing Chambira Hammocks and Bags in the Village of Brillo Nuevo, Northeastern Peru." *Economic Botany* 56(1): 27–40.
Wachtel, Nathan. 1994. *Gods and Vampires: Return to Chipaya.* Chicago: University of Chicago Press.
Walker, Charles. 1987. "El uso oficial de la selva en el Peru republicano." *Amazonía Peruana* 8(4): 61–89.
Warren, Kay, and Jean Jackson, eds. 2003. *Indigenous Movements, Self-Representation, and the State in Latin America.* Austin: University of Texas Press.
Warren, Patrizio. 1992. "Mercado, escuela y proteinas: Aspectos históricos, ecológicos y económicos del cambio del modelo de asentamiento entre los Achuar Meridionales." *Amazonía Peruana* 11(21): 73–107.
Watson-Franke, M.-B. 1987. "Women and Property in Guajiro Society." *Ethnos* 52: 229–45.
Watt, Robin. 1986. "On 'Inalienable Wealth.'" *American Ethnologist* 13: 157–58.
Weiner, Annette. 1985. "Inalienable Wealth." *American Ethnologist* 12: 210–27.
———. 1992. *Inalienable Possessions: The Paradox of Keeping-While-Giving.* Berkeley: University of California Press.
———. 1994. "Cultural Difference and the Density of Objects." *American Ethnologist* 21(1): 391–403.
Werlich, David. 1990. *Admiral of the Amazon: John Randolph Tucker, His Confederate Colleagues, and Peru.* Charlottesville: University of Virginia Press.
Westermarck, E. 1901 [1891]. *The History of Human Marriage.* London: Macmillan.
White, D. 1988. "Rethinking Polygyny: Co-Wives, Codes, and Cultural Systems." *Current Anthropology* 29: 529–72.
Whitehead, H. 1987. "Fertility and Exchange in New Guinea." In *Gender and Kinship: Essays toward a Unified Analysis,* ed. J. Collier and S. Yanagisako, 244–67. Stanford, Calif.: Stanford University Press.

Whitehead, Neil. 2002. *Dark Shamans: Kanaimà and the Poetics of Violent Death.* Durham, N.C.: Duke University Press.

Whitehead, Neil, and Robin Wright, eds. 2004. *In Darkness and Secrecy: The Anthropology of Assault Sorcery and Witchcraft in Amazonia.* Durham, N.C.: Duke University Press.

Whitten, Norman. 1976. *Sacha Runa: Ethnicity and Adaptation of Ecuadorian Jungle Quichua.* Urbana: University of Illinois Press.

———. 1988. "Historical and Mythic Evocations of Chthonic Power in South America." In *Rethinking History and Myth: Indigenous South American Perspectives on the Past,* ed. J. Hill, 282–306. Urbana: University of Illinois Press.

———. 2007. "The Longue Durée of Racial Fixity and the Transformative Conjunctures of Racial Blending." *Journal of Latin American and Caribbean Anthropology* 12(2): 356–83.

Wiener, Carlos. 1884. "Viaje al río de las Amazonas y las cordilleras, 1879–1882." In *América pintoresca: Descripción de viajes al nuevo continente por los más modernos exploradores.* Barcelona: Montaner y Simon.

Wilbert, Johannes. 1987. *Tobacco and Shamanism in South America.* New Haven, Conn.: Yale University Press.

Wilbert, Johannes, and Karin Simoneau, eds. 1992. *Folk Literature of South American Indians.* Vol. 80. Los Angeles: UCLA Latin American Studies.

Williams, Raymond. 1977. *Marxism and Literature.* Oxford: Oxford University Press.

Wilson, Fiona. 2003. "Reconfiguring the Indian: Land-Labour Relations in the Postcolonial Andes." *Journal of Latin American Studies* 35(2): 221–48.

Wolf, Eric. 1982. *Europe and the People without History.* Berkeley: University of California Press.

———. 1990. "Facing Power: Old Insights, New Questions." *American Anthropologist* 92: 586–96.

Wood, Charles, and Roberto Porro, eds. 2002. *Deforestation and Land Use in the Amazon.* Gainesville: University Press of Florida.

Worsley, Peter. 1970. *The Trumpet Shall Sound.* New York: Schocken Books.

Wright, Robin. 1998. *Cosmos, Self, and History in Baniwa Religion: For Those Unborn.* Austin: University of Texas Press.

Wright, Robin, and Jonathan Hill. 1986. "History, Ritual, and Myth: 19th-Century Millenarian Movements in the Northwest Amazon." *Ethnohistory* 33(1): 31–54.

———. 1992. "Venancio Kamiko: Wakuénai Shaman and Messiah." In *Portals of Power: Shamanism in South America,* ed. E. J. Langdon and G. Baer, 257–86. Albuquerque: University of New Mexico Press.

Yalman, Nur. 1967. "'The Raw:the Cooked:Nature:Culture.'" In *The Structural Study of Myth and Totemism,* ed. E. Leach, 71–90. London: Tavistock.

Zutter, Pierre de. 1976. "El contrabando de pieles." In *Los condenados de la selva: Amazonia y capitalismo,* ed. R. Rumrrill and P. de Zutter, 56–59. Lima: Editorial Horizonte.

Index

abortion, 45, 176–77, 269
achiote (annatto tree seed), 47, 61, 90, 192
Achuar, 33, 45, 48, 65, 78, 163, 226, 264
adultery, 158, 162, 170–72, 174, 175, 177, 183
affinity, 3, 20, 53, 148, 157, 159, 162–63, 165, 180–82
affliction, 26, 182, 193, 194, 221, 235, 246, 255
agro-extractive, 99, 101, 104, 114, 139
aguaje (palm tree and palm fibers), 46, 147, 188, 193, 196
aguardiente (cane alcohol), 22, 66, 124, 126, 136, 220, 266
AIDESEP (Asociación Interétnica de Desarrollo de la Selva/Inter-Ethnic Association for the Development of the Peruvian Amazon), 82–83
Airico River, 28, 72, 120
Ajidi (hummingbird), 194, 196
Ajkaguiño (boa), 147, 196–97
Alamas Quichua, 5
alienation, 4, 24, 209–10, 231–32, 236, 251, 259, 272
alliances, 39, 81, 110, 127, 137, 138, 144, 159, 163, 165, 166, 184, 267
alterity, 12, 134, 142, 143, 231, 242
Amazon Basin, 88, 104, 114
Amazonia, western, 86–87, 146, 158, 266, 271
Amazonian societies, 85, 113, 145, 146, 149, 165, 169, 202, 204, 257
Amazon River, 44, 59, 104, 106, 112, 139, 141
ambivalence, 8, 21, 20, 26, 127, 129, 218–19, 233, 234, 240, 241, 249, 256, 272
ammunition, 50, 66, 124, 126, 136, 213, 215, 220, 223–27, 243, 265
anacondas, 145–46, 207, 267–68
anazairi (foreigners, mestizos), 136, 143, 150, 208, 210, 218, 253
Andean highlands, 74, 86, 104, 111, 265
Andes, 11, 14, 27, 74, 78, 85–86, 88, 100, 108, 145, 186, 236, 264
Andoas, 203
animals, 23, 30, 35, 41, 42, 57, 146, 194, 207, 209–10, 218–20, 222, 223, 224–30, 232, 241, 248–49, 250, 271, 272. *See also specific animals*

anteaters, 220, 227
Arawakan, 149, 186, 190, 261, 271
archaeological findings, 85, 86, 96, 265, 272
armadillos, 42, 211, 220
arrows, 211, 228, 248–49
Aséij, 248
Asháninka, 236, 242, 272
assembly meetings, 155, 168–69, 170, 174
assets, 20, 21, 40, 150, 175–76, 182
assimilation, 2, 75, 84, 106
Augustinians, 109–10, 119–21 *See also* Catholicism; Christianity; Franciscans; Jesuits
Autonomy: cultural, 26, 96; political, 12, 54, 57–58; territorial 72
aviados (suppliers of rubber), 112
ayahuasca shamanism, 25–26, 31, 42, 47, 207, 234–35, 237–38, 240, 242, 244, 251–52, 255

Bajkagá, 143, 197, 242, 249
Bakirí, 32
bamboo shafts, 212
bananas, 10, 26, 45, 58, 60, 63, 65, 87, 108, 210, 222, 264
barbasco (plant), 117; for fish poisoning, 14, 68, 123
bardiguë, 22, 62, 165, 169, 172, 192
bargaining, 10, 24–25, 144, 205, 226–27
barter, 9, 10, 22, 63, 70, 86, 89, 95, 124, 130–31, 136, 152, 190, 191, 197, 203, 206, 207, 217, 224, 225, 226, 227, 252
bashful fiancés, 171, 173, 176–78
baskets, 43, 50, 63, 193, 202, 264
beads, 10, 47, 50, 132, 138, 145, 187, 198, 200, 205
beans, 108, 210
beliefs, 4, 5, 8, 19, 26, 44, 54, 126, 146, 178, 190, 193, 209, 232, 235, 236, 242, 248, 250, 252, 258
bestowal, 38, 130, 159, 160, 165, 171, 172, 175, 181, 190, 197, 198, 240
birds, 6, 9, 42, 50, 60, 71, 101, 146, 225, 228, 251, 272
birth, 13, 45–46, 50, 150, 165, 177, 194, 197, 200, 237, 244, 257
blood, 33, 45, 221, 243, 261, 263

blowguns, 43–44, 86, 169, 203, 208, 211, 221–22, 225–26, 248, 251. *See also* curare (dart); darts; poisoning
boas (snakes), 146–47, 197. *See also* reptiles; serpents
body (human), 44, 48, 219, 244, 246, 250–51, 267
Bolivia, 34, 81, 82, 128, 146, 241, 262
bones, 57, 145, 212, 216, 219, 220, 223, 268
Bora, 2, 11, 188, 270
Borja, 89, 91, 92
Bororo, 161, 177
boundaries, 23, 28, 33, 57, 64, 97, 104, 132, 133, 148
Brazil, 27, 28, 33, 34, 95, 101, 104, 105, 106, 107, 111, 129, 138, 146, 149, 202, 258, 263, 265, 266, 267, 268, 271
bridegrooms, 157, 160, 164, 176, 178, 179, 180, 181, 183
bride price, 157, 182–83
bride service, 20–21, 62, 157–62, 164–65, 170, 176–77, 269
bride-service societies, 20–21, 47, 157–59, 161, 172, 177, 179–81, 183
bride wealth, 157, 159, 183, 269
British, 108, 111, 187
brothers, 63, 121–22, 137, 147, 158, 172, 176, 240
brothers-in-law, 158, 175. *See also* daughters-in-law; fathers-in-law; in-laws; mothers-in-law; sons-in-law
burial, 45, 48, 194, 195, 198, 200, 246
bushmasters (snakes), 147, 268. *See also* reptiles; serpents
bushmeats, 22, 24, 26, 207–9, 210, 212, 213, 215, 216, 217, 218–19, 223, 224, 226, 227, 229, 231–33, 234, 240, 249, 251, 252, 254, 255. *See also* game
butterflies, 62, 247

caboclo peoples, 33–34
cacao, 61, 87, 90
Cahuapanan, 186, 248
Cahuapanas, 203
caimans, 42, 67, 68, 101, 207, 224, 227, 271
Cajamarca, 95, 187
cannibals, 197, 235, 249, 253, 267, 269, 272
capital, cultural and/or financial, 1, 4, 12, 15, 18, 66, 99, 103, 108, 111, 113–15, 123, 125, 144, 217, 225, 258, 266

capybaras, 42, 67, 210, 224, 225
Carijona, 87
cascarilla, 90, 101
Cashinahua, 136, 178, 241, 246
cassava, 22, 46, 50, 58–62, 63, 70, 101, 117, 126, 141, 169, 210, 215, 216, 220, 224, 247, 263, 264. *See also* manioc
cassava beer, 21–22, 46, 62, 133, 152, 169, 170, 171, 172, 192, 196, 215, 216, 221, 222, 233, 245, 246, 247, 253
Catholicism, 47, 109–10, 120–21, 203, 237, 239. *See also* Augustinians; Christianity; Franciscans; Jesuits
cattle, 116, 126
caucheros (gatherers of rubber sap), 111, 112, 117, 118, 119
CEDIA (Centro de Desarrollo del Indígena Amazónico), 83, 168
cedro, 69, 134
cemeteries, 48, 198–99, 246
ceremonial items, 24, 44, 46, 58, 164, 197–98, 201, 216, 252
Chachapoyas, 16, 88, 90, 94, 95, 101, 102, 109, 112, 187, 223, 265
Chambira Basin, 1, 3, 5–6, 8–9, 10, 11, 12, 28–31, 34, 36, 39, 42, 53–55, 65–71, 73–75, 86, 92, 95, 110, 116–17, 119–25, 138, 139, 143, 144, 167, 168, 186, 188, 232, 234, 259, 261, 264, 266, 270, 271
Chambira fiber, 193, 212
Chambira River, 12, 28–30, 33–35, 48, 54, 55, 62, 64–66, 70, 83, 86, 93, 116, 117, 118, 120, 122, 123, 126, 138, 139, 173, 264, 266
chants, 5, 25, 45, 47, 48, 147, 148, 149, 243, 244, 245, 247, 251, 255
Chayahuita, 5, 248
chickens, 43, 50, 59, 87, 183, 210, 230
children, 9, 10, 21, 38, 42, 43, 45, 46, 47, 61, 63, 89, 108, 124, 133, 134, 136, 139, 150, 151, 162, 164, 165, 166, 174–76, 177, 181, 192, 201, 205, 215, 216
Chile, 106
Chinese immigrants, 108
Christianity, 17, 46, 89, 109, 235. *See also* Augustinians; Catholicism; Franciscans; Jesuits; Protestants
chunchos (indigenous Amazonian peoples), 17, 96, 106
citizenship, 16, 17, 98, 107, 111, 138–39, 153

civilizing project, 2, 15–16, 17, 106, 110, 121, 234
civil war, 3, 76, 82, 264
clans, 39, 262, 270
class, 2, 3, 14–16, 18, 34, 97, 99, 111, 125, 129, 154, 159, 167
clients, 77, 107, 124, 129, 154, 267
cloth, 22, 23, 66, 85, 86, 101, 126, 132, 136, 138, 145, 185–89, 192, 196, 201, 203–6, 226, 242, 267
clothes, 120, 141, 174, 181, 183, 203–5. *See also* garb
clubs, 121, 166, 168, 190, 252
co-residents, 144, 164, 166, 212, 213, 215, 216, 240
co-wives, 38, 61, 164, 167, 172, 173, 176, 181, 200, 213, 215
coca, 2, 3, 14, 15, 80, 82, 86, 90, 103
Cocama, 5, 33, 59, 66, 82, 85, 86, 91–93, 95, 105, 119, 141, 186, 209, 237, 262
Cocamilla, 33, 82, 91, 92
COICA (Coordinadora de Organizaciones Indígenas de la Cuenca Amazónia), 81, 269
Colombia, 27, 28, 111, 138, 159, 248, 267
colonialism, 1, 13, 14, 16, 18, 28, 34, 54, 64, 87, 88, 92, 94, 95, 96, 97, 98, 99, 114, 115, 129, 182, 186, 202, 235, 256, 258, 265, 271
colonization, 1, 3, 34, 59, 76, 87, 99, 100, 102, 104, 106, 107, 114, 186, 258
commerce, 17, 43, 101, 102, 103–7, 112, 116, 120, 187, 202, 204, 230, 270
commodities, 1, 4, 14, 18, 19, 22, 24, 25, 26, 62, 66, 73, 124, 130, 131, 136, 143, 150, 152, 164, 182, 185, 190, 192, 204, 218, 220, 223, 231, 234, 243, 252, 253, 254, 255, 266
commoditization, 113, 178, 182, 185, 190, 202, 232, 254
commodity peonages, 122, 123, 140, 217, 219, 224, 225, 226
communal work, 62, 169, 216, 264
compadrazco (spiritual compeership), 23, 124, 201
compensation model, 157, 158, 160, 179, 180
comunidades nativas (native communities), 64, 72, 74, 75
CONAP (Confederación de Nacionalidades Amazónicas del Perú/Confederation of Amazonian Nationalities of Peru), 82, 83
Concordia, 93, 117, 120, 134
confinement, 47, 87, 171, 173

conflict, 1, 31, 39, 41, 68, 71, 74, 82, 87, 91, 100, 122, 129, 138, 141, 165, 170, 171, 172, 177, 180, 181, 197, 201, 207, 236, 240, 241, 242, 255, 258, 259
Conibo, 60, 186
conquests, 14, 86, 87, 88, 92, 100, 108, 114, 203
conscription, 88, 138, 139, 267
consumer goods, 26, 132, 217, 224, 234, 241, 255
consumption, 3, 14, 19, 22, 23, 25, 42, 45, 53, 61, 62, 69, 70, 83, 96, 108, 132, 136, 145, 146, 152, 179, 185, 189, 197, 200, 201, 207, 208, 209, 210, 213, 215, 216, 217, 220, 221, 222, 224, 228, 230, 232, 238, 246, 253, 254, 257, 266
cooking pots, 42, 50, 147, 215, 225
cordage, 119, 134, 186, 188, 192, 196, 198, 211, 270
corn, 59, 61, 70, 117, 126, 147, 264
Corrientes River, 5, 31, 55, 78, 83, 86, 117, 131, 227
cosmology, 3, 7, 12, 21, 25, 26, 32, 41, 44, 46, 54, 64, 134, 167, 181, 182, 189, 190, 193, 194, 197, 232, 234, 235, 236, 237, 241, 244, 245, 250, 252, 256, 257
cotton, 9, 15, 61, 86, 87, 101, 186–87, 192, 194, 200, 203–4, 270
cousins, 164
couvade, 46
creation myth, 55, 194, 200, 209, 247, 257
credit (financial), 18, 71, 72, 100, 112, 114, 118, 120, 123–24, 126, 130, 132, 151, 213, 226, 267
Crusader Order 237
culinary traditions, 215, 221, 225, 227, 271
cultivation, 38, 58, 60–61, 63, 66, 70, 115, 116, 125, 126, 192
cultural, 7, 8, 23, 31–32, 84, 99, 125, 147, 150, 179, 204, 210, 237, 265, 270; area, 65, 186; autonomy, 26, 17, 64, 65, 96; capital, 1, 108 (*see also* capital, cultural and/or financial); homogeneity, 17; heterogeneity, 25, 155; identity, 6, 11; knowledge, 194, 242; material, 5, 19, 24, 270; power, 145; practices, 23, 84, 254; survival, 82, 156, 251
cumala (tree), 46, 69
curare (dart poison), 50, 86, 90, 188, 208, 211, 220, 222, 225, 226, 227. *See also* blowgun; dart; poisoning

darts, 86, 198, 208, 211, 212, 220, 221, 222, 225, 228, 251, 271. *See also* blowguns; curare; poisoning

datura, 26, 228, 230, 243, 245
daughters, 22, 62, 109, 137, 160–61, 164, 165, 173, 174, 175, 194, 205, 245, 246, 270
daughters-in-law, 63. *See also* brothers-in-law; fathers-in-law; in-laws; mothers-in-law; sons-in-law
dead, 41, 55, 65, 148, 175, 191, 198–201, 246–49
death, 26, 48, 59, 65, 76, 147, 175, 197–98, 200, 218–20, 230, 239, 241, 245, 246, 249, 257
debt peonage, 1, 3, 13, 14, 19, 23, 25, 65, 111, 114, 116, 119, 121, 123, 124, 127, 128, 132, 136, 151, 152, 186, 189, 190, 232, 243, 254, 267
debts, 69, 84, 98, 114–15, 120, 123, 126, 127, 130–32, 136, 139–40, 144, 145, 160, 161, 204, 217, 237
deer, 42, 149, 218, 225, 227, 248–49
deforestation, 3, 69
demand sharing, 213, 216–18, 232, 243
deme (hamlet), 38–40, 64, 65, 134, 137, 152, 158, 163–67, 171, 177, 212, 213, 215, 216, 217, 222, 262
demons, 23, 247, 248–49, 253
desire, 1, 3, 7, 8, 10, 19, 20, 26, 31, 65, 73, 89, 114, 123, 124, 127, 141, 147, 152, 160, 162, 164, 165, 176, 179, 182, 190, 194, 201, 203, 241, 246
development, 1, 2, 13, 15, 18, 28, 74, 77, 81, 82, 100, 102–5, 142, 255, 258, 264
discourse, 3, 11, 13, 14, 16, 21, 34, 40, 41, 48, 55, 57, 96, 97, 100, 142, 143, 148, 152, 153, 158, 180, 181, 183, 184, 191, 231, 242, 259, 264, 269; mythological, 5, 19, 55, 145, 151, 232, 239, 256, 257
discursive formations, 145, 148, 150, 152, 253, 269
disease, 1, 9, 26, 31, 47–48, 54, 55, 65, 87, 88, 89, 91, 110, 171, 194
disputants, 166, 170, 181
distribution, 10, 22, 83, 90, 110, 114, 116, 120, 169, 187, 205, 207, 208, 209, 213, 215, 216, 226, 227, 232, 233, 236, 240, 242, 243, 254
divorce, 145, 164, 176, 180
dogs, 44, 210, 218–22, 225, 227, 253, 271
Dog Spirits, 218–19, 253
dolphins, 29, 245
domestication, 85, 87, 219
domestic platforms, 50, 53, 133, 134, 193, 215, 216, 267
domination, 14, 15, 81, 91, 109, 127, 142, 148, 161, 242, 261, 268

domus, 22, 41, 53, 58, 71, 158, 177, 208, 218, 224
downstream, 11, 30, 33, 38, 41, 44, 54, 68, 130, 138, 139, 173, 176, 215, 262
dreams, 238, 245, 246, 250, 251
Dukaiya, 12
dyes, 61, 71, 192, 270

earth, 12, 57, 64, 194, 235, 245, 247, 255
economy: kinship, 19, 20 22, 23, 132, 150, 208; moral, 4, 253, 261; political, 1, 3, 4, 74, 112, 114, 156, 158, 182, 258
Ecuador, 27–28, 33, 78, 81–82, 86, 119, 126, 138, 172, 188, 226, 247. *See also* Quito
eggs, 30, 41, 50, 71, 147, 227
ejlá (palm-bast cloth), 188, 192, 196, 198, 200, 201, 211
elderly, 61, 118, 119, 121, 165
elders, 5, 43, 47, 139
El Dorado, 14, 86, 97, 100, 103, 107
elites, 1–2, 14, 17, 98–100, 116, 185
encomiendas (estates granted by Spain), 31, 89, 92, 98, 115
encompassed, 151–52
encompassing, 151–52
encroachments, 3, 72, 82, 102, 118
endogamy, 163–64, 170
enganchadores (labor recruiters), 111, 115
English: country, 105, 108; language, 7
entanglements, 13, 24, 123, 124, 127, 142, 208, 243
entradas (military-ecclesiastical raids), 89, 93
Ese Ejja, 44, 241
ethnicity, 3, 11, 14, 32, 33, 34, 64, 65, 82, 141, 153, 154, 155, 189, 264, 264
ethnography, 1, 4, 5, 7, 8, 19, 31, 44, 84, 158, 177, 179–80, 231, 240, 253, 255, 269, 271
ethnology, 16, 34, 54, 65, 92, 254, 257, 258
evangelical efforts, 109, 110, 122, 237, 266
evil, 61, 140–44, 147, 223, 230–31, 237, 247, 249–50, 255, 272
evil *patrónes*, 141–42, 143, 144
exchanges, 1, 3–4, 8, 14, 18, 19–25, 39, 40, 43, 62, 65, 66, 68, 72, 84, 85, 87, 90, 96, 99, 101, 112, 113, 116, 119, 122, 123, 124, 125, 129–30, 131, 132, 133, 136, 137, 142, 143, 144, 145, 148, 151, 152, 155, 157, 158, 159, 160, 161, 165, 166, 170, 178, 179, 181, 183, 184, 185, 186, 187, 188, 189, 190, 197, 201–2, 203–4, 205, 206, 207–9, 212, 215, 217–18, 219, 224–26, 227,

231, 232–e3, 235, 240, 241, 242–43, 250, 251, 252–53, 254, 256, 259, 265, 266, 267, 271
exclusions, 20, 81–82, 129, 133, 148, 150, 152–54
experiences, 3, 5, 7, 15, 16, 22, 35, 40, 41, 57, 132, 140, 143, 144, 151, 152, 162, 170, 179, 182, 226, 231, 239, 240, 241, 245, 246, 247, 256, 257, 258, 267
exports, 15, 69, 77, 100, 101, 102, 103, 105, 112, 224,
extractions, 18, 54, 69, 70, 71, 72, 77, 82, 100, 102, 108, 111, 112, 114, 115, 117, 118, 119, 124, 126, 129, 203, 209, 227
extractive bargaining, 24–25
extractive entrepreneurs, 23, 71, 73, 75, 96, 99, 100, 111, 118, 138, 139, 143, 201, 266

fabric, 9, 113, 183, 185, 187, 188, 193, 197, 198, 200, 201, 202, 203, 204, 205, 211, 266. *See also* cloth
factionalism, 12, 13, 31, 38, 54, 82, 122, 139, 144, 166
fans, 30, 50, 135, 193, 198, 200, 238, 251, 259
FARC (Fuerzas Armadas Revolucionarias de Colombia), 138
fathers, 12, 43, 46, 62, 118, 137, 139, 158, 160, 164, 172, 174, 175, 176, 177, 180, 250, 263
fathers-in-law, 62, 145, 157, 160, 164, 180, 214, 221. *See also* brothers-in-law; daughters-in-law; in-laws; mothers-in-law; sons-in-law
fear, 129, 138, 139, 142, 143, 144, 152, 178, 218, 247, 252, 269
feathers, 14, 30, 44, 86, 186, 198, 202, 207, 238, 245, 259, 268
felines, 223, 224, 249, 271
females, 11, 19, 21, 23, 24, 37, 40, 42, 44, 45, 46, 47, 48, 50, 63, 68, 132, 133, 144, 145, 146, 149, 155, 158, 160, 165, 169, 170, 172, 175, 178, 179, 181, 182, 183, 191, 192, 195, 205, 208, 216, 246, 261
feral creatures, 31, 207, 219, 222, 224
fermentation, 42, 63, 169, 216
fiancés. *See* bashful fiancés
fieldwork, 4, 7, 30, 32, 83
fire, 42, 43, 45, 50, 60, 96, 134, 147, 193, 200, 215, 246, 252
firearms, 113, 213, 220, 225, 226. *See also* guns
fish, 6, 14, 18, 29, 35–36, 42, 48, 62–63, 66–69, 95, 101, 105, 108, 147, 209, 212, 215, 216, 224–25, 228, 232, 251, 268

fishing, 9, 10, 31, 36, 42–44, 50, 55, 62, 63, 67–68, 70, 72, 74, 134, 209–11, 220, 225, 228, 245
floods, 27, 28, 29, 35, 60, 66, 68, 93, 125, 232, 269, 245, 252, 267
food, 30, 42, 50, 60, 62, 66, 78, 85, 94, 101, 105, 115, 116, 118, 119, 126, 141, 151, 152, 164, 169, 171, 175, 204, 207–9, 212–14, 216–17, 219, 221, 225, 227, 228, 229, 230, 231, 232, 233, 240, 245, 249, 252, 271; crops, 59, 61, 63, 116, 125, 126, 198; exchanges, 22, 187, 212, 217; gardens, 17, 38, 41, 58–59, 194; scarcity, 29, 70, 267
foraging, 70, 74, 160, 208, 220, 225
forests, 1, 6, 8–9, 27, 28, 29, 30, 31, 35, 38, 42, 44–45, 48, 57–59, 62, 64–65, 89–91, 103, 118, 173–74, 177, 218, 228, 247–48. *See also* game, forest
Franciscans, 94, 187. *See also* Augustinians; Catholicism; Christianity; Jesuits
frogs, 9, 196, 227
frontiers, 2, 14, 15, 16, 28, 64, 86–87, 100, 101, 104, 105, 107, 108, 114, 142, 202
Fujimori, Alberto, 76, 77, 78, 80, 168, 264
fundos (work camps), 35, 39, 55, 59, 66, 99, 116–20, 122, 126–28, 139, 251

game, 9, 18, 19, 21, 22, 23, 24, 26, 30, 42, 66, 70, 90, 91, 117, 123, 125, 165, 166, 207, 208, 209, 210, 212–13, 215–17, 218, 219–21, 222–23, 224, 225, 226, 227, 229, 230, 231, 232, 233, 235, 250–51, 252, 255, 259, 272. *See also* bushmeats
game, forest, 18, 19, 42, 66, 90–91, 125, 165, 166, 207–9, 215–19, 220, 222, 224–27, 229–32, 250, 251, 255, 259; commoditization of, 209, 219, 233, 255, 272; consumption of, 23, 208, 213, 216; exchange of, 21, 22, 23, 24, 208, 212, 216, 217, 218, 232–33, 225, 227, 252
garb, 85, 110, 198, 223. *See also* clothes
gardens, 42, 43, 44, 46, 55, 58–59, 61–63, 65–66, 117, 134, 137, 147, 173, 192, 232, 247
Gê, 161
gender, 3, 4, 19, 20, 21, 40, 41, 42, 47, 132, 133, 134, 136, 145, 147, 148, 149, 151, 152, 153, 154, 155, 161, 169, 178, 182, 183, 193, 197–98, 233, 246
generosity, 161, 166, 179, 181, 216, 217, 255

geographic distinctions, 17, 28, 56, 57, 144
gifts, 4, 10, 20–22, 24, 130, 157, 182, 197, 209, 218, 231, 243, 254
globalization, 1, 3, 23, 81, 107, 123, 124, 125
gossip, 9, 10, 72, 170, 171, 173
gringos, 33, 34, 239, 262
grooms. *See* bridegrooms
guayusa, 90
guns, 41, 44, 50, 66, 112, 113, 126, 136, 201, 204, 211, 213, 220, 222, 225, 226, 232, 234, 252. *See also* firearms

habilitación (debt peonage), 3, 20, 113, 115, 124, 127, 253
hacienda, 97, 99, 101, 116, 119, 126
hallucinogenics, 25, 26, 41, 193, 198, 201, 228, 230, 239, 246, 250, 251, 252
hammocks (beds), 90, 95, 101, 105, 185, 188, 190, 193, 197–98, 201–2, 203, 270
handicraft production, 189, 201–2, 206
hardwood, 50, 69–70, 77, 124, 126, 168
harpy eagles, 198, 238, 251, 259, 262
headhunters, 113
headmen, 8, 19, 24, 31, 38, 40, 50, 54, 78, 119, 123, 130, 137, 139, 140, 142, 151, 163, 166–68, 170, 172, 174–75, 213–14, 217, 244–45, 251, 253
headwaters, 30, 54–55, 64, 65, 91, 92, 94, 118, 122, 266
health, 1, 2, 35, 46, 263
heart, 221, 229, 252
hearth groups, 38, 50, 163, 173, 175, 177, 213, 215, 216, 218
hegemony, 15, 18, 78, 126, 148, 208, 256, 261
hierarchy, 21, 24, 42, 100, 124, 133, 157, 168, 183, 186, 194, 214, 220, 265, 271
hoarding, 217, 219
homesteads, 53, 60, 61, 62–64, 66, 72, 119, 122, 126, 134, 139, 168, 173, 247
honey, 30, 42, 71
hosts, 23, 62–63, 133, 172, 208, 212, 213, 215, 216, 255
howler monkeys, 57–58, 218
huairuro seeds, 61, 223
Huallaga, 5, 59, 86, 89, 91, 93, 103, 105, 186, 270
Huánuco, 88, 100, 106
Huaorani, 126, 250
Huitoto, 2
hunting, 12, 14, 22, 23, 26, 40, 41, 43, 44, 58, 62, 63, 66, 70, 74, 83, 91, 123, 134, 136, 167, 174, 197, 207, 208, 209, 210–11, 213, 215, 219, 220, 221, 222, 224, 225, 226, 227, 228–29, 231–2, 234, 244, 245, 248, 249, 250, 255
husbands, 36, 38, 47, 63, 134, 137, 147, 158–62, 164–65, 167, 170–75, 177–82, 184, 197, 210, 267

Ibo'tsa, 12
identity, 6, 24, 33–34, 57–8, 139, 154–55, 191, 197, 200, 208, 220, 241, 262, 263
ideology, 1, 25, 98, 107, 127, 142, 145, 152, 180–81, 183, 237
iguanas, 42, 70
in-laws, 160, 161, 164, 173, 178, 181–82. *See also* brothers-in-law; daughters-in-law; fathers-in-law; mothers-in-law; sons-in-law
inalienability, 4, 80, 189, 200, 270
inalienable wealth, 189, 198, 208, 245
independence, national, 97, 99, 101, 202
indigenismo (pro-indigenous), 13, 81, 153, 154, 155
indigenous communities, 3, 73, 75, 76, 78, 80, 82, 89, 96–99, 107, 116
indigenous movement, 78, 81, 82, 153–55, 268
individuals, 8, 65, 73, 84, 113, 120, 130, 131, 132, 143, 144, 153, 157–59, 164, 165, 172, 206, 217, 248, 267
inequality, social, 157, 159, 206
infanticide, 177
infants, 45–46, 177, 197, 223, 247, 270
infidelity, 20, 21, 157, 158, 162, 170–74, 179, 181, 183
Inka (Inca), 241, 242, 272
Iquitos, 9, 35, 38, 41, 44, 54, 69, 71, 101, 102, 105, 106, 108, 109, 110, 112, 117, 120, 121, 125, 130–31, 134, 137, 139, 141, 154, 202, 211, 224, 230, 232, 262, 267, 270
ishanga (plant), 61
isolation, 4, 12, 13, 47, 54, 131
Italians, 104, 108
Itucales, 87, 92–93

Jaén, 90, 265
jaguars, 197, 198, 224, 248, 249, 252
Jeberos, 11, 33, 89, 95, 109
Jesuits, 28, 30, 87–90, 91–92, 93–96, 102, 108–9, 116, 189–90, 202, 203, 265, 266. *See also* Augustinians; Catholicism; Christianity; Franciscans

Jews, 108, 110
Jíbaros, 33, 261
Jivaro, 78, 91, 113, 143, 150, 162, 166, 171, 189, 197, 242, 249
journeys, 17, 43, 104, 141, 173, 243, 246, 248, 250, 262

Kachá, 30, 48, 210, 253
Kachá eje, 32, 151
kaj laitjíra (longhouse groups), 35, 38, 42, 46, 64, 131, 136, 139, 163, 165, 166, 169, 172, 173, 175, 176, 177, 181, 212, 215, 216, 232
Kandozi, 33, 189
Karajá, 202
Kayapó, 146, 202, 258, 267
killing, 91, 210, 247, 249, 251
Kuánra, 54, 55, 57, 59, 67, 148–49, 151, 193, 194, 195, 200, 209, 210, 218, 219, 228, 229, 230, 231, 239, 243, 245, 252, 253, 255, 263
kuichá (shamans), 24, 26, 228, 244, 245, 246, 250, 251
kurana (headmen), 24, 40, 54, 57, 58, 62, 73, 133, 137, 144–45, 166, 168, 176, 177

labor bosses, 8, 31, 55, 65, 73, 75, 112, 121, 126, 127, 128, 131, 141, 143, 144, 208, 217, 237, 241, 253, 255. *See also patrón/patrones*
labor power, 12, 14, 21, 23, 48, 58, 62, 63, 65–66, 69, 73, 89, 90, 94, 95, 101, 113–16, 117, 122, 123, 126, 131, 136, 137, 139, 145, 157, 160, 162, 169, 175, 177, 187, 192, 201, 203, 205, 207, 232, 235
Lagunas, 66, 89, 91–93, 95, 96, 101, 105, 117, 203, 204
Lamas, 33, 90, 187, 223, 265
land titles, 76, 80
land-titling, 76, 83
leaders, 26, 40, 57–58, 75, 78, 81, 88, 91, 96, 98, 107, 131, 143, 153–55, 218, 241
legislation, 72, 74–75, 78, 82, 83, 98, 99, 100, 107
Lévi-Strauss, Claude, 20, 53, 161, 177–78, 188, 197, 208, 210, 220, 229, 256, 267, 268
liberalization, 100, 105, 106, 120
lightning, 252
Lima (Peru), 15, 27, 34, 81, 88, 95, 98, 100–107, 109, 112, 141, 262, 270
linguistics, 5, 7, 11–12, 17, 32, 34, 48, 112, 121, 151, 153, 179, 189, 251, 261, 262, 263, 265, 268, 271

liver, 248, 252
logging, 43, 69–70, 73, 80, 266
longhouse groups, 8, 18, 20, 35, 38, 46, 48, 63–64, 66, 118, 122, 152, 158, 165, 166, 172–73, 176, 177, 189, 216, 217
looms, 90, 187, 192, 196, 251
Loretano Spanish, 6–7, 139, 153, 189, 225, 251, 262, 263, 267, 272
Loreto (Peru), 16, 17, 28, 34, 42, 72, 75, 92, 102–4, 105, 107–8, 110, 111–12, 116, 118, 119, 120, 125, 139, 202, 247, 261, 264, 266, 270
lowlands, 11, 27, 74, 86, 88–90, 100, 108, 207, 265
lowland South America, 13, 32, 47, 85, 87, 99, 159, 166, 169, 175, 179, 183, 234, 235, 256, 257, 267, 268, 269, 270
ludéri (permanent longhouses), 22, 41, 43, 48, 50, 53, 72, 134, 152, 158, 163, 198
lumber, 3, 18, 43, 62, 64, 69–73, 76, 81, 82, 117, 126, 134, 138, 164, 209, 266
lupuna (tree), 45–46, 69, 177, 247

machete, 60, 62, 68, 122, 141, 171, 211, 225, 248
Machiguenga, 186, 270
Madre de Dios (Peru), 82, 117
magic, 41, 44, 90, 149, 197, 221, 222, 244, 251, 263, 271
mahogany, 69, 270
Mainas, 87, 88, 89, 91, 93, 95, 186, 203, 265
Maipuco, 54, 117, 119, 131
Makuna, 248
Manao, 190
manatees, 101
manioc, 42, 61, 63, 65, 123, 207, 263. *See also* cassava
Marañón, 38, 50, 66, 138–39, 125, 202, 265
Marañón River, 5, 27, 28, 29, 33, 35, 44, 54, 59, 60, 64, 68, 69, 79, 86, 88, 89, 91, 92, 93, 95, 101, 103, 105, 110, 116, 117, 119, 120, 121, 123, 138, 139, 186, 203, 226, 232, 262, 265
marginality 1, 3, 18
marriage, 23, 38, 39, 110, 120, 158–66, 172, 174–85, 195, 197, 201, 216, 265
Marx, Karl, 12, 23, 25, 192
Matsigenka, 38, 165–66, 212, 258
Mauss, Marcel, 178, 189, 197, 209, 252, 272
Maybury-Lewis, David, 3, 47, 81, 98, 150, 158, 178, 246, 261

320   Index

Maynas (province), 28, 88, 89, 91, 94–95, 98–100, 102
Maynas missions, 89–90, 92, 94, 96, 99, 109, 116, 189, 203, 264, 265, 266
Mehinácu, 149
Melanesia, 44, 182, 183, 235, 254, 271
memories, 19, 41, 142, 233, 259
mercantilism, 101, 125, 128, 151, 237, 240, 256
merchants, 9, 15, 87, 99–101, 111–12, 114, 115, 119, 120, 124, 130, 139, 187, 213, 217, 219, 226, 227, 241. *See also* traders
mestizos, 14, 19, 33, 64, 66, 68, 73, 82, 94, 96, 98, 100, 117, 119, 123, 127–29, 133, 141, 143, 150, 153, 167, 190, 204, 208, 210, 216, 218–20, 224, 225, 230, 231, 237, 240, 242, 243, 253–54, 255, 256, 265, 267, 271
metaphors, 12, 33, 143, 194, 210, 219, 220, 241, 255
migration, 31, 57, 65, 66, 68, 125, 140, 141, 171, 262, 265
millenarianism, 31, 235–37, 240, 272
mining, 3, 76, 77, 80, 82
missionaries, 13, 17, 32, 48, 85, 87, 88, 89, 90, 91, 99, 104, 110, 120, 121, 201, 239, 262
missionization, 1, 55, 89, 109, 110, 152
missions, 14, 31, 46, 88–96, 99, 102, 109, 115, 116, 119, 122, 187, 189, 203–4, 265, 266
mita (forced-labor recruitment), 98, 115
mitayo (forest game), 22, 90, 91, 123, 136, 207–8, 217, 218, 224–27, 230, 231, 232, 243, 248
modernity, 11, 15–16, 76, 107–8, 112, 182, 240, 268
moena (tree), 46, 69
money, 4, 130, 182, 240, 243, 253
monkeys, 9, 42, 44, 57–58, 150, 194, 210, 215, 218, 225, 248–49, 263
montaña (high forest), 17, 27, 74, 86, 87, 94, 100, 102, 187, 261–62
mothers, 11, 12, 42–43, 45, 46, 47, 63, 139, 145, 146, 158, 162, 170, 172, 174–75, 180, 197, 215, 247, 250
mothers-in-law, 42, 63, 137, 157, 174–76, 180, 196. *See also* brothers-in-law; daughters-in-law; fathers-in-law; in-laws; sons-in-law
mother spirit, 177, 247, 250, 263
movement, indigenous rights, 13, 80, 153–54
Moyobamba, 88, 90, 95, 100–102, 187, 202, 265
MRTA (Túpac Amaru Revolutionary Movement), 76, 138

multiple regimes of value, 22–23, 83, 185, 190
Munichi, 12
murder, 141
music, 5, 19, 46, 63, 149, 244

Napo River, 203, 261
narcotic substances, 221–22, 238, 246, 250, 259
narcotraficantes (narcotics traffikers), 138–39
narratives, 5–6, 9, 11, 40–41, 55, 140–44, 147–48, 150, 185, 194, 197, 209, 210, 218–19, 228, 230, 236, 240, 242, 246, 249, 252, 253, 256, 257, 259, 271
national expansion, 13, 15, 18, 64, 74, 97, 100, 150, 231, 240, 258
national society, 1, 13, 25, 81, 111–12, 127, 152, 256, 258
nation-states, 13, 14, 15, 78, 97, 107, 125
Native Communities Law, 74, 75, 76
natural resources, 2, 3, 63, 71, 76, 77, 78, 81
Nauta, 38, 41, 44, 66, 71, 73, 101, 105, 110, 117, 131, 134, 202, 232, 262, 265
necklaces, 61, 198, 200, 223, 224
negotiation, 19, 20, 24, 57, 63, 127, 132, 136, 137, 141, 144, 145, 152, 153, 155, 158, 159, 165, 179, 181, 205, 213, 240
net bags, 63, 185, 188–93, 198, 201, 203, 248
non-Urarina, 11, 47, 132, 144, 150, 153, 168, 173, 206, 242, 265

objects, 20, 22, 24, 25, 40, 130, 157, 172, 179, 183, 185, 189–91, 194, 198, 201, 205, 208, 209, 210, 223, 224, 225, 232, 238, 249, 252, 252, 254
obligations, 20, 22, 38, 39, 42, 47, 48, 62, 97, 98, 124, 129, 137, 144, 145, 151, 157, 160, 163, 165, 166, 175, 176, 177, 180, 181, 183, 191, 197, 214, 217, 240, 254
oil, 1, 3, 14, 32, 72, 77–80, 82, 125–26. *See also* petroleum
ojé (plant), 61
Ollanta, 29, 69, 72, 117
Omagua, 11, 85, 86, 92, 186, 203
Omurana, 32–33, 54, 96, 189
ontology, 44, 194, 247
order, social, 25, 74, 138, 160, 237, 256, 257
Orejón, 12
outsiders, 1, 7, 8, 9, 10, 17, 19, 31, 34, 129, 134, 136, 137, 142, 203, 204, 234–35, 241, 242, 256, 262, 272

ownership, 12, 21, 54, 59, 64, 71, 76, 80, 98, 116, 231, 232
Oxapampa, 76, 102

pacas, 42, 44, 210, 211, 218, 220, 225, 232, 251, 263
Pacific coast and coastal areas, 27, 90, 100, 102–4, 106, 126, 185
palm-fiber cloth, 85, 185, 190, 191, 192, 195–96, 198, 200, 201, 203–4
palm-fiber goods, 19, 152, 189, 190, 192, 197, 201, 203, 204, 205, 259, 270
palm-fiber wealth, 19, 23, 132, 183, 185, 189–90, 193, 197, 201, 202, 206, 231
palm swamps, 28, 30, 66, 122, 134, 193, 248, 255
panama hats, 102–3
Pangayacu, 8, 9, 11, 28, 35, 36, 37–39, 49, 55, 62, 66, 69, 92, 119, 122, 123, 124, 128, 130, 137, 139, 140, 149, 166, 169, 172, 173, 174, 175, 176, 181, 195, 200, 213, 214, 221, 226, 239, 243, 244, 251, 253, 263, 267, 271
Panoans, 32, 136, 186, 247, 261, 270
papayas, 10, 50, 59, 61
Paranapura, 5
Paranapura River, 5
parents, 42–43, 46, 159, 160, 164, 172, 174, 180–81, 182, 183, 214, 268, 269
Parinari, 119, 265
parrot, 14, 44, 198, 238, 245
Pastaza River 30, 32–33, 55, 65, 88, 89, 91, 189, 223, 261, 272
Patayacu River 28, 29, 38
Patoyacu, 75, 117
patrón/patrones, 8, 18, 24, 31, 37, 41, 47, 53, 55, 57, 63, 66, 68, 69, 73, 75, 111, 112, 115, 116, 117, 118–23, 124, 125–26, 127–28, 129, 130–31, 132, 137, 138, 139–42, 143, 144, 151, 204, 208, 217, 219, 225, 226, 227, 231, 241, 243, 251, 252, 253–54, 255, 261, 266, 267
patronazco, 119, 127, 141, 142, 208, 248
patron-clientalism, 125, 129, 141, 153
payment, 115, 123, 182, 188, 217, 267
peanuts, 57, 61, 70, 225, 228–29
Pebas, 86, 202
peccaries, 42, 57, 193, 210, 213, 218, 220, 223, 224, 225, 226, 227, 228–29, 230, 245, 248–49, 255, 259, 271
pelts, 18, 71, 117, 207, 213, 224, 227, 252, 271
peons, 112, 114, 115, 118–19, 122, 126, 127
peppers, 46, 61, 86, 108, 207, 221, 222

perdiz (bird), 42
performance, 6, 7, 106, 110, 115, 141, 170, 238, 257
personhood, 44, 142, 154, 155, 163, 200, 246, 272
perspectivism, 250
petroleum, 14, 69, 72, 76, 77, 78, 80, 125–26. *See also* oil
pets, 44, 86, 210, 249
petty-commodity production, 1, 19, 22, 42, 62, 66, 118, 120, 126, 133, 142, 148, 243, 253 254
pigs, 87, 210, 230
pineapples, 61, 188
Piro, 186
plantains, 42, 46, 50, 58, 60, 61, 70, 71, 101, 117, 125, 126, 136, 166, 210, 215–16, 247, 264
poisoning, 67, 68, 72–73, 209, 253. *See also* blowguns; curare (dart poisoning); darts
police, 139, 168
polygyny, 21, 118, 165, 166, 167,
population, 11, 12, 17, 29, 31, 34, 37–38, 48, 89, 92, 93, 94, 118, 265
postcolonial life, 1, 16, 64, 72, 178, 186, 202, 237, 256, 258
postnuptial residence, 170, 176, 180
potatoes, 210
poultry, 18, 116, 136, 225
power, 3, 4, 13–14, 18, 24, 26, 39, 40, 41, 42, 73–74, 77, 81, 82, 98, 107, 112, 116, 119, 122, 124, 129, 132, 133, 137, 138, 142–43, 145, 148, 149, 151, 152, 153, 155, 156, 160, 161, 166, 169, 190, 194, 218, 236–37, 239, 240, 242–43, 245, 246, 247, 248, 269, 270, 272
pregnancy, 45, 147–48, 172, 176–77, 193
prestation, 20–22, 24, 161, 183, 209, 216, 223, 271
prestige, 22, 40, 42, 44, 58, 137–38, 148, 151, 153, 173, 177, 182–83, 185, 204–5, 214, 217, 232, 240, 255
production, 1, 3, 4, 14, 19, 20, 22, 23, 25, 38, 41, 43, 53, 61, 65, 70, 78, 90, 93, 96, 99, 101, 104, 107, 111, 116, 118, 119, 123, 124, 125–26, 132, 136–37, 145, 151, 152, 163, 165, 166, 168–69, 186, 188–89, 191, 193, 194, 197, 201, 202, 203, 204, 206, 207, 208, 225, 226, 230, 232, 241, 242, 243, 244, 253, 270
Protestants, 110, 120, 239
Pucayacu River, 34, 61, 73–74, 75, 119, 264, 266
Pucunayacu River, 120
Pucuyacu River, 28, 32, 53, 118

Index 321

purma (secondary growth), 55, 59, 60
putrification, 227–30
Putumayo River, 2, 112, 115

Quechua, 17, 30, 90, 189, 221, 223, 247, 248, 252, 261, 263, 271, 272
quinine, 14, 105, 117
Quito, 14, 28, 88, 90, 95, 100, 101, 203, 265. *See also* Ecuador

reciprocity, 4, 21, 22, 23, 62, 129, 165, 179, 181, 190, 197, 208, 216–17, 227, 232–33, 240, 242–43, 254
reducción (mission posts), 87, 88, 91, 93, 94, 108
regatón/regatones (itinerant river-traders), 31, 68, 73, 101, 112, 118, 122, 127, 129–30, 130–31, 143, 144, 173, 243, 253, 262
remarriage, 137, 145
repartimiento, 114–15, 204
repartos, 204
reproduction, 1, 3, 21, 23, 25, 90, 149–50, 163, 165, 189, 194, 201, 208, 242, 251
reptiles, 68, 71, 146. *See also specific snakes. See also* serpents
resistance, 1, 15, 25, 31, 89, 127, 130, 139, 153, 209, 235, 237, 239, 255, 258
ribereños (river dwellers), 5, 11, 17, 29, 33–35, 38, 39, 46–47, 50, 57, 59, 60, 64, 66, 69, 72, 73, 83, 92, 93, 96–97, 101, 121, 128, 134, 167, 168, 171, 202, 204, 209, 216, 220, 225, 226, 228, 232–33, 264, 265
rice, 9, 63, 66, 70, 87, 108, 123, 125, 126, 130, 136, 210, 225
rights, 13, 17, 22, 38, 39, 47, 53, 64, 71, 74, 77, 78, 80–81, 82, 99, 103, 115, 153–54, 156, 158, 159, 160, 162, 177, 178–79, 180, 182, 191, 213, 232, 255
Rimae Santú, 218–19
rituals, 20–22, 25, 39, 41, 43–44, 46–48, 55, 66, 155, 190–91, 193–94, 197–98, 207–8, 210–11, 221, 244
Roamaina, 32, 54, 203
rubber, 2, 15, 34, 77, 101–2, 105, 108, 110–15, 116, 117, 118–19, 123, 141, 167, 203, 225, 257, 261, 264, 266, 269
rules, 62, 83–84
Runa, 30, 247

Rurú (headman), 172–75
Rurú (red howler monkey), 57–58, 218, 248, 263

sacraments, 110, 120
sacred, 4, 5, 25, 26, 44, 47, 54, 55, 57, 61, 149, 183, 189, 193, 197, 198, 201, 257
salt, 9, 14, 50, 66, 68, 86, 90–91, 95, 101, 105, 119, 124, 126, 144, 203, 204, 213, 215, 222, 224, 226, 227, 228, 230, 232, 265, 270
salvajes (savages), 16, 17, 35, 96, 204
San Antonio, 118, 120
San León del Amazonas, 109
San Martín, 16, 38, 66, 76, 99
San Pedro, 119, 120
Santa Beatriz, 35, 37, 39, 49, 78, 122
Santa Rosa, 68, 75, 117, 120
San Xavier, 93–94, 203
Saramuro, 117
Sarayacu, 187
sarsaparilla, 14, 101, 105, 187
Satipo, 76
scarification, 44, 47, 61, 194
scavenging, 2, 67, 70, 71, 134, 165, 166, 209, 219
schools, 1, 17, 34–35, 50, 89, 102, 110, 118, 121, 122
selva baja (Peruvian tropical lowlands), 11, 27, 28, 94, 100–101, 105
Sendero Luminoso (SL), 76, 138, 264
serpents, 6, 145–47, 227, 245, 267, 268. *See also specific snakes. See also* reptiles
sexuality, 19, 21, 34, 40, 133, 137, 145–48, 150, 162, 164, 169–73, 175, 178–79, 181–83, 194, 196, 211, 221, 222, 237, 245, 267, 268
shamanism, 21, 23, 25, 26, 31, 42, 47, 207, 222, 227, 231, 234–35, 236, 237, 238, 240, 242, 244, 246, 247, 249, 250, 251, 252, 253, 255, 271
shells, 186, 198, 223, 238, 259, 264
Shipibo, 60, 91, 185, 186, 272
Shuar, 143, 172, 204
signification, 6, 21, 256, 259
signs, 5, 23, 33, 58, 108, 247, 255
siíji (soul), 245, 246, 250, 252
Summer Institute of Linguistics (SIL) 12, 34, 48, 121–22, 262
SINAMOS (Sistema Nacional de Apoyo a la Movilización Social), 74–75

Sirionó, 32, 146
sisters, 11, 58, 62, 137, 147, 161, 164, 165, 167, 170, 172–74, 176, 180, 246, 268
sky, 8, 58, 222, 228, 230, 239, 255
slaves, 14, 85, 87, 89, 91, 99, 113–14, 117, 118, 160, 218
sloths, 44, 198, 215, 227, 232
snails, 223, 238, 259
sociality, 6, 158, 161, 197, 198, 204, 242, 243, 250, 254
social life, 6, 14, 19, 21–22, 26, 72, 129, 132, 148, 151, 155, 186, 201, 210, 216, 228, 231, 232, 234, 239, 242, 246, 259; commodification of, 21, 183, 209, 253
soil, 27–28, 60, 93, 222, 263
songs, 5, 6, 10, 41, 221, 238, 243, 254, 259
sons, 33, 54, 59, 67, 68, 89, 137, 175, 176, 180, 200–201
sons-in-law, 40, 48, 62, 137, 145, 151, 160, 161, 164, 166, 175, 179, 180–82 196, 269. *See also* brothers-in-law; daughters-in-law; fathers-in-law; in-laws; mothers-in-law
sorcery, 170, 258
sororal polygyny, 21, 38, 159, 167, 171
Spanish, 7, 14, 17, 18, 35, 45, 46, 47, 65, 83, 86, 87, 88, 89, 91, 92, 94, 95, 96, 97, 98, 99, 104, 114, 121, 123, 151, 186, 193, 198, 203, 205, 225, 236, 245, 246, 252, 261, 263, 267
spears, 50, 68, 113, 197, 209, 211, 225, 228
spirits, 9, 23, 45, 48, 55, 57–58, 62, 65, 134, 149, 169, 177, 193, 201–2, 209, 218–19, 221, 245–48, 250–53, 267, 272
squash, 61, 117, 210
status, 2, 3, 10, 20, 39–40, 47, 53, 71, 92, 97, 99, 142, 149, 151, 154, 159, 162, 165, 167, 168, 174, 176, 180–82, 186, 197, 205, 210, 216, 236–37
steamboats, 69, 105, 108
stingrays, 67
stockades, 118, 168, 171, 173
stories, 5–7, 9, 10, 32, 40–41, 141–43, 148, 150, 158, 191, 194–95, 219, 241, 242, 252, 261, 271
subalterns, 4, 12, 33, 73, 96, 99, 155
subsistence, 12, 18, 42, 44, 54, 62, 63, 65–66, 68–69, 83, 90, 99, 101, 122–25, 133, 134, 136, 207, 210, 225–27, 241, 247
swamps, 28–30, 55, 66, 122, 134, 188, 193, 196, 248, 255

sweet potatoes, 61
swiddens, 32, 38, 43, 58–60, 74, 123, 136, 173
swine, 43, 59, 116
symbolic density, 255

Tabatinga (Brazil), 101, 105, 187, 202
tabus (taboos), 46, 47, 137, 146, 150, 193, 194, 211, 227, 268
Tapirapé, 32
tapirs, 42, 86, 210, 211, 213–15, 218, 225, 227, 245, 248–49, 271
Tarapoto, 102, 187
Taushiro, 12
teeth, 198, 212, 223, 248–49, 259
teniente gobernador (lieutenant governor), 168, 172, 173, 174, 269
termites 50
territory, 28, 32, 55, 57, 64, 65, 71, 72, 75, 78, 80, 88, 89, 95, 100, 131, 163, 219, 229, 230, 266
Ticuna, 86, 261
Tigre River, 5, 31, 32, 55, 65, 92, 110, 117, 118, 126, 127, 204, 262, 264, 265
Tigrillo River, 28, 32, 34, 38, 55, 61, 66, 120, 122, 131, 166, 245
Timbira, 202
tobacco, 26, 90, 101, 105, 124, 207, 222, 246, 250, 266
tocuyo (cotton fabric), 113, 187, 203, 204
tools, 43, 50, 62, 87, 89–90, 105, 118, 141, 204, 225, 232, 235, 241–42
tortoises, 30, 41, 50, 67, 101, 219, 220, 227, 245, 265
toucans, 42, 228
tourists, 3, 202, 211, 224
trade, 14, 25, 61, 66, 90, 101, 104, 105, 106, 107, 111, 113, 126, 130, 137, 140, 142, 145, 151, 153, 187, 190, 197, 201, 202, 203, 205, 208, 209, 220, 224, 226, 227, 234, 239, 242, 262, 265
traders, 8–9, 13, 17, 18, 24, 25, 26, 31, 47, 63, 73, 83, 87, 95, 97, 99, 100, 104, 112, 120, 122, 123, 124, 126, 127, 128, 129–31, 138, 141, 142, 143, 144, 173, 190, 203, 208, 215, 217, 219, 225–27, 231, 237, 241, 252, 255, 261, 262, 266, 267. *See also* merchants
transactions, 22, 71, 83, 124, 130, 133, 139, 145, 183, 203, 204, 207, 217, 231, 234, 241, 254
trees, 45, 46, 48, 60, 61, 62, 63, 69, 70, 72, 111, 114, 118, 119, 136, 166, 266

Tucanoan, 32, 187
Tukano, 20, 149, 185, 218, 267, 271
Tukúna, 202
Tupian 32, 86, 92, 186, 189, 217, 261, 270, 271

Ucayali River, 17, 38, 66, 91, 105, 111, 116, 186, 187, 262
ujkuaná (gardens), 55, 58–59
ujtiya (men's ceremonial stave), 197, 252
uña de gato (cat's claw, prickly shrub), 61
uncivilized peoples, 2, 35, 106, 160
unequal exchanges, 18, 85, 99, 122–23, 125, 130, 131, 142, 148, 185, 190, 206, 243, 253, 256, 266
United States, 77, 111, 141
upriver, 28, 33, 66, 69, 93, 119, 173, 202
upstream, 31, 33, 54, 117, 130, 218
Urituyacu River, 5, 12, 54, 55, 59, 64, 65, 66, 83, 93, 96, 131, 261, 265
utopia, 97, 235–37, 240
uxorilocality, 20, 21, 38, 63, 65, 66, 167, 159, 161, 164, 165, 167, 170, 172, 176, 180, 269

valorization, 17, 23, 42, 53, 167, 182, 216, 217, 225, 256, 269
valuables, 162, 179, 185, 190, 254, 259
value, 3, 5, 10, 14, 19–24, 58, 83, 94, 147, 162, 172, 178, 179, 185, 186, 189, 190, 194, 200, 208, 229, 232, 240, 265, 271; conversion, 157; cultural, 4, 7, 12, 54, 78, 179, 244, 259; economic, 24, 190, 255; extraction, 14, 85; political 217; surplus, 112, 123; use, 12, 190
vanilla, 90, 105
vessels, sacred inalienable, 201, 245
Viceroyalty, 88, 95, 97
violence, 1, 11, 15–16, 87, 107, 113, 127–28, 130, 138, 139, 141, 142, 143, 153, 166, 241–42, 245
viracochas (new converts), 88, 93
virilocalty, 170

Waiâpi, 202
Waiwai, 202
Wakuénai, 209, 267
War of the Pacific, 106
water, 28–29, 46, 47, 69, 78, 103, 106, 141, 146–47, 164, 197, 230, 239, 247, 262, 264, 268, 271
Wayâna-Aparai, 202
wealth, 1, 4, 7, 8, 12, 14, 19, 21–25, 26, 30, 53, 107, 108, 111, 150, 179, 185, 186, 195, 198, 207, 208, 223–24, 234, 235, 237, 242, 245, 249, 252, 255, 259
weaving, 42, 43, 47, 90, 135, 136, 169, 185, 186, 187, 191, 192, 193, 194, 196, 197, 201, 250, 270
weaving swords, 147, 192, 196–97, 252
widows, 19, 40, 62, 137, 162, 172, 175, 196–97, 205
wife, 36, 38, 59, 130, 134, 147, 157, 160–62, 164, 165, 166, 167, 171, 173, 175–78, 179, 180, 183, 197, 213, 215, 246, 269
wives, 21, 22, 42, 62, 63, 137, 151, 159–60, 162, 165–67, 170, 171, 173, 174, 175, 176, 177, 178, 180, 181, 182, 205, 210, 213, 214
Women's Catholic Union (Unión Católica de Señoras), 109. *See also* Catholicism

Xavánte, 178, 202, 234
Xerente, 202

Yacumama, 146, 247
Yagua, 39, 185, 202, 237, 261, 270
Yameos, 117, 270
Yamináwa, 247
Yanomami, 1, 202, 268
yinánja (plant), 221–22, 271
Yurimaguas, 38, 89, 90, 105, 117, 146, 190, 202, 270

Zápara, 268
Záparoans, 32, 113, 186, 202, 261, 270
Zapas, 32

Bartholomew Dean is associate professor of anthropology at the University of Kansas, as well as visiting professor at the Universidad Nacional Mayor de San Marcos, Lima. He is the coeditor of *At the Risk of Being Heard: Identity, Indigenous Rights, and Postcolonial States* and *The Varieties of Human Experience: An Anthropological Reader.*